CHINA AND HER POLITICAL ENTITY

(A STUDY OF CHINA'S FOREIGN RELATIONS WITH REFERENCE TO KOREA, MANCHURIA AND MONGOLIA)

BY

SHUHSI HSÜ, Ph.D.

ASSOCIATE PROFESSOR OF POLITICAL SCIENCE IN PEKING UNIVERSITY
(YENCHING); SOMETIME LECTURER ON INTERNATIONAL
LAW IN THE UNIVERSITY OF HONG KONG

"The policy of the United States is to preserve the
territorial and administrative entity of China."
JOHN HAY.

NEW YORK
OXFORD UNIVERSITY PRESS
AMERICAN BRANCH: 35 WEST 32ND STREET
LONDON, TORONTO, MELBOURNE & BOMBAY
1926

To

My Mother

"There is no doubt that within a decade Japan's prosperity and power will be considerable. . . . I earnestly hope that those who are at the helm of state will occupy their attention with the problem while there is still time."

LI HUNG-CHANG.

PREFACE

" THE policy of the United States ", declared John Hay as Secretary of State, " is to preserve the territorial and administrative entity of China ". This celebrated declaration was made at the height of the Boxer Rebellion of 1900, when there was a general apprehension that some powers might seize the opportunity to precipitate anew the scramble for Chinese territory that had occurred two years previously.

The Boxer Rebellion ended with Russia in military occupation of Manchuria, and this in turn led directly to the intervention of Japan in 1904 and to the subsequent transfer to the latter of the lease of Port Arthur and Talienwan, together with the section of the Southern Manchurian branch of the Chinese Eastern Railway south of Changchun. In order to complete the task which the McKinley administration disinterestedly took upon itself the American government during the two succeeding administrations first interposed to localize the Russo-Japanese armed conflict, then lent the good offices of the United States to China to obtain American capital for the development of Manchuria, and finally proposed to the Powers the " neutralization " of Manchurian railways.

Following the Portsmouth Conference in 1905, Japan took great pains to convert her late enemy into a virtual ally. When the last of the steps mentioned was taken by the United States, Japan came forward with Russia and brought it to nought. Encouraged by success, she even launched with the latter further encroachments upon China. Within a few years her partner turned Outer Mongolia into an autonomous state, while she herself converted southern Manchuria and eastern Inner Mongolia into what was practically an exclusive sphere of influence. Russia's hold upon Chinese territory has since been much weakened by the revolution at home; but Japan, free from domestic troubles, has shown no sign of retreating from her entrenched position.

By the correspondence relating to the formation of the four-power financial consortium, as well as by the result of the Washington Conference, the United States has shown herself disposed to acquiesce in "accomplished facts". This attitude, let us hope, is merely one of those aberrations of American foreign policy initiated by the Wilson administration. The United States has not ceased to have important economic and cultural interests in China, and hence cannot remain long indifferent to the fate of that country. Already she has reaffirmed the principle of the territorial and administrative integrity of China and canceled the Lansing-Ishii agreement. Is it possible that a frank return to the active policy of restoring the complete control of Manchuria to China as pursued consistently by the McKinley, Roosevelt, and Taft administrations, is thereby presaged?

There seems to be no limit to Japanese ambition. The blocking of the "neutralization" scheme for Manchurian railways in 1909 took place but one year after a Japanese protectorate was securely established over Korea; and the presentation of the Twenty-one Demands in 1915 with an attempt to impose a vassalage upon China came immediately after Japan found that her hold upon southern Manchuria and eastern Inner Mongolia was to pass unchallenged. It is evident that this continuous march of the Japanese must be stopped somewhere. American statesmen from 1900 to 1912 did not take the Great Wall of China as the line of defence, but chose the Manchurian-Korean frontier. In doing so they were undoubtedly right. Manchuria has in the past repeatedly served as the base for hostile descents upon China, and also forms today the only outlet for the surplus of the Chinese millions of the north. If Korea is but a limb of the Chinese political entity, Manchuria is easily as vital as the throat. To compromise with Japan upon Manchuria would be equivalent to letting China remain in the death embrace of her neighbor.

In the following pages an attempt will be made to trace the problem of Manchuria back into remote antiquity, taking also some account of the bearing of Liuchiu, Korea, and Mongolia upon the main question, ever mindful of the maxim that what is not forgotten of the past will provide a guide for the future.

It is proper to make some mention in this place of the materials used in this monograph. For convenience these materials may be classified into document collections and works; and works further into classical and modern; and both document collections and works further into official and private, making six classes in all. The first five of these classes, with the exception of about one dozen "gazetteers" of less importance and certain collections of documents that have not been replaced after their loss in transit during the last Japanese earthquake, are given with descriptive notes in the "List of Special Abbreviations" below, to which the reader is referred.

As to the last class, the modern private works, it may for convenience be treated under two heads — Chinese, and non-Chinese. Under the latter head the memoirs, and other works of a similar nature, are found indispensable. The memoirs are not all written by men of a scholarly turn of mind, and statements contained in them are often inaccurate when examined in the light of documents. Besides, the writers generally have some object in view, often personal, and are apt to be biased. But such works are based upon a personal experience, and thus supply suggestions for further research, if not also valuable information of primary importance. Other modern works are as a whole not very helpful. Most of them apparently suffer from a lack of first-class source material, particularly of Chinese material, which, it is hardly necessary to point out, is essential for a subject like that of the present study.

What has been said is in general also true of modern private Chinese works. As in other fields in China, art and learning are going through a period of transition. Students who are ardent about things Western are apt to forget what they have at home, particularly in the question of source material. Fortunately, the tradition of scholarship, of which China in the past was justly proud, is not entirely dead. In writing the monograph two excellent modern works have been found helpful. As these fall outside the "List of Special Abbreviations" they may be given here. They are: Chen Chung-tsu's *Contemporary Outer Mongolia* (Shanghai, 1922), and Hsu Hsi's *The Eastern Three Provinces* (Shanghai, 1915). The latter is a study in the old Chinese tradition, while the former is a digest from records kept in the Residency-General in Urga.

A word may also be added concerning another point of technique. In the Romanization of Chinese words the Wade system is employed with certain modifications. One of these is the adding of the consonant *y* before the vowel *i* when the latter begins a word. This is for insuring the correct pronunciation by readers not familiar with the system. Another is the omission of the sign indicating an aspirate, and of the signs distinguishing one *e* or *u*, the two vowels that vary in Chinese, from another. It is thought that these signs are more important to sinologues than to general readers. Aside from the foregoing, effort has been made to abstain from deviations.

It remains for the author to acknowledge his indebtedness. His profoundest gratitude is due to Judge John Bassett Moore, Dr. Julius Goebel, Jr., and Professor Joseph P. Chamberlain, of Columbia University. It was under the inspiring supervision of Judge Moore that the study was commenced, and it was with the painstaking criticism of Dr. Goebel and Professor Chamberlain that the work was completed. He is also under great obligation to his wife's mother, Mrs. S. K. Lew, Dr. T. T. Lew of Peking University, Judge Y. K. Kuo of the Supreme Court of China, and Mr. Chuan Chao of the Chinese Ministry of Foreign Affairs, for their assistance in collecting Chinese materials in China, while he was in America; and to Mr. Olin D. Wannamaker of Princeton-in-Peking, Dr. Albert B. Marshall, formerly President of the Omaha Theological Seminary, and Mrs. Marshall for reading the manuscript and making many valuable suggestions.

CONTENTS

LIST OF SPECIAL ABBREVIATIONS

A.   Book A or books A.   Special book or books found in the beginning of some Chinese works.

Ai hui hsien chih.   "Gazetteer" of the *hsien* of Ai-hui (Aigun) by Hsu Hsi-lien in 14 bks., 1920.

Braddeley.   *Russia, Mongolia, China,* a collection of records concerning the relation between Russia and Mongolia and China, 1602–76, by J. F. Baddeley, in 2 vols. (London, 1919).

Chen pao.   A Chinese daily of Peking.

Cheng fu kung pao.   Chinese government gazette published daily since Oct. 25, 1907, and known at different times as *Cheng chih kuan pao, Nei ko kuan pao,* and *Lin shih kung pao.*

Cheng te fu chih.   "Gazetteer" of the prefecture of Cheng-te, by Hai-chung and others in 28 bks., 1830 (revised edition, 1887).

Chi fu tung chih.   "Gazetteer" of Chihli, by Huang Peng-nien and others in 300 bks., 1884.

Chi lin tung chih.   "Gazetteer" of Kirin, by Li Kuei-lin and others in 122 bks., 1891.

Chi lin wai chi.   A work on Kirin, by Sa-ying-e in 10 bks., (Canton edition, 1900).

Chia.   The reign of Chiaching (1797–1820).

Chin shih.   History of the Chin dynasty, by To-ko-to and others of the Yuan dynasty, in 135 bks.   (Han-fen-lou edition).

China, No. — (year).   British Parliamentary Papers.

China Weekly.   The *China Weekly Review,* formerly the *Millard's Review,* published at Shanghai.

Chine (year).   Documents diplomatiques du ministère des affaires estrangères.

Ching-shan Diary.   "The Diary of H. E. Ching Shan," chap. xviii of *China under the Empress Dowager,* by J. O. P. Bland and E. Bakhouse (Philadelphia, 1910).

Chiu pien kao.   *Huang ming chiu pien kao,* a work on the frontiers of the Ming dynasty by Wei Huan of the Ming dynasty in 10 bks., 1541.

Chiu tang shu. History of the Tang dynasty by Liu Chu and others of the Posterior Tsin dynasty in 214 bks. (Hfl. ed.).

Chou li. *Chou li chu su* of the Thirteen Classics Series (1781 edition).

Chou shu. History of the Northern Chou dynasty, by Ling-hu Te-fen of the Tang dynasty in 50 bks. (Hfl. ed.).

Chun yi chih. *Feng tien chun yi chih,* a geography of Fengtien, by Wu Ting-hsieh in 5 bks., published as vol. xxii of *Tung san sheng cheng lueh* (see *Hsu*), being a portion of a projected new "gazetteer" of Manchuria that has never been completed.

Cm. or Cmd. — (year). Also British Parliamentary Papers.

Customs. *Treaties, Conventions, etc., between China and Foreign States,* published by the Chinese Maritime Customs in 2 vols. (Shanghai, 1908) with a supplement (1917).

F. E. Review. *The Far Eastern Review,* published monthly at Shanghai.

Fang pu yao lueh. *Huang chao fang pu yao lueh,* an account of the feudatory tribes of the Tsing dynasty by Chi Yun-shih in 16 bks., 1839 (Hangchou edition, 1884).

Fang yu chi yao. *Tu shih fang yu chi yao,* a historical geography of China by Ku Tsu-yu of the Ming dynasty in 130 bks. (1879 edition).

For. Rel. *Foreign Relations of the United States.*

H. The reign of Hsuantung (1909–11).

Hai chun han kao. Section of 4 books of *Li wen chung kung chuan chi,* the documents of Li Hung-chang, published by Wu Ju-lun in 150 bks. (100 vols.), 1905.

Han shu. History of the Han dynasty by Pan Ku of the Later Han dynasty, in 120 bks. (Hfl. ed.).

Herald. *The North-China Herald,* the weekly edition of the *North-China Daily News* of Shanghai.

Hertslet. *Hertslet's China Treaties* (3rd ed.) London, 1908.

Hou han shu. History of the Later Han dynasty by Fan Yeh of the Liu Sung dynasty in 100 bks. (Hfl. ed.).

Hsien. The reign of Hsienfeng (1851–1861).

Hsu. *Tung san sheng cheng lueh,* a collection of documents and maps relating to Manchuria under the administration of Hsu Shih-chang, 1907–8, edited by himself, 1911, in 40 vols. (12 bks.), 1911.

Hsu liu chiu chih. *Hsu liu chiu kuo chih lueh,* a continuation of *Liu chiu kuo chih lueh* by Chao Hsin in 2 bks., 1882.

Hsu sin fa ling. *Hsuan tung sin fa ling,* a continuation of *Kuang hsu sin fa ling* (see *Sin fa ling*) (Shanghai, 1909).

Hu lan fu chih. "Gazetteer" of the prefecture of Hulan, Heilung-kiang, by Huang Wei-han, in 12 bks., 1915.

Hui tien. *The Institutes of the Ta Tsing Dynasty* (*Ta tsing hui tien shih li*), compiled by Li Hung-chang and others in 1,220 bks., 1886 (2d edition, Shanghai, 1909).

Japan Treaties. *Treaties, Conventions, etc. between Japan and other Powers*, published by the Japanese ministry of foreign affairs (1899 edition).

K. The reign of Kuanghsu (1875–1908).

Kang. The reign of Kanghsi (1662–1722).

Kien. The reign of Kienlung (1736–1795).

Kuang hsu cheng yao. A collection of the more important documents of the reign of Kuanghsu, 1875–1908, by Shen Tung-sheng in 34 bks., 1909.

Kun yu tien. Section of *Ku chin tu shu chi cheng*, the grand "Chinese Encyclopedia" (Tsungli Yamen edition).

l. Left — the left front or reversed side of a Chinese page.

Lepsius. *Die Grosse Politik der Europäischen Kabinette, 1871–1914*, a collection of diplomatic documents of the German foreign office, by Johannes Lepsius and others (Berlin, 1923).

Liang shu. History of the Liang dynasty by Yao Ssu-lien of the Tang dynasty, in 56 bks. (Hfl. ed.).

Liao shih. History of the Liao dynasty, by To-ko-to and others of the Yuan dynasty, in 115 bks. (Hfl. ed.).

Lin chiang pao kao. *Tiao cha lin chiang pao kao shu*, a report by Fu Chiang on the upper Yalu, published as part of vol. vi of *Tung san sheng cheng lueh* (see *Hsu*).

Liu chiu chih lueh. *Liu chiu kuo chih lueh*, "gazetteer" of Liuchiu, by Chou Huang in 16 bks., 1757 (Japanese reproduction edition).

Lung chiang shu lueh. A work on Heilungkiang by Hsu Tsung-liang, in 6 bks., 1891.

Lung chiang wai chi. *Hei lung chiang wai chi*, a work on Heilungkiang by Hsi-ching (Canton edition, 1900).

Malloy. *Treaties, Conventions, etc. between the United States and other Powers, 1776–1909*, compiled under a resolution of the Senate by W. M. Malloy, in 2 vols. (1910) with a continuation as vol. iii, *1910–1923* (1923).

MacMurray. *Treaties and Agreements with and Concerning China*, edited by J. V. A. MacMurray in 2 vols. (New York, 1921).

Man chou yuan liu. *Man chiu yuan liu kao*, an official account of the origin of the Manchus by A-kuei and others in 20 bks., 1777.

Meng ku yu mu chi. An account of the Mongols by Chang Mu in 16 bks., 1867.

Ming shih. History of the Ming dynasty by Chang Ting-yu and others in 332 bks., 1739 (Hfl. ed.).

Moore. A Digest of International Law, compiled under an act of Congress by John Bassett Moore, in 8 vols., 1906.

Pei chi shu. History of the Northern Chi dynasty, by Li Pai-yo of the Tang dynasty, in 50 bks. (Hfl. ed.).

Pei shih. History of the Northern Dynasties, by Li Yen-shou of the Tang dynasty, in 100 bks. (Hfl. ed.).

Pien yi tien. Section of *Ku chin tu shu chi cheng* (see *Kun yu tien*).

Ping lo fang lueh. Ping ting lo cha fang lueh, an official account of the campaigns against the Russians, 1682–89, published from MMS as bks. v-viii in *Shou fang pei cheng.*

R-J Corres. Correspondence Regarding the Negotiations between Japan and Russia, 1903–1904, presented to the Japanese diet, March, 1904 (a translation).

Rockhill. Treaties and Conventions with or Concerning China and Korea, 1894–1904, edited by W. W. Rockhill (Washington, 1904) with a supplement (1908).

S. & P. S. Review. The Chinese Social and Political Science Review, published quarterly in Peking.

S-J Negotiations. Chinese Official Statement Respecting the Twenty-one Demands, 1915 (New York edition).

S-R Corres. Correspondence between the Directorate-General of Sino-Russian Negotiations and the Russian mission in Peking (by courtesy of the Directorate-General).

San ting chih. Kou pei san ting chih, "gazetteer" of Kalgan, Tu-shi-kao and Dolon Nor by Huang Ko-jun in 17 bks., 1758.

Sen. Doc. Senate Documents.

Scott. The Consortium, text of the four-power agreement for Chinese loan business and relevant documents, edited by J. B. Scott (Washington, 1921).

Shang shu. Shang shu cheng yi of the Thirteen Classics Series (1781 edition).

Sheng ching tung chih. "Gazetteer" of Shengking by Wang Ho and others in 46 bks., 1736. (There is a revised and enlarged edition by A-kuei and others, 1778.)

Sheng wu chi. An account of the military operations of the Tsing dynasty down to the reign of Taokuang by Wei Yuan in 14 bks., 1842.

Shih chi. The "Mémoires historiques" of Ssu-ma Chien of the Han dynasty, in 130 bks. (Hfl. ed.).

Shuo fang pei cheng. A work on Sino-Russian relations by Ho Chiu-tao, presented to the emperor Hsienfeng in 1860 and published from MMS by Li Hung-chang in the eighties.

Sin fa ling. Kuang hsu sin fa ling, official documents of the reign of Kuanghsu since 1900 (Shanghai, 1909).

State Papers. British and Foreign State Papers.

Sui shu. History of the Sui dynasty, by Wei Cheng of the Tang dynasty, in 85 bks. (Hfl. ed.).

Sung shih. History of the Sung dynasty, by To-ko-to and others of the Yuan dynasty, in 496 bks. (Hfl. ed.).

Tang shu. History of the Tang dynasty, by Ou-yang Hsiu and Sung Chi of the Sung dynasty, in 273 bks. (Hfl. ed.).

Tao. The reign of Taokuang (1821–1850).

Tiao yo. Treaties, conventions, etc., of the Tsing dynasty, issued with relevant documents for official use by the Chinese Ministry of Foreign Affairs in a series of 5 sets (60 vols.) and a supplement. (To be quoted by number.)

Tien kao. Section of 40 bks. of Li Hung-chang's documents (see *Hai chun han kao*).

Tsin shu. History of the Tsin dynasty, by the emperor Tai-tsung of the Tang dynasty, in 130 bks. (Hfl. ed.).

Tsou kao. Section of 80 books of Li Hung-chang's documents (see *Hai chun han kao*).

Tung. The reign of Tungchih (1762–1774).

Tung fan chi yao. A work on Korea by Hsieh Pei-jung in 12 bks., 1882.

Tung hua chuan lu. Official history of the Tsing dynasty down to the reign of Tungchih, by Wang Hsien-chien and Pan Hsi-fu, in 594 bks. (1911 edition).

Tung hua hsu lu. Continuation of *Tung hua chuan lu* for the reign of Kuanghsu by Chou Shou-peng, in 220 bks., 1909.

Wai chiao kung pao. A monthly published by the Chinese Ministry of Foreign Affairs since July, 1921.

Wai chiao wen tu. Diplomatic documents issued by the Chinese Government.

Wei shih. Section of *San kuo chih,* history of the Three Kingdoms, by Chen Shou of the Tsin dynasty, in 65 bks. (Hfl. ed.).

Wei shu. History of the Northern or Later Wei dynasty, by Wei Shou of the Northern Chi dynasty, in 114 bks. (Hfl. ed.).

Wu tai shih.   History of the Five Dynasties, by Ou-yang Hsiu of the Sung dynasty, in 74 bks. (Hfl. ed.).

Yen chi pao kao.   *Yen chi pien wu pao kao shu,* a report by Chen Chao-chang and Wu Lu-chen on the "Chientao" dispute, published as vol. iv of *Tung san sheng cheng lueh* (see *Hsu*) and also in independent edition.

Yen ko piao.   *Li tai ti li yen ko piao,* a historical geography by Chen Fang-chi in 47 bks., 1667 (Canton edition, 1895).

Yi shu han kao.   Section of 20 bks. of Li Hung-chang's documents (see *Hai chun han kao*).

Yuan shih.   History of the Yuan dynasty, by Sung Lien and others of the Ming dynasty, in 210 bks. (Hfl. ed.).

Yung.   The reign of Yungcheng (1723–1735).

CHINA AND HER POLITICAL ENTITY

CHAPTER I

HISTORICAL BACKGROUND

Sec. 1. Early Chinese Colonization

THE Chinese nation had its origin in the Yellow River basin. As it grew it expanded both southward into southern China, and northeastward into Manchuria and Korea.

Of the northeastern region, southern Manchuria and northern Korea, being the closest to the Yellow River basin, were the sections colonized first. Students of the Chinese classics claim that long before the reign of Yao (2357–2258 B.C.), from which the first documents of the classic *Shu ching* are dated, southern Manchuria and northern Korea had formed a part of two of the nine provinces into which China was then divided.[1] They also claim that at the time of the ruler Shun (2257–2208 B.C.) the regions in question were organized into two separate provinces which, together with a third, formed the three new provinces recorded to have been added to China by that ruler.[2] However this may be, the descriptions of the classic *Chou li* concerning the northeastern country are such as to leave us without doubt that the regions under discussion constituted the greater part of one of the nine prov-

[1] *Shang shu, 5/10 et seq.*
[2] *Ibid., 2/15 l.; cf. Tsiu shu, 13/22 l.*

I

inces into which China at the beginning of the Chou
dynasty (1122–250 B.C.) was divided.[3]

Although northern Korea and southern Manchuria
formed a part of the Chinese world at the very beginning
of Chinese history, extensive Chinese colonization of those
regions seems, however, not to have taken place until during the Chou dynasty. We have left us the record of a
dramatic migration headed by Chi-tzu, a prince of the
dynasty that was displaced by the Chou, who declined to
become a subject of the new ruling house, and migrated
with his men into the country east of the Liao river and
founded for himself a state known as Chao-hsien.[4] There
is no doubt as to the existence of Chi-tzu, for the classic
Shu ching included a document recording Chi-tzu's advice
on principles of government to Wu-wang, the founder of
the Chou dynasty. As to Chi-tzu's founding Chao-hsien,
it is probable that this is only a legend told by the inhabitants of a Chinese colony founded at a much later date.
In any event, it is certain that by the middle part of the
Chou dynasty there was in existence a Chinese colony in
northern Korea which was ruled by the Chis, who claimed
that both the colony and the ruling house were founded by
Chi-tzu.

As to southern Manchuria, there are no allusions in
Chinese history as to how it was colonized. Judging by
its geographical position it could not have been left un-
occupied long after the establishment of Chao-hsien. It
is probable that it was colonized even before northern
Korea, but that on account of its proximity to the powerful feudal state of Yen, which had its capital on the site
of Peking, no feudal state like Chao-hsien was developed
there.

[3] *Chou li*, 35/15 *l*.   [4] *Han Shu*, 28 ii/3; *Shih chi*, 38/2–8.

Southern Manchuria and northern Korea are separated from the Yellow River basin by the sea and by the Jehol hills. The Yangtze valley, the section of the southern region closest to the Yellow River basin, is different. With the exception of its upper section, which is surrounded by mountains, its physical conformation is such that it forms a natural geographical unit with the Yellow River basin. For this reason Chinese migration to that valley began much earlier than to the northeast. Indeed, we learn that by the latter part of the Chou dynasty, while southern Manchuria and northern Korea were still not yet fully developed, the states in the middle and lower sections of the Yangtze valley had already played important parts in the politics of the Chinese world as equals of the states of the Yellow River basin.

Simultaneously with the colonizing activities there was, as the nation grew, a tendency among the feudal states to consolidate by absorbing one another. In the twelfth century before Christ, when the Chou dynasty was established, there were 1,800 feudal states of various sizes in the Chinese world. By the time of Confucius (551–479 B.C.), shortly after the entrance of the Yangtze states into the politics of the Yellow River basin, there were about 160 states left. The Yangtze states, being more favored by nature than the Yellow River states, were greater and more powerful. Their appearance in the political arena of the Chinese world had the effect of upsetting the existing political equilibrium and hastening the natural process of consolidation already at work. Consequently, by the time of Mencius, only about a century after Confucius, the 160 states of the latter's time had been reduced to eight, including Chao-hsien in northern Korea.

As a notable part of the process of consolidation, the

feudal state of Yen extended its rule over southern Manchuria.   In doing so it came into conflict with the desert
tribe known as the Tung-hu, who occupied the Jehol hills
and were able to threaten the communication between Yen
and southern Manchuria, and to present a constant menace
to Yen itself.   Under the great ruler Chao-wang (311–
278 B.C.) Yen therefore carried on a campaign against the
tribesmen, drove them off the hills, and constructed a wall
known as the Great Wall of Yen, to protect the hills and
southern Manchuria.   In consequence it also established a
prefecture known as Yu-pei-ping over the hills, another
prefecture known as Liao-hsi over the west of the Liao,
and a third known as Liao-tung over the east of that river.[5]

Throughout the process of consolidation the ruling Chou
dynasty as a matter of policy did not take part.   Consequently it became more and more insignificant as the feudal
states grew, until by the time the Chinese world was divided among eight states it had long ceased to wield an
unifying influence.   It became necessary therefore that
some of the states should assume the leadership in its place.
Consequently the tendency to consolidate assumed also the
direction of unification.   By 255 B.C., a century after the
time of Mencius and a few decades after Yen extended its
rule over southern Manchuria, Ts'in, the westernmost state
which occupied the strategical section of the country, the
present province of Shensi, had conquered all fellow states
except Chao-hsien.

Having the resources of the six states added to its own,
Ts'in or more appropriately the Ts'in dynasty (255–207
B.C.), as its ruling house is recognized by Chinese historians
as having succeeded the Chou dynasty from 255 B.C. on,
carried the process of unification further.   Within a short

---

[5] *Han shu*, 94/4; *Yen ko piao*, 11/2, 7, 13, 14, 29.

time it extended its influence beyond the boundaries of the defunct states. In the northeast it acquired the allegiance of Chao-hsien.[6] In the south it constituted what are now the provinces of Fukien, Kuangtung and Kuangsi and a part of Annam — sections of country beyond the Nanling mountains which had hitherto been to only a small extent colonized by the Chinese — into four prefectures.

The Ts'in dynasty soon fell as a result of the revolt of the people of the lower and middle Yangtze valley. The Han dynasty (206 B.C.–24 A.D.), which succeeded it, had also difficulties with the same region. Consequently it was not until the reign of Wu-ti (140–87 B.C.) that the process of unification was carried further. Under that great ruler Chinese direct rule was established over the Yunnan plateau in the south. As to the northeast, attention was directed to Chao-hsien. By that time the Chis there had long been displaced by the Weis.[7] The latter had fled into that country from the old territory of the feudal state of Yen after taking part in an unsuccessful revolt against the Han dynasty. True to their original antagonism to the ruling dynasty in China they adopted an aggressive policy towards it. This supplied a good occasion. The Han forces invaded Chao-hsien by land and sea, deposed the Weis, and constituted the country into two prefectures,[8] that southeast to Liao-tung being known as Lo-lang, and that northeast to Liao-tung as Yuan-tu.[9]

South of Lo-lang and Yuan-tu was the country of the Han tribes. Farther south across the sea were the islands inhabited by the Japanese, or rather the Wo tribes, as they

[6] *Shih chi,* 105/1.

[7] *Ibid.,* 115/1; *Hou han shu,* 115/9.

[8] *Shih chi,* 115/2–4; cf. *Chi lin tung chih,* 10/2–5.

[9] *Hou han shu,* 115/9–10; *Chi lin tung chih,* 10/1, 6, 8, 9–10.

were known to the Chinese. Long before the establishment of the prefectures in northern Korea Chinese migration had also reached these countries.[9a] The eastern coast of southern Korea according to local tradition was colonized by Chinese refugees who migrated across the sea at the time the Ts'in dynasty fell, while the western coast was for some time under the rule of the Chis, who migrated there after they were expelled from Chao-hsien. Southern Korea, if not also Japan, was therefore in just as favorable a position for absorption into China as the country south of the Yangtze valley. Indeed, it seems that the Han dynasty might have advanced a step further after taking Chao-hsien, and established direct rule over southern Korea, if not also the Japanese islands. The Han dynasty, however, was then occupied with campaigns against the desert nomads known as the Hsiung-nu, who, since the Ts'in dynasty, had formed a constant menace to the existence of the Chinese nation. These campaigns led finally to the subjugation of a section of that powerful desert people, and the expulsion from the Far East of another section, which spread into the West and were known there as the Huns. On the other hand, it also led to the cessation of the process of unification in the Far East. The tribes of southern Korea and certain sections of Japan, however, soon learnt to admire Chinese power and culture. In this way Chinese influence was extended over these regions, not by conquest, but by voluntary homage of local chieftains, who received in return appointments as hereditary governors to rule over their own people, thus laying a foundation for the system of suzerainty later developed.[10]

[9a] It is said that not a few of the Japanese families of today can trace their ancestral lines back to the early Chinese settlers.

[10] *Wei chih*, 30/10 *et seq*; *Hou han hsu*, 115/10-12.

North of Liao-tung, Lo-lang, and Yuan-tu was the country of the tribes who were known in Chinese history generically with those of the Korean peninsula and the Japanese islands as the "Tung-yi". They were known in the west by mistake as the "Tungus",[11] but will be known for our purpose simply as the "Manchurian tribes" or "Manchurian nomads". In the age of the Chinese classics they were known to the Chinese as the Shu-shen. Both the Bamboo Books and *Shih chi* record that they appeared at the court of Shun.[12] However this may be, they certainly appeared in the court of Sheng-wang (1115–1079 B.C.) of the Chou dynasty. *Shu ching* bears witness by including one document, now lost,[13] in which the ruling

[11] The term the "Tungus" has, since Chinese students have been going to Japan, crept into Chinese history textbooks and therefore deserves some passing criticism. Western authorities in general seem to agree that the term the "Tungus" is derived from the term the "Tung-hu". (See E. G. Ravenstein, *The Russians on the Amur* — London, 1861, p. 4.) If so, we have a case of misnomer. The Tung-hu or Hsien-pie or Chitan and the Shu-shen or Nuchen or Manchu, as each was known at different periods of history, were two different peoples, one related to the desert nomads and the other to the original tribes of northern Korea. They appeared in history at different times, the latter at least seven centuries earlier than the former; inhabited different parts of the land of nomads, the latter in the Sungari valleys, and the former in the Cherim prairie and Jehol hills; and lived independent lives as two peoples until the latter was merged mainly into the Chinese and the former mainly into the Mongols. They were consistently classified in all Chinese records — except *Tang shu* which is better known for its literary style than for its scientific accuracy — under two different generic names, the "Pei-ti" and the "Tung-yi". It, therefore, seems strange to hear students of history call one by the name of the other.

[12] *Man chou yuan liu*, 1/4–5.
[13] *Shang shu*, 17/10.

dynasty exhorted their chieftain to loyalty. When the
Weis ruled over Chao-hsien a number of these Manchurian
tribes that lived close to that colony were subdued. When
the Han dynasty annexed Chao-hsien more of these tribes
tendered their allegiance.[14] In fact, conditions favored
Chinese expansion into the valleys of the Sungari as much
as into southern Korea and the Japanese islands. Yet the
military exhaustion that prevented China from growing in
one direction prevented her from growing in the other.
The tribes in the north, however, like the tribes in the south,
also learnt to admire Chinese power and culture. During
the Later Han dynasty (25–219) the tribe of the upper
Sungari known as the Fu-yu, which was closest to the prefectures and more subject to Chinese cultural influence,
had founded a kingdom after the Chinese model, the first
of its kind in Manchuria. This state not only admitted
Chinese suzerainty, but also constantly fought on their side
against the descendants of the Tung-hu nomads known as
the Hsien-pie until it was conquered by the latter at the end
of the Wei dynasty (221–264).[15]

. The northeastern prefectures were handed down from
dynasty to dynasty. During the Han, Later Han, and Wei
dynasties, the prefectures of Yu-pei-ping, Liao-hsi, Liaotung, Lo-lang, and Yuan-tu formed part of one of the
thirteen provinces into which the China of those dynasties
was divided.[16] During the Tsin dynasty (265–316) the
northern part of Liao-tung was organized as a prefecture
known as Chang-li, and the southern part of Lo-lang an-

---

[14] *Hou han shu*, 115/3–10; 120/1–15; cf. *Chi lin tung chih*,
10/5–10.

[15] *Wei chih*, 30/10–11; *Tsin shu*, 97/2.

[16] *Han shu*, 28 ii/9–10; *Hou han shu*, 33/14–15; 115/2, 8–9,
10; *Wei chih*, 8/12–13; 30/15, 21.

other known as Tai-fang, and, furthermore, the prefectures east of the Liao river were united into a new province to rank as one of the nineteen of that dynasty.[17]

Sec. 2. Rise of Separate Kingdoms

Between the present Great Wall of China and the chain of mountains formed of the Alashan, the Yinshan, and the Great Khingan, there lies a twilight zone between nomadism and civilization, which has more than once served in history as a base for nomadic descents upon the Yellow River basin. Students of the Chinese classics claim that the third province Shun added to the nine of Yao lies in that twilight zone, and this indicates that the strategical importance of that region was early recognized by Chinese statesmen. Certainly the raids made by the nomads from that region in the latter part of the Chou dynasty must have convinced the feudal states along the northern frontier of the necessity of driving them off. It was in pursuance of such a policy that the feudal state of Yen occupied the Jehol hills. About the same time Yen's western neighbor, the feudal state of Chao, occupied the Chahar steppes and the section of the Yellow River at the foot of the Yinshan range. Finally, the Ts'in dynasty occupied the Ordos region.

After the subjugation of the Hsiung-nu nomads by the Han dynasty Chinese statesmen grew forgetful of the necessity of keeping the wandering tribes at a distance. At the beginning of the Later Han dynasty the Hsiung-nu were allowed to settle down in the Ordos region and a branch of the descendants of the Tung-hu nomads, known as the Wu-huang, to settle down in the Jehol hills.[18] With the decline of the Later Han dynasty, the unwisdom of the

[17] *Tsin shu*, 14/21–23.   [18] *Wei chih*, 30/4–5.

measure became apparent. The Wei dynasty (220–264) therefore removed the Wu-huang, who had revolted, into the interior of China,[19] and divided the Hsiung-nu, who still remained loyal, into smaller and more manageable units. The lesson learnt from the Wu-huang revolt, however, was ignored by the Ts'in dynasty, for that dynasty not only let the Hsien-pie, a cousin tribe of the Wu-huang, settle down in the Jehol hills after the latter were removed from them, but also admitted more of the Hsiung-nu into the Ordos region.[20] The result was most unfortunate, for, shortly afterwards, when a fratricidal war took place among the imperial princes, the nomads, led by the Hsiung-nu, revolted, compelled the ruling dynasty to retire to the Yangtze valley, and converted the Yellow River basin into a battleground for over a century (317–439) — a period known in history as the Barbarian Rebellion.

By the beginning of the fifth century after Christ a branch of the Hsien-pie nomads under their chieftains, the Tobas, descended upon these war-worn barbarians, destroyed one by one the kingdoms the latter had set up in the Yellow River basin, and established the first of several barbarian dynasties known in history as the Northern Dynasties (439–580), thus ending the Rebellion as far as that basin was concerned.

The effects of the Rebellion were to tell yet more seriously upon China. The nomadic problem which confronted the statesmen of the feudal states of the latter part of the Chou dynasty and of the Ts'in and Han dynasties, and had been practically solved by the subjugation of the Hsiung-nu nomads, had become serious again through the subversion of Chinese power by the Barbarian Rebellion.

[19] *Wei chih*, 30/4–5.
[20] *Tsin shu*, 97/17–19.

The following century and a half, *i.e.*, during the existence of these barbarian dynasties in the Yellow River basin and before the unification of China by the Chinese Sui dynasty (581–617), presented, therefore, a condition of things similar to what existed at the latter part of the Chou dynasty, not only in the division of the nation into independent units, but also in the relation between these units and the nomads. The barbarian dynasties, however, on account of their alienage, could not elicit the same support which the people had given to the feudal states of the Chou dynasty, and hence the barbarian rulers were compelled, on the whole, to remain on the defensive. Indeed, from the last days of the Tobas (about 535) onward, the barbarian dynasties were so hard pressed by the nomads that they had to construct walls for protection.[21] Being different in purpose from the walls built by the feudal states, *i.e.*, defensive, rather than offensive, the walls of the barbarian dynasties which formed the basis of the modern Great Wall of China, did not follow the old track[22] of the walls of the feudal states, but struck out in an easterly direction from the Yellow River at the foot of the Chahar steppes to the coast of the Pohai,[22a] abandoning the Chahar steppes and the Jehol hills to the nomads, and leaving the northeastern prefectures to whatever fate might befall them.[23]

[21] *Wei shu*, 3/14; *Pei chi shu*, 4/14, 18, 20; *Chou shu*, 7/6.

[22] The section east of the Yellow River appears to coincide more or less with the dividing line between Outer Shansi, Outer Chihli, and the intra-Palisade Shengking on the one side, and Inner Mongolia and the land of the Manchurian nomads on the other. See *Cheng te fu chih*, 3/5–11; *San ting chih*, 1/1–14.

[22a] Known to the West as two regions of water, the Gulf of Liaotung and the Gulf of Pechili.

[23] For further information about the Wall see *Sui shu*, 1/15,

At the opening of the Barbarian Rebellion southern Manchuria and northern Korea, being nearest to the Hsien-pie nomads,[24] fell conveniently into the hands of a branch whose chieftains were known as the Mujungs. With the resources of the northeastern prefectures at their disposal, the Mujungs found no difficulty in descending upon the Yellow River basin and taking part in the general struggle to master that section of the country. Indeed, they succeeded in remaining on the field till almost the end of the Rebellion.[25]

The position of the Mujungs in the northeastern prefectures, however, became precarious as soon as their centre of interest moved into the Yellow River basin. From the very beginning a Manchurian tribe known as the Kao-ku-li,[26] who lived side by side with the Hsien-pie on the border of the northeastern prefectures, had cast a covetous eye upon that section of the country, and on several occasions the Mujungs had to drive them back across the border.[27] After the Tobas descended into the Yellow River basin and ended the Mujung power, taking advantage of the situation the Kao-ku-li occupied the three remoter prefectures, Lo-lang, Yuan-tu, and Tai-fang,[28] and there founded a barbarian

---

23, 24; 3/11–12; 13/20; *Fang yu chi yao*, 9/26 *l.*; 10/24 *l.*–26 *l.* For further information about the northeastern prefectures see *Wei shu*, 105/35–38; *Sui shu*, 30/20; *Tang shu*, 39/20–21; *Wu tai shih*, 72/8; *Yen ko piao*, 34/27–32; 35/1–30; *Fang yu chi yao*, 5/12, 30–31.

[24] *Hou han shu*, 120/10–14; *Wei chih*, 30/7–9; *Tsin shu*, 108/1; *Yen ko piao*, 35/11 *l.*

[25] *Tsin shu*, books 109–110 and 123–124.

[26] *Wei chih*, 12/15; *Liang shu*, 54/21–22.

[27] *Tsin shu*, 109/7–8.

[28] *Ibid.*, 110/5 *l.*; 111/12 *l.*; 123/11; *Liang shu*, 54/54–55.

kingdom known after the tribe as Kao-ku-li or Kao-li. The Tobas were naturally not as interested as the Mujungs had been in that section of the country. Furthermore, they were fully engaged first, in the conquest of other barbarian kingdoms in the Yellow River basin, and then, in the struggle against newcomers from the desert. Consequently Kao-li was able not only to hold on, but presently also to annex the prefectures of Liao-tung and Chang-li, thus extending her territory as far west as the Liao river.[29]

The Barbarian Rebellion did not end in the northeast with the establishment of the kingdom of Kao-li. We had occasion above to speak of southern Korea and the Japanese islands as having been brought up to a high degree of civilization through Chinese immigration. It is quite natural that the example of Kao-li was readily followed in those regions, and within a comparatively short period of time three more kingdoms made their appearance in the northeast, one of them in the Japanese islands known as Wo, after the name of the tribe of the islands; another on the western coast of southern Korea, known as Pai-chi; and a third on the eastern coast of the same section of the peninsula known as Hsin-lo.

Thus, as a result of the Barbarian Rebellion, a separatist tendency was set in motion in the northeast. But if this was due to the temporary eclipse of China, the tendency was from the very outset checked by the potentiality of her power. When the Hsiung-nu nomads started the Rebellion by revolt against the incompetent Tsin dynasty, their chieftains based their claim to the throne on the fact of their being descendants of the Han dynasty by a female line.

[29] *Pei shih*, 94/7.

When the Mujungs descended upon the northeastern prefectures they applied for authorization to act as governors [30]
to the Eastern Tsin dynasty (317–419), by which name
the Tsin is known in history after its retirement to the
Yangtze valley. It is curious that, despite their military
power, the nomads continued to regard China as the fountain head of authority in the Far East. Settled communities, being children of Chinese cultural influences, of course,
were not slow to do the same thing. After the rise of the
kingdoms in the northeast their rulers, therefore, one after
another applied for authorization to hold their kingly offices
to the Chinese dynasties — known in history as the Southern
Dynasties (420–589) — which followed the Eastern Tsin
dynasty in the Yangtze valley, and which represented the
legitimate line of succession.[31] These rulers were appointed
as governors and at the same time invested as kings. For
example, the first titles the king of Kao-li received were
" Commander-in-Chief of the Forces of Ying-chou, King
of Kao-li, and Prefectural Duke of Lo-lang ", and the
first titles the king of Wo received were " Commander-in-
Chief of the Forces of Wo, Pai-chi, Hsin-lo, Jen-na, Tsin-
han, and Mu-han Nations, East-Tranquilling Marshal, and
King of Wo ".[32]

[30] *Tsin shu*, 108/3 *et seq.*

[31] For *Pai-chi* see *Tsin chu*, 9/3 *l.* For Kao-li see *Pien yi
tien*, 13/34; *Wei shu*, 4 i/17. For Wo see *Sung shu*, 97/18 *l.*–
19. For Hsin-lo see *Liang shu*, 54/25. See also *Sui shu*, 81/1 *l.*,
6, 8, for all.

[32] The five kings of Wo that were recorded as having received
investitures from the Sung of the Southern Dynasties have been
identified by an eminent Japanese authority with the following
Japanese mikados: O-sazaki, Mizuha-wake, O-asazuma-wakago-
sukune, Anaho, and O-hatsuse-waka-take. See Wang Tung-leng,
History of Eastern Asia (in Chinese) (Shanghai, 1922), vol. i,
p. 194.

In 589 the Sui dynasty (581–617) effected the unification of the country within the Wall, as the Ts'in dynasty
had also done in 255 B.C., and it was inevitable that the
question of China's relation with the kingdoms of the northeast should again present itself. The northeastern country,
however, was at this time more detached from the rest of
the Chinese world than had been the case in the third century before Christ, on account of the simple fact that China
was not in possession of the twilight zone of nomadism and
civilization that lay between the two sections. Furthermore, the northeastern kingdoms had developed a greater
local sentiment than had previously been the case in Chao-
hsien. This was particularly true in the northeastern prefectures, where a nomadic conquest had taken place. Consequently, if the question of the relation of China with
those kingdoms was to be solved successfully, it could not
be made in the same way as before.

As records show, neither the Sui dynasty, nor the Tang
(618–906), which followed immediately, had any desire
to reconquer Kao-li, and still less the other kingdoms in
southern Korea and the Japanese islands. Therefore, had
the petty rulers of the time been able to recognize the relative position of their kingdoms with China, or at least respected the relationship which their predecessors had already
established for them, the *status quo* in the Far Eastern
political system would doubtless not have been disturbed.
The petty rulers were unable to do either.

The unification of China, coupled with the reëstablishment of Chinese control over the nomads, naturally enough
disquieted the kingdom of Kao-li, and moved her to undertake warlike preparations. Wen-ti (581–604), the first
Sui emperor, took offense at these evidently disloyal acts,
but being a man of moderate nature he confined himself

merely to sending the king of Kao-li a personal letter of remonstrance. In view of the revelation the letter makes of the attitude and policies of China towards the north-eastern question at that time, it may be justifiable to reproduce it in part: [33]

. . . Although the people and the territory of the out-of-the-way kingdom of your highness are insignificant, they are just the same my people and my territory. If we were to depose your highness, we could not leave the post vacant and would have to select some one to fill it. Should your highness be able to cleanse your heart, modify your conduct, and hereafter act in conformity with the fundamental laws of the empire, we would already have had a good minister, and why should we trouble ourselves to send other talents! In administering laws, the rulers of old were guided above all by the principle of justice; reward is for the good, and punishment for the evil. The people within the four seas will know what we do. If we should impose armed forces upon your highness without a just cause, what would they think of us? We hope your highness will consider what we have said and desist from further designs. . . . [34]

The letter did not bring the desired effect, and the Sui dynasty resorted to force. The successor of Wen-ti, on whom the task fell, was, however, not competent to carry it out. He not only failed to enforce the suzerain claims of China, but also so discredited himself with his badly conducted campaigns that the malcontents in the country were able to bring about a widespread rebellion and overthrow the dynasty itself.

The failure of the Sui dynasty also discredited China in the eyes of the other kingdoms, and under the Tang dynasty

[33] *Sui shu*, 81/3–4.   [34] *Ibid.*, 81/1–3, 5.

their attitude towards the suzerain was found likewise not at all satisfactory.[35] The first years of the new dynasty, however, passed without any serious conflict, as China was then fully occupied with attempts to subdue the Tu-chueh nomads, who had again gone beyond control as a result of the fall of the Sui dynasty. But towards the close of the reign of Tai-tsung (627–649) and the beginning of the reign of Kao-tsung (650–683), when Chinese rule was reëstablished throughout the land of nomads, the attention of the dynasty was again directed eastward. On the occasion Hsin-lo appealed to the Tang dynasty for protection against attacks from Kao-li and Pai-chi, the dynasty readily despatched forces to her aid.[36] Against a powerful dynasty like the Tang the latter kingdoms had little chance of success. In 660 Pai-chi was conquered, and eight years later Kao-li underwent the same fate.[37]

True to its original purpose — the enforcement of suzerain claims — the Tang dynasty refrained from annexing the kingdoms. In 665, as soon as tranquillity was restored in Pai-chi, and still three years before the conquest of Kao-li, the dynasty created the son of the deposed king "Prince of Tai-fang" and restored the kingdom to him.[38] In 677, under similar circumstances it restored Kao-li to her deposed king.[39] In this case the process had to be arrested on account of the complicity of the king in a rebellion which led to his deposition the second time. A little later the Tang dynasty, however, reconsidered the question of reëstablishing Kao-li. In 687 it created the twice-deposed king's grandson "Prince of Chao-hsien". In 698 it despatched him home. In the following year it further

---

[35] *Tang shu*, 220/2–4.
[36] *Ibid.*, 220/4–5, 16, 20.
[37] *Ibid.*, 220/5–11, 12–14, 17.

[38] *Ibid.*, 220/19.
[39] *Ibid.*, 220/21 *et seq.*

appointed an uncle of the young prince " Protector-General of Antung " — the title borne by the Tang governors of Kao-li since the conquest — thus terminating direct control over the kingdom.[40]

The once proud, though petty, kingdoms of Kao-li and Pai-chi were, however, destined to disappear from the peninsula; for their old enemy, the kingdom of Hsin-lo, which had fought them when they were at their height of power, could not be expected to abstain from taking advantage of them now that they were in this plight. During a short civil disturbance in China occasioned after the death of Kao-tsung by the usurpation of the imperial throne by his widow, Pai-chi was practically absorbed by Hsin-lo. Later, during another civil disturbance in China, known in history as the An-Shih Rebellion, which closed the reign of Hsuan-tsung (713–755), southern Kao-li was also absorbed by Hsin-lo.[41] In the civil disturbance after the death of Kao-tsung, a kingdom was set up by a Manchurian tribe in the upper Sungari, which was then included in the northern confines of Kao-li. This kingdom was later known as Po-hai, after the title " Prince of Po-hai " conferred upon its king by the Tang dynasty. During the An-Shih Rebellion, when Hsin-lo absorbed the southern half of Kao-li, Po-hai absorbed the northern.[42] Thus Pai-chi and Kao-li both disappeared from history.

The fate of the kingdom of Wo was equally eventful. The titles conferred upon the king of Wo by the Southern Dynasties given above indicate that the interests of this kingdom at that time were not confined to the islands. When the kingdoms of Kao-li, Pai-chi, and Wo made their

[40] *Ibid.*, 220/15.
[41] *Ibid.*, 220/15, 19, 22.
[42] *Ibid.*, 219/14 *et seq.*

appearance, the eastern coast of southern Korea was still in an unorganized state. While Kao-li was much occupied in the north, and while Pai-chi was comparatively small and weak, Wo did not fail to take upon herself the pleasant task of dominating that southeastern section of the peninsula. This aggression did not pass unnoticed. A native kingdom known as Hsin-lo made its appearance there, drove out the Wos and ended this almost legendary Japanese overseas activity.[43]

Before Wo finally withdrew to live for the next thirteen centuries, except a decade or two, a peaceful life in the islands as a respectable member of the Far Eastern world, she was to appear yet again to test with the rest of the petty kingdoms the power of the Tang dynasty. This conflict took place during the Tang campaigns against Pai-chi when Wo sent assistance to the peninsula kingdom. Her part, however, was not sufficient to tip the balance in favor of Pai-chi, for her second and larger detachment of forces, consisting of 27,000 men and 400 vessels, was met by a Tang fleet before landing and completely annihilated.[44] With this failure Wo immediately set about to prepare for a worse fate. The Tang commander of the expeditionary forces, however, not only did not follow up his success but even sent Wo a mission of good will. This resulted in Wo's sending periodical missions of homage to the Tang court until the decline of that dynasty.[45] It was during that dynasty that Wo first adopted the present name of Jih-pen, or Japan as it appears in the Anglicized form.

[43] *Pien yi tien,* 28/2 *l.,* 8 *l.,* 9, 11.

[44] *Tang shu,* 108/2 *l.;* 220/18 *l.*

[45] *Ibid.,* 220/26 *et seq.*

Sec. 3. Remerging of Manchuria into China

Down to the Barbarian Rebellion there was no such division of functions between the civil and the military as in later ages. Under such circumstances local governors were primarily trained administrators and secondarily successful soldiers, if they must be also soldiers at all; for even in border provinces where a governor had the duty of warding off invasion and even of inflicting punishment upon the border tribes for offenses not great enough to demand national attention, that duty would yet be small in comparison with the duties of administering justice for the people, of preventing drought and flood or remedying their effects, of providing facilities for education, of collecting national revenues, and of maintaining post-roads. This system had the result, that on the one hand there was not such prejudice against professional soldiers as in later ages, and on the other, the military elements in the country did not constitute a menace to the state.

A new condition of things, however, was brought about in consequence of the Barbarian Rebellion. The barbarians who came to establish dynasties in the Yellow River basin after the Rebellion found themselves not only unable to rule the country owing to the lack of experience but also compelled to maintain an army to insure safety among an alien people. Under such circumstances they instinctively delegated civil administration to the Chinese who were better versed in the art of government and retained for themselves military administration. This operated first to divorce the military function from the civil, and then, naturally enough, to assure the domination of the former over the latter.

In later ages the military, though never again united with

the civil function as in the early ages, was always held subordinate to the latter. The Tang dynasty, having followed
close on the heels of the barbarian dynasties, had no earlier
experience to profit by, and therefore was to suffer through
the consequences of the change. Although it did not place
the civil below the military, for the necessity of so doing
had disappeared with the end of the barbarian dynasties, it
never hesitated to treat the two as mutually independent.
Thus in the country military governors were in control of
the armies of the nation side by side with civil governors
who attended to judicial, economic and educational matters,
and on the border where the Han dynasty would have only
maintained civil prefects who were also soldiers, the Tang
dynasty stationed military defence commissioners with large
armies under their command.[46] At the beginning of the
dynasty when the central government was itself in control
of large armies and the emperors and ministers of state
were often themselves great soldiers the system not only
worked well but even made the dynasty one of the most
glorious in military achievement in the history both of
China and of the world. But when peace brought about
general disarmament and converted soldier emperors and
ministers into civil administrators pure and simple, local
military authorities began to absorb civil functions and make
themselves more or less independent of the central government. Thus in the latter part of the Tang dynasty a system of military feudalism came into existence in China and
the vigorous control exercised by the early Tang dynasty
over the nomads was gradually slackened; and when the
dynasty came to an end, China fell into a number of petty
states and the nomads again became uncontrollable.[47] After

---

[46] *Fang yu chih yao,* 5/31 *et seq.*
[47] *Tang shu,* 210/1-3.

the lapse of half a century known in history as the Five Dynasties (907–959), the Sung dynasty (960–1126) was established and the nation was again unified; but the nomadic situation had been so developed as to pass beyond remedy.

The effect of the fall of the Tang dynasty upon the nomads was both immediate and tremendous. In 911, only four years after the fall of that dynasty, the descendants of the Hsien-pie nomads that lived on the Cherim prairie and were known as the Chitans [48] had shown signs of restlessness. By 924 they had conquered their cousins in the Jehol hills in the south, the Manchurian tribes in the north, the Tu-chueh nomads in the west, and the kingdom of Po-hai in the east. [49] In 923 they seized the two prefectures on both sides of what is now Shanhaikuan — remnants of the ancient prefectures of Yu-pei-ping and Liao-hsi. [50] In 936 they occupied the Pei-ho basin. [51] In 946 they even marched upon the Yellow River basin and proclaimed the establishment of a dynasty known as the Liao to succeed the Tang dynasty. [52] This, however, they failed to maintain.

The Sung dynasty, after the unification of the nation, was not only unable to end the Chitan power but was even unable to recover the Pei-ho basin, and so the entering wedge of the nomads upon the nation was not removed. [53] But as by that time the vigor of the Chitans had already

[48] *Ibid.*, 219/1, 7–9.

[49] *Liao shih*, 1/4, 9; 2/4–7.

[50] *Ibid.*, 2/3; *Wu tai shih*, 72/11; *Fang yu chih yao*, 6/31.

[51] *Liao shih*, 3/9–11; 4/2.

[52] *Ibid.*, 4/13–15.

[53] *Sung shih*, 4/8 *et seq.*; 5/2–4; 7/6; 11/3–4; 15/11. For similar attempts of the petty dynasties preceding the Sung dynasty see *Liao shih*, 6/4–5; *Wu tai shih*, 73/4.

declined, no disaster immediately fell upon China. In the twelfth century, however, a new nomadic tide arose, when the Manchurian tribe of the Amur river, known as the Nuchen,[54] revolted against the Chitans and succeeded in displacing them. In face of this new tide of nomadism with the dyke washed away by the previous tide, the Sung dynasty had no alternative but to abandon the Yellow River basin and retire to the Yangtze valley — known in history henceforth as the Southern Sung dynasty (1127–1279) — and the Nuchens thereupon founded a barbarian dynasty in northern China known as the Chin.[55] But the end was not yet, for nomadism, unless checked, recurs. Another century passed and the Mongols,[56] cousins of the Chitans, did not fail to follow the footsteps of the Chitans and the Nuchens before them. They revolted against the Nuchens and replaced them much in the same manner as the Nuchens had done with respect to the Chitans.[57] Before this third tide of nomadism with now only one-half of the resources of the nation at its disposal the Southern Sung dynasty could not but forfeit its existence. This took place a quarter of a century after the Nuchens had succumbed. Upon the ruins of the Chin and Sung dynasties the Mongols established the Yuan dynasty (1280–1367), the first barbarian dynasty that ever ruled over the whole of China.[58]

The conquest of southern China by the Mongols removed an incompetent dynasty and gave the people an opportunity

[54] For the tribes of Manchuria before the rise of the Nuchens see *Tang shu*, 219/2–6, 8–9, 12–13.

[55] *Chin shih*, 2/6–8, 12, 20–21; 3/8; 4/8.

[56] For the origin of the Mongols see *Tang shu*, 219/10–11; *Chiu tang shu*, 199 ii/15 *l.*–17.

[57] *Yuan shih*, 1/14.

[58] *Ibid.*, 1/15–17; 2/2–3.

to attack the nomadic problem themselves. On the other hand, the Mongols were not as ready to lose their identity in the Chinese people as the Tobas and the Nuchens had been, although they were equally ready to be assimilated in ideas. Consequently, the culmination of nomadic ascendency turned out to be its end. In 1531, just about half a century after the death of Kablai Khan (1264–94) the founder of the Yuan dynasty, the Yangtze valley revolted, and fifteen years afterwards the Ming dynasty (1368–1644) was established,[59] and the Mongols were driven back to their desert home [60] and made to submit to Chinese control even as the equally proud Hsiung-nu and Tu-chueh nomads before them.[61]

The sage Laocius has it that blessing and disaster like chums are often found together. If during the nomadic ascendency China found her territory bit by bit taken away from her, when the process was over she found herself in possession of one-half of the northeast which she had long lost. Had the Chitans and the Nuchens confined themselves to Manchuria as the Kao-ku-li did with respect to the Korean peninsula they might have developed a kingdom separate from China even as Kao-li. But from the very beginning they were not bent so much upon the establishment of a separate kingdom as upon the establishment of a dynasty in succession to the Tang dynasty, as in the case of the Chitans, or to displace the Sung dynasty, as in the case of the Nuchens. The result was as natural as it was contradictory, that the twilight zone of nomadism and civilization and southern Manchuria, with all the possibilities that came with their acquisition, were restored to China.

[59] *Ming shih*, 2/1.
[60] *Ibid.*, 2/2–3, 5; 327/1; *Fang yu shih yao*, 9/10.
[61] See *infra*, sec. 5.

The kingdom of the Chitans was divided into five " provinces ", the Pei-ho basin constituting two, the Jehol hills, the Liao basin, and the Cherim prairie one each.[62] The Nuchens added the upper Sungari basin as a fourth to the three established by the Chitans in the extra-mural country.[63] The Yuan dynasty gave the Cherim prairie back to the desert tribes, converted the upper Sungari basin into a special territory, established one prefecture on the hills and four in the Liao basin, and constituted the entire region into one of the eleven provinces into which the China of the Yuan dynasty was divided.[64] The Ming dynasty restored autonomy to the tribes of the upper Sungari, converted the hills and the Liao basin into two units, divided by the Liao river, of a military zone along the northern frontier, and constituted the unit west of the Liao, known as Ta-ling, part of Chihli and the unit east of the Liao, known as Liao-tung, part of Shantung — Chihli and Shantung being two of the fourteen provinces into which the China of the Ming dynasty was divided.[65]

Sec. 4. China and the Kingdoms

(1) Korea

About the time the Chitans conquered the kingdom of Po-hai, Hsin-lo, the co-heir of the terrtory of Kao-li, also fell into its constituent parts with two new kingdoms set up in the territories of the old kingdoms of Kao-li and Pai-chi and bearing the old names. The problem of the peninsula, however, proved simple of solution. Under the

[62] *Liao shih*, 38/2; 39/1-3; 40/1-2.
[63] *Chin shih*, 24/1-18.
[64] *Yuan shih*, 59/1-6; *Pien yi tien*, 21/55; *Sheng ching tung chih*, 10/2-3.
[65] *Ming shih*, 37/2 et seq; 41/10-15.

leadership of one Wang Kien, Kao-li absorbed Hsin-lo, conquered Pai-chi and unified the peninsula (936).[66]

As early as 923, *i.e.*, thirteen years before the unification of the peninsula, Kao-li had taken upon herself the duty of Hsin-lo in paying homage to the Chinese court, then represented by one of the petty dynasties that followed after the Tang dynasty in quick succession.[67] But in 995 when the Sung dynasty was not able to protect her from the Chitans she was compelled to transfer her allegiance to the latter.[68] This transfer of allegiance, however, was only temporary, for with the merging of the kingdom of the Chitans into China, when the Nuchens conquered it together with northern China, Kao-li's allegiance reverted to China.

Five centuries had elapsed since the Tang dynasty enforced China's suzerain claims in the peninsula. During this half of a millennium the peninsula was left much to itself either because its right to separate existence was recognized as during the powerful Tang dynasty, or because nobody was strong enough to question it as during the time of the Chitans and Nuchens. A new condition of things now came into existence with the rise of the Mongols, who were more powerful than the Chitans and the Nuchens and less considerate than the Tang dynasty. When the Mongols first appeared, they made periodical raids [69] upon Kao-li as upon northern China. When Kablai Khan became a Chinese monarch the Mongols ceased their raids and laid suzerain claims upon her instead.[70] The change, how-

---

[66] *Pien yi tien*, 28/54–55; 16/34–37.
[67] *Wu tai shih*, 74/11–12.
[68] *Liao shih*, 13/4; 115/2–4.
[69] *Yuan shih*, 208/1–4.
[70] *Ibid.*, 258/4; 208/14.

ever, was only in form and not in kind, for the suzerainty exercised by the Mongols differed fundamentally from what was exercised by former dynasties. On one occasion a king was deposed, and two of his ministers publicly flogged by the imperial government.[71] On another a minister was summoned to the imperial court for punishment.[72] On still another a king not only was deposed, but also exiled to the south coast of China,[73] *i.e.*, sent from one end of the empire to the other. And these were but single instances of the exercise of that suzerain power. It is probably more correct to describe the China of the time as the " protector " than as the suzerain. In fact in 1321 a provincial government was established in the kingdom to rule, in theory, side by side with the king but in practice, in his place.[74] In the latter circumstances Kao-li really differed from the provinces only in the respect that she still had a king. Indeed, in 1323 the abolition of the kingship which had evidently become superfluous was discussed, but this measure was abandoned when a Chinese minister of state differed from his Mongol colleagues and advised to the contrary. Aside from the question of the competency or incompetency of the house of the Wangs, he based his opinion against annexation upon the ground that the race, language, and culture of the peninsula kingdom were sufficiently different from those of China to justify a separate national existence.[75]

If the barbarian kingdom of Kao-li was considered as distinct enough to exist separate from China after the development of only two centuries, how much more would the native kingdom of Kao-li be so considered after the de-

[71] *Ibid.*, 20/1.
[72] *Ibid.*, 21/9.
[73] *Pien yi tien*, 22/15–16.

[74] *Yuan shih*, 63/26.
[75] *Ibid.*, 178/11.

velopment of another six centuries? It is true that during
the Sui and the early Tang dynasties the peninsula, being
virtually cut off from China, could not serve as a colonizing ground. But it is equally true that during the Yuan
dynasty and early Ming the peninsula, like southern China
of the time, had sufficient population of its own to provide
for. The attempt of the Yuan dynasty therefore would
undoubtedly not have been followed up, even if it had been
consummated. When Hung-wu-ti (1368–1398) the first
Ming emperor came to power, instead of maintaining the
provincial government established by the Yuan dynasty in
Kao-li, he merely announced to the latter the fact of his
ascension to the Chinese throne. The act of Hung-wu-ti
reminds one of that of Wen-ti of the Sui dynasty. But
the native kingdom of Kao-li, which had become wise
through a period of difficulty, differed greatly from the
barbarian kingdom of Kao-li which was arrogant because
of her unchallenged position of two centuries. The result
of Hung-wu-ti's announcement was, therefore, not war, as
on the previous occasion, but the inauguration of a new
period of harmonious relation between the suzerain and the
vassal lasting to our own time — a duration of half a
millennium. On receiving the announcement, the king of
Kao-li applied to the Ming dynasty for investiture. This
was accordingly granted.[76] In order to give a further token
of good will the emperor, having learned from the envoys
of Kao-li that the king devoted himself to religion to the
neglect of government, sent him a present of books consisting of the Six Classics, the Four Books and *Tung chien* —
the last a political history of China showing causes of success and failure in government — together with a personal
letter,[77] which, both for itself and for its prophetic indica-

[76] *Ming shih*, 320/1.   [77] *Ibid.*, 320/1–2.

tion of the trend of subsequent history, may be justifiably reproduced here. The emperor, himself an ex-Buddhist monk, had the following to say:

The rulers of old paid special attention to the defence of the country, to the means of subsistence of the people, and to the maintenance of a proper place as the centre of government. We have learnt that, on the contrary, your highness has sheltered your people with no wall, abandoned the land of Po-hai as waste, and housed even the person of your highness in mean huts. We can hardly consider this advisable. The important functions of government are the vicarial and the military. If one devote himself to the offering of prayers to Buddha instead, let him acquaint himself with the fate of Wu-ti of the Liang dynasty. The kingdom of your highness is adjacent to the Nuchens on the north and to the Wo tribe on the south. May your highness neglect not vigilance.

The house of the Wangs, however, was destined to vacate its place for others to enjoy the peace of half a millennium, for the successor of the king, an adopted son, was less competent a person and soon brought an end to the Wang line. This came about thus:

The fertile basin of the river Yalu formed originally a part of the kingdom of Po-hai.[78] When the Chitans conquered that kingdom, the kingdom of Kao-li, which had just been set up by Wang Kien, seized the opportunity and pushed her boundary north to that river. The Chitans, however, considered that region too vital to their interests, and in spite of best friendly relations did not hesitate to push her back from that place as soon as they could afford to do so (1010–1020).[79] In the thirteenth century,

[78] *Liao shih,* 115/1.   [79] *Ibid.,* 115/3.

after the lapse of about two hundred and fifty years Kao-li,
availing herself of the fall of the Chin dynasty in China,
again pushed to the Yalu.[80] This time her success was final,
for although during the Yuan dynasty she was again pushed
back, she was after the lapse of two decades given the possession of the territory she so much coveted.[81] Kao-li,
however, did not remain contented. When the Yuan dynasty fell, she even advanced beyond the river and occupied
the right bank of the upper course. In 1387, when the
question came up, the Ming court ruled that since the Yalu
had been the boundary between China and Kao-li in the
Yuan dynasty, it should remain so. By this decision the
new king refused to abide. This, of course, meant war
with the suzerain, and therefore led to dissension in the
court of the kingdom itself. The general who was sent to
garrison the territory in defiance of the imperial ruling, revolted and replaced the Wangs. In 1392, the new ruler,
whose name was Li Cheng-kuei, applied to the imperial
government for recognition as well as a new designation
for his kingdom. In consideration of the cause that led to
the change of ruling house the imperial government readily
accorded him recognition and conferred upon his kingdom
the name of the ancient colony Chao-hsien.[82] As to the
name of Kao-li which has so long been associated with the
nation, it is natural that it could not be easily forgotten.
In fact, outside of official communications, that nation up
to the present is equally known as Chao-hsien and Kao-li,
and in the West it is even known almost exclusively by the
latter, which in its Latinized form is written as Corea or
Korea.

[80] *Chin shih*, 2/12.
[81] *Sheng ching tung chih*, 10/2-3.
[82] *Ming shih*, 320/4-6.

With the establishment of the kingdom of Chao-hsien, or Chosen as the Japanese write it, the good will of the Ming court found response. Throughout the Ming dynasty Chao-hsien never failed in her duty towards the suzerain. On the other hand, the favor of the Ming dynasty to Chao-hsien was an object of envy among the vassal states.[83] And this good relationship was not confined to form and sentiment. When Chao-hsien was overrun by the Japanese in the end of the sixteenth century the Ming dynasty readily came to her rescue. When the Ming dynasty fought against the rising Manchus at the beginning of the seventeenth century Chao-hsien hastened to send aid. Indeed, it was in days of trial that the strong tie between the suzerain and the vassal was best demonstrated. Before the Manchus entered China, Chao-hsien was twice overrun by them and finally (1636) compelled to transfer her allegiance to them even as Kao-li had had to do with respect to the Chitans during the Sung dynasty; and yet during the struggle between the Ming dynasty and the Manchus that followed, Chao-hsien avoided every duty that would require her to go against her former suzerain.[84] The Tsing dynasty (1644–1911) made no departure from the policy of the Ming dynasty towards Chao-hsien [84a] and the happy relation established between China and that vassal kingdom by the founder of the Ming dynasty was continued until it was terminated by the Japanese War of 1894–95.

(2) *Japan*

Towards Japan the policy of the Yuan dynasty was no less vigorous. Ever since the decline of the Tang dynasty

[83] *Pien yi tien*, 23/51.

[84] *Sheng wu chi*, 6/18 *et seq.*

[84a] For details of Sino-Korean relations during the Tsing dynasty see *Hui tien*, bks. 502–514.

Japan had ceased to send missions of homage to the Chinese court either as represented by the Sung dynasty or the Chin.[85] In 1266 as soon as Kablai Khan felt that he had sufficient hold upon Korea he summoned Japan to renew the mission by the following letter:[86]

His Mongol majesty the emperor to his highness the king of Japan:

As even the rulers of the petty states of old, whose territories were limited, felt it their duty to promote friendship and good will, what is to be said of us, whose ancestors had the mandate of heaven to rule over the universe and the respect and love of the multitudes of distant and strange lands! On our ascension to the throne we took pity upon the innocent people of Kao-li, who had long suffered from arrows and spears, and ordered the cessation of fighting and the restoration of territory and banners. The king of Kao-li and his ministers were so deeply moved that they came in person to do us homage with such gladness of heart as existed in children towards their father, though their relation to us was but that of servant and master. This, we presume, is known to your highness and the ministers. Kao-li is now our eastern vassal. Why has not Japan, who is just next to her and has had official relation with the Middle Kingdom since the beginning of her national existence, sent us a single mission to show her good will? In order that the kingdom of your highness might realize the significance of this, we now send envoys with this letter to empty our heart. We hope that friendly communication will be henceforth opened and intimate relationship established. The sages regard what is within the four seas as one family. If this is so, there must not be discord. Should it be necessary to resort to force, it would be entirely against our wish. We hope your highness will give this matter due consideration.

[85] *Pien yi tien*, 33/25.   [86] *Yuan shih*, 208/20.

Japan, however, declined this and other overtures,[87] and in 1273 Kablai Khan, after he had taken the Quelpart island, sent his victorious fleet of 390 vessels and 15,000 men to intimidate her.[88] This did not produce the desired effect. Instead, it made the Japanese desperate, and they murdered the envoys subsequently sent them. In 1281 the Khan, therefore, decided upon an expedition consisting of 100,000 men from China and a smaller force from Korea. On the arrival of the two forces a junction was formed without any interference, but when they advanced from that point they were struck by a typhoon, which destroyed the entire fleet from China and the greater part of the fleet from the peninsula.[89] In 1283 the Khan planned another expedition, but he was then opposed in the country. Besides, his attention was soon diverted to Annam,[90] and Japan was spared.

When Hung-wu-ti established the Ming dynasty he reversed the policy of the Yuan dynasty towards Japan as he did its policy towards Korea, and to Japan as to Korea he merely sent a messenger to announce his ascension to the throne. In this case the response did not come immediately, as Japan had, since the middle part of the Yuan dynasty (1355), split into two and was then engaged in civil war. On the other hand, the Ming dynasty abstained from going to the extreme. Unlike the Yuan dynasty, it brought no force to bear upon her. Hung-wu-ti's good will, however, proved much wiser than the military force of Kablai Khan. In 1402, shortly after the Ashikagas unified Japan, Yoshimitsu, the greatest of that house, despatched his first

[87] *Ibid.*, 208/20–22.
[88] *Ibid.*, 208/18–19.
[89] *Ibid.*, 208/23; *Pien yi tien,* 21/44–45.
[90] *Yuan shih,* 208/24.

mission of homage to the Chinese court. In 1408 his son reported Yoshimitsu's death to the Ming dynasty and was accordingly invested as " King of Japan ". And this voluntary admission of Chinese suzerainty continued for several generations.[91]

China's relations with Japan, however, were destined to be less smooth than with Korea. In the latter part of the Ming dynasty two dictators in turn ruled Japan. The last of the two, Iyeyasu, was a statesman. He utilized his military power to found the Tokugawa house which lasted until 1867 when it gave place to the Empire. The first dictator, Hideyoshi, was a mere soldier. Typical of a man of his type, he found no better way to dispose of his troops than to send them across the sea to plague his neighbors the Koreans (1592), probably not without the vain hope that some chance success might even bring him to China as in the cases of the Nuchens and of the Mongols. Hideyoshi's host caught the poor peninsula kingdom unprepared and overran it in a short time. But he was destined to achieve nothing beyond creating a strong hatred which was to be surpassed only by that created in the twentieth century. First of all his fleet was swept from the sea by the Koreans, just as the Koreans were swept from the land by his troops. Then came the rescuing forces of the suzerain power, which compelled the invaders to retreat from Pingyang as fast as they had advanced from Fusan, and to sue for peace instead of dictating it. Peace was granted, and the invaders were permitted to retire to the coast for embarkation. But Hideyoshi could not admit his defeat. While making preparations to renew the campaign he on the one hand ordered his troops to hold on to the coast and on the other opened negotiations with the Ming court to gain time; and as soon

[91] *Ming shih*, 322/5 *l.; cf. Pien yi tien*, 34/28.

as he was ready, he broke off negotiations and ordered his troops to take the field again (1596). But China and Korea were ready for him, and he was held in check both on land and at sea. While he was doomed to lose his dictatorship at home by his defeat abroad, death mercifully removed him (1597), and the Japanese withdrew to their islands to live contentedly for another three centuries.[92]

Hideyoshi's diplomacy consisted in nothing more than representing himself to the Ming court as if he was in need of an investiture for replacing the Ashikagas. His craftiness left a bad impression upon the Ming court, and later when the Tokugawas sought to revive official relationship with both China and Korea, the Ming dynasty though giving permission to Korea to accept the overture, declined to entertain it itself. From this policy the Tsing dynasty made no departure until the seventies of the nineteenth century.

(3) *Liuchiu*

South of the Japanese group there was another group of islands known as the Liuchiuan, or, as often spelled, Loochooan group. We have so far not spoken of this group, for Chinese influence, having been checked in its march towards that group from the north by the loss of the northeastern prefectures, did not manage to reach it until the southern route by way of the Pescadores islands and Formosa was opened. Under Kublai Khan the first attempt was made to bring the group into the empire, but his envoys never reached their destination.[93] When Hung-wu-ti despatched a mission (1372) to announce the establishment of the Ming dynasty to the Japanese and the other oceanic peoples, the Liuchiuans readily tendered their allegiance. Later, when the Liuchiuan king sent students to the national

[92] *Ibid.*, 322/14–22. [93] *Yuan shih*, 210/13 *l.*

academy at the Chinese capital, as the kings of Japan, Hsin-lo, and Po-hai during the Tang dynasty, and of contemporaneous Chao-hsien had done, the emperor was so pleased that to facilitate communication he undertook to promote the migration of thirty-six families of sailors from Foochow — the port of entry for the Liuchiuans as Ningpo was for the Japanese.[94] It was after the tendering of allegiance that the islanders first adopted the Chinese name of Liuchiu for their nation. During the reign of Yung-lo-ti the Liuchiuan king first applied to the Ming court for a surname and was given that of " Shang ".[95]

As we have seen, the Japanese group at a later day also tendered their allegiance to the Ming dynasty. But, while the Japanese group broke off at the first sign of the decline of that dynasty, the Liuchiuan group remained loyal to the very end, weathering even the most trying period of Japan's short-lived ascendency. Some time after the Japanese failed in their attempt on Korea, a Japanese feudal lord of the Satsuma clan invaded Liuchiu, carried off her king (1609), annexed five of his forty-two islands, and compelled him to pay an annual tribute as ransom.[96] In spite of the fact that the Ming dynasty was not able to send him succor as it did in the case of Korea, the king did not let his allegiance to the Ming dynasty suffer any change. Under the Tsing dynasty his relations with China remained the same.[97]

[94] *Ming shih*, 323/3 *l.*; *Pien yi tien*, 100/13.
[95] See memorandum submitted by Hsiang Te-hung, envoy of Liuchiu, K., 5/6/24, *Yi shu han kao*, 9/23 *l.*; also *Ming shih*, 323/4.
[96] See the Hsiang memorandum above cited; also *Ming shih*, 323/10.
[97] *Pien yi tien*, 100/35 *et seq*; see also *Hui tien*, bks. 502-514.

Sec. 5. China and the Mongols and Manchus

We have seen that the nomadic ascendency consequent to the fall of the Tang dynasty resulted in reopening the vast extra-mural country, and that so far as the settled communities, such as Korea and Japan, were concerned, China's policy, in spite of the attempts of the Mongols to modify it, in the end remained the same as that adopted by the Tang dynasty. To China's policy toward the nomads we may now turn.

From the Han dynasty, especially after the subjugation of the Hsiung-nu, down to the Barbarian Rebellion the nomads did not form a serious problem to China. The nomads of northern Manchuria and Outer Mongolia were yet insignificant politically. Those on the border, since they had been repeatedly subdued by Chinese military power and long subjected to Chinese cultural influence, were not difficult to manage. During the Han dynasty they were merely placed under the nearest prefects like their settled neighbors. During the Later Han dynasty and afterwards, they were given chieftains of their own, who in turn were subject to the supervision of Chinese " protectors ".

While the Barbarian Rebellion was going on, these border tribes were absorbed by the settlers. When the Tang dynasty attacked the problem, it found in place of these familiar nomads new tribes from the north and the west. Consequently it had to change the methods of dealing with them. As the desert nomads of the Cherim prairie and Jehol hills and the Manchurian nomads tendered their allegiance voluntarily, the Tang dynasty appointed their chieftains hereditary governors just as the Later Han did with respect to the tribes of southern Korea and the Japanese islands, and placed these chieftains only nominally under the nearest military governors acting as " protectors ". As the Tu-chueh nomads had to be compelled by force to tender their allegiance, the dynasty established four " protectors-general ", one in Inner Mongolia, one in Outer Mongolia, and two in what is now the province of Sinkiang, to rule over them directly.

An important period of transition had intervened between the Tang and Ming dynasties as between the early dynasties and the Tang. No fundamental change, however, was produced in consequence of this later transition as had been the case in the earlier transition; for when the Ming dynasty came to grips with the nomadic problem, it too found that the nomads east of the Great Khingan mountains were as tractable as they had been during the Tang dynasty, while those west of that range were as defiant. Consequently, in the nomadic problem as in the relation with the settled communities the Ming dynasty did not make any departure from the policies adopted by the Tang dynasty.

The Ming dynasty, however, was not as powerful as the Tang. Besides, the Mongols, the principal nomads it had to deal with, were in possession of an imperial tradition — a tradition of which the Tu-chueh nomads never dreamt — and were at the same time more powerful than their nomadic predecessors. Consequently, the same task which was accomplished by the Tang dynasty in one generation, was to take the Ming and the Tsing dynasties together to complete.

After the Mongols were expelled from China they still held out in Outer Mongolia, with occasional raids across the Gobi desert. This led to campaigns which lasted for two decades.[98] In the end Mongol power was crushed, but Hung-wu-ti, the founder of the Ming dynasty, did not

[98] *Ming shih*, 327/2-5.

proceed further, partly because of his old age, and partly because of the need of reconstruction at home.

Under Yung-lo-ti (1403–1424) the Ming dynasty's attention was redirected to the extra-mural country. As in the Tang dynasty no difficulty was found with the nomads east of the Great Khingan mountains. At the invitation of the Chinese court all chieftains tendered their allegiance and hence were required only to appear periodically with nominal tributes at the seat of government of the nearest defence commissioner.[99] Again as in the Tang dynasty the nomads west of the Great Khingan mountains were defiant, and campaigns for their subjugation were launched. The Mongols had in the meantime recovered from the crushing blows of Hung-wu-ti, but Yung-lo-ti was able not only to defeat them again but also to bring them this time to admit Chinese suzerainty.[100] However, before any further steps could be taken to tighten control over them, the soldier emperor Yung-lo-ti died, leaving no successor equally endowed to carry on his work. Thus left free, the Mongols did not fail to take advantage of the opportunity. Shortly afterwards, when they were again sufficiently recovered, they began to make occasional raids across the Gobi desert, and when the Ming showed signs of decline they even moved southward *en masse* and settled in the zone outside the Great Wall, the Tatas (Mongols east of the Altai mountains) east of the Alashan range,[101] and the Oelots (Mongols west of the Altai) west of the Alashan,[102] thus again depriving China of the control of the twilight

[99] For the desert nomads of Cherim prairie see *ibid.*, 328/8. For the Manchurian nomads see *Fang yu chi yao*, 9/22; *Chi lin tung chih*, 12/1–2.

[100] *Ming shih*, 327/5 *l. et seq.*, *Fang yu chi yao*, 9/20–21.

[101] *Ming shih*, 327/8 *et seq.*; see also *Fang yu chi yao* 9/23–24.

[102] *Ming shih*, 328/1 *et seq.*; *Sheng wu chi*, 3/23 *l.*, 26.

zone of nomadism and civilization so necessary for her security.

The days of the Mongols as a menace to China were, however, over. After a few decades of pressure against the Great Wall they settled down as the Hsiung-nu nomads of the distant past had done.[103] But the Ming dynasty was not destined to be free of nomadic cares. While it was watching these Mongols with large armies, unable to forget that they were once a great nomadic people, a tribe of the border of Liaotung, later known as the Manchu, an insignificant group[104] of the generally tractable Manchurian nomads, suddenly revolted (1618), occupied Liaotung as far west as the Liao river (1621), and set up a kingdom with Mukden as capital.[105]

The rise of the Manchus has features which resemble the rise of the Chitans, for both border nomads had long been under Chinese influence, political and cultural, and in each case the revolt resulted in the establishment of a barbarian kingdom on Chinese soil. But the two differed in several very important respects. First of all, while the rise of the Chitans took place after the fall of the Tang dynasty when China was for half a century disorganized, the rise of the Manchus took place when China was under a unified government though in the decline of a dynasty. Again, while the Chitans succeeded in founding their kingdom on the Liao basin as well as on the Pei-ho basin, and thus were not only secured from the Chinese but also in a position to keep the latter eternally vigilant, the Manchus were to the very end unable to go much further than the Liao river and thus were forever exposed to attacks by the Ming forces. It was

[103] *Ming shih,* 327/17 *et seq.;* 327/31–33.
[104] *Chiu pien kao,* 2/15 *et seq; Sheng wu chi,* 1/3.
[105] *Sheng wu chi,* 1/4–6, 18–26.

therefore reasonable to expect that, although the Manchus like the Chitans were able to deprive China of practically all the territory beyond the Great Wall, they would not be able to hold out like their nomadic predecessors but would come to an end speedily. The Manchus, however, had the " Mandate of Heaven " as they later arrogated it to themselves. While the first of the Manchu chieftains had fallen a direct victim to, and the second died broken-hearted in, futile attempts to take the territory west of the Liao river,[106] and while the Manchus had so far given up their hope of any further advance as to make overtures to the Ming dynasty with the hope of holding Liaotung under some color of a Chinese suzerainty, the Ming dynasty itself fell.

By the time of the Ming dynasty southern China was no longer able to absorb the surplus of population of the Yellow River basin, and yet the dynasty through its failure to exercise effective control over the nomads deprived China of the alternative ground of colonization in the extra-mural country. Given these conditions without the modern means of remedy, the Malthusian law of population did not fail to work itself out. For some time rebellion had been rife in the Yellow River basin. When troops were withdrawn from the west to check the Manchus in the east, the southern rebels entered Shensi and Shansi; and when they had thus gained the vantage ground, they entered Chihli and sacked Peking before troops from the frontier could be recalled to check them. With a country as centralized as the China of the Ming dynasty the fall of the national capital was fatal, for it left the nation powerless to resist any nomadic invasion. Under such circumstances the Manchus were not only able to enter China but were also able to effect a

[106] *Ibid.,* 1/18–26, 29 *et seq.*

wholesale conquest, the second of its kind in Chinese history.[107]

Nature is its own remedy. The very ease with which the conquest was effected saved China from a period of division and political impotence such as was consequent to the Barbarian Rebellion or the Nuchen descent upon the Yellow River basin. Thus there was no break in government or policy as a result of the change, and the Tsing dynasty (1644–1911) which the Manchus established became a real successor to the Ming. Indeed, when tranquillity was restored in the country the Manchus turned their attention northward and carried on what the Ming dynasty had not yet completed.

By this time the Tatas both north and south of the Gobi desert as well as the Oelots on the Chinese frontier were already as tractable as their cousins east of the Great Khingan mountains, but the Oelots of what is now Sinkiang were still defiant. In the time of the emperor Kanghsi (1662–1722) they even attempted to absorb the Tatas, probably with the hope of welding the nomadic forces for a revival of Mongol power. It is highly probable that had the Manchu descent upon China ended similarly to the Nuchen descent, the Oelot attempt might have led to something as serious as the Mongol conquest. But the Oelots had now to oppose a unified China, and in so doing they courted disaster. China not only expelled them from Outer Mongolia but also followed them into their home west of the Altai mountains, and in a series of campaigns spreading over a period of eighty-three years (1677–1760) finally subdued them. Thus the task of controlling the nomads was completed.[108]

After the establishment of the Tsing dynasty the Man-

[107] *Ibid.*, 1/43 *et seq.* [108] *Ibid.*, 3/30–38, 59 *l.*–68; 4/1–15.

chus made Mukden the auxiliary capital of the dynasty as Nanking was in the Ming. They furthermore gave the territory of Liaotung the dignity now due it as the home of the dynasty, by constituting it into a province known as Shengking of equal rank with the eighteen intra-mural provinces, with two prefectures known as Fengtien and Chinchou, and nine *hsiens* under it.[109]

With regard to the Manchurian nomads the Tsing dynasty made no departure from the Ming policy. It only required the nomads to appear periodically with nominal tributes at Mukden, the seat of the Military Governor of Shengking, the nearest defence commissioner to them, and left them otherwise much to themselves.[110]

As to its policy towards the desert nomads, the Tsing dynasty found its model in the acts of the Tang. These nomads were organized into " banners " each under a hereditary chieftain, and the " banners " were grouped into leagues each with a captain-general and a deputy captain-general, who were elected subject to the approval of the imperial government. The " banners " and leagues were then in turn placed under the imperial government or its agents.[111] Thus those of Inner Mongolia were directly under the Court of Colonial Affairs in Peking, those of Outer Mongolia under the Military Governor of Uliassutai, those of Kukunor under the Imperial Commissioner at Sining, and those in Sinkiang under the Military Governor of Ili. In Inner Mongolia the Chahar Tatas [112] and the Tumet Tatas of Kueihuacheng [113] lost their tribal government through revolt and were placed under the direct control of the Deputy Military Governor of Chahar and the

[109] *Sheng ching tung chih,* 10/4.
[110] See *ibid.,* 10/14 *l.*–15.
[111] *Sheng wu chi,* 3/2 *l.*–3 *l.*

[112] *Ibid.,* 3/6.
[113] *Ibid.,* 3/7.

Military Governor of Suiyuan respectively. Besides these, the Tatas there numbered forty-nine "banners," grouped into six leagues. In Outer Mongolia, as found in the reign of Kienlung (1736–1795), there were eighty-two "banners" of Tatas, grouped into four leagues, and an additional number of "banners" of Oëlots. Attached to Outer Mongolia there was also another nomadic people known as the Urianghai, of whom we have heretofore not spoken. These nomads, having been under the Mongols, passed over to China with their overlords. They were organized into "squadrons" and placed either directly or indirectly under the Military Governor of Uliassutai.[115] About the Oëlots of Alashan, the westernmost section of Inner Mongolia, of Kukunor and of Sinkiang we shall not trouble ourselves, as we shall have little occasion to speak of them. Suffice it to say that the Oëlots of Sinkiang have been in the process of being assimilated by the Chinese since the organization of the province of Sinkiang in the eighties, while those of Kukunor and Alashan are still enjoying their nomadic life as before, subject only to supervision from the nearest defence commissioner.

Sec. 6. China and the Russians

During the latter part of the period under discussion, roughly beginning with the end of the Ming dynasty, a new people, the Russians, began to make their appearance on the outskirt of the great nomadic land of the Chinese world. Whether this people will prove to be the Tu-chueh of the next half a millennium just as the Mongols proved to be but the reincarnation of the Hsiung-nu nomads, history has yet

[114] *Ibid.*, 3/15–19.
[115] *Ibid.*, 3/20–21; *Shuo fang pei cheng*, 5/7.

to reveal. For although the Russian attempt to control Outer Mongolia in recent years suggests that they are striving consciously or unconsciously to succeed the Mongols as a problem to China just as the Tu-chueh succeeded the Hsiung-nu, yet the fact that they, except their vanguards the Cossacks, are not nomads, will probably disqualify them for the task. However this may be, their arrival had a great historical significance both in itself and for China's policy towards the land of nomads.

Russia, like China, was conquered by the Mongols, but she was at the same time both more unfortunate and more fortunate than the latter. She was more unfortunate because while China bore the Mongol yoke only eighty-eight years, she languished under it two hundred and forty-four years (1236–1480), almost three times as long. She was more fortunate for two reasons. In the first place, while China's chief debt to the Mongols was the completion of a unification which she could have effected herself, Russia owed to the Mongols the creation of a nation out of chaos. In the second place, while China expelled the Mongols only to find her task but partially completed, Russia at the close of the Mongol rule found open to her not only the steppes of southern Russia which gave access to western and central Asia, but also the vast undeveloped region of northernmost Asia from the Russian border to the Pacific Ocean.

As might be expected from the fact that there were no powerful nomadic tribes in Siberia to oppose the Russian advance, its progress was rapid. In 1582 the Russians first crossed the Ural mountains; half a century later they had already reached the Lake Baikal region, the land of the Buriates (a branch of the Mongols) and the northern slope of the Outer Khingan mountains[115a] beyond which China

[115a] Known to the Russians as the Stanovoi.

exercised authority. It was here that their advance brought
them into conflicts with both China and the Buriates.

Russian advance across the Outer Khingan mountains
into the vast Sungari system [116] took the same form as elsewhere in Siberia, *i.e.*, depredation. An English authority
in summarizing the Russian activities of the first nine years
(1643–52) in the Amur and lower Sungari rivers has the
following [117] to say:

The natives appear to have been exposed to all sorts of
extortion: tribute was levied to an unlimited extent, without
any commensurate good being conferred upon the natives.
No settlements of peasants or tillers of the soil were
founded; the resources of the country were soon exhausted
by perpetual foraging expeditions of Russian adventurers.
When the Russians first arrived on the Amur, the natives
cultivated fields and kept cattle. Ten years afterwards
these fields had become desert; and a country which formerly exported grain, could not even support its own reduced population.

The Manchurian nomads were not as helpless as their
cousins in Siberia, for behind them stood the Chinese government. In 1652, the latter government finally gave
orders to drive the Russians out of the country. The Russians, chiefly Cossacks, were nomads, but unlike those whom
China had dealt with before, they were in possession of

[116] According to Russian usage the Sungari is a tributary of the
river Amur; but according to Chinese, and also to Manchu and
Nuchen usage the position is the reverse. In this treatise we shall
follow the Chinese and older usage. For the sake of clearness we
shall, however, designate the Chinese and Russian sections of the
Sungari as "upper" and "lower" respectively when only the
sections are spoken of.

[117] E. G. Ravenstein, *The Russians on the Amur*, (*London*,
1861), p. 25.

firearms. Besides, they had the experience of half a century's exploration. Wherever they went they entrenched themselves behind barricades. Such tactics were excellent in a country where the besiegers had no advantage over the besieged in the matter of provisions to offset the advantage of security. Consequently, the Chinese authorities were at first unable to make any headway with the Russians. But they were soon able to profit by experience. Instead of taking the trouble of seeking the Russians out and at the same time running the risk of being repulsed or compelled to raise a siege through lack of provisions, they took up a few strategical points along the rivers, intercepted them here and there, and with comparative ease cleared the Amur and lower Sungari. By 1660 there were no more Russians in these parts.[118]

Russian advance upon the Lake Baikal region turned out in their favor. The Buriates were stronger nomads, the kind of people the Russians consistently avoided in their early expansion across the continent and were only compelled to attack, it is said, on account of the necessity of maintaining communication between the Yenisei and the Lena rivers at the upper waters. But the Buriates, being separated from China by Mongolia over which Chinese control was then not yet fully reëstablished, did not have the advantage of Chinese protection. Consequently the Russians were able to occupy that region.

The occupation of the Lake Baikal region was significant, not so much because that region was traditionally a part of the Chinese world, but because it gave the most convenient access to the Sungari valleys. In their descent upon the Amur and the lower Sungari the Russians had

[118] *Ping lo fang lueh,* A 5/1; *cf.* Ravenstein, *op. cit.,* pp. 21, 29, 32–33.

hitherto to ascend the long rivers Aldan and Olekma from Yakutsk, but now with the possession of the Lake Baikal region they could simply cross the Outer Khingan mountains at will. When they reached that point their activities in the Sungari system were just at their height. So they crossed the easy mountain passes eastward, descended the Shilka, and founded (1654) Nertchinsk as a base for the exploration of the rivers lower down.[119]

As we have seen, Russian activities on the Amur and lower Sungari rivers were shortly afterwards brought to an end by Chinese authorities. But as the Chinese government was yet occupied with affairs in southern China which came to a head in the rebellion of 1673–80, no attempt was made to follow up the success and Nertchinsk was left as it stood.

For not expelling the Russians from the Shilka river as from the rest of the Sungari system the Chinese government was probably not to be blamed, in view of China's internal situation. Nevertheless it was a mistake. In 1670, only a decade after their expulsion, the Russians returned, this time with great earnestness of purpose, for in place of pillaging they now encouraged permanent settlement, and furthermore founded Albazin to serve as an advanced base.[120]

No sooner had the Russians entered the Amur again than the Chinese government despatched a note of protest to Nertchinsk. In the meantime the rebellion we spoke of above broke out (1673), and nothing was done as a result. But the Chinese government did not cease in its attempts to induce the Russians to withdraw peacefully, of which the chief instance was the emperor Kanghsi's protest to the

[119] Vladimir, *Russia on the Pacific and the Siberian Railway* (London, 1899), pp. 78, 127–9; Ravenstein, *op. cit.*, pp. 34–37.
[120] *Ibid.*, 38–39.

Russian envoy, Nicolas Spafarik, who came to Peking in 1675,[121] evidently as a result of the note despatched to Nertchinsk.[122] And as conditions remained unchanged after the rebellion was quelled, China resorted to force.

In the fifties the Russians were devoted to pillaging and the campaigns against them could very well be entrusted to local authorities. In the eighties the Russians carried on a plan of colonization and built Albazin as headquarters. Consequently, the central government had to take the matter into its own hands. In 1682 a high military authority was despatched to make a detailed study. On the strength of his report that 2,000 troops would be enough to undertake the task, 1,500 troops were despatched to the mouth of the Zeya and at the same time two lines of communication, one by water and the other by land, were established.[123] When the preparations were completed, order was given for the opening of the campaign. In 1684, therefore, the lower Sungari was cleared of the Russians.[124] Next year the troops at the mouth of the Zeya, which had been in the meantime brought up to the recommended strength, advanced upon Albazin [125] and within two days compelled the Russian stronghold to capitulate. The Russian prisoners were, however, not detained, but were, as a sign of good will, allowed to return with their belongings including arms.[126] [127] Good will which worked well for Russian

---

[121] *Ping lo fang lueh*, A 5/1 *l.*; A 7/1 *l.*

[122] Ravenstein, *op. cit.*, p. 39.

[123] *Chi lin wai chi*, 3/4 *l.*; *Ping lo fang lueh*, A 5/1–2, 4–5, A 6/5 *l.*

[124] Ravenstein, *op. cit.*, p. 46; *Ping lo fang lueh*, A 6/1.

[125] *Ibid.*, A 6/2; A 6/3 *l.*

[126] *Ibid.*, A 6/4 *l.*; Ravenstein, *op. cit.*, p. 48.

[127] Of the two English works consulted, which are based upon Russian authorities, Ravenstein gives the number of Chinese troops

prisoners at Albazin, however, had no deterring effect upon Russian officials at Nertchinsk, for shortly afterwards the

---

engaged in the two-day siege of Albazin as 18,000 men (p. 47) and Vladimir as 15,000 (p. 135). As far as we can ascertain from Chinese official records the strength of the besiegers was never greater than 2,000 as recommended by the officer sent to study conditions in preparation for the campaign. The number sent to Aigun in 1683 in consequence of the recommendation was 1,500. It was later reënforced by 400 armed with cane shields and long sabres from the province of Fukien where that kind of troops was extensively employed. When the campaign was about to open, 500 more were despatched north to Aigun from Mukden to take over garrison duties. Beyond these figures we cannot find any more. Indeed, on the contrary, we come across incidents that tend to prove that the strength of 2,000 men was never exceeded. Before the reënforcement was sent, the commander at Aigun applied for 1,000 additional troops armed with firearms. This was turned down by the government on the ground that his 1,500 men were already well equipped with the instruments he specified. Again, shortly after order was given for the 400 troops from Fukien referred to above it was reported that the expenses involved in transportation were too great, and it was therefore decided to send for only a commander and the equipments in order that the contingent could be made up and trained for service in Peking instead. If the Chinese forces before Albazin could be augmented at all, such could only have come from the sailors and transporting hands. But these, too, were limited in number. According to the records the entire force engaged in maintaining water communication between Kirin and Aigun was 150 sailors and 1,050 transporting hands. These, of course, could not be all present at the siege. Even granting the improbable, the entire number of Chinese before Albazin could only be about one-fifth of Vladimir's figure, the smaller of the two cited. The campaign against Albazin was difficult because it was conducted in a distant land, not because the Russians were formidable. Once communication between Kirin and Aigun was established, it took only two days to compel the Russian stronghold to capitulate. If this fact is recognized it is hardly worth while to exaggerate.

same set of prisoners were reënforced and ordered to resume their post at Albazin.[128]

The return of the Russians convinced the Chinese government that they were not a gang of irresponsible adventurers. Consequently, while it ordered local authorities to invest Albazin,[129] it also sought to communicate with the Russian government through a Dutch mission which was then in Peking.[130] The last campaign against the Russians had not, however, been entirely futile, for it demonstrated to the Russian government the determination of China to check Russia's expansion into the Sungari valleys and the unwisdom of persisting in a course which might eventually lead to the loss to Russia of eastern Siberia. In 1685, the year following the clearing of the lower Sungari of Russians, it had appointed a special envoy, Fedor Alexevitch Golovin, to effect a settlement with China. Golovin was preceded by a messenger bearing a letter from the Russian government to the Chinese. This letter expressed surprise at the warlike measures of China after Spafarik's mission of amity; acknowledged the receipt of a message from China — probably one of the notes of warning China despatched to the Russians before the commencement of the last campaign; announced the appointment of a special envoy to delimitate the common boundary; and finally requested that pending the arrival of the envoy China should

---

In the case of artillery force of the Chinese before Albazin, while Ravenstein gives it, on the authority of Witsen, as fifteen guns, Vladimir speaks, upon that of Müller, even of 150 pieces of field artillery and forty to fifty siege guns! (See note, Ravenstein, p. 47.)

[128] Ravenstein, *op. cit.*, pp. 49–50.
[129] *Ping lo fang lueh*, A 7/1.
[130] *Ibid.*, A 7/1 l.

raise the siege of Albazin and make known her complaints more fully.[131]   The messenger arrived in Peking in 1686, a couple of months after a message to the Russian government was sent through the Dutch mission and about half a year after Albazin was invested.   The Chinese government accordingly ordered the raising of the siege [132] and gave the details of its complaints in a letter to be taken back by the messenger.[133]

Golovin was provided with an escort of three regiments, of which one, 1,500 strong, was composed of regular militia from Moscow and two were raised later on his way in Siberia.   He left Moscow in 1686, reached Selinginsk the next year, and in the latter place notified the Chinese government of his arrival.[134]   The Chinese government accordingly appointed So-e-tu, a member of the Grand Secretariate, and several other high officials as plenipotentiary to meet him.   Before their departure from Peking the Chinese envoys submitted the following memorial [135] to the emperor Kanghsi at his request as to the terms on which they proposed to come to agreement with the Russian plenipotentiary:

Nestchinsk is originally the pasturage of our Mao Mingan tribe.   Albazin is the old home of Pei-li-erh, our Daurian chieftain.   The territories occupied by the Russians are neither theirs, nor a "neutral" country.   The Amur has a strategical importance which must not be overlooked.   If they descend it, they can reach the Sungari.   If they ascend the Sungari in the south, they can reach the

131   For text of message see *ibid.*, A 7/2.
132   *Ibid.*, A 7/2; Ravenstein, *op. cit.*, p. 52.
133   For text of letter see *Bradley*, ii, 425.
134   Ravenstein, *op. cit.*, p. 56.
135   *Ping lo fang lueh*, A 8/1.

Nonni and the Ku-erh-han, Kirin, and Ninguta, and the land of the Sibos, the Khorchins, the Solons, and the Daurians. If they descend the Sungari towards the mouth, they can reach the sea. Into the Amur flow the Amgun, the Bureya, and the Zeya. Along these rivers live our people the Orochons, the Gilyaks, the Birars as well as the Hochen and the Fei-ya-ko. If we do not recover the entire region, our frontier people will never have peace. Nertchinsk, Albazin, and all rivers and rivulets flowing into the Amur being ours, it is our opinion that none should be abandoned to the Russians. The deserters, the three officers, Gantimur and others, and the several that went over later, too, must be extradited. If they can concede these, we shall give up their deserters, expatriate the prisoners, draw the boundary and enter into commercial relations; otherwise, we shall return and make no peace with them at all.

The memorial was sanctioned by the emperor, and the mission left Peking for Selenginsk by way of Outer Mongolia with a guard of 800 troops. While it was on its way news of the Oelot invasion of Outer Mongolia which began a struggle of eighty-three years between China and that nomadic people, reached Peking, and in order to prevent the mission from falling into the hands of the invaders, it was recalled by express messengers, and the Russian mission notified of the incident. Finally Nertchinsk was agreed upon by both parties as the place to meet instead of Selenginsk.

The Oelot invasion of Outer Mongolia, however, had a greater consequence than the mere interruption of the settlement with Russia. With Outer Mongolia in the hands of a hostile party it was no longer possible for China to meet the Russians outside the disputed territory without risking the safety of her mission. Then, should peaceful settlement prove hopeless, it would be impossible for her to deal with them in any effective way now that they were well protected on their flank. And yet a settlement with them had to be made, not only because there was no time to wait, in view of the war with the Oelot — the kind of war which was always lasting, but also because there was the danger of the Russians' throwing in their lot with the hostile nomads. Therefore, when the Chinese mission prayed for fresh confirmation of the old instructions on the eve of its second departure from Peking, the Grand Secretariate transmitted to it the following edict: [136]

It is his majesty's opinion that if you insist upon having Nertchinsk and leave it not to the Russians, then their trading missions will have no shelter and their communication with us prove difficult. At the opening of the conference you ought still to hold to the line covering Nertchinsk. But if they pray for Nertchinsk, you may have the Argun river as the boundary.

The same changed circumstances which influenced the Chinese government to moderate its terms also led it to take precautionary measures to prevent the Russians from taking undue advantage of them. Besides slightly increasing the body-guards of the mission, order was issued to the commander of troops at Aigun to proceed to Nertchinsk with 1,500 troops.

The historic conference of 1689 was finally held. In eight days [137] the first treaty [138] between China and a Western power was drawn up, signed and exchanged. The boundary as desired by the Chinese government was secured.

---

[136] *Ibid.*, A 8/1 *l.*

[137] *Ibid.*, A 8/2; Ravenstein, *op. cit.*, pp. 60–61.

[138] For text see *Tiao yo, Kang*, 1/10.

Beginning with the Argun river it ran northward to the Amur river; thence further northward by the Kerbechi river, a small stream nearby, to the Outer Khingan mountains, and thence eastward along the crest to the sea. As the Outer Khingan mountains did not end at the coast but turned northward after reaching the coast, it was provided, in the absence of precise geographical information, that the territory between the Ud river and the Outer Khingan mountains after it turned northward — territory through which the eastern end of the boundary line was to run — was to remain "neutral" until further determination.[139] Besides settling the boundary question the treaty also provided that both countries were not to let hunters wander across the frontier [140] or to give asylum to fugitives,[141] but only to permit persons furnished with passports to trade.[142] The text on the last point, for the reason that it has formed a subject of misrepresentation, may be conveniently given here from the Chinese text:

Since peace has been permanently established between the two countries, henceforth travellers *coming and going* shall be permitted to trade if they are provided with passports.[143]

In the next spring boundary stones with the terms of the treaty inscribed on them in Chinese, Manchu, Russian, Latin, and Mongol were by order of the Chinese government set up, one on the Argun river, another on the Kerbechi river, and another on the point where the boundary line left the crest of the Outer Khingan mountains for the sea.[144] The boundary that ran between the Ud river and the Outer Khingan mountains was never determined,

[139] Arts, i & ii.
[140] Art. iv.
[141] Art. vii.
[142] Art. vi.
[143] *Cf.* text in Ravenstein, *op. cit.*, p. 63.
[144] *Shuo fang pei cheng*, 8/6 *l.*

but in the treaty of Kiakta (1727),[145] which deliminated
the Mongolian-Siberian boundary, it was expressly provided
that both parties were barred from the occupation of the
territory through which the first mentioned line was to
pass.[146]   Shortly after the conclusion of the treaty of
Nertchinsk China recovered Outer Mongolia from the
Oelots, and as Russian merchants gathered at Kiakta, Nertchinsk never became the trade centre as contemplated.

As might be expected, the Russian attempts did not end
without leaving some effect upon China's relation with the
land of Manchurian nomads.   In 1653, the year after
China gave order to drive the Russians out of the country,
a special defence commissioner, known later as the Military
Governor of Kirin, was stationed at Ninguta.   In 1676,
shortly after the Russians renewed their activities, that defence commissioner was moved to Kirin, which being on
the point of the main course of the Sungari nearest to the
Liao river, was more strategically located.   In 1683, in
preparation for campaigns that led to the Nertchinsk Conference, another defence commissioner known as the Military Governor of Heilungkiang was stationed at Aigun on
the junction of the Zeya and Amur rivers.   After the conclusion of the treaty of Nertchinsk the defence commissioner at Aigun was moved to Tsitsihar (1699), but not
only Aigun and Ninguta were retained as seats of deputy
defence commissioners, but Mergen (1685), Petuna
(1692), Sansin (1728), and A-li-chu-ko, a little way
south of what is now Harbin (1756), were one after
another also added for similar purposes.[147]

In spite of the extension of control over their land

---

[145] For text see *Tiao yo, Yung*, 2/5.
[146] Art. vii.
[147] See *Sheng ching tung chih*, 10/14-15.

China's policy towards the Manchurian nomads remained much the same as before. Only they were now required to appear at Kirin and Tsitsihar instead of at Mukden. According to the rules which they followed in the next century and a half, *i.e.*, during the period the Russians settled down as respectable neighbors, the tribes inhabiting the country round the junction of the Amur and Sungari rivers were to appear at Ninguta annually, and those inhabiting the lower Sungari, including the Gilyaks at the mouth of the river, triennially, both between the fourth and the sixth moon of the year. Those inhabiting the Amur were to appear at Tsitsihar annually in the fifth moon. As to the Gilyaks on the island of Sakhalin and the Orochons and Birars of the mountains north of the Amur river, they were met by tribute collectors sent respectively from Kirin and Heilungkiang annually at the sixth moon instead of being required themselves to appear in the latter cities.[148]

[148] *Shuo fang pei cheng*, 1/7; 2/7.

Chapter II

DECLINE OF THE TSING DYNASTY

Sec. 1. A New Manchu Policy

NEVER were conditions as favorable for Chinese colonization of the extra-mural country as at the beginning of the Tsing dynasty, for not only was the Yellow River basin able to yield a surplus population, but China was in the closest of control of the nomads, as we have seen, as a result of the work of two dynasties. Given these conditions, Chinese colonists steadily pushed beyond the Great Wall and the Palisade into the land of nomads, and shortly after the Nertchinsk Conference the government found it necessary to constitute Jehol (1723) and Pingchuan (1729) of the Jehol hills, Kalgan (1724), Dolan Nor (1732), and Tushihkao (1735) of the Chahar steppes parts of the province of Chihli,[1] and Kirin, Petuna, and Ninguta (1726) parts of the prefecture of Fengtien.[2]

There is no doubt that had the Manchus been more farsighted, they would not have stopped at founding garrison cities in strategical points along the rivers of the Sungari system but would have gone a step further and utilized the natural tendency of Chinese colonization to develop the country and thus cut Russian ambition at the bottom. Unfortunately, they were not only unable to do so but were soon even to check the very tendency.

[1] *Chi fu tung chih,* 16/2 *l.,* 5; *Hui tien,* 152/2.
Sheng ching tung chih, 10/10.

Under the emperor Kanghsi (1662–1722) not only were all anti-dynastic activities in China stamped out, but China's rule was also reëstablished in Outer Mongolia, Alashan,[3] Kukunor,[4] Tibet,[5] and a part of what is now Sinkiang. In these circumstances it was difficult for the average Manchu to remember that being originally a border nomadic people they were really more Chinese than nomads, or to recognize that having established themselves in China their interests were identical with those of the nation. Kanghsi, being born in time of difficulty and brought up among statesmen, was not likely to be swept off his feet. But Yungcheng, his successor, who was born in time of success and brought up among scholars on the one hand and lawless elements on the other, did not have the same firmness of character, and with his accession a change in Manchu policies took place. Just a year after he took over the control of the empire, Yungcheng had the following [6] to say in reply to a memorial from the defence commissioner of Kirin praying for a temple of Confucius and a number of schools:

Arts and military skill both require training and neither is more important than the other. In the world few are qualified for both. We Manchus who lived in the land of the Chinese are apt to deviate daily from our original mode of life. Fortunately, the men at Ula and Ninguta do not have to undergo the same change. If we now promote arts, the slightly brighter youngsters will devote their attention to books to the neglect of military skill. Even if they should be industrious, they could hardly compete with the Kiang-nan Chinese. Why should they give up what they are gifted for and compel themselves to learn what they

---

[3] *Sheng wu chi*, 3/55 *l.*   [5] *Ibid.*, 5/8.
[4] *Ibid.*, 3/35 *l.*   [6] *Chi lin tung chih*, 1/17.

can never acquire? We Manchus are devoted to the superiors, single-mindedly sincere, filial to parents, not covetous of wealth, not open to shameful and mean acts even in extreme poverty and direst need. We Manchus excelled in all these. The aim of education is only to know these and put them into practice. We rather act without education than fail to act with it. . . . Let our edict be published with the contents of the memorial to the people of Ula and Ninguta that they may know our wishes. Let also the Military Governor of Heilungkiang be acquainted with the same that he may be able to coöperate. Let them all keep to the Manchu mode of life with earnestness and without hesitation! . . .

Yungcheng failed to achieve the same success as Kanghsi, but he was able to consolidate China's rule newly reestablished in Kukunor,[7] Tibet,[8] and Outer Mongolia.[9] At his death he was succeeded by Kienlung (1736–1795). It seems that there was no greater need at this juncture than to have a person who could strike out independently, if not back to the sanity of Kanghsi, at least out of the reaction of Yungcheng. Unfortunately, Kienlung was not the man, for he not only had been spoiled by others' success like his predecessor but was to be further spoiled by his own. During his reign the Oelot nomads were finally subdued (1757), and with this followed the reëstablishment of China's control over the Tarim basin (1758–60), the acquisition of the allegiance of the Burut, the Kozak, and some khanates of Central Asia. Indeed just about one-half of his reign had expired when the Tsing dynasty had reached the height of its power, which later acquisitions relating to Nepal, Burma, Siam, and Annam did not ma-

---

[7] *Sheng wu chi*, 3/55–59; 3/26, 58.
[8] *Ibid.*, 5/17 et seq. [9] *Ibid.*, 3/59 l.–66.

terially increase. In these circumstances it was even more difficult for Kienlung than for Yungcheng to remain steady. Indeed, if Yungcheng had only attempted to prevent the Manchu assimilation by the Chinese, Kienlung was to go the length, as we shall presently see, of creating a Manchu entity in the body politic of China.

Shengking being one of the nineteen provinces of China, was ruled like the rest. During the ninety-two years before the ascension of Kienlung there were altogether 52 metropolitan prefects of Fengtien, who were *ex officio* governors of the province, and 292 lesser officials from the assistant of the metropolitan prefect down to the magistrates of the *hsiens*. Of the 52 metropolitan prefects 34 were Chinese, 17 were Chinese " bannermen ", *i.e.*, members and descendants of the Chinese contingents that assisted in the establishment of the Tsing dynasty, and one was Manchu. Of the 292 lesser officials 247 were Chinese, 28 were Chinese " bannermen ", and 18 were Manchus.[10] This preponderating Chinese influence in the government of the province was the centre of Kienlung's attack. As soon as he came to the throne he placed Kirin, Ninguta, and Petuna — cities beyond the Palisade, that had lately been made parts of the prefecture of Fengtien — under the military governor of Kirin,[11] who by law was a Manchu. Then, when the Oelot War was over he immediately set about to take the rest of Shengking out of the hands of the Chinese. In 1751 he laid it down as a rule that none except Manchus were eligible for magistracy in the province.[12] In 1762

[10] For the foregoing figures see *Sheng ching tung chih*, 20/19 *et seq.*

[11] *Ibid.*, 10/11; Hui tien, 1093/1; Hsu Hsi, *The Eastern Three Provinces* (in Chinese) (Shanghai, 1915), pp. 62, 68.

[12] *Hui tien*, 1093/1.

he made the metropolitan prefect of Fengtien, the *ex officio* governor of the province, a subordinate of the military governor of Shengking, who like his colleagues of Kirin was by law a Manchu. In taking the last step Kienlung was, however, not well advised, for it was soon revealed that Manchu military men were not yet fit to be civil administrators, and in 1765 he had to order that the post of the metropolitan prefect be held concurrently by one of the vice-presidents of the Metropolitan Boards of Mukden instead. But evidently he was not yet fully satisfied with the last steps, for in 1789 he further ordered that the choice of the vice-president to act concurrently as the metropolitan prefect be limited to the Manchu members of that vice-presidential group.[13] With the foregoing measures Kienlung, so to speak, snatched Shengking from the Chinese and gave it to the Manchus. After this Shengking ceased to rank with the intra-mural provinces, and came to be associated with Kirin and Heilungkiang as a group. This latter group has been known in China as the "Eastern Three Provinces" (Tungsansheng) and in the West as "Manchuria".

Two more measures were, however, yet to be taken before Kienlung could rest in peace. One was the exclusion of Chinese from the land of the Manchurian nomads. There is no doubt that if he could, he would have moved all Chinese into the intra-mural country or elsewhere. But failing to have an opportunity to do so, he was determined to see that at least Kirin and Heilungkiang would be free from the Chinese. In 1776, therefore, he issued the following edict[14] for Kirin and by inference for Heilungkiang:

Shengking and Kirin are the home of the dynasty. To

[13] *Ibid.*, 32/1.   [14] *Chi lin tung chih*, 1/34.

permit immigrants to settle down there would greatly affect the Manchu mode of life. In Shengking, which is adjacent to Shantung and Chihli, immigrants have, during years of peace, gradually gathered. It is not possible to order them to leave without at the same time depriving them of their means of subsistence, and thus we have established civil governments to accommodate them. As to Kirin, which is not adjacent to Chinese territory, they ought not to be allowed to stay there. Report has it that new settlements have gradually been formed in it. Let Fu Sen be commissioned to investigate and settle the matter, and orders be given out that immigrants are forever prohibited from entrance.

The other measure was the creation of a link to connect Shengking, the home of the dynasty, with Chihli, the seat of government. Ever since the occupation of the Jehol hills by the desert nomads in the Ming dynasty, China had been suffering from a double evil: the isolation of the Liao basin and the exposure of the national capital. This Kienlung now remedied by encouraging Chinese colonization in the Jehol hills, despite his effort to check this movement in the country outside the Palisade. In 1778 when the time was ripe he organized the Jehol region into a prefecture known as Chengteh with six *hsiens* under it.[15]

Sec. 2. *Colonization of the Extra-Palisade Country*

The shortsighted policies of Yungcheng and Kienlung with regard to the Manchus and Manchuria were, however, but instances of a general change of the Manchus' attitude towards the sacred trust which they held under the " Mandate of Heaven ". Into the details which mean the history of the Tsing dynasty itself, we do not need to enter. Suffice it to say that, as a result of this change which culminated

[15] *Chi fu tung chih,* 16/2 *l.,* 5; *Cheng te fu chih,* 3/31 *l.*

in the subjugation of the Oelots in the middle part of the reign of Kienlung, the Tsing dynasty declined.

As early as a score of years before the close of the sixty-year reign of Kienlung, anti-dynastic agitations, which had subsided as a result of the enlightened rule of Kanghsi, broke out again.[16] Finally, in 1796, the year Kienlung abdicated in favor of his son Chiaching (1796–1800), the Pai-lien Rebellion[17] broke out, lasted eight years, devastated the northwestern quarter of intra-mural China, took the joy out of Kienlung's last three years of life, which he planned to spend happily in nominal retirement, and sent him to the grave with great anxiety for the future of the Manchu dynasty.

The reactionary policy of the Manchus, of course, was but one phase of a general degeneration of that people, which again we have to leave to the specialist to treat. For our purposes we shall merely observe that with the death of Kienlung the Manchu dynasty was left without any capable ruler. After the death of Kienlung, Chiaching reversed several of his predecessor's policies under the pressure of circumstances,[18] and finally brought the Pai-lien Rebellion to a close. On the other hand, as soon as immediate danger was over, he followed up his early wise policy with no constructive measures. In other words, he ended where he started, and the decline of the dynasty was allowed to continue indefinitely. The nomads had long been subdued and the anti-dynastic agitation had again subsided. Under such circumstances in an ordinary time incapables like the successor of Kienlung were probably just as good as any, for if they were not able to carry on constructive work,

[16] *Sheng wu chi*, 8/60.
[17] *Ibid.*, 9/1.
[18] *Ibid.*, 9/34 *et seq.* 10/41 *et seq.*

they were at least unable to drag the nation further down. Unfortunately, the century that followed the death of Kienlung was destined to be an extraordinary time in the history of China and the Far East. The day of trial came in the reign of Taokuang (1821–1850), when the Opium War (1840) broke out between Great Britain and China.

By the middle of the nineteenth century European expansion had reached such a stage that, if it had not made its influence felt in the Far East in 1840, it would have made it felt at some other date not far remote. In view of this situation, it was probably right for China not to prolong the war with Great Britain. But the right thing done by the wrong person resulted as disastrously as would have the wrong thing done by the right person. As soon as the war broke out, Taokuang hastily repudiated the act of his agent, Lin Tse-hsu, in spite of the fact that what Lin had done to the British was in line with what Yungcheng and Kienlung had done to the Russians on three occasions.[19] When the British ignored the apology, or what amounted to an apology, and carried on the war for an extension of trade privileges, he vacillated between war and peace as if China were entirely in the wrong. When peace was decided upon, he blindly appointed as plenipotentiaries men like Kiying, who were unable even to distinguish between issues or to understand the significance of their acts, and whose claims to high trust were no more than that they were Manchus. Finally, when peace was purchased on the humiliating terms of the payment of an indemnity, the cession of Hong Kong, and the granting of extra-territorial jurisdiction, he neither repudiated it, nor took measures to provide against the future, but meekly swallowed all and

[19] For these instances see *Shuo fang pei cheng*, 37/1–11.

let things drift as before. This, of course, could not but have serious consequences. Inasmuch as it discredited the dynasty, it brought about the Taiping Rebellion of the fifties and sixties, which lasted twice as long and devastated an area thrice as great as did the Pai-lien Rebellion before. Inasmuch as it discredited the nation, it invited foreign aggression, through which China has suffered until this day. At last Taokuang's acts turned the decline of the dynasty into a problem of the nation.

Returning to the question of Manchuria, where we left off, the new policy with reference to that section of country, in view of its shortsighted nature, did not work smoothly in every respect. It was difficult to expect the Manchus of Kirin and Heilungkiang to be willing to remain beyond the pale of civilization as decreed by Yungcheng, while their compatriots in Peking and other parts of China were fast being assimilated by the Chinese. Thus, during the three reigns following that of Kienlung the Manchus of Kirin once and again agitated for schools and had to be each time reminded of the edict of Yungcheng.[20] It was no less impossible, too, to expect the Manchus to be able to take over the civil administration of the entire province of Shengking as planned by Kienlung, since they had not learnt the art of government. Shortly after the death of Kienlung, therefore, it was found necessary to reopen the civil service of Shengking to Chinese, with the exception of four *hsiens* on the Mongolian border, where the problem of administration was simple.[21] Consequently, from the very beginning, only two aspects of the new policy merited consideration. These were the exclusion

[20] Edicts, *Kien*, 24/9/jen shen, *Tao*, 2/6/hsin wei, *Tao*, 13/12/ping chen, *chi lin tung chih*, 1/28, 3/5 *l.*, 3/24.

[21] *Hui tien*, 1093/2 *l.*

of Chinese from the extra-Palisade country and the reservation of higher control of Shengking for the Manchus.

The policy of the Manchu dynasty did not kill the natural tendency of the Chinese to migrate northward. Nevertheless it had at first the effect of heading that tendency off into a channel of less resistance, the Cherim prairie. This prairie forms a part of the zone that lies between the Gobi desert and the arable country to the south and east. But, as it borders upon the Sungari valleys which were inhabited by comparatively weak tribes, it had not only never passed out of the hands of the desert nomads, as had the rest of that zone, but had served throughout history as a base for the Tung-hu nomads and their various descendants, as had Outer Mongolia for the Hsiung-nu nomads and the Mongols. Conditions had changed since Chinese colonists invaded the Sungari valleys. If things had been allowed to run their course, the prairie might have remained free from Chinese colonization for yet some period of time. On top of the invasion of the Sungari valleys by Chinese colonists, however, came the Manchu policy to reserve that region for the Manchus. Consequently the Cherim prairie became a colonizing ground for the Chinese before it would normally have been. As soon as Chinese colonists were barred from Kirin they entered what are now Changtu and Changchun on the edge of the prairie, as well as the section known as Hsinmin, which, though inside the Palisade, was not yet colonized because of the fact that it was occupied by the desert nomads in the Ming dynasty.

The fact that the Cherim prairie formed geographically an integral part of Manchuria was evident to the Court. The colonization of the section of what is now Hsinmin, occurring within the Palisade, of course, called forth no intervention. But when the colonization of sections outside the Palisade was reported, investigation was ordered. According to the report of 1799 concerning what is now Changchun, the land cultivated there had amounted by that year to 265,648 *mou*, and the population to 3,330 families. However, as these colonies were there neither in violation of the wishes of the desert nomads, nor in violation of the law of Kienlung, the Court, which was then fully engaged by the Pai-lien Rebellion, readily accepted the accomplished fact and started to regularize the situation by including the colonized sections of the land of the desert nomads as parts of the province of Kirin, adding the injunction that " not one more settler " should be permitted to come there again.[22]

A tendency as strong as the Chinese migration towards the northwest could not, however, be checked by mere injunction. In 1812, when just a little more than a decade had elapsed, it was reported that alone in the section of what is now Changchun 7,000 additional colonists had in the meantime arrived, and that the entire settlement already formed there had an area of 80 miles by 60.[23] In the face of such a situation the Court could do no better than to acquiesce.[24] [25]

The Cherim prairie is fertile on the edge that borders upon the rivers Liao, Sungari, and Nonni and sandy from the centre westward. Having colonized the sections on

---

[22] Edict, *Chia*, 5/7/mou tzu, *Chi lin tung chih*, 2/8.

[23] Edict, *Chia*, 15/11/ jen tzu, *ibid.*, 2/8; see also *Hsu*, 10/43 *l.*

[24] See edicts of *Tao*, 5, *Chi lin tung chih*, 3/18–23.

[25] For further information concerning the colonization of the southern section of the Cherim prairie, see *Hsu*, 10/41 *l.*; *Hui tien*, 1913/2–3. *Cf.* Hsu Hsi, *op. cit.*, p. 38 *et seq.*

the rivers Liao and Sungari, Chinese immigrants instinctively turned away from the centre into the forbidden land of Kirin, which was separated from the prairie by no stronger obstacles than the letter of the law and a flimsy willow palisade. By this time, however, if the violation of the law was more obvious, the Court had also become more conscious of its impotence. Although it was not willing to repeal the law which embodied the " holy will " of the " sacred ancestors ", it was not prepared to enforce the exclusion in order to incur fresh expressions of resentment from a resentful people. It resorted eventually to the counteracting measure of colonizing Kirin with Manchus from Peking, which was by that time congested with a surplus population of that people.

The plan as decided upon was to send 3,000 Manchu families at the rate of 300 a year, beginning with 1824. In order to make the way smooth for these high class settlers orders were given that 1,000 local Manchus be chosen to reclaim the land before their arrival,[26] and that dwellings be also erected for them.[27] The Manchus of the metropolis, however, were not at all attracted by their ancestral home, where the government used to send their unteachable relatives to get permeated with the " unsoiled mode of life " which Yungcheng, being sick of the life of his own court, and probably also of himself, so often longed for and was so anxious to preserve. In the first year, therefore, only 53 out of the quota of 300 families were reported as having enrolled. Finally, after five years' experiment the original number of 3,000 was reduced to 1,000, with more land allotted to each and with permission to employ farm hands to cultivate the land: in other words,

[26] Edict, *Chia*, 19/11/ kuei chou, *ibid.*, 2/15.
[27] Edict, *Tao*, 1/1/ mou wu, *ibid.*, 3/1.

with the additional inducement that they would become landlords instead of farmers.[28]

The Manchu attempt to colonize the Sungari valleys with Manchus was no more successful than was their policy of excluding Chinese from these lands. In the case under discussion there were yet several hundred families enlisted. In another case, which was tried in the seventies in Heilungkiang, it is said that, of the small number of thirteen families which enlisted, ten families returned to Peking in less than a year and the remaining three, which could not return because of poverty, pitifully begged authorities to send them home, as exiles in this region were accustomed to do when amnesty was granted them.[29] The luxurious life of the metropolis was too attractive a hotbed of degeneration for the common people no less than for the ruling class. By resorting to the immigration of the metropolitan Manchus for maintaining the mistaken notion of Kienlung, the Court merely declared bankruptcy on its Manchurian policy.

The tendency of Chinese migration into Manchuria, however, was soon to grow so strong that, even if the counter measures of the Manchus could have been carried out, they would, nevertheless, have proved to be of no avail. By the sixties the already strong natural tendency to migrate in this direction was reinforced by the aid of steam navigation, in consequence of the opening of New-chwang as a treaty port. On the other hand, the already weakened Manchu government was further reduced in

---

[28] Edicts, *Tao*, 3/12/ ting ssu, *Tao*, 4/2/ chi yu, *Tao*, 5/10/ keng shen, *Tao*, 9/31 kuei mao, *Tao*, 11/12 mou hsu, *Tao*, 23/12/ chia chen, *Tao*, 24/3/ chia hsu, *ibid.*, 3/8 *l.*, 11, 17 *l.*, 28, 31, 40 *l.*, 42.

[29] *Lung chiang shu lueh*, 4/6 *l.*

vitality by the Taiping Rebellion. By the early seventies, when the Rebellion was over, not only were the districts around the cities in Shengking and Kirin, as well as the southern section of the Cherim prairie, more thickly populated, but the virgin districts, such as the extra-Palisade Shengking on the right bank of the Yalu river, and the districts around what is now Hailung, and such as the Sungari basin around what is now Harbin both in Kirin and in Heilungkiang, were also colonized.

In these circumstances, the Manchus could no longer merely acquiesce, and they threw open the extra-Palisade Shengking and Kirin and divided them into administrative units like the intra-Palisade country. In consequence they added in Manchuria three more prefectures — Changtu for the province of Shengking, and Changchun, and Kirin for the province of Kirin; and twenty-one lesser units down to the *hsien* — eight in eastern Shengking up to the Yalu river, five in the northern section of the Cherim prairie, and eight along the Kirin side of the upper Sungari.[30]

By this time, one-half of Manchuria had been lost to the Russians for more than ten years,[31] and not only could Manchuria no longer serve as a home for the dynasty, but it was also exposed to the danger of further Russian absorption. If not in the interest of the nation, the Manchus should have reversed the entire policy for the sake of the dynasty itself. And yet, beyond recognizing the accomplished fact of the colonization of extra-Palisade Shengking and of Kirin, they went no further. Indeed, instead

[30] Memorials by Chung-hou, *K.*, 2/1/- and 2/3/-, *Kuang hsu cheng yao*, 2/1, 24; memorial by Chi-yuan, *K.*, 4/7/-, *ibid.*, 4/22; memorial by Ming-an, *K.*, 8/4/-, *ibid.*, 8/8 *l.*

[31] *Infra*, sec. 3.

of reversing their policy, they even added a few fatal finishing touches to it. First of all, while throwing open Kirin, they still maintained exclusion for Heilungkiang.[32] Next, instead of adding a civil governor for the civil administration of Kirin, they entrusted the civil administration to the military governor of that province. Thirdly, they again made the metropolitan prefect of Fengtien, the *ex officio* governor of Shengking, a subordinate to the military governor of Shengking. Finally, they raised the latter to the position of a senior to his colleagues at Kirin and Tsitsihar by giving him the rank of a viceroy.[33] If the reservation of Heilungkiang was but a continuation of the old discredited policy, the entrusting of civil administration to military governors was an aggravation of a proven mistake.

In the meantime, Chinese migration into Manchuria continued steadily. By the end of the century the northern section of the Cherim prairie, the left bank of the Tumen, eastern Kirin, as well as the left bank of the Sungari in the province of Heilungkiang, where the official bar was not yet let down — or, in other words, all colonizable territory except the outlying districts along the Amur and the Ussuri, and west of the Great Khingan mountains — was colonized, and the entire population of Manchuria amounted to 14,000,000, of which eighty per cent were Chinese.[34] [35]

[32] *Cf. Lung chiang shu lueh*, 4/8; see also memorial, K., 13, *ibid.*, 4/9 *l.*

[33] Edict, *K*, 1, *Hui tien*, 1913/2 *l.*; 23/1 *l.*

[34] For a good account of Manchuria at the close of the 19th century, see "Notes on Manchuria" by Col. Brown, enclosed in no. 53, *China, No. 1* (1899) (British Parliamentary Papers), p. 34.

[35] For further development, see *infra*, chap. v, sec. 5.

Sec. 3. *Russian Descent upon Manchuria*

(1) *The Lower Sungari and Trans-Amur Regions.*

After the check they had received on the Amur and the lower Sungari rivers in the seventeenth century, the Russians had practically forgotten the Sungari valleys. The British success in the Opium War instantly quickened their memory. Shortly after the war numerous accounts of early Russian adventures on those rivers began to appear in Russian papers, including several government organs,[36] and in 1848, Nicolas Muraviev was appointed governor of Eastern Siberia, evidently for the purpose of reviving Russian activities on those rivers.

We have had occasion to speak of the strategical importance of the Shilka river to the entire Sungari system. In the present period of Russian activities, that river, as we shall see, proved to be the source of trouble as it had in the past. With, however, a military post at Aigun, and boundary stones on the Kerbechi and Argun rivers inscribed with five languages, including the Russians' own, and inspected annually in their presence, the Russians did not feel free to descend from the Shilka as soon as they started. Accordingly they first followed the coast down to the mouth of the lower Sungari and the Gulf of Tartary,[37] places which, being far removed from Russian territory, were left much in the state in which they had been a century and a half before.

There were not lacking men in Russia who were not yet ready to depart from the century-old tradition of peace

---

[36] E. G. Ravenstein, *The Russians on the Amur* (London, 1861), p. 114.

[37] Vladimir, *Russia on the Pacific and the Siberian Railway* (London, 1899), pp. 185–92.

with China, and when the occupation of the lower Sungari was reported, they severely criticized it. But the expansionists had the advantage of having Nicholas I on their side and they, therefore, won the day, finally inducing the Russian foreign office to resort to the pretext of boundary delimitation with the view of acquiring a legal title by peaceful methods for territories adversely occupied.[38]

It is not known whether the note to the Chinese government, asking for boundary delimitation, took as a point of departure the provision of the treaties of Nertchinsk and Kiakta relating to the territory between the Outer Khingan mountains and the Ud river, or whether it was merely made with the simple pretext of retracing the old boundary to avoid possible misunderstanding, as relations on the frontier had grown much closer and more complicated after the lapse of a century and a half. Whatever the method might be, the Chinese government, being yet unaware of Russian designs, appointed commissioners and despatched them to Urga to await the arrival of their Russian colleagues.[39]

The Russian commissioners, however, never came. By this time (1853) the Taiping leaders had set up a government at Nanking and despatched expeditions in two directions to converge upon Peking. This not only paralyzed China for any active opposition to Russian advance, but also emptied Heilungkiang and Kirin of garrisons for service in intra-mural China and opened the way for that very advance. Of this the Russian expansionists were fully aware. Worse still, while conditions were so tempting in the East, the Crimean War broke out in the West. If hitherto the expansionists had been checked by the saner elements, they now could do almost anything by virtue of

[38] *Ibid.*, p. 185.   [39] *Ibid.*, p. 200.

the war-power. In these circumstances they merely ignored the arrangement already made between the Russian government and the Chinese. Indeed, they even felt that they did not need to confine their activities to the coast any longer, and on May 18, 1854 (O. S.), wilfully violated the treaty of Nertchinsk by a solemn entrance into the Amur river from the Shilka with an expeditionary force destined for the mouth of the lower Sungari.[40]

In descending the Amur river in violation of treaty stipulations Muraviev, of course, did not fail to go through the procedure of a nominal notification to the Chinese government. The latter, though still quite in the dark as to Russia's designs, could not but be alarmed by the new development, and accordingly ordered the commissioners, who were still waiting at Urga, to proceed down the Amur and lower Sungari, in company with local commissioners from Kirin and Heilungkiang to meet Muraviev.[41]

On September 9, 1855 (O. S.) the Chinese commissioners arrived at Mariinsk where Muraviev had his headquarters. To their surprise the latter, instead of delimiting the boundary with them, proposed that China recognize Russia's title to the lower Sungari river, and furthermore permit her to establish a chain of settlements along the Amur river, to insure uninterrupted communication.[42] The Chinese commissioners declared that the proposal was beyond their power to entertain, and when the Chinese government was informed of it, a protest was immediately sent to Russia.[43]

---

[40] *Chi lin tung chih*, 55/6; Vladimir, *op. cit.*, pp. 207–9.

[41] Edicts of *Hsien*, 4 & 5, *Chi lin tung chih*, 55/6–7.

[42] Edict, *Hsien*, 5/10/ping wu, *ibid.*, 55/7 *l.*; Vladimir, *op. cit.*, pp. 241–42.

[43] Edict, *Hsien*, 5/11/ keng shen, *Chi lin tung chih*, 55/8 *l.*

The general ignorance of the geography of northeastern Asia on the part of the Anglo-French naval forces in operation in the East, coupled with the probably certain foresight of Muraviev in his defence measures, freed Eastern Siberia from any war misfortunes. This, by comparison with the general failure of the Russians in the Crimean War, made Muraviev a hero. It was therefore natural that his act would be speedily ratified, rather than criticized. The Russian government, instead of replying to the Chinese protest, created out of the territory already occupied the province of Primorskaya (1856),[44] and at the same time renewed its activities to acquire from China a legal title to it.

In the meantime events in China took a new turn. Hitherto she had been only engaged by the Taiping Rebellion. At this moment she had also drifted into war with Great Britain and France. Russia was not slow to avail herself of the opportunity. When Great Britain and France despatched special commissioners and troops to China in 1856, Russia also appointed an envoy, Count Euthyme Putiatin, to proceed to the East.

Putiatin traveled overland, had a conference with Muraviev, and proceeded to the mouth of the Peiho, where he requested admission to Peking to settle with the Chinese government, he declared, the boundary question.[45] Upon receipt of his request the Chinese government appointed Yi-shan, military governor of Heilungkiang, as plenipotentiary, and as it saw no good reason to settle the boundary question in the capital, designated Aigun as the place of conference, and requested the Russian envoy to repair there.[46] Putiatin, however, had another object in view:

---

[44] Vladimir, *op. cit.*, p. 251.   [45] *Ibid.*, p. 252.
[46] Edict, *Hsien*, 7/7 kuei ssu, *Chi lin tung chih*, 55/9.

to secure whatever advantages the British and French might acquire. Accordingly, he declined, upon the pretext that he needed more instructions,[47] and traveled south to watch events.[48] The Russian government therefore appointed Muraviev to act on the Manchurian question, and on receiving the latter's communication, the Chinese government ordered Yi-shan to take up the matter with him instead (1858).[49] Yi-shan proceeded to Aigun, sent agents to meet Muraviev, who was then on his annual trip down the Amur river, and invited the Russian to meet him at that place.

The conference at Aigun was held on May 11, 1858 (O. S.), about the same time negotiations were being carried on by China with Great Britain and France at Tientsin. If in the latter place China was constrained to make all concessions demanded of her, in Aigun it was not likely that she could do better. In his memorial submitted after the conference, Yi-shan had the following to say:

. . . All edicts I have received have enjoined upon me not to incite hostilities. During these years of activities on the river the Russians have constructed dwellings, stationed troops, and accumulated provisions and ammunition in abundance. They have now further declared that in the summer they will despatch more men and officers to guard, they say, the English. Their heart is indeed unfathomable. On the other hand, the tide of rebellion inland has not subsided, and the men of Kirin and Heilungkiang have not returned from service. Evidently it is not practical to appeal to arms. . . .[50]

[47] Edict, *Hsien*, 7/8/ hsin hai, *ibid.*, 55/10.
[48] Henri Cordier, *L'expedition de chine de 1857–58* (Paris, 1905), p. 169.
[49] Edict, *Hsien*, 8/3/ chia wu, *Chi lin tung chih*, 55/11 *l.*; *Tiao yo, Hsien*, 2/5 *l.*   [50] *Chi lin tung chih*, 55/12.

Yi-shan was prepared to grant the Russians the right to
settle on the left bank of the Amur; but he made no headway with Muraviev, who insisted upon an outright cession.
Finally, with a small concession on the part of the latter
regarding the Manchu villages on the left bank of the
Amur at the mouth of the Zeya, the treaty of Aigun was
signed on the 16th (O. S.). The part dealing with the
boundary runs as follows:

The left bank of the river Hei-lung [Amur] and the
river Sung-hua [Sungari] from the river Argun to the sea
mouth of the river Sung-hua shall be the territory of the
Russian Empire; as to the right bank, that following the
stream to the river Ussuri shall be the territory of the Ta
Tsing Empire, and that from the river Ussuri to the sea —
as if it lies between clearly defined boundaries of the two
countries — shall be under the joint control of the Ta
Tsing and Russian Empires. The navigation of the rivers
Hei-lung, Sung-hua, and Ussuri shall hereafter be reserved
to the vessels of the Ta Tsing and Russian Empires and no
vessels of other nationalities shall be permitted upon them.
The Manchu inhabitants who settled on the left bank of
the river Hei-lung, south of the river Zeya to the village
of Hormoldzin, shall be permitted to reside in their villages
in perpetuity and be under the control of the Manchu authorities; and the Russians shall remain on terms of peace
with them and desist from molesting them.[51]

(2) *The Trans-Ussuri Country*

The treaty of Aigun, however, was not the end of Russian encroachment, for the same conditions that compelled
China to agree to the cession of the left bank of the Amur
and the lower Sungari seemed also to have made the Rus-

[51] A translation from Chinese text in *Tiao yo, Hsien,* 2/13; *cf.*
French text in Cordier, *op. cit.,* 417.

sians more insatiable. When Putiatin communicated with the Chinese government on the question after he repaired to the south, he had already suggested that the boundary should follow the Amur down to the Ussuri, and then " up the latter and thence to the sea by some river that rose near its source " [52] — a suggestion entirely different from the proposal made by Muraviev at Mariinsk. Now that the left bank of the Amur and the lower Sungari had been acquired, Muraviev felt no more need of confining himself to what had been gained, and he thereupon launched upon the absorption of the territory further south. Under color of the treaty of Aigun he first despatched men to survey the interior,[53] and in the next year (1869) himself made an extensive cruise on the coast, occupying on his way the harbor of Vladivostok and Possiet Bay.[54]

While Muraviev carried out the actual absorption of territory on the spot, Putiatin, who had followed the British and the French from the south to the north, again raised the question of right with the Chinese government. He now spoke of the Ussuri and Suifen rivers, instead of the Ussuri and some such river as rose near the source of the Ussuri.[55] The Chinese government referred the matter to local authorities for report, and having been informed that what was mentioned by Putiatin had no relation to the treaty of Aigun,[56] it instructed these authorities to

[52] Putiatin to Chinese Government, *Hsien*, 8/1/25, *Tiao yo, Hsien*, 2/3; edict, *Hsien*, 8/2/ kuei chou, *Chi lin tung chih*, 55/10 *l*.

[53] Memorial by Yi-shan, *Hsien*, 8/7/ chia hsu, *ibid.*, 55/16.

[54] Vladimir, *op. cit.*, 262–3.

[55] Memorial by Tan Ting-hsiang, *Hsien*, 8/3/29, and edict of even date, *Tiao yo, Hsien*, 2/62 and 7 *l.; Chi lin tung chih*, 55/12.

[56] Memorial by Yi-shan, *Hsien*, 8/12/20, and edict of even date, *Tiao yo, Hsien*, 2/10 *l.; Chi lin tung chih*, 55/16 *l*.

proceed to the delimitation only when the Russians desisted from making unreasonable demands.[57]

There are writers who are in the habit of accusing the Chinese government of procrastination whenever it refuses to let China's rights be encroached upon, and here as elsewhere they join in a chorus of condemnation. It is therefore pertinent to ask whether China had ceded the trans-Ussuri country by the treaty of Aigun. To this we must reply in the negative. The treaty speaks of the bank of the Amur and of the lower Sungari, but nowhere of the bank of the Ussuri. If the name of this latter river appears in that document, it appears only as a point on the bank of the lower Sungari, or, in other words, only as a landmark. The territory that is left by the treaty for further delimitation can therefore only mean the right bank of the Sungari, from the mouth of the Ussuri downward. It is true that Putiatin in his communication to the Chinese government referred to above had spoken of the Ussuri as a part of the boundary, but this, like the rest of his pretensions, was never entertained by the Chinese government.[58] It is also true that Muraviev broached the question in a similar way to Yi-shan at Aigun, but there the proposal was peremptorily rejected.[59] Indeed, by neither the terms of the treaty nor the attending facts can we come to the conclusion that the trans-Ussuri country was ever ceded.

The Chinese government readily ratified the treaty of Aigun as it was drawn, by an edict issued to the military governors of Heilungkiang and Kirin,[60] and consented to

---

[57] Edict, *Hsien*, 8/12/21, *Tiao yo, Hsien*, 3/3 *l.*

[58] Edict, *Hsien*, 8/2/8, *ibid.*, 2/4; *Chi lin tung chih*, 55/11.

[59] See memorial of Yi-shan above cited.

[60] Edict, *Hsien*, 8/5/ mou yin, *Chi lin tung chih*, 55/15.

the cession of the left bank of the Amur and of the lower Sungari, but was determined not to give way on the question of the trans-Ussuri country. On the occasion of Muraviev's party proceeding independently to the survey of the interior, it made direct representation to the Russian government.[61] Pending the reply from that government, it also ordered local authorities to use all pacific means to bar the Russians from entering their respective jurisdictions, removed Yi-shan from office and sent the military deputy governor of Aigun in cangue to the Ussuri, and instructed the new military governor of Heilungkiang to make clear to Muraviev China's stand on the treaty and to take military measures to provide against emergencies.[62]

Circumstances, however, favored the Russians. In 1859 General Nicolas Ignatiev came to Peking to exchange the ratifications [63] of the treaty [64] which Putiatin succeeded in concluding with China in the wake of the Anglo-French forces in the previous year. While he was still there, the British and French, who came on a similar mission, started to hack their way to Peking instead of following the route indicated to them.

When Putiatin was with the Anglo-French forces in Hong Kong in 1858, he advised the allies to leave Canton and menace Peking by occupying Tientsin.[65] But later, when he was in Tientsin, he offered to supply the Chinese government with arms and ammunition to resist the aggression.[66] The same policy Ignatiev now followed. On June

[61] Edict, *Hsien*, 8/12/21, *Tiao yo, Hsien*, 3/3 *l*.

[62] Edicts, *Hsien*, 9/5/ yi yu and 9/8/ chi hai, *Chi lin tung chih*, 55/22, 24.

[63] For text see *Tiao yo, Hsien*, 2/14.

[64] For text see *ibid.*, 3/15. [65] Cordier, *op. cit.*, 179.

[66] Memorial by Tang Ting-hsiang, *Hsien*, 8/3/29 and edicts of even date and of 8/3/25, *Tiao yo, Hsien*, 2/6, 7 *l.*, 3/8 *l*.

15, 1860, Ignatiev traveled to Shanghai and counseled energetic action and a blow at Taku. Later, he joined the French at Chefoo and proceeded with them to the mouth of the Peiho,[67] thus, as he said, demonstrating the solidarity of the great maritime powers.[68] After he had returned to Peking he of course did not fail also to demonstrate similar solidarity of the great continental powers by offering arms and ammunition to China.[69] When Peking was finally in the hands of the Anglo-French forces, Ignatiev came forward for the cession of the trans-Ussuri country, and a number of other concessions.[70] In these circumstances Prince Kung, then head of the government at Peking, submitted a memorial in favor of the cession. In the memorial he had the following to say:

England and France have come at the instigation of that country [Russia]. As long as she plays the part of the devil . . . there is no hope of English evacuation [of Peking]. This deeply exercises our thoughts.[71]

The Throne consented, and the "honest broker" obtained his fee.[72] [73]

[67] Henri Cordier, *L'expedition de chine de 1860* (Paris, 1906), pp. 184, 230, 244.

[68] *Ibid.*, 186.

[69] Edict to Sengkolintsin & Hengfu, March 27, 1860, *China* (1859–1860), 119; see also H. B. Morse, *The International Relations of the Chinese Empire* (London, 1910), vol. i, p. 613.

[70] Memorial by Prince Kung, *Hsien*, 10/9/20, *Tiao yo*, *Hsien*, 7/2.

[71] See also Ignatiev to Baron Gros, Peking, Oct. 16–18, 1860, Henri Cordier, *Histoire des relations de la chine avec les puissances occidentales 1860–1900* (Paris, 1901), vol. i, p. 94.

[72] Edict, *Hsien*, 10/9/ yi ssu, *Chi lin tung chi*, 55/25 *l*.

[73] The supposed ability of Ignatiev in dealing with the Chinese as demonstrated in the cession of the trans-Ussuri country led to his

In the treaty of Peking [74] (November 14, 1860) thus concluded, the boundary between China and Russia was to follow the Ussuri south and then its tributary, the river Songatcha, to the lake Khanka. From that point it was to cut the lake in the direction of the river " Pai-leng ". From the mouth of the " Pai-leng " it was then to follow the crest of the mountains to the mouth of the river Houpi-tou, and thence the crest of the mountains between the river Hung-chun and the sea to a point on the river Tumen not more than twenty *li* (seven miles) from its mouth.[75] The treaty has also the following provision:

What has been said above refers to uninhabited territory. Russia engages not to occupy territory inhabited by Chinese subjects or occupied by them for fishing and hunting purposes, but to permit them to fish and hunt as before.

After the signing of the treaty an investigation was ordered by the military governor of Kirin on the location of Chinese subjects in the ceded territory and a copy forwarded to the Tsungli Yamen.[76]

As to the delimitation of the boundary between the lake Khanka and the Tumen, the treaty also fixed a special date. In due course of time the commissioners of both countries proceeded to the spot. The question immediately arose as to what was the river " Pai-leng " referred to in the treaty. The Russian commissioners insisted upon the river Mu-leng, a tributary of the Ussuri far inland, but later receded from their position. Finally the two parties agreed upon

---

appointment as Russian minister to Turkey in 1864, where he stayed until his mischiefs culminated in the Russo-Turkish War of 1877, and he himself fell into disfavor and was retired for the rest of his life.   [74] For text see *Tiao yo, Hsien,* 7/8.
[75] Art. i.   [76] For text see *ibid.,* 11/15.

a rivulet known as the Tu-erh-pi-la as a compromise.[77] The delimitation then proceeded swiftly and on June 28, 1861, maps and records of the delimitation were signed and exchanged on the spot as supplements to the treaty.[78] After this a tablet carved with the terms of the treaty relating to the boundary was set up by the Chinese commissioner.[79] Later the military governor of Kirin was ordered to proceed with local Russian authorities to erect boundary stakes.[80]

In 1886 the attention of the Chinese government was called by local authorities to the fact that the Russians had in several places pushed beyond the boundary. An investigation revealed that several of the stakes had disappeared. At the suggestion of the Chinese government commissioners were sent by both countries to the frontier to determine upon the line as drawn before. They met on May 25, 1886, and found that among other questions they could not agree upon the point where the boundary was to meet the Tumen, for while the Chinese commission pointed to a place twenty *li* from the sea, the Russian commission pointed to another place forty *li* from the sea, but twenty *li* from where the sand bank of the river began. They, however, made the compromise of taking a point midway between the two points, *i.e.*, thirty *li* from the sea but ten *li* from the sand bank, and an agreement was drawn up and signed between them as a supplement to the records of 1861.[81] [82]

[77] For relevant documents see *ibid.*, 11/2–10.

[78] For records see *ibid.*, 11/12.

[79] For text see *ibid.*, 11/14.

[80] Memorial, *Hsien*, 11/9/11, *ibid.*, 11/10.

[81] For text see *ibid.*, 7/17 *l.*

[82] For various accounts relating to the delimitation of 1886 see *Chi lin tung chih*, 55/37–54.

Both the treaty of Aigun and the treaty of Peking touched also upon the question of trade privileges. In Article II of the former treaty, it was provided that " in order to promote good relationship the subjects of the two countries inhabiting the Ussuri, the Hei-lung and the Sung-hua rivers shall be allowed to trade among themselves, and authorities on both banks shall reciprocally extend them protection ". In Article IV of the latter, it was also provided that on the new common frontier " the subjects of the two countries shall be allowed to trade at will and be exempted from taxation ", and that " frontier authorities shall assist the traders and supervise their trade ".

The treaty of Peking contained provisions concerning trade privileges also of Mongolia and Sinkiang. By Article V the Russians could trade in Urga and Kalgan, on the main trade route to Peking from Transbakalia, in addition to Kiakta, and appoint a consul to Urga. By Articles VI and VIII, Kashgar in Sinkiang was open to trade " as an experiment ", as Ili and Tarbagatai had been in 1851,[82a] and Russia was given the privilege of stationing a consul there, as in the latter places.

Russian trade privileges in Mongolia and Sinkiang were later extended by the treaty of St. Petersburg of February 24, 1881,[83] as a compensation for the restoration of the Ili district. In that treaty Russians were permitted to trade in Mongolia and Sinkiang free of taxation until " when, trade having become prosperous, the two countries shall agree upon the rates of duties and terminate the exemption ".[84] Furthermore, Russia was given the privilege of stationing consuls at Suchow, the Shanhaikuan of the western end of the Great Wall, and at Turfan.[85]

[82a] See treaty of Ili, 1851, *Tiao yo, Hsien*, 1/19.
[83] *Tiao yo, K.*, 5/15.   [84] Article xii.   [85] Article x.

Sec. 4.   Reappearance of Japan

The impact of the West, which brought about rebellion in China, had similar effects upon Japan. On account of the simple insular life and the limited island territories, Japan, however, emerged from her difficulties not only with comparative ease, but also with positive advantage. The year 1858 witnessed the fall of the Tokugawa house, and the establishment of a new régime known as the Restoration.

The condition in which the Japan of the Restoration found herself in respect to China was similar to that in the end of the sixteenth century. But with the lesson of the upstart Hideyoshi's utter failure before her, Japan was cautious. By the time Japan was free from her domestic troubles Great Britain and Russia were well entrenched in the Far East and France had started to secure a foothold; and the universal rule of China in that region of the world had again fallen into abeyance. We have heretofore seen how the petty kingdom of Wo took advantage of the impotence of China during the period following the Barbarian Rebellion to meddle with the affairs of southern Korea, and how she was first checked by the reaction she created there and then compelled to withdraw to the islands by the appearance of the all-powerful Tang dynasty. To that distant period the condition of the Far East in the latter half of the nineteenth century was similar. To leave one's own home in order to establish a dynasty at the centre of power and influence is the work of the nomads. For settled folks it is more congenial to stay where they are and enslave their neighbors. Rather than pursue a sure failure as did Hideyoshi, Japan of the Restoration employed the same energy generated by a successful civil strife to play high politics after the example of the petty kingdom of Wo.

In 1862 and 1864, shortly after Japan entered into treaty relations with Western powers, she twice sought to appoint a consul to reside at Shanghai. The Chinese government was not willing to depart from the practice of non-intercourse with the Japanese, which had been adopted from the time of the Hideyoshi invasion, and declined the approach on both occasions.

In 1870, shortly after the Restoration, Japan again approached China, this time not only in regard to the appointment of a consul, but also for a treaty of friendship and amity. On the former occasion, Japan merely asked for the resumption of official relations which had been broken off since the end of the Ming dynasty; now she asked for recognition as an equal. In other words: if Japan's former approach involved only the change of a temporary measure, the present called for the modification of an established system. Thus it would be natural if the Chinese government declined the approach as before. The year 1870 was, however, more opportune. The Taiping Rebellion had terminated several years before, and Chinese statesmen like Tseng Kuo-fang and Li Hung-chang, men who were able to recognize the change of circumstances, had been released from war service to be civil administrators. If these men were not in control of national destiny, they at least were in a position to influence the decisions of those who were. Through their advice, therefore, the Court signified its readiness to entertain the Japanese approach.[86] The next year, when the Japanese returned with proper commission for the purpose of concluding a

[86] Memorials by Tsungli Yamen, *Tung*, 9/9/24, 10/7/29, 9/10/18, *Tiao yo*, *Tung*, 20/2, 10 *l.*, 4.

treaty, Li Hung-chang, viceroy of Chihli, was appointed
to treat with them, and on September 13th a treaty of
friendship and amity of eighteen articles, with thirty-one
trade regulations appended to it, was signed at Tientsin
between Li and Date Muneki, the Japanese plenipotentiary.[87]

The Japanese treaty of 1871 is important, not only for
its bearing upon subsequent Sino-Japanese relations, but
also as an example of how far China would be willing to
go in entering into treaty relations under normal conditions. One of the features of the treaty was the reciprocal granting of extra-territorial jurisdiction.[88] Supplementary to this were the provisions that foreign residence
was to give no protection to native servants,[89] that foreign
subjects were not to wear arms,[90] and that foreign mob vio-
lence was to be dealt with according to local law.[91] Another feature was the mutual confinement of trade to the
treaty ports.[92] Still another feature, negative in this instance, was the omission of the most-favored-nation clause
which was present in all treaties concluded between China
and foreign powers previous to that time. Of the less
important provisions that merited notice are those which
prohibited war vessels from entering ports not declared
open by the treaty, nor " rivers, lakes, and streams of the
interior ",[93] and another which stipulated that consuls were
not to engage in trade, nor to act for a non-treaty power,
and were to be subject to the withdrawal of exequatur in
case of improper conduct.[94] At the head of the treaty, in
Article I, there was the following declaration:

[87] *Ibid., Tung,* 20/21, 26.
[88] Art. viii.
[89] Art. x.
[90] Art. xi.
[91] Art. xiii.
[92] Regs. xiv and xv.
[93] Art. xiv.
[94] Art. xvi.

Henceforth China and Japan shall cultivate amicable relationship with doubled effort to last as long as heaven and earth; and even the nations and territories belonging to each shall receive courteous treatment from the other and not the slightest of molestation, to the end that they may enjoy peace and security forever.[95] [96]

The reëstablishment of friendly relationship between the two countries proved, however, to be merely the beginning of trouble, notwithstanding the declaration that these relationships were " to last as long as heaven and earth " and to apply equally to " nations and territories belonging to each ".

Ostensibly to congratulate China on the assumption of government by the emperor Tungchih, Japan sent Soyesima Tanewomi, her foreign minister, as special ambassador to China. Soryesima exchanged the ratifications of the treaty of 1871 in Tientsin with Li Hung-chang, and then proceeded to Peking.[97] While there awaiting the audience granted to the diplomatic representatives, including himself, he sent Yanagiwara Sakimitsu, a member of his suite, to the Tsungli Yamen on an informal visit. In his conversation there Yanagiwara said that a number of Liuchiuan sailors had been murdered by the aborigines of Formosa and that the Japanese government contemplated making an investigation. The member of the Yamen who received him replied that the aborigines had hitherto been left much to themselves on account of the fact that they had their own peculiar mode of life, but China would look

---

[95] Art. i, a translation; *cf.* current text in *Customs*, ii, 1236.
[96] For reports on the negotiation of the treaty see memorials, *Tung*, 10/7/6, 10/7/15, *Tiao yo, Tung*, 20/5, 9 *l.*
[97] Memorial, *Tung*, 12/4/7, *Tiao yo, Tung*, 20/19; *cf.* memorial, *Tung*, 11/6/1, *ibid.*, 20/13.

into the matter this time. Yanagiwara rejoined that he meant only to impart some information and not to request an investigation.[98] With this Soyesima deemed that he had done his part, for nothing was again mentioned either in conversation or in note to either the Tsungli Yamen or Li Hung-chang,[99] and in 1874 Japan sent an expedition to Formosa, consisting of 3,000 men and an equal number of transport hands, with two generals in command, assisted by three foreign military and naval advisers.

Some time before Soyesima's mission, when report came to China of Japan's intention to intervene in the name of the Liuchiuan sailors, the Chinese government had ordered the viceroy of Fukien and Chekiang under whose jurisdiction Formosa was, to make a thorough investigation and to take appropriate measures concerning it.[100] This must have been known to Soyesima before Yanagiwara ever appeared at the Yamen. Besides, when Yanagiwara broached the subject he was plainly informed that China would look into the matter. Therefore, when Japan nevertheless persisted in despatching an expedition, China could not but regard it as an act of aggression, and accordingly protested on the one hand, and on the other despatched a high official with troops to the scene.

Japan was evidently not devoid of a sane element in her government, and when China's position was made known

[98] See memorandum of a conversation with the American minister, *Tung*, 13/9/10, *Yi shu han kao*, 2/52 *l.*; also memo. on conversation with Yanagiwara, enclosed in despatch to Yamen, 13/6/11, *ibid.*, 2/36.

[99] Soyesima mentioned nothing to the viceroy either before or after he went to Peking. The statement in *Herald*, July 26, 1873, cited in Morse, *op. cit.*, ii, 271, seems incorrect. See despatch to Yamen, 12/4/7, *Yi shu han kao*, 1/43.

[100] To Yamen, 12/4/7, *ibid.*, 1/43, see p. 46 especially.

this element gained ground. Consequently, after having made sure of China's temper, Japan commissioned Okubo Toshimitsu to China to effect a settlement. The Chinese government was not at all bent upon extreme measures. Besides, it seemed to have been over-conscious of the unprepared state of coastal defence and at the same time unbelievably credulous of Okubo's plea of Japan's domestic difficulties.[101] So, with the mediation of the British minister at Peking an agreement composing the differences was signed on October 31, 1874.[102] The agreement in part reads as follows:

Article I. — The present proceedings having been undertaken by the Government of Japan for the humane object of affording security to its own subjects, the Government of China will not therefore impute blame to it.

Article II. — The Government of China will give a certain sum to compensate the families of the shipwrecked Japanese who were murdered [in Formosa]. The roads made and buildings erected by the Japanese on the ground, the Government of China is prepared to retain for its own use and it agrees to make a further payment on this account. The details of the engagements on these points will be elsewhere stated.

The sum was later fixed at 100,000 taels for the families of the murdered and at 400,000 taels as expenses occasioned by the construction of roads and erection of buildings. In another article both parties agreed to drop the matter forever and China engaged to take steps for due control of the savage tribes.

[101] Memorial by Yamen, *Tiao yo, Tung,* 21/5.

[102] *Ibid.,* 21/7; Wade to Derby, Nov. 16, 1874, *China No. 2* (1875).

Sec. 5.   Japanese Annexation of Liuchiu

The Formosan incident was thus closed, but in fact it was merely the beginning of Japanese advance upon China, for the incident itself was but a part of a plan to detach Liuchiu from China preparatory to its annexation.

From the standpoint of the Chinese government, the question of Formosa was settled without reference to the status of Liuchiu.   It had been the practice of China as suzerain not to interfere with her vassals in their relations with other nations, either of the same standing or independent, so long as she was not called upon.   When Japan announced that she would espouse the cause of the Liuchiuan sailors, the king of Liuchiu declared to Japan that he was not concerned,[103] but neglected to communicate on the matter with China.   Thus China was not only not called upon to interfere in the case, but was not even officially informed of it, and it was therefore consistent on her part not to take issue with Japan on the point.   Furthermore, rightly or wrongly she regarded the Liuchiuan issue as a mere pretext.   To her indeed the Formosa question was not raised when Japan championed the cause of the Liuchiuan sailors, but when Japan, to use the expression of the Tsungli Yamen, " violated covenant and despatched troops " to Formosa.[104]   Thus in the agreement she spoke of " Japanese subjects " and not of " Liuchiuan sailors ", or in other words they assumed certain Japanese subjects to be the victims for the purpose of settling the case irrespective of whatever nationality they really possessed.

Though this point of view must have also been that of

[103] See memorandum by Hsiang Te-hung, Liuchiuan envoy, 5/6/24, *Yi shu han kao*, 9/23 *l.*

[104] Memorial by Yamen, *Tiao yo, Tung*, 21/5.

Japan when she later accepted the good offices of ex-President Grant of the United States to discuss the question of Liuchiu with China, it was evidently not hers immediately after the settlement of the Formosan question. Indeed, the Japanese seemed to have assumed that as China took no issue with her on the question of Liuchiu, China had tacitly abandoned her vassal.

We have heretofore seen that from the beginning of the seventeenth century onward Liuchiu was compelled by a certain Japanese feudal lord to pay an annual tribute. If, in the Formosan case, Japan saw an occasion for the absorption of Liuchiu, in the question of the annual tribute she saw another. So, while she announced that she would champion the cause of the Liuchiuan sailors, she also made the king of Liuchiu a feudal lord of the new Japanese Empire (1871). Now that she considered the case with China settled, she accordingly advanced one step further with Liuchiu itself by transferring its affairs from the ministry of foreign affairs to that of the interior. The next year Japan also prohibited Liuchiu from sending the biyearly tribute mission to China then due, as well as from sending the customary congratulatory mission and adopting the new year title on the occasion of the accession of the emperor Kuanghsu.

The so-called transfer of the rights of the Japanese feudal lords to the Japanese national government was so subtle that the Liuchiuan king did not know what objection to raise and he rested content with an assurance from Soyesima that such did not affect his relation with China.[105] But the prohibition of sending missions to China was too evidently a departure from the past to escape anybody, especially after the solemn assurances had been given by the

[105] From Ho, recd. *K.*, 4/4/28, *Yi shu han kao*, 8/2.

Japanese foreign minister, and the king therefore sent his uncle to Foochow with an urgent appeal to the suzerain. The Chinese government were then sending diplomatic representatives abroad. The matter was, therefore, referred to the Chinese minister to Japan.

As may be expected, Japan refused to discuss the matter. When the Chinese minister went to the Japanese ministry of foreign affairs, the foreign minister said the matter lay within the province of the minister of the interior. Later, when the Tsungli Yamen took the matter up with the Japanese legation, the minister declared that he had no instructions to discuss it. Worse still, in 1879, while China was still protesting, Japan took another step forward, deposed the king, and annexed Liuchiu outright.[106]

When the last event took place the king's uncle, who had been waiting at Foochow, the port of entry for Liuchiuan envoys, immediately proceeded north to Tientsin to make a personal appeal to Li Hung-chang. To the envoy we owe three valuable documents on the Liuchiuan question: the first,[107] an appeal for help in general, with the case stated; the second,[108] also an appeal urging China to take military measures, citing as a precedent the case of the seventh year of Hung-wu (1374), when the Ming emperor despatched troops to guard Liuchiu against Japan; and the third,[109] rebutting all Japanese arguments for annexation when these were submitted to him by Li Hung-chang on consultation. As an example of the patriotism of the envoy, if not also for the light it might throw on

---

[106] See petition from Hsiang, *K.*, 5/5/14, *ibid.*, 9/19 *l.*; also Stevens to Evarts, May 13, 1879. *For. Rel.*, 1879, p. 637.

[107] *K.*, 5/5/14, cited above.

[108] *K.*, 5/6/5, p. 22, *Yi shu han kao*, 9/22.

[109] A memorandum, *K.*, 5/6/24, also cited above.

the subject, we reproduce here the first of these documents:

In the intercalary third month of the current year stranded Liuchiuan sailors who landed at Foochow brought with them the news that Liuchiu had been annexed by Japan. On learning of this . . . which was regularly submitted to the High Authorities at Foochow, I prepared to come personally to appeal to your Excellency for rescue, but in fear that publicity might invite dangers of a kind still worse, I finally sent Tsai Ta-ting and others north to have the matter confidentially submitted first. . . . However, on the seventeenth of the fourth month, there came a secret letter from the Heir Apparent brought by a Fukien merchant returning from Japan which gave the following information: On the third day of the month one ——, a member of the Japanese ministry of interior, came to Liuchiu at the head of a score of officers and several hundred troops. As soon as he arrived, he, roaring and angered, started to rebuke the King for having sent the tribute and other missions to the Celestial Court, and for ignoring the Japanese injunction in making an appeal to the Court for mediation, and then informed him that, on account of what they called the disloyal acts, the feudal status of Liuchiu was abolished and the country constituted into a district. Although all, from the King downwards, were determined not to submit, the King, with a weak, small nation backed by no military forces, was constrained to leave the capital, to the great suffering of the entire nation. In addition, he gave the King a time limit to leave for Japan to await orders. The King, being sick abed, officials and people joined in intercession to spare him the trip, but he refused to make any concession. The Heir Apparent, who had gone to Tokyo after the intercalary third month, with the hope of gaining time for the Celestial Court to come to the rescue, petitioned the Japanese government to extend the time limit. This the Japanese government also declined to

do. The Heir Apparent therefore decided to submit the
matter to His Majesty's Minister at Tokyo, but as the Japanese kept such close watch as to prevent any communication
with him, he was compelled to send a secret letter to me
through the Fukien merchant instead, instructing me to
proceed north immediately with my appeal. With tears
streaming down his face as he wrote, he declared that if
the nation could not be restored, he would resort to a hun-
ger strike and die, in order not to humiliate the nation and
fail his master. . . .

In the fifth year of Hung-wu [1372] Liuchiu became
an integral part of China. When the Celestial Dynasty
was established at Peking, she hastened to tender her allegiance. During the successive Holy Reigns she received
increasing favor, and on her part she dutifully observed the
rule of bi-yearly tribute payment in accordance with the
Institute of the Ta Tsing Dynasty without any deviation.
On the first year of Kuanghsu [1875] Japan suddenly
barred the payment of tribute, as well as the sending of
the congratulatory mission on the accession of His Imperial
Majesty. Having explained her status to Japan, pleaded
with her, and been declined consideration, the King specially despatched me with his commission to Foochow to
submit the case, and the matter through the memorializa-
tion of their Excellencies the Viceroy and the Governor
at Foochow was referred by an Imperial Edict through the
Tsungli Yamen to his Majesty's Minister to Japan. His
Excellency on arrival at Tokyo — when the Liuchiuan
official stationed there further appealed to him — made
representation to the Japanese ministry of foreign affairs.
The Japanese, however, were not only obstinate enough
not to take note of the case, but were even bold enough to
exhibit their sinister power, and end the century-old line
of the vassals of the Celestial Dynasty. " When the
master is worried, the servants ought to feel ashamed;
when the master is humiliated, the servants ought to sacrifice their lives." What right have we to exist any longer

in this world? When living, we shall not be Japanese subjects! When dead, we shall not be Japanese ghosts! We care not even if our bodies are ground and our skulls powdered! We pondered and pondered during our days of waiting in Foochow: we would shave our heads, change our costume, and early proceed north rather than waste time and let the nation perish; we would weep in the Imperial Capital in accordance with the Great Principles until we died, rather than swallow disgrace, endure humiliation and live like cowards in Liuchiu. And when all letters from home either from officials or from the people, either from men of business or from farmers, urged us on our way after the examples set by Shen-pao-hsu of Chu and Pei Po-chi of Annam, we chose not to avoid penalties and came to Tientsin. We have full confidence that your Excellency, world-wide known and reverently respected in the insular nation, would be able to measure up to the Grace of the Son of Heaven and save Liuchiu from the disaster of extinction. We beseech Your Excellency to submit the facts to the Throne, devise means for our rescue and raise a punitive expedition. Such will not only make all from the King down to the people and to all generations grateful to His Majesty and Your Excellency, but will end the bullying of Japan and preserve Siam, Korea, Annam, Formosa, and Hainan to the Imperial Government forever.[110]

When the matter was first taken up with Japan the Chinese government was bent upon conciliation in spite of the advice of extreme measures of her minister at Tokyo.[111] Now that Japan had heaped insult upon injury, the Chinese government began to contemplate the severance of diplomatic relations.[112]

While the relations of the two countries were being

[110] Here follows a request for protection against Japanese spies.

[111] From Ho, recd. 4/4/28, *Yi shu han kao*, 8/2; to Yamen, 4/5/9, *ibid.*, 8/1.

[112] To Yamen, 5/intercalary 3/16, *ibid.*, 8/20 *l.*

strained to the breaking point, ex-President Grant of the United States arrived in China on his world tour. The Chinese government saw still a chance of peaceful solution. When the ex-President arrived in Peking, Prince Kung presented the case to him, and requested him to mediate. To this the ex-President readily consented.[113]

In Japan ex-President Grant invited the governor of Hong Kong, who happened to be there, to mediate with him. Towards such dignitaries the Japanese government felt constrained to show consideration, in spite of the attitude they had held with regard to the matter. They, however, complained to the ex-President that China had unnecessarily called in Western powers into the controversy,[114] and made the uncompromising attitude of the Chinese minister at Tokyo the excuse for not taking up the matter with China before. Nevertheless, they accepted the ex-President's advice as to conferring with China.[115] So when the Tsungli Yamen again approached the Japanese government, upon receipt of the ex-President's letter reporting the result of his mediation, the latter government accordingly instructed its representative at Peking to take up the matter.[116]

On August 11, 1879, the Chinese minister to Japan reported that John A. Bingham, American minister at Tokyo, had intimated to him that he had thought out a plan for the settlement of the Liuchiuan case with the ex-President, by means of which the central group of the Liuchiuan Islands

[113] To Yamen, 5/4/24, *ibid.*, 8/40; memo. of conversation with ex-President Grant, *ibid.*, 8/41.

[114] China approached none else except ex-President Grant.

[115] For details see correspondence between the viceroy and ex-President Grant and Col. J. R. Young in *Yi shu han kao*, books 9 & 10 *passim*; also despatches from Ho, recd. 5/6/24, from same, recd. 5/7/4, to Yamen 5/7/22, *ibid.*, 9/28, 33, 44.

[116] To Yamen 5/8/10, 5/10/26, *ibid.*, 10/2, 10.

was to be restored to the king and the northern and southern groups were to be ceded to Japan and China respectively; and that the ex-President hoped to effect a general settlement before his departure, leaving only the details to the minister.[117]   Bingham was one of the foreign representatives at Tokyo to whom Liuchiu had made appeal when Japan decided upon annexation, and was reported to be in sympathy with the unfortunate nation.   The plan as reported was evidently practical, for if China should decline the cession of the southern group of islands, Liuchiu could yet purchase her peace from Japan, and Japan given an honorable exit, having a group of islands to accommodate the magistrate whom she had rashly appointed for Liuchiu and could not recall without appearing ridiculous.   There is little doubt that the plan was actually suggested to the Japanese government, though possibly in view of the fact that the State Department was inclined to regard the mediation of ex-President Grant as personal, its consideration was not pressed.[118]

The Bingham plan, if it was ever accepted by the Japanese government at all, came out in a distorted form. When it entered into negotiation with China, it suggested that Japan turn over the southern group to China in exchange for a revision of the treaty of 1871 in Japan's favor.   When pointing out to it that it failed to take into consideration the northern group, it replied that that group had " always " been considered as part of Japan, and therefore could not enter into the settlement.[119]   In spite of the strange nature of the proposal, the Chinese government

[117] To Yamen, 5/7/22, *ibid.*, 9/44.

[118] On view of the State Dept. see Blaine to Angell, April 4, 1881, *For. Rel.*, 1881, p. 243.

[119] To Yamen, 6/2/17, 6/7/23, 6/7/29, *Yi shu han kao*, 10/26, 28, 31 *l.*

showed itself well disposed to give the matter consideration. Japan, however, showed no desire to yield on the stand she had taken, *i.e.*, the retrocession of the southern islands in exchange for a revision of the treaty of 1871 in favor of Japan. Furthermore, she refused to restore the deposed king to the southern islands, even should her terms be accepted. Seeing that no more concessions could be wrested from Japan without resorting to other measures than mere negotiation, the Chinese government submitted the case to the Liuchiuan envoy. We have the envoy's reaction in the following quotation from Li Hung-chang's report to the Tsungli Yamen: [120]

Hsiang Te-hung is a member of the Liuchiuan royal family, was formerly an official of the rank Tzu-chin, and has been in various high positions. He is balanced in judgment, loyal, and strong in character — a man of great distinction. If you contemplated appointing a person [as regent] none can equal him. But he points out that Miyako and other islands are barren, not possible to stand as a nation, and declares definitely that he can never accept the proposal of carving out the southern islands and establishing a regency there. When finishing [his protest] he prostrated himself and wept and refused to rise. His personality demands respect. His loyalty calls out for sympathy. . . .

In concluding his report Li Hung-chang recommended that the settlement of the case be delayed, and so it was delayed. Shishido Tamaki, the Japanese minister, declared this irregular, entrusted the legation to a *chargé* and withdrew from Peking,[121] thus formally terminating the

[120] To Yamen, 6/9/16, *ibid.*, 11/37.
[121] For Shishido's argument see enclosure in Angell to Evarts, Jan. 25, 1881, *For. Rel.*, 1881, p. 229.

negotiations opened as a result of ex-President Grant's mediation.[122] The Liuchiuan king, upon receiving the report of China's action, signified to the Chinese minister at Tokyo his concurrence.[123]

The case, however, was not abandoned by either party for some time. Informal discussion was still held between Takezoye, the Japanese consul at Tientsin, and Li Hung-chang on the one hand, and the Chinese legation in Tokyo and the Japanese foreign office on the other. At one point China seemed willing to end the case if Japan would further retrocede the island on which the old Liuchiuan capital, Shuri, stood, even at the expense of a revision of the treaty of 1871 in favor of Japan. This Japan refused to entertain, and so the informal discussion dragged on indefinitely and the case was never settled.[124]

As late as 1882 and 1886, when Japan approached China for a revision of the treaty of 1871, China still asked that the Liuchiuan case be settled.[125] The popular belief that China recognized Japan's claims over Liuchiu in 1881 seems to be entirely groundless. Until today China has never recognized the annexation of Liuchiu unless long silence on the subject can be construed to mean acquiescence. But it is an error to assign a date for it, as some writers do.[126]

[122] To Yamen, 6/12/16, *Yi shu han kao*, 11/45.

[123] Memorial, 6/10/9, *Tsou kao*, 39/1.

[124] To Yamen, 8/1/5, *Yi shu han kao*, 13/1; 8/1/15, 13/1 *l.*; 8/2/12, 13/19; 8/2/25, 13/24 *l.*; 8/12/24, 13/59 *l.*; 9/1/8, 14/1; also from Li, recd. 8/12/25, and reply, 8/12/30, *Tien kao*, 1/11, 11 *l.*

[125] To Yamen, 12/5/17, *Yi shu han kao*, 18/31.

[126] For further information on Liuchiu's relation to China see Seward to Evarts, Dec. 11, 1879, *For. Rel.*, 1860, p. 194.

Chapter III

THE KOREAN PROBLEM

Sec. 1. *Action and Counteraction*

JAPAN's expansion into Liuchiu led her in a direction that did not vitally affect China. With regard to her activities towards Korea the case was entirely different. Korea was not only a vassal state of China as was Liuchiu, but she was also the shelter of Manchuria and the entire coast of northern China. If China's live-and-let-live policy had allowed Korea to maintain a separate existence in common with all other Far Eastern settled communities, her sense of security, apart from the duty of a suzerain or the feeling of neighborliness, had also actuated her to see to it that the peninsula fell into no hostile hands. Hence it was but natural that, if China acquiesced in the annexation of Liuchiu, she would not let the same fate overtake Korea.

As early as 1868, the very year the present régime in Japan came into existence, and fully three years before Japan descended upon Liuchiu, this state had begun her activities with Korea. According to an account of Japanese origin,[1] though not of Japanese authorship, in the first year of Meiji Japan sent the lord of Tsushima to Korea to renew relationships which, the writer says, had not been cultivated since the beginning of the disturbance in Japan, and to announce the Restoration. The Korean government,

[1] Liu Yen, *Diplomatic History of China* (in Chinese) (Shanghai, 1921, 3rd edition), p. 174.

however, objected to the employment of terms such as " His Imperial Japanese Majesty ", on the ground that such dignity rightly belonged to China, and declined to receive the mission. On his return the lord of Tsushima advocated military demonstrations. According to another account [2] of Japanese authorship, after the revolution of 1868 a lord of Tsushima was sent to Korea as an envoy " formally to announce the resumption by the Mikado of the imperial sovereignty, and to invite the Koreans to reëstablish the old relations " which, the writer claims, was Korea's vassalage to Japan, but the lord returned without any " satisfaction ", and " such obstinacy of the Koreans so incensed General Saigo that he insisted upon an immediate expedition for their chastisement ".

Judging by these accounts there seems to be no doubt that the mission of 1868 was designed as an imposition upon Korea. It is safe to assume that Japan was fully aware of Korea's relations with China. It is also safe to assume that she was familiar with the existing political system in the Far East, and that she understood that the announcement to another's vassal of the assumption of imperial dignity with an invitation to establish relationships was tantamount to a summons to tender allegiance. With such impositions Korea was indeed not at all unfamiliar. It was only a few years after the Hideyoshi invasion, when she was just free from a Japanese conquest, that such a demand came from the Manchus at Mukden, and in that case she preferred an invasion to the imposition. Having failed in one policy, Japan was not slow to adopt another. On Korea's rejection of her advances Japan quickly held up that nation to the world as backward. For the time being, however, her ac-

[2] S. G. Hishida, *International Position of Japan* (New York, 1905), p. 163.

tive attention followed the line of least resistance by concentrating on Liuchiu, and her activities in Korea were confined to a naval demonstration after the fashion of the
Western powers. This took place about the time the treaty
of 1871 was being negotiated at Tientsin between the
viceroy Li Hung-chang and the Japanese plenipotentiary,
Date Muneki. It was this bellicose gesture of Japan towards Korea that caused the viceroy to insert the declaration
in the treaty that " courteous treatment " was to be accorded
by each to " the nations and territories " belonging to the
other.

After the settlement of the Formosan question Japan not
only deemed it a good time to take decisive steps towards
the acquisition of Liuchiu, but also to resume her activities
with respect to Korea. In 1875, again adopting Western
tactics, she sent a surveying party to the mouth of the Han
river, which was the sea gate of the Korean capital, and
on being fired upon, sent a squadron of six vessels and a
detachment of troops there the next year. But in her adventure here, as in Liuchiu, she never forgot China. Preceding the expedition, she sent Mori Yurei to Peking. On
his arrival Mori presented to the Chinese government his
request for credentials for the mission to Korea.

In view of China's relations with Korea the request was
equivalent to a demand that China order that nation to receive the Japanese. This was no less a problem to the
Chinese government than Japan's former request that China
enter into treaty relations with her on terms of equality.
The present request involved a departure from the past, as
did the former, for in the Far Eastern political system, it
had never been considered right for the vassal to have relations with nations other than those of her own status, much
less for the suzerain to order her to have such relations.

Besides, while the early request concerned China alone, the present request involved the wishes of Korea. In this relation the king had made his stand very clear four years previously when the Chinese government lent its good offices to the United States by forwarding to him a letter of F. F. Low, American minister to China, who was commissioned by the government of the United States to conclude a treaty with Korea.[3] In his communication to the Board of Rites, the king, after arguing against the points raised by Low, and laying down the principle that "a minister of the Emperor must not have relations with a foreign state", said in conclusion:

I humbly hope that the honorable board will lay before the throne all the facts connected with this matter, and that the Emperor will send forth a special edict to exhort and instruct the envoy of the nation in question so as to overcome the doubts and dispel his anxiety and thus each of us be left to himself without trouble.[4]

Because of the foregoing points of difference the Chinese government declined to grant the request of the Japanese envoy, who therefore repaired to Paoting to seek the good offices of Li Hung-chang.

In the present case as in the earlier Li was in favor of making the departure demanded by new circumstances. Before the Japanese envoy repaired to Paoting he had already suggested to the Tsungli Yamen that it confidentially advise Korea to receive the Japanese.[5] He gave as his opinion that, should China fail to take the step, Korea would resist Japan, and that would mean either a war be-

[3] Low to Fish, April 3, 1871, *For. Rel.*, 1871, p. 111.
[4] King to Board of Rites, *For. Rel.*, 1871, p. 133.
[5] To Yamen, 1/12/23, *Yi shu han kao*, 4/30.

tween China and Japan or the conquest of Korea by the latter, which in turn would mean the exposure of Manchuria to Japanese invasion. As to Korea's attitude, he thought that a word from China would be sufficient to effect a change. When he saw the Japanese envoy he readily promised to use his influence with the Chinese government, and as the latter had already declined to issue credentials, he suggested as a compromise that a promise be made to communicate the Japanese request to Korea.[6] Thus it came about that when the Japanese mission arrived at Korea, it was received and the treaty of 1876 was concluded between the two powers.[7] By this treaty Japan was to have the right to establish a permanent legation in Seoul; to trade in two more ports in addition to Fusan,[8] to which Japanese traders had hitherto been confined; to station consuls in these ports and to enjoy extra-territoriality;[9] to be free from "all former usages, such as the practice of Sai-ken-sen"[10] in the port of Fusan to which she was hitherto subjected,[11] as well as "all rules and precedents that are apt to obstruct friendly intercourse".[12]

By the conclusion of this treaty Japan was able to begin operations with Korea by showing the latter, with herself as

[6] To Yamen, 2/1/1, *ibid.*, 4/33.

[7] *State Papers*, vol. 67, p. 530.

[8] Arts. ii, iv and v.

[9] Art. viii.

[10] " Junk annually sent to Chosen by the late Prince of Tsushima to exchange a certain quantity of articles between each other ", Henry Chung, *Korean Treaties* (New York, 1919), p. 207. Is it compulsory on the part of the Prince and hence an annual tribute to Korea?

[11] Art. iv: On conditions at Fusan see Von Brandt to Baron de Rehfues, enclosed in despatch from Peking Legation, Nov. 22, 1876, *For. Rel.*, 1877, p. 74.   [12] Art. i.

an example, how a nation could achieve independence by asserting it. As inconsistent as it was natural, the attitude of Japan was at the same time as bellicose towards Korea as before.[13] Hence, before Korea began to think of Korean independence, Japan had brought upon herself anti-Japanese demonstrations, as revealed in the incident of 1882, which we shall presently discuss. It must have appeared to the Japanese of the time that, in serving the ends of Japan, Korea resentful was as good as Korea tractable, for as long as Korea became active in one way or the other she would thus offer an opportunity for Japan to step in. The Japanese were, however, to discover soon that they were mistaken.

Shortly after China had lent her good offices to Japan in entering into treaty relations with Korea, the Liuchiuan question came to a head. If China was not yet aware of Japan's ambition when Formosa was invaded, she fully realized it when Liuchiu was annexed. Thus the year 1879 witnessed a change in Chinese attitude towards Japan: she began to take precautionary measures. One of these was to advise Korea to reconstruct her army to prepare for an emergency, and at the same time to enter into treaty relations with Western powers to weaken the hold of Japan upon her. To carry out these measures Li Hung-chang, being in close touch with the situation, was given the commission.[14] [15]

Since the year 1875, when Japan renewed her activities towards Korea, some of the foremost Korean statesmen of

[13] See memorial, 5/7/14, *Tsou kao,* 34/44.
[14] Memorials, 5/17/14, 6/9/4, 6/9/27, same date, 7/2/2, *ibid.,* 34/44, 38/24, 37, 27, 46, 40/11; also to Yamen, 5/7/12, 7/2/2, *Yi shu han kao,* 9/34, 12/6.
[15] Ordinary Sino-Korean relations remained to the end in the charge of the Board of Rites.

the time had been in constant communication with the viceroy, cultivating his friendship and seeking his advice.[16] The suggestions of the Chinese government, therefore, did not come to them as a surprise. They immediately sent commissioners to the viceroy to consult with him in person, and a plan for the reorganization of the Korean army was forthwith drawn up.[17]

While the viceroy was looking for an opportunity to carry the second of the foregoing suggestions into effect, Commodore R. W. Shufeldt, of the United States Navy, appeared on the scene. In 1880 Shufeldt had obtained a commission from the State Department to repeat Low's attempt to establish treaty relations with Korea. Upon his arrival in the Far East he sought the good offices of the Japanese government. But there he met with failure, for his letter to the Korean king was first, when sent through the Japanese consul at Fusan, returned by the local authority, and then, when sent through the Japanese foreign office in company with a personal letter from Inouye Kaoru, the Japanese foreign minister, it was returned to him by the Korean government. So he repaired to China. At Tientsin he found the viceroy ready to lend him his good offices. In March, 1882, after arrangements had been made — by the viceroy with the Korean government [18] and by Shufeldt with the State Department — negotiations were instituted between the viceroy on behalf of Korea and Shufeldt on behalf of the United States.[19]

---

[16] See memorial, 5/7/14, *Tsou kao*, 34/44.

[17] Memorials, 6/9/4, 6/9/27, 7/12/2, *ibid.*, 38, 24, 37, 42/44.

[18] To Yamen, 6/11/21, 7/2/2, *Yi shu han kao*, 11/42, 12/6; memorial, 7/2/2, *Tsou kao*, 40/11.

[19] For a full account of the Shufeldt mission, based upon the Shufeldt and other official papers, see C. O. Paullin, *Diplomatic*

The draft [20] of a treaty which was taken as the basis of negotiations was drawn up by the viceroy in consultation with Korean commissioners sent to him for the purpose. It was similar to the treaty of 1871 concluded between China and Japan, with modifications as demanded by circumstances, such as the stipulation that the enjoyment of extraterritorial rights was temporary [21] in place of a mutual grant, or as favored by circumstances, such as the stipulation that foreign settlements in treaty ports were to be under local jurisdiction [22] which, in view of existing conditions, did not find its way into the treaty with Japan. Shufeldt signified his general concurrence with the provisions of the draft, but raised strong objections to a declaration which headed the draft that "Chao-hsien is a dependency of China, but in matters relating to internal administration or foreign intercourse she has always enjoyed autonomy".[23]

In the treaty Korea concluded with Japan in 1875 there was the declaration that "Chao-hsien, being an autonomous state, shall enjoy the rights of equality with Japan".[24] This was, of course, nothing more than a declaration of historical facts, for Korea had been an autonomous state ever since she came into existence, with the possible exception of a short period during the Yuan dynasty, and had always enjoyed the rights of equality with Japan, not excluding the days of the Hideyoshi invasion. On account of

---

Negotiations of American Naval Officers, 1778–1883 (Baltimore 1912), pp. 293–328.

[20] *Yi shu han kao*, 13/10.

[21] Art. iv.

[22] Art. vi.

[23] Art. i.

[24] Art. i. For Chinese text of the treaty of Kianghua, see *Japan Treaties* (1899), i, 1.

the fact that nothing was said of China's suzerain rights in that treaty, those who were working against China were able to twist that declaration to their own advantage. Thus we see that, after its translation into English, it was transformed into the following unrecognizable phrase:[25] " Chosen, being an independent state, enjoys the same sovereign rights as does Japan." It was to provide against this contingency that the viceroy proposed to have the declaration of the draft, " lest ", to use his own language, " the Powers shall soon forget that Chao-hsien belongs to us ".

The declaration, as proposed, was not only a statement of the facts, but also had the full concurrence of the Korean commissioners, and in view of the fact that it was China, rather than Korea, that was entering into a treaty with the United States, the viceroy thought it was but just to have it inserted. Shufeldt, however, reasoned differently. He rejected the declaration on the simple ground that it was irrelevant to the conclusion of the treaty between the United States and Korea.[26]

When the matter was reported to the Tsungli Yamen, the latter took it up with Chester Holcombe, American *chargé d'affaires* at Peking. Holcombe was reported as seeing nothing irregular in the proposed declaration, and promised to use his influence with Shufeldt, as he was about to proceed to Tientsin to assist in the negotiations. At Tientsin Hol-

[25] For current text see *State Papers*, vol. 67, p. 530.

[26] Shufeldt objected not only to the declaration but also to the provision for good offices in the same article. It is the provision and not the declaration that he characterized as placing Korea under the joint protection of the United States and China. See Shufeldt to the Viceroy, *Yi shu han kao*, 13/23 *l*. *Cf.* statement in Tyler Dennett, *Americans in Eastern Asia* (New York, 1922), p. 459.

combe reported to the viceroy that Shufeldt refused to yield on the point.[27]   Before the arrival of Holcombe, however, Shufeldt had made the concession that the declaration be made by the Korean government supplementary to, but separated from, the treaty.   In the hope that he might yet induce him to go the full length, the viceroy now requested Shufeldt to consult the State Department on the point, which the latter did on April 12th.   By the 19th the treaty was completed in every particular except the point relating to the inclusion of the declaration in question.   Then, as Shufeldt stated that he had not received any instructions from Washington,[28] the viceroy accepted his early concession as a compromise.   The treaty as agreed upon was then brought to Korea by a Chinese war vessel, and on May 22, 1882, on Korean soil it was signed by Shufeldt and Korean plenipotentiaries.[29]   As to the declaration, it was embodied in a letter from the king to the President of the United States, dated May 15, 1882, transmitted through Shufeldt. According to the translation communicated to the State Department by Holcombe [30] this letter read as follows:

Cho-sen has been from ancient times a state tributary to China, yet hitherto full sovereignty has been exercised by the Kings of Cho-sen in all matters of internal administration and foreign relations.   Cho-sen and the United States in establishing now by mutual consent a treaty, are dealing

[27] *Cf.* Paullin, *op. cit.*, p. 317.

[28] For possible causes of the failure of the State Department to reply to Shufeldt see *ibid.*, p. 324.

[29] To Yamen, 8/2/9, 8/2/24, 8/3/3, *Yi shu han kao*, 13/7 *l.*, 23, 31; memorial 8/3/6, *Tsou kao*, 43/34.   For text of treaty see *Malloy*, i, 334.

[30] See Bayard to Denby, Feb. 9, 1888, *For. Rel.*, 1888, p. 225. In the same instruction may be found also a translation transmitted by Shufeldt.

with each other upon a basis of equality. The King of Cho-sen distinctly pledges his own sovereign power for the complete enforcement in good faith of all the stipulations of the treaty in accordance with international law.

As regards the various duties which devolve upon Cho-sen as a tributary state to China, with these the United States has no concern whatever.

Having appointed envoys to negotiate a treaty it appears to be my duty, in addition thereto, to make this preliminary declaration.

Following the treaty and mainly modelled after it were also concluded a number of treaties with European powers, with Great Britain [31] and Germany on November 26, 1883; with Italy on June 26, 1884; with Russia on July 7, 1884; and with Austria on June 23, 1892.[32]

Trade between China and Korea was originally limited to the border. Now that Korea had entered into commercial relations with the world a change in the old condition had necessarily to be effected. Accordingly, even before the signature of the Shufeldt treaty, the matter was discussed, but it was delayed for a while on account of the absence of the viceroy in mourning. After his return the matter was taken up again and trade regulations of eight articles were drawn up and promulgated.[33] The preamble reads as follows:

[31] For revision of treaty by Great Britain see to Yamen, 9/10/28, 9/11/8, 9/12/13, *Yi shu han kao*, 15/13, 14, 19.

[32] For the question of Chinese suzerainty as connected with the Austrian treaty, see from Tang Shao-yi, 18/3/21, and reply of even date, *Tien kao*, 14/7 *l.*, 8; to Yamen, 18/4/12, *Yi shu han kao*, 20/28.

[33] Memorial, 8/8/29, *Tsou kao*, 14/36; to Yamen, 8/8/29, *Yi shu han kao*, 13/38. For text of regulations see *Tsou kao*, 44/40, or *Customs*, ii, 1521.

Chao-hsien has long been ranked among the vassal states. All that pertains to the rites has been definitely regulated and no change is required there. But as now that various countries have entertained trade [with Korea] by water, it becomes necessary to remove at once the maritime prohibitions and let the merchants of both countries enter into commercial relations and share in the benefit. The regulations for the frontier trade will also, as required by new circumstances, be accordingly modified, but the regulations for the maritime and overland trade are now decided upon. Be it understood that they are made out of China's favor for the vassal and shall not be subject to equal participation by the various peer nations.

In the next year twenty-four regulations for the trade on the frontier were also drawn up between the authorities of Shengking and Korean commissioners. A similar declaration was also made in the preamble.

Sec. 2. The Li-Ito Convention

Unfortunately, the above measures were hardly carried out when the problem of Korea became even more complicated. The king who succeeded his childless uncle as a boy of twelve years in 1863, with his father as regent (known as the Ta-yuan-chun), was a weak person. After his marriage he allowed himself to come under his consort's influence, and permitted her to oust his own father, the regent, from power, thus sowing the seeds of trouble.

Incensed by Korea's weakness and smarting under a sense of personal injury the Ta-yuan-chun took advantage of some dissatisfaction in the army and incited a palace revolution just about two months after the signing of the Shufeldt treaty. Being in the main a patriotic movement, the anti-Japanese feeling which had been generated in the country found in the rebellion an occasion to manifest itself. The Japanese legation was burned by a mob and the Japanese minister, Hanabusa, who headed the naval demonstration of 1871, escaped with his staff to the coast. The Japanese government, advised of the events, promptly sent a large military force to Korea and entered Seoul, the capital.

The viceroy Li Hung-chang was then in mourning at his home in the province of Anhui. Upon hearing of the disturbance, the Chinese government immediately hurried him back to his post, while despatching Ma Kien-tsung, one of the viceroy's secretaries, with troops to Korea. The matter, however, did not need the viceroy's presence, for on September 1st, while he was on his way north, report had already reached him that all was over. In ordinary circumstances China would have left such a revolution alone, reserving to herself the right to approve or disapprove the change that might be brought about. Under the present circumstances, however, with Japan involved, China could not but act differently. Rather than give Japan an opportunity to begin hostilities against Korea, Ma promptly quelled the disturbance and arrested the instigator, the Ta-yuan-chun. The Chinese government approved the measure and ordered the detention of the Ta-yuan-chun at Paoting, the provincial capital of Chihli.[34]

The cause of complaint being removed, Japan had to content herself with whatever indemnity she might exact. On August 30, 1882, Hanabusa, the unfortunate Japanese minister, who had returned with Japanese troops, succeeded in obtaining a convention of six articles from the Korean government for an indemnity of $500,000 (Mex.) and

[34] To Yamen, 8/7/24, 8/8/3, *Yi shu han kao*, 13/35, 35 *l.*; memorials, 8/7/8, 8/7/27, 8/8/10 (in 3), *Tsou kao*, 44/4, 6, 11, 15, 21.

the right to maintain a legation guard with quarters provided by the Korean government. In addition, he also exacted a supplement to the treaty of 1876, granting rights and privileges in addition to what had been obtained before.[35]

The Ta-yuan-chun was not a demagogue like those of whom we shall presently speak, but a man of responsibility, being the ex-regent, father of the king, and brother of the late king. Had he succeeded in his *coup d'état* the next few decades of Korea's history, and hence, that of the Far East, might have been entirely different. Unfortunately his acts involved the Japanese and he failed. Worse still, his failure further accentuated the very situation which he aimed at remedying, for by his removal and by the coming of the Japanese guards, the demagogues who had hitherto lain low could now raise their heads.

In the year 1884 China drifted into war with France on behalf of Annam, another vassal which was facing the same situation as Korea. These demagogues, with the assistance of Takezoye, the Japanese *chargé d'affaires* at Seoul, and of course his guards, immediately became active. On being threatened with the penalty of exile by the Korean government, they hastened to carry out their *coup d'état*. On the night of December 4, 1884, on the occasion of a dinner given to the diplomatic corps to celebrate the opening of a Korean postal system, the conspirators murdered six ministers of state and seized the king and queen. In the trouble of 1882 the Chinese government had despatched six battalions of troops to Korea. When the French War became imminent half of these troops were recalled and the remainder were entrusted to Yuan Shih-kai, who was a mem-

[35] From the king, *ibid.*, 44/31. For convention and supplementary commercial treaty see *ibid.*, 44/33.

ber of the staff and at the same time commander of the
new Korean army.[36]

About a month before the incident Yuan had reported
to the viceroy the possibility of trouble and was ordered to
make ready to meet it.[37]   The morning after the murders
Yuan duly notified Takezoye, who was in the palace, that
he would come to rescue the king from the rebels.   In the
afternoon when he came, at the head of Chinese troops, he
was, however, fired upon.   He consequently returned the
fire and drove whosoever resisted him out of the palace.   In
the evening he further effected the rescue of the king,
whom the fleeing rebels had carried away.

The Japanese saw their cause lost, burned the legation
and retreated to the sea coast.   The mobs fell upon them,
as well as upon the Japanese traders in the Korean capital, and several lives were lost.   The Chinese troops rescued
the traders and escorted them to Chemulpo to join their
chargé.[38]   When the report came to China, the Chinese
government immediately appointed two imperial commissioners to investigate the matter, and at the same time re-
enforced the three battalions in Korea with another.[39]

If on the previous occasion of her intervention Japan
lost her cause of complaint through China's action, in the
present instance she had none at all, because her *chargé* was
implicated in it.   Nevertheless she again sent Count Inouyé
Kaoru with a large military force to Korea to exact what-

[36] Memorial, 10/4/4, *ibid.*, 49/34.

[37] From Yuan, recd. 10/9/25, *Yi shu han kao*, 16/10 *l.*; to
Yamen, same date, *ibid.*, 10/10.

[38] To Yamen, 10/11/4, *Tien kao*, 4/31. See also minutes of
Tientsin Conference cited below.

[39] Memorial, 10/11/3, *Tsou kao*, 52/5; to Yamen, 10/10/23
(2), 10/11/15, *Tien kao*, 4/23, 32; to Yamen, 10/11/20, *Yi shu
han kao*, 16/14.

ever reparation was possible. On January 9, 1885, Inouyé succeeded in obtaining a convention by which Korea engaged to make apology to Japan, to punish the rioters, to pay $30,000 as indemnity, and to reconstruct barracks for the Japanese legation guards.[40]

Unlike the preceding case, the present crisis did not merely involve Korea, and Japan also sent Count Ito Hirobumi to China. Ito proceeded to Peking to take up the matter with the Tsungli Yamen, and being referred to the viceroy returned to Tientsin. There he had his first meeting with the latter on April 3, 1882.

In taking up the matter with the viceroy Ito assumed the part of an injured party, and laid the blame to the Chinese troops in Korea, alleging that they had started hostilities and had taken part in the interception of the retreating Japanese troops and in the pillaging of the Japanese traders. Then he demanded that China recall her troops from Korea, punish the officers connected with the incident, and compensate the Japanese traders who had suffered loss of life and property.

In this case, as in the Formosan, China was ready to compose whatever difficulties lay between the two nations, and to settle, as far as possible, to the satisfaction of Japan. The stationing of troops in Korea was after all a temporary measure. On the other hand, the right of maintaining a guard at Seoul, which the Japanese had exacted from Korea as a result of the earlier incident, constituted a constant source of danger, as evidenced by Takezoyi's part in the second *coup d'état*.

The viceroy, therefore, accepted Ito's point on the recalling of Chinese troops from Korea, on condition that Japan

[40] Bingham to Frelinghuysen, Dec. 22, 1884, *For. Rel.*, 1885, p. 553.

would also recall her legation guards. As to the two other points, he peremptorily rejected them on the ground that, in undertaking to quell the disturbance, Chinese officers were acting in accordance with their duty and that there was no proof that the loss of life and property incurred by the Japanese traders was inflicted by the Chinese soldiers as alleged. On April 8th, after three meetings, Ito sent Admiral Enomoto Takeaki — Japanese minister at Peking, who had come to assist Ito in the negotiations — to the viceroy with the threat to break off negotiations unless the latter acceded to his demands on the two points.

On March 23, 1885, just after Ito's arrival from Japan, the viceroy wrote to the Tsungli Yamen, pointing out the close relation of the French and the Japanese problems, and urging the government not to waver in its purpose of concluding peace with France,[41] which was then being negotiated. Accordingly, on April 4th, a peace protocol was signed in Paris. Yet, in spite of this, the viceroy was conciliatory in his attitude. On April 8th, the day after the third meeting with Ito and a little while before Enomoto came with his threat, the viceroy wrote to the Tsungli Yamen asking if the Court would not make the concession of granting a sum, as in the Kung-Okubo convention, to the families of the Japanese traders who died in the incident, in order to meet Ito half way.[42] Ito's threat, however, gave him no retreating ground. When he heard it, he immediately questioned the origin of the trouble, and declared expressly that China was ready for whatever measures Japan might take. Ito, however, did not break off the negotiations. In the next meeting, held on April 10th, he peacefully took up the question of recalling troops.

[41] To Yamen, 11/2/7, *Yi shu han kao*, 16/16.
[42] To Yamen, 10/2/23, *ibid.*, 16/27 *l.*

As the principle of recalling troops had been agreed to by China, negotiations on the point went on smoothly. Having ascertained from Ito his reaction concerning Chinese instructors in the Korean army, the viceroy communicated, in writing, his proposals for a settlement: (1) the two countries were simultaneously to withdraw their armed forces from Korea within four months; (2) China was to recall her instructors in the Korean army after a certain number of years, the number of instructors being limited in the meantime to ten or twenty; (3) neither country was to despatch troops along with her commissioners in case their presence in Korea was demanded; and (4) any troops China might hereafter send to Korea at the request of the king for quelling rebellions, were to be recalled as soon as their mission was fulfilled. To the last three proposals, particularly the last two, Ito raised objections. In place of the second he proposed that Korea employ instructors of other nationalities for continuing the training of her army. In place of the last two he proposed that notice be given previously in case either nation deemed it necessary to despatch troops to Korea in future. The viceroy readily accepted the first counter-proposal. As to the second, he referred it to the Court, and having obtained permission he also accepted it. In the meantime a convention embodying what they had agreed upon was drawn up, and on the seventh meeting, held on the 18th, it was signed by both parties.[43]

The Li-Ito convention was in three articles.[44] In Article I China agreed to withdraw her troops and Japan her legation guards, both within four months, but to embark at

---

[43] For details of the conference see the minutes, *Yi shu han kao*, 16/17 *l.*–17/8 *l.*; also memorial, 11/3/5, *Tsou kao*, 53/24.

[44] *Yi shu han kao*, 17/7; *Customs*, ii, 13, 16.

different ports, the Chinese at Masanpo, and the Japanese at Ninsen. In Article II China and Japan agreed to urge the king of Korea to organize his forces under instructors who should be neither Chinese nor Japanese. In Article III occurred the following passage:

In case any disturbance of a grave nature occurs in Korea which necessitates the respective countries, or either of them, to send troops to Korea, it is hereby understood that they shall give, each to the other, previous notice in writing of their intention so to do, and that after the matter is settled they shall withdraw their troops and not further station them there.

At the fifth meeting after the viceroy had accepted all Ito's counter proposals, Ito again brought up the question he had dropped before. In order to meet him half way, the viceroy promised that he would counsel the Chinese officers against future hasty action and order an investigation into the charges against the Chinese troops by Japanese traders, with due punishment in case the charges were found to be true. This promise was embodied in a note [45] and handed to Ito at the same time the convention was signed.

When discussion first began, the viceroy questioned Takezoyé's part in the *coup d'état*, but as Ito was able to produce a document alleged to be from the king of Korea to Takezoye calling for his aid, the viceroy did not press the point. Later, as we have seen, when Ito threatened to break off negotiations, the viceroy again raised the question, but again, as Ito showed conciliation, he dropped it. However, when the viceroy promised to counsel Chinese officers, Ito also intimated that he would recall Takezoye. This he accordingly did, when he returned to Japan.

[45] *Yi shu han kao,* 17/8.

As to the Korean demagogues, they fled to Japan after the failure of the *coup d'état*, and were found at the end of 1885 plotting there with some Japanese for another attempt to overthrow the Korean government.[46] The discovery, however, put an end to the conspiracy, and they remained there until 1894 when, in the month of March, one was enticed by the agent of the king to Shanghai and there assassinated, while another had his life attempted in Tokyo. In the former case the Korean government, having secured the corpse, had it quartered, against the advice of Yuan Shih-kai and some other foreign representatives, and thus supplied material for Japanese propaganda on the intervention in Korea which brought about the Sino-Japanese War of 1894–5. In the latter case the Korean minister to Tokyo acted no more wisely. He first declined to let one of his secretaries be subpoenaed by the Japanese court to appear as a witness in the case, and when the Japanese police forcibly entered the legation to take the secretary, he withdrew from Japan without waiting for instructions from home. The incident, however, was patched up by the Korean government, on the advice of Yuan, by appointing one of the secretaries of the Tokyo legation as *chargé*.[47]

The incident of 1884 fully demonstrated the weakness of the Korean king. In reporting the settlement with Japan and enjoining upon him the training of his army, which China had helped to reorganize, and was now barred from interfering with by the agreement with Japan, the viceroy concluded as follows: [48]

[46] To Yamen, 11/2/4, *Yi shu han kao*, 18/20 *l.*

[47] For correspondence relating to the two cases see telegrams in *Tien kao*, 15/23–30 *passim.*

[48] To king of Korea, 11/3/20, *Yi shu han kao* 17/10.

Korea has met two great disasters within three years. Your Highness, repenting the past and guarding against the future, will undoubtedly understand the cause of the trouble and be deeply grateful to his Majesty, the Emperor, for its solution, and hence become painfully averse to partisanship and doubly cautious in the cultivation of neighbors' friendship. The *Chuan* has it: "A nation might become secured because of difficulty!" I hope your Highness will rouse yourself to it.

The viceroy did not stop with admonitions. When the incident of 1884 first occurred he had decided to send the Ta-yuan-chün back to serve as a check on the weak king.[49] This he now carried out. In addition he also appointed Yuan Shih-kai, who had distinguished himself in the last two incidents, as "Trade Commissioner" to Korea. The commissionership, as established after the promulgation of regulations for trade with Korea, was to look after trade alone. Now it was also invested with power to advise the king on behalf of the Chinese government, or, in other words, converted into a residency. In the summer of 1885 the Ta-yuan-chün and Yuan Shih-kai left for Korea together.[50]

There is no doubt that Ito's willingness to compose differences with China was due just as much to China's fast recovery from the effects of the Taiping Rebellion, and Russia's becoming interested in the question of Korea — the latter problem we shall presently review — as to his desire to conserve Japanese energy for internal reorganiza-

---

[49] From Yuan, 10/9/25, *Yi shu han kao*, 16/10 *l.*; to Yamen, 10/10/27, 11/6/27, 11/7/10, *ibid.*, 16/12, 17/42, 50; to king of Korea, 11/7/11, *ibid.*, 17/55 *l.*; memorial, 11/8/15, *Tsou kao*, 54/45.

[50] To Yamen, 11/7/28, *Yi shu han kao*, 17/57 *l.*

tion. In any event, he showed statesmanlike qualities which left a good impression upon the viceroy. After the conference the viceroy wrote to the Tsungli Yamen [51] saying in part as follows:

This envoy [Ito] has traveled extensively in Europe and America and has done his utmost to learn from them. He is in possession of statesmanlike qualities; applying himself diligently to commerce, to neighborliness, to the welfare of the people, and to the training of the army and navy; not prone to bellicose talk, nor to aggression against small nations. There is no doubt that within a decade Japan's prosperity and power will be considerable. This is a distant and not an immediate danger to China. I earnestly hope that those who are at the helm of state will occupy their attention with the problem while there is still time.

The viceroy's judgment was accurate. Japan did not come out to challenge China's position in Korea until exactly a decade later. Meanwhile her policy underwent a change. Hitherto Japan had ignored China's claims and had taken independent action; henceforward she recognized China's paramount position and sought her coöperation. In 1885, when the Korean court flirted with the Russians, Count Inouyé, Japan's foreign minister, submitted a memorandum of eight articles to the viceroy, suggesting more active Chinese intervention and closer Sino-Japanese coöperation.[52] Again in 1889, when the Japanese minister at Seoul had some difficulty with the Korean foreign office, he unhesitatingly sought the coöperation of the Chinese Trade Commissioner,[53] and in 1893, when the Japanese

[51] 11/3/5, *ibid.*, 17/8 *l.*
[52] To Yamen, 11/5/24, 11/7/28, *ibid.*, 17/27, 57 *l.*; for memorandum submitted by Inouyé see *ibid.*, 17/29.
[53] From Yuan, 15/9/16, *Tien kao*, 11/46.

government failed to get satisfaction from Korea for loss alleged to have been caused by a Korean embargo upon rice, Ito communicated with the viceroy, counting upon him to arrange a settlement.[54]   In the last case the Japanese minister, Oishi, advanced Japanese claims against Korea for the loss beyond what was originally made by the Japanese government, and in addition presented an ultimatum for payment within fourteen days.   In seeking the viceroy's help Ito intimated, as in the case of Tokezoye, that he would have the minister recalled, which he accordingly did.[55]

It may also be added that towards the several chief measures taken by China after 1885, such as the release of Ta-yuan-chun and the appointment of Yuan Shih-kai, Japan generally expressed her friendly concurrence.   In short, during the decade that followed the Li-Ito convention, Japan actually maintained the sort of normal relations with her neighbors, Korea and China, which she should have done.   Indeed, this was so much the case, that the Russian representative at Seoul was finally led to the conclusion that there must exist certain secret agreements between China and Japan.[56]

Nor did this policy undergo any material change.   At least there was no sign of it, even in the early days of the Tung-hsueh Rebellion.   It is recorded that, when that rebellion first became serious, the Japanese *chargé* sent his secretary to the Trade Commissioner to express his opinion in favor of China's putting down the rebellion for Korea, and when he learnt that Korea had applied for such assistance, he came in person to express his wish that China

---

[54] To Yuan, 19/3/20, *ibid.*, 14/31; see also other correspondence, pp. 14 *l.*–37 *l.*, *passim.*

[55] To Yamen, 19/4/10, *Tien kao*, 14/40.

[56] To Yamen, 19/6/30, *ibid.*, 14/48 *l.*

would not decline. There is little doubt that, on both occasions, the *chargé* was sincere and acted in conformity with
the Japanese policy of that time.[57]

As to Japan's attitude towards Korea, although she was
still apt to be bellicose even after 1885, she became more
and more conciliatory as time went on. Even in the case
of the assassinations referred to above, which later furnished good material for propaganda purposes, Japan's attitude was not extreme. It is interesting to note that this very
case, which has been given by writers as one of the immediate causes of the war of 1894–5, was satisfactorily settled
more than a month before the outbreak of the Tung-hsueh
Rebellion,[58] which led directly to the war.

Sec. 3. The Russian and British Complications

To all intents and purposes Japan was thus kept out of
Korea, but the action and counteraction which preceded the
settlement of 1885 could not but have indirect results,
which only time and energy could render innocuous.

After the conclusion of the Shufeldt treaty a foreign
office, after the style of the Tsungli Yamen, called the
Tungli Yamen, was created, and P. G. von Möllendorff,
a German subject who had come to China for the Chinese
Customs Service and who was then in the German consular
service, was employed through the viceroy to act as adviser.
Möllendorff arrived at Korea in 1883 and applied himself
diligently to the introduction of reforms for Korea, among
which was the creation of a postal system, at the celebration
of which occurred the *coup d'état* of 1884.

Möllendorff's loyalty to his work, however, got the better
of his judgment. Failing to see what he could do for

[57] From Yuan, 20/4/28, 20/5/1, *ibid.*, 15/32, 34.
[58] See from Yuan, recd. 20/13/23, *ibid.*, 15/30 *l.*

Korea after the *coup d'état*, when Japan was hostile and while China was fully occupied in the French War, he turned to Russia for assistance. When approached, Russia naturally became interested. After some negotiations between Möllendorff and the Russian legation at Tokyo, first by correspondence through one Alexis de Speyer, a secretary of the Russian legation, and later in person, when Möllendorff went with the mission of apology provided for in the convention settling the incident of 1884 between Korea and Japan, a provisional secret agreement was drawn up, by which Russia was to grant certain kinds of protection to Korea and to supply her with military instructors in return for the lease of Port Lazarev on the east coast of Korea.[59]

For some time Great Britain, the old rival of Russia, had contemplated [60] the occupation of Port Hamilton on a group of islands off the southern end of the Korean peninsula, evidently to serve as an outpost for watching the Russians. When the arrangement of Möllendorff with the Russian legation at Tokyo came to the knowledge of Great Britain, her relations with Russia over boundary questions in Central Asia were greatly strained. Accordingly she hastened to occupy the desired port on April 15, 1885.[61] The nervousness of Great Britain, however, did not cause her to forget that the territory was Korean. On the day next to that of the occupation, her foreign office notified Tseng Ki-tse, Chinese minister at London, commonly known as Marquis Tseng, of the fact,[62] apologizing for not having come to a

[59] See memorandum of conversation between Yuan and Chin, 11/9/1, *Yi shu han kao*, 18/2 *l*.

[60] See *China, No. 1* (1887), *passim*.

[61] Admiralty to Dowell, April 14, 1885, *China, No. 1* (1887), p. 1.

[62] Granville to Tseng, April 16, 1885, *ibid*., p. 1.

previous understanding with China on the subject on the ground of the port's " probable occupation . . . by another power", disclaiming that she had any wish to injure the prestige of China, and declaring herself prepared to come to an agreement " which would not be harmful to Chinese interests in those parts ".

In June, 1885, Speyer came to Seoul to consummate the Russian arrangement with the Korean government. But he came too late, for the Japanese question had already been settled, and, besides, Great Britain also had shown herself interested. Under such circumstances the saner element of the Korean government easily carried the day, and the king had no alternative but to repudiate Möllendorff's act and finally also to dismiss him from the foreign office.[63]

The correct disposal of the Möllendorff case made it easy for China to take up the case of Port Hamilton with Great Britain. On October 13th, the viceroy approached N. R. O'Conor, British minister at Peking, on the question, suggesting that Great Britain " should take down the British flag, remove the military shanties which had been erected, and extend the cable [which, with the consent of the Chinese government Great Britain had laid from Shanghai] to Chemulpo, where it would be connected with the Korean land-line, thus rendering it useful to both governments ". O'Conor replied that the time was not opportune for a discussion on the matter owing to impending elections in Great Britain, but he would communicate with his government.[64]

At this time Great Britain had nothing to complain of

[63] To king of Korea, 11/3/20, *Yi shu han kao*, 17/11 *l.*; to Yamen, 11/4/5, 11/4/11, *ibid.*, 17/14, 18.

[64] O'Conor to Salisbury, Oct. 14, 1885, *China, No. 1* (1887), p. 19.

on the score of Russian aggression. Besides, she had also found out that the port was of little value to her unless converted into a first-class fortress like Malta.[65] Upon being informed of China's wishes Lord Salisbury instructed O'Conor on December 12th to ascertain from the viceroy, in case the latter raised the question again, whether, if Great Britain withdrew from Port Hamilton, " the Chinese government would undertake that it should not be occupied by any other foreign country." [66] The viceroy waited until the election in Great Britain, which ended in the overthrow of the conservative government, was over, and then opened the question again.[67] The new British foreign minister directed O'Conor to take up the matter on the basis of Salisbury's instructions. Having been informed of the British wishes the viceroy turned next to the Russian government.

While the settlement with Great Britain was being delayed, matters in Korea threatened to become even more complicated. The return of the Ta-yuan-chun seemed to have supplied material for mischief makers to work upon the king for independence from China. Now the delay of the settlement with Great Britain also furnished a basis for them to point out to him the mistake in repudiating Möllendorff. The result was renewed activity to befriend Russia. With the experience of Speyer before him, the Russian representative at Seoul, Waeber by name, grew cautious, and demanded proof that the matter had the approval of the king. Accordingly sometime in the autumn of 1886 a state document [68] invoking Russian assistance

[65] Dowell to Admiralty, May 20, 1885, *ibid.*, p. 6; also other documents same to same, *ibid.*, *passim.*

[66] Salisbury to O'Conor, Dec. 12, 1885, *ibid.*, p. 20.

[67] Rosebery to O'Conor, April 1, 1886, *ibid.*, p. 25.

[68] For text see *Hai chun han kao*, 2/7.

in favor of Korean aspirations to independence was communicated to him under the seal of the king, and the countersignature of the minister of the interior, the foreign office not being in favor of the measure.

When the matter had reached this stage, Min Yung-yi, a minister of state and nephew of the consort of the king, saw the danger the step would involve, communicated the secret to Yuan, and requested China to take immediate action before it was too late.[69] On receiving Yuan's report the viceroy instructed the Chinese minister at St. Petersburg to induce the Russian government not to accept the document, and at the same time secured from the Court freedom of action with regard to the matter. China being prepared, the matter settled itself. The Korean government hastened to put the blame on the mischief makers and promised to get back the document from Waeber. Waeber himself denied that he ever received the document. Such being the case, the Korean government, on Yuan's advice, sent a circular to the foreign representatives at Seoul declaring invalid all documents communicated to them unless countersigned by the minister of foreign affairs.[70]

When this had been done, Ladygensky, Russian *chargé d'affaires* at Peking, was instructed by his government to come to Tientsin to meet the viceroy, ostensibly to answer his approach for a declaration concerning Port Hamilton. To the viceroy Ladygensky declared that Russia had no territorial ambitions in regard to Korea. But when he

[69] For details of the case see *ibid.*, 2/3 *l.*, 13; to Yamen, 12/8/8, 12/8/21, *Yi shu han kao*, 18/31 *l.*, 35; from Yuan, recd. 12/8/4 and 12/8/8, *ibid.*, 18/34.

[70] For circular and note to Chinese government on the circular see *ibid.*, 48/33.

was requested to put this in writing he proposed in its place an agreement between the two countries covering the entire subject of Korea, and accordingly submitted a draft on October 1st, which was revised on October 6th, as bases of discussion. According to the revised draft, China and Russia were to preserve the existing status of Korea; to declare that they had no territorial ambition towards her; and to consult with each other in case any change proved necessary.[71] The viceroy showed much interest in the proposal and submitted the draft to the Tsungli Yamen, but he was compelled to decline the Russian overtures when the Yamen declared itself not in favor of such an arrangement.[72] Later, in 1888, the Russian foreign office again approached the Chinese minister at St. Petersburg on the same subject, but as the idea never met with the approval of the Court, nothing resulted.[73]

Ladygensky, on the other hand, refused to give in writing his declaration that Russia had no territorial ambitions towards Korea. To meet British wishes the viceroy therefore notified the Yamen officially of the verbal promise.[74] This on November 5th was in turn transmitted to the British legation; and on December 10th the evacuation of Port Hamilton was ordered by the British government.[75]

When, upon his release in 1885, the Ta-yuan-chun was consulted, he recommended that China appoint a dignitary to rule Korea in conjunction with the king after the prece-

[71] For text of the two drafts see *ibid.*, 18/45 *l.*

[72] See to Yamen, 12/9/4, 12/9/11, 12/9/25, 12/9/27 and various memoranda enclosed, *ibid.*, 18/39, 44, 49, 52; also to Alexis Coumany, 12/11/8, *ibid.*, 18/57.

[73] To Yamen, 14/4/11, *ibid.*, 19/20 *l.*

[74] For text see *ibid.*, 18/54; for note transmitting it see Walsham to Iddesleigh, Nov. 5, 1886, *China, No. 1* (1886), p. 38.

[75] Iddesleigh to Walsham, Dec. 10, 1886, *ibid.*, p. 30.

dents of the Yuan dynasty.[76] After the plot to invite Russian interference was revealed, the question was mooted in Chinese government circles. However, as the king readily denied his complicity in the plot, the matter was allowed to drop. On the other hand, the viceroy did not fail to make it very clear to the king that such would be the consequence in case he did not arrest his disloyal tendencies. On the occasion of the reply to a letter from the king, clearing himself of the blame,[77] the viceroy wrote a sharp letter [78] which, for the light it throws upon the entire case, we will here reproduce:

. . . In the correspondence of recent years I have diligently and repeatedly enjoined upon your Highness the necessity of being earnest in your relations with the suzerain and careful in your cultivation of neighbors' friendship, keeping close to decent people and distant from the indecent. I have done this, not because I do not know that such loyal advice would not agree with the ear and keep your Highness from me, but because both duty and friendship have urged me on, and because I am fully aware that your Highness is pliable in nature and capable of improvement. . . .

In her relations with the vassal states China is guided by the " rites ". She seeks to be considerate without once encroaching upon their rights, and yet goes to their rescue whenever there is need, as if they were under her direct rule. Take your country . . . : in the troubles of 1882 and 1884 she came to your rescue without any thought of the hardship, but the duties which the relation has imposed upon her and from which she cannot escape. In the West

[76] Memorandum by Ta-yuan-chun, 11/6/23, *Yi shu han kao*, 17/46 *l.*

[77] For king's letter, recd. 12/8/18, see *ibid.*, 18/35 *l.*

[78] 12/9/3, *ibid.*, 18/47.

such is not the rule. The nations that are under the protection of others can never stand on the same plane. No,
under power and oppression they would not remain feudatory states even if they were willing to, for the protector
would not only interfere with their national policies but
would also count their people, control their military forces,
tamper with their power of appointment and collect their
taxes and, worse still, even pension their kings off as private citizens with empty titles to live the lives of exiles. I
do not need to cite to you the distant examples of Egypt
and India: Annam has afforded one. I cannot understand
why they want your Highness to give up the glory of a
fief of several thousand square miles in exchange for the
position of a prisoner. . . .

In international intercourse national dignity is held most
important. The Tungli Yamen of your government has
the same functions as the Tsungli Yamen in the Celestial
Court or the foreign office in other countries. Matters of
foreign relations, be they important or unimportant, must
pass through it. Such is the general practice of all nations,
and that must not be deviated from. How can a nation
be respected by the world if the palace communicates with
the outside over the head of the foreign office and in the
ignorance of the government to the confusion of order and
procedure? When Chin Yung-yuan secretly entered into
an agreement with the Russians, it still could be pleaded
that there was no evidence of full powers authorizing such
procedure. But when Chin Yu-chun invited the Japanese,
there was already a document stamped with the royal seal
which supplied the Japanese envoy a basis of argument
when he took up the case with me at Tientsin. This ought
to be put up as a warning for all generations. How could
it be ignored and repeated again and again? If the palace
were cleared of traitors and order and dignity properly
maintained, eunuchs and maids would not be able to sell
the country to powerful neighbors in the name of author-

ity on high, nor would the national seal be repeatedly employed by the rebels. Your letter informs me that last month suddenly there were traitors using state documents, etc. . . . Stepping on frost one is reminded of the coming of ice. The matter has come to such a pass as almost to involve your Highness in treason and incur the hostilities of the enemy and actually cause relatives to suspect and the people to stir! This is terrible! If one does not repent the past and guard against the future, with efforts to raise one's self; if " the four pillars fall ", I am afraid there will be nothing left to support the nation.

Matters between the Chinese government and your country are just like those of one family. If they can be covered up, then in accordance with the principle of the Spring and Autumn Annuals in ignoring personal misdemeanor, why should we not be willing to cover them up considerately in order that general interests may not be affected and a laughing stock not supplied to the world. But if matters become widely known, and cannot be covered up, then we shall have to act regretfully in accordance with the fundamental principles of the laws of the Empire.

Sec. 4. *The United States and Chinese Claims*

Another incident, however, was yet to take place before Korea settled down to her normal life. After the dismissal of Möllendorff, his place at the Korean foreign office was taken, at the suggestion of the viceroy, by O. N. Denny, an American citizen who had been in the American consular service in China. In 1887, on the advice of Denny and others, the king decided to establish permanent legations in the United States and Europe. The viceroy saw nothing irregular in the measure, and on receiving Yuan Shih-kai's report, proceeded to lay down rules governing the style of correspondence between envoys of the suzerain and of the vassal in foreign capitals.[79] The measure of establishing legations abroad was conceived by its promoters as an instrument to interest the American and possibly the European governments in the aspirations of the king to independence. This soon became known to Yuan who, therefore, instead of communicating the rules to the Korean government, recommended to the viceroy that he withhold his approval. In order to prevent the mission to the United States from starting before the viceroy could take action, he protested to the king on the ground that no memorial had been submitted by the latter to him on the subject. Yuan's recommendation was not accepted by the Chinese government but his protest to the king was sustained. Accordingly the king memorialized the Throne, and the matter was referred to the viceroy for consideration.[80]

Being acquainted with the motive for the measure, the viceroy ruled that Korean envoys abroad should be of the rank of minister resident, in order that they might not by chance take precedence of the envoys of the suzerain. The envoy appointed for the United States had been gazetted as envoy extraordinary and minister plenipotentiary. The Korean government therefore submitted a memorandum, asking as a favor the exemption of this particular case from the rule.[81] This the viceroy granted, on condition that this particular envoy would (a) call upon the Chinese minister on arrival at the country to which he was accredited,

---

[79] To Yamen, 13/7/26, *Tien kao*, 8/32.

[80] To Yuan, 18/8/7, *ibid.*, 8/35. For memorial of the king see *For. Rel.*, 1888, p. 237. For edict in reply, 13/9/4, *Tien kao*, 9/1.

[81] Recd. 13/3/23, *ibid.*, 9/4.

and be presented to the foreign minister; (b) give precedence to him on state occasions; and (c) consult with him on matters of importance. The king accepted the conditions [82] but subsequently again requested modification as to the rule regarding presentation.[83] The viceroy again acceded to the request and authorized the Chinese minister at Washington to waive the right, if he deemed the course expedient. The envoy to the United States, however, ignored all requirements on his arrival, and on his return he was, at the request of the Chinese government, degraded.[84]

In this connection it may be interesting to make a study of the official stand taken by the United States with regard to China's claims over Korea, in view of the fact that quite a number of private American citizens and not a few officials and ex-officials had taken sides on the subject during the year following Shufeldt's mission.[85]

On January 9, 1888, Chang Yin-huan, Chinese minister at Washington, wrote to T. F. Bayard, Secretary of State, that he had received a communication forwarding a note from the Korean government stating that the Korean envoy would report his arrival at the legation and request him to present him at the State Department, and that he would do so in due course of time.[86] Next day Chang was informed by Bayard that, shortly after he was advised by

[82] To Yuan, 13/9/24, *ibid.*, 9/6 *l.*; also king to viceroy, *For. Rel.*, 1888, p. 249.

[83] To Yamen, 14/1/5, *Tien kao*, 9/25.

[84] Korean Foreign Office to Yuan, recd. by the viceroy, 13/12/25; same to same, despatched to Yamen, 16/7/23; same to Tang Shao-yi, 17/9/25; *ibid.*, 9/24, 12/32, 13/26 *l.*

[85] See in this connection W. W. Rockhill, *China's Intercourse with Korea from the XVth Century to 1895* (London, 1905).

[86] Jan. 9, 1888, *For. Rel.*, 1888, p. 380.

this note, the Korean envoy had asked for an interview for the purpose of making an arrangement for the presentation of his credentials to the President, and that he had appointed January 13th for such presentation.[87] On the 12th, while reporting the matter to the Chinese government, Chang called on Bayard and expressed his satisfaction and that of his government with the manner in which the Korean minister had been received by him.[88] In writing to H. A. Dinsmore, American minister resident at Seoul, Bayard stated his position as follows:

As the United States has no privity with the inter-relations of China and Korea, we shall treat both as separate governments customarily represented here by their respective and independent agents.

On October 6, 1887, on Dinsmore's representation that Yuan had interfered with the sending of the mission, Bayard directed Charles Denby, minister to China, to express to the Chinese government " the surprise and regret with which the United States learned of obstructions being placed by Chinese officials in the way of Korea's diplomatic representation in the United States as stipulated in existing treaties ".[89]

Denby replied that, a representation being made to the Chinese government, the latter alleged that Korea was tributary, adding that the king of Korea, having memorialized the Throne had been authorized to act under the provision of the treaty between Korea and the United States. On receiving this information Bayard wrote on November 4, 1887:[90]

[87] Jan. 10, 1888, *ibid.*, p. 381.
[88] Bayard to Dinsmore, Jan. 26, 1888, *ibid.*, p. 443.
[89] Oct. 6, 1887, *ibid.*, p. 220.   [90] *Ibid.*, p. 225.

It may be premature, in advance of a full report of the correspondence had by you with the Chinese government on this subject, to lay down instructions for your guidance. But it is right and proper to suggest a line of thought within which our treatment of the question should be confined. The essential thing is to fix the responsibility of execution of treaty stipulations, and to determine where lies the discretion which guides the acts of independent sovereign states in their mutual relations. Whether the act performed is obligatory or permissive is not material, so long as it is done by the one contracting party in pursuance of a treaty compact with the other.

The reciprocal sending and receiving of diplomatic and consular officers is provided for in the treaty between the United States and Corea. No act of national sovereignty is more express and decided than this, and it is necessarily an attribute of the power to manage her own affairs, domestic and foreign, which, as the United States was assured when her treaty with Corea was negotiated, belonged to Corea, notwithstanding her tributary relation to China. That treaty sprang, logically, from the announcement of the Chinese government that its treaties with foreign powers did not extend to Corea, and that it was in no way internationally responsible for any acts of Corea toward foreigners. By treaty Corea assumes that responsibility.

It seems, now, from your telegram, that the accepted sovereignty of Corea in her foreign relations is not absolute. It seems to be claimed by China that one of the simplest and most ordinary provisions of the treaty can not be executed without the King of Corea memorializing the Emperor of China and being accorded permission to do so.

The right to accord permission necessarily involves the right to refuse it, but the exercise of the latter right suggests a responsibility which has not heretofore been admitted and is expressly disclaimed. What would have been the consequences if the Emperor of China, in the exercise of a sovereign claim of right, had refused to allow Corea to maintain a diplomatic mission in the United States?

I do not think the advisers of His Majesty the Emperor have considered the necessary inference from the premises on which they act. For if the treaties with sovereign states cannot be executed without the authority and consent of China, they can not be violated without the responsibility of China.

The Department's instructions to your legation during the last few years, show the concern felt here at the indeterminateness of the question of China's relation to Corea. The object of this instruction is to impress like solicitude upon you, so that in any discussion affecting this question you may ascertain the real position of China, and avoid any admission that might be construed as approving China's singular claim of ultimate control without ultimate responsibility.

Before he reported the reply of the Chinese government, Denby wrote on October 13, 1887, to Bayard [91] on the question of the suzerainty of China as a whole, and when referring to the case of Korea he said:

China can not now be heard to object to the sending by Corea of ministers abroad, because she consented that Corea should make treaties with the foreign powers. Nevertheless the condition is peculiar. Here Corea, preliminary to the making of a treaty, solemnly notifies the power with which it treats that it is tributary to China.

What restrictions, if any, on the intercourse with other powers, the suzerain may impose, are to be carefully considered. I simply make the suggestion as worthy of some consideration.

In order to support his suggestion, Denby a little later [92] forwarded the memorial from the king of Korea to the

[91] *Ibid.*, p. 222.   [92] Dec. 9, 1887, *ibid.*, p. 236.

Emperor of China, and at another time [93] a letter from the king to the viceroy Li Hung-chang, adopting the rules laid down by the viceroy for the Korean envoys. On the former occasion he wrote in part:

Vattel discusses, at page 2, the status of dependent states with reference to foreign powers. This discussion furnishes little information applicable to the peculiar relations existing between China and her dependent states. The text has little application to countries which, in their history, antedate international law, of which, also, they never had any knowledge. What unwritten law or tradition controls the relations of China with her dependencies remains unknown.

Then, after giving the position of the United States with reference to Korea, he continued:

The co-equality of Corea with the United States being thus recognized, it would seem that no questions but those of expediency remain.

In the solution of such questions the geographical locality of Corea, its distracted condition internally, its possible relations to Japan, Russia, England, and China, if complete independence be assured, are all to be looked at.

After reading the above observations Bayard wrote, on February 9th: [94]

Your comments upon this singular memorial attracted my consideration. I quite agree with you that the agitation of the subject of Corea's complete independence of China, by representatives of the United States is neither desirable nor beneficial; nor do I think it incumbent on this Department now to pursue any question heretofore raised as to the relations of Corea to China, unless called upon to do so by an actual case requiring affirmative action.

[93] Jan. 21, 1888, *ibid.*, p. 248.   [94] *Ibid.*, p. 255.

After reciting the two translations of the letter of the king of Korea on May 15, 1882, in the possession of the Department, he continued:

The position of the United States is that of simply requiring the observance of treaty obligations, and it is not thought expedient to pursue any controversy as to the relations of China and Corea further than may be necessary to enable us to secure such observance. The interest of this government is not political. It seeks merely the protection of American citizens and their commerce and is not disposed to go beyond the point where such protection can be obtained.

Sec. 5.   *The Defence Measures*

Before closing this chapter, it is important that we review the defensive measures which China adopted, in addition to the devices of diplomacy, to meet problems created by such situations as those narrated above, for upon them just as much as upon the good-will of her neighbors will, as we shall see, ultimately depend not only the fate of her future policies, but also her entire position in the Far East.

(1)   *The Navy*

After the solution of the Formosan question the Tsungli Yamen memorialized the Throne, urging the immediate carrying out of the measures of maritime defence which had been for some time projected by liberal statesmen such as Tseng Kuo-fang and Li Hung-chang. One of the measures was the creation of a navy of three squadrons, one for the Pohai, one for the East China Sea and one for the South China Sea, with two ironclads and fourteen auxiliary vessels for each.[95]   The memorial received the

[95] Memorial, *Tung*, 13/11/2, *Tsou kao*, 24/10.

attention of the Court, and on May 29, 1875, the viceroys of Chihli and of the Kiang Provinces were appointed respectively Defence Commissioners of Peiyang and Nanyang with the object of creating two squadrons, the defence of the South China Sea being entrusted to authorities at Foochow and Canton.[96] The government, however, was not yet prepared to spend such a large sum of money as was required for the project, and as late as 1879 only eight gunboats were purchased from Great Britain and divided equally between Peiyang and Nanyang.[97]

The annexation of Liuchiu by Japan and her defiant attitude towards China not only turned China's attention to Korea, but also reminded her of her navy program.[98] An annual appropriation of 4,000,000 taels was therefore made from national revenues and voluntary contributions were asked for from the people. As the funds were forthcoming orders were placed with British and German firms for vessels. The program, though only two-thirds of the original was, however, not destined to be completely carried out. In 1884, when about one-third of the vessels had been ordered, the French War broke out, and with this more urgent need went all funds. But the French War was only a temporary check, for it came to an end in a year.

After the death of Hsienfeng in 1861 China was ruled by the defunct emperor's widow, the Empress Dowager Tsuhsi, and his brother, Prince Kung. The post-Boxer Rebellion policies of Tsuhsi will more than prove that the Empress Dowager was one of the ablest women who ever ruled an empire, but in the early days of her power, though

[96] Memorial, *K.*, 1/5/10, *ibid.*, 25/18.
[97] Memorial, 5/10/16, *ibid.*, 35/22.
[98] See memorial, 5/11/26, *ibid.*, 35/45.

a person of strong character she made the mistakes of ignorance.   She aspired to rule supreme herself, and in 1884
during the French War she finally ousted her brother-in-
law from office.   Prince Kung was fundamentally a weak
person, like all Manchu nobles since the time of Kienlung;
but he was, nevertheless, enlightened.   Although he was
unable to put vigor into constructive measures advocated by
the liberal statesmen of the times, he was sympathetic; and
although he was unable to entrust the direction of the destiny of the nation to the Chinese, he was not jealous of
their power.   For this reason, although China did not
emerge from the chaos of the Taiping Rebellion over
night, she was progressing all the time, and while still
far from being ranked among the most powerful of the
nations, actually came to enjoy a decade of peace and honor
between 1885 and 1894, in which, be it noted, there was
not a single instance of foreign aggression.   There is no
doubt that, had the same régime been allowed to continue
for another decade or so, China would have gone beyond
the danger zone.   Unfortunately, this was not her fate.

Prince Kung was succeeded by Prince Chun, father of
the emperor Kuanghsu.   Chun was probably a weak prince
like his predecessor, but certainly without his liberal mind
acquired through the difficult days of the Taiping Rebellion and the long years of foreign aggression.   Unable to
appreciate the services of the liberal Chinese statesmen to
the dynasty and the nation, he was inclined to grow jealous
of their power and to attempt to curb it.   Deeply indebted
to his sister-in-law, the fountain head of his power and
position, he was apt to lose his sense of proportion and to
recompense her beyond proper means.   As soon as he took
up his office he caused, on the one hand, the repairing of
the winter palace and the construction of the now desolate

Summer Palace to accommodate his imperial mistress; and, on the other hand, the creation of a new army of 30,000 in Manchuria, under the command of a Manchu imperial commissioner, to be stationed at Mukden.[99] All this meant expenses which must be provided for in one way or another.

By the time of Chun's coming to power the vessels ordered from Europe were about to be sent to China, and a board of the navy was therefore created. This was opportune for Chun. He conveniently stepped in, made himself the president of the new board, diverted part of the navy fund for his Manchurian army and another part for his palace program, and converted the board itself into a headquarters for ransacking the empire to make up the rest of the needed funds.

In consequence of this depredation upon the navy funds, not only was there no means to create the second third of the navy program, but even the process of creating the first third was checked. A fight was naturally started by Li Hung-chang, one of the original advocates of the navy, and the actual creator of the first squadron. The fight was unequal, indeed, in view of the power of the Prince. It resulted in nothing more than the granting of a minimum for the current expenses of the vessels already built, and of permission to carry on the construction of the docks at Port Arthur, then under way, to completion, as well as to add a minimum amount of defence works at Weihaiwei for the accommodation of those vessels. As to Li's entreaty for a few additional destroyers to the existing squadron, the Prince turned a deaf ear to him. Prince Chun died in 1891, only a few years after the inauguration of his policies, but the new Manchurian army had to be main-

[99] *Chi lin tung chih,* 53/5 *et seq.; Lung chiang shu lueh,* 5/16.

tained, and the construction of the Summer Palace had yet to be completed, and the navy was left as it stood in 1884. Shortly before the Japanese War of 1894–5, Li wrote to the Board of the Navy, asking for funds to replace the boilers of the vessels. The Summer Palace was by that time completed, but the sixtieth anniversary of the birth of the Empress Dowager was about to take place, and the request naturally was also put aside.[100]

The squadron, thus denied everything except bare minimum funds for current expenses, formed the ill-fated Peiyang Squadron. It consisted of two light cruisers from Great Britain, arriving in China in 1881;[101] two ironclads and one armed cruiser from Germany, arriving in 1885;[102] and four ordinary cruisers, two from Great Britain and two from Germany, arriving in 1888.[103] This fleet was manned by Chinese officers trained in the British navy, organized with the assistance of Captain W. M. Lang of the British navy, " lent " at the request of China, and commanded by General, and later Admiral, Ting Ju-chang, a gallant soldier.

In this connection we may also briefly review the much talked of Chinese aggressive designs. On various occasions of Japanese aggression there never lacked memorialists who urged the government to take measures to root out the trouble, by an invasion of Japan herself, for instance. It may be safely said that men of responsibility like Li Hung-chang never entertained such an extreme view. During the dispute with Japan over the annexation

100 For details see *Hai chun han kao*, *passim*.

101 Memorials, 5/10/28, 7/10/11, *Tsou kao*, 35/27, 42/17.

102 Memorials, 6/6/3, 7/4/27, 9/2/8, 11/10/18, *ibid.*, 37/32, 40/52, 46/7, 55/16.

103 Memorials, 9/2/8, 14/2/19, *ibid.*, 46/7, 62/14.

of Liuchiu memorials were poured in advocating aggressive measures to check aggression. When they were submitted by imperial order to Li and others for their opinion, Li said in part: [104]

Japan is a small and poor country and therefore by nature not as powerful as the Western powers. But in recent years she has learned much from the Westerners and to matters of military organization and manufacturing of weapons she has devoted no small attention, and hence she is rising. China as yet has neither her navy constructed nor the funds for it sufficiently provided. It would seem better that we continue our discussion with her on treaty basis, unless she again shows unrestrained activities. Of course as the Japanese are bellicose by nature, we should be ready, lest she might become over ambitious. This is the reason why not one day can be lost in getting on our feet.

The incident of 1882 in Korea again called forth a number of memorials advocating drastic measures. For carrying out these the memorialists naturally pointed to Li Hung-chang. It was then, probably at the suggestion of Li, that Chang Pei-lun, his son-in-law, and a member of the Hanlin Academy, submitted his two memorials, one of which,[105] while echoing the extreme view of the other memorialists to take the wind out of their sails, pointed out that there was no necessity for an immediate invasion of Japan, and the other [106] by advocating certain lines of policy to meet the problem arising from the 1882 incident, gave Li an opportunity to vindicate the wisdom of not resorting to hostile measures. It is interesting to note that the first of Chang's memorials, together with one from

[104] Memorial, 5/11/26, *ibid.*, 35/45.
[105] See memorial, 8/8/22, *ibid.*, 44/27.
[106] See memorial, 8/10/5, *ibid.*, 45/7.

Li in reply to an edict submitting Chang's memorial for his opinion, were unearthed twelve years later, and nine years after the Tientsin Conference, and published in London [107] as a proof that China was the aggressor; and it is even more interesting to note that such an idea could have found general acceptance.

(2) *The Railways*

Another constructive measure which the liberal statesman attempted to carry out may also be reviewed here. We refer to the construction of a system of railways. This subject had been mooted as early as the navy program, but the occasion for its presentation to the Court did not come until 1880, when China's relations with Russia were strained over the treaty of Livadia. Taking advantage of this state of mind, Liu Ming-chuan, later defender of Formosa during the French War, memorialized the Throne,[108] advising the construction of railways, beginning with one from Tsing-kiang-pu on the Huai river, over which route Li Hung-chang had in the previous year established a telegraph line. When the memorial was submitted by the Throne to the provincial authorities for their opinion, Li boldly came out as a champion for the idea and went on to advocate an extensive system of four lines radiating from Peking, one in the direction of the lower Yangtze as recommended by Liu, one to Hankow, one into Sinkiang, and one into Manchuria, with recommendations that Liu be made president of a railway board to carry out the project.[109] The railway project, however, fared worse

[107] Also appended in A. M. Pooley (editor), *The Secret Memoirs of Count Tadasu Hayashi* (New York, 1915).

[108] For memorial see *Kuang hsu cheng yao*, 6/17.

[109] Memorial, 6/12/1 (2), *Tsou kao*, 39/20, 27.

than the navy. First of all, in its decision the opinion of the conservatives had as much weight as that of the liberals, because the project was economic as well as military in nature. Then, in its carrying out, the part of the central government was just as important as that of the provincial authorities, for it concerned not only the jurisdiction of one viceroy or governor, but several at one time. Consequently the project was shelved. The liberal statesmen were, however, not discouraged. When Liu Ming-chuan became the first governor of the province of Taiwan (Formosa) after the French War, he experimented with railway construction on the island.[110] On the other hand, Li gave encouragement to the administration of the Kaiping coal mines to construct a line to connect the mines with Taku, and finally in 1887 he submitted a plan to the Board of the Navy for the extension of the line eastward to Shanhaikuan and westward to Tungchou as a project of maritime defence. The plan having been approved by the Throne, work was commenced and in the next year the section between Taku and Tientsin was completed.[111]

In spite of Li's care to avoid the conservatives by making his plan a project of maritime defence, opposition soon gained strength, when work for the extension beyond Tientsin was about to commence,[112] and as a result the question of railway as a whole was again referred by the Throne to the provincial authorities for their opinion.[113]

When the memorials came in, three were selected by

[110] To Admiralty, 13/4/20, *Hai chun han kao*, 3/3 *l.* Cf. statement in Morse, *op. cit.*, iii, 78, note 16.

[111] To Admiralty, 12/10/16, 12/10/16, *Hai chun han kao*, 2/17 *l.*, 18 *l.*

[112] To Admiralty, 14/9/9, 14/12/28, *ibid.*, 3/9, 14.

[113] Edict, 15/1/15, *ibid.*, 3/27 *l.*

the Grand Council for presentation to the Throne. These were from Liu Ming-chuan, Huang Peng-nien, and Chang Chih-tung. All were for railways, but while Liu and Huang were uncompromising towards the opposition, and advocated immediate construction either for commerce or for defence, Chang stooped to the level of the opposition and advocated lines not exposed to attack from the sea, beginning with one from Peking to Hankow. When they were presented to the Throne, Chang's memorial received especial attention.[114] With this the extension from Tientsin to Tungchou was ended, though the line from Peking to Hankow was started. The extension from Kaiping to Shanhaikuan, not being opposed, was begun in 1891 and completed in 1894.

In 1880, on the same occasion of strained relations with Russia referred to above, the Chinese government, at the suggestion of Li Hung-chang, sent Wu Ta-cheng to Manchuria to make a study of the defence conditions there. On his return Wu recommended the strengthening of southeastern Kirin. In consequence Hungchun was made the seat of a deputy military governor, and a special army of 5,000, foot and horse, later increased to 7,000, was created for that region, with the military governor of Kirin and the deputy military governor of Hungchun as *ex-officio* Defence and Assistant Defence Commissioners of Kirin Frontiers, to command it.[115]

In 1890, shortly after the failure of the plan to extend the railway from Tientsin to Tungchou, Li Hung-chang also projected a line from Yingkow to Hungchun via Kirin, as a measure to strengthen that defence, as well as to develop Manchuria. The project, however, was later aban-

[114] To Admiralty, 15/4/20, *ibid.*, 3/28 *l*.
[115] *Chi lin tung chih*, 53/1-4.

doned for one consisting of an extension from Shanhaikuan to Kirin via Chinchou, Kuangning, Hsinmin, and Mukden, with a branch from the latter to Newchwang, and a possible extension from Kirin to Hungchun.[116] At the time of the Japanese War, the line was constructed to Chunghouso, forty miles beyond Shanhaikuan.[117]

[116] To Admiralty, 16/3/19, 16/11/18, 17/2/12, *Hai chun han kao*, 4/2 *l.*, 9 *l.*, 13 *l.*

[117] For further railway development see *infra*, chap. iv., sec. 6.

Chapter IV

THE JAPANESE WAR AND SOME CONSEQUENCES

Sec. 1. The Occasion

In the spring of 1894 an anti-foreign movement known as the Tung-hsueh Rebellion broke out in the south of Korea. When it was reported the viceroy Li Hung-chang ordered the Chinese navy to assist in transporting troops and at the same time sent ammunition from the munition works at Tientsin [1] — thus rendering all assistance possible short of despatching troops to Korea. The Korean government, however, failed to quell the rebellion and appealed to the viceroy for troops.[2] The latter consequently despatched 1,500 soldiers to Korea and instructed the Tokyo legation to notify the Japanese government in accordance with the Li-Ito convention.[3]

When Ito entered into the above-mentioned convention with the viceroy he was engaged at home in drawing up a constitution. This task he completed in 1889. Ito evidently thought that the situation in Japan was similar to

[1] To Yamen 20/4/4, *Tien kao*, 15/31; 20/4/21, 15/32.

[2] For the Korean note see enclosure to Yamen 20/5/1, *ibid.*, 15/33 *l.*

[3] For Japanese official translations of Sino-Japanese correspondence concerning the war see appendix B, Vladimir, *China-Japan War* (New York, 1896), p. 338 *et seq.* For the Chinese note see no. 1, p. 338.

that in Prussia, and in order to meet it he modelled his constitution upon that of the latter country. The similarity, however, was more apparent than real; for, whereas in Prussia the parties the constitution sought to harmonize were the people and the king, in Japan they were the people and a clan oligarchy. Consequently the promulgation of the Japanese constitution, instead of ending difficulties, meant their beginning. When the Korean question came up, the constitutional squabble in Japan was just at its height. Suddenly there came a war, then the cessation of that squabble, then the triumph of the clan oligarchy, and henceforth the Japanese people followed their military lords into the continent and forgot their democratic leaders in the islands. A student of constitutional history has said that, whatever may be said of Ito's statesmanlike qualities previous to 1885, " he will go down in Japanese history as a man of distinctly second-rate ability " and " damned by the constitution of 1889, as well as by his action in 1894 in distracting the attention of the nation from the problems of political progress by bringing on the war with China ".[4] Judged by the circumstances, this conclusion is probably true. But however this may be, we may be certain that the step Japan was about to take was novel to her decade-old policy and that the change came abruptly [5] — both these facts suggesting some strange force at work.

On June 7th, the very day the Chinese minister at Tokyo notified the Japanese foreign office of China's intention to despatch troops to Korea, the Japanese government declared in its reply to the note that " although the words

[4] W. W. McLaren, *A Political History of Japan during the Meiji Era, 1867–1912* (New York, 1916), p. 229; on Japan's constitutional crisis see pp. 203–229.

[5] *Supra,* chap. iii, sec. 2.

' tributary state ' appear in your note, the Imperial Government has never recognized Korea as a tributary state of China ", and at the same time instructed its legation at Peking to inform the Chinese government that " owing to the existence of a disturbance of a grave nature in Korea necessitating the presence of Japanese troops there ", it was the intention of the Japanese government to send a body of Japanese troops to that country.[6]

On June 9th the Chinese government pointed out in a note that the despatching of Chinese troops to Korea was in accordance with the practice hitherto pursued by China in protecting her tributary states; that no necessity existed on the part of Japan to send a large number of troops, and that there was danger of conflict between troops of the two countries, should Japanese troops also join in suppressing the rebellion.[7]   On the 12th the Japanese government replied that it had never recognized Korea as a tributary state of China; that Japan despatched her troops in virtue of the convention with Korea that closed the 1882 incident, and in doing so she had followed the procedure laid down in the Li-Ito convention; that it was compelled to exercise its own judgment as to the number of troops to be sent; and that " although no restriction is placed upon the movement of Japanese troops in Korea " they would not be sent where their presence was not deemed necessary.[8] In the meantime claiming rights under the convention of 1882 by which Korea consented to Japan's stationing guards for her legation at Seoul, the Japanese government despatched detachment after detachment, in spite of con-

[6] Nos. 2 and 3, Vladimir, *op. cit.*, p. 340; to Yamen, 20/5/5, *Tien kao,* 15/35.

[7] No. 4, Vladimir, *op. cit.*, p. 341.

[8] No. 5, *ibid.*, p. 342.

stant protest from Korea, until by July 18th there were 18,000 Japanese troops around the Korean capital.[9]

The rebels in Korea dispersed on learning of the arrival of Chinese troops, and China accordingly requested Japan to withdraw her troops simultaneously with the Chinese forces as provided in the Li-Ito convention.[10] In reply to this, however, Count Mutsu Munemitsu, Japanese foreign minister, submitted on June 16th a memorandum proposing that China and Japan should first jointly suppress the rebellion and then appoint a joint commission charged with the duty of reforming the financial, civil, and military administration in Korea — in short, assume whatever there was of government in that poor country.[11] On June 22nd the Chinese government pointed out the absurdity of such a proposal. It called attention to the fact that the rebellion had already been suppressed, that even Chinese troops did not need to trouble themselves on behalf of Korea, and that there was even less necessity to consider the proposition of joint suppression. It indicated further that reform was a question for Korea herself, that even China would not interfere with the internal administration of Korea, and that Japan, having from the very first recognized the independence of that country, had no right to interfere. The Chinese government also reminded Japan that there was an engagement between the two countries to withdraw troops from Korea after the necessity of their presence there was over.[12]

---

[9] Sill to Gresham, July 18, 1894, *For. Rel.*, 1894, app. i, p. 31.

[10] See correspondence in *Tien kao*, 15/40–43.

[11] To Yamen, 20/5/14, *ibid.*, 15/44; no. 6, Vladimir, *op. cit.*, p. 343.

[12] No. 7, Vladimir, *op. cit.*, p. 344; *cf.* to Yamen, 20/5/18, *Tien kao*, 15/48.

Japan's mind, however, was made up. On the very day of the receipt of the note she declared that " the interests of Japan in Korea, arising from propinquity as well as commerce, are too important and far-reaching to allow her to view with indifference the deplorable condition of affairs in that kingdom ", and that " therefore the withdrawal of their forces should be consequent upon the establishment of some understanding that will serve to guarantee the future peace, order, and good government of the country ".[13]

Sec. 2.   Korean " Reform " versus the Status Quo

Upon receiving Japan's notification of her intention to send troops to Korea the viceroy Li Hung-chang immediately perceived the coming of trouble. On June 9th, N. R. O'Conor, British minister to China, made a visit to the viceroy on his way through Tientsin. The viceroy availed himself of the opportunity and sounded the minister on the question whether the British government would not advise Japan against sending troops to Korea. O'Conor readily declared that he saw no necessity for Japan to take such action, and he undertook also to consult with his government on the question. He was able on the 20th to report to the viceroy that the British minister to Japan had been instructed to advise the Japanese government accordingly.[14] On the same day O'Conor, however, also informed the Tsungli Yamen that, according to what he had learnt from Komura Jutaro, Japanese *chargé d'affaires* at Peking, the Japanese government did not have any ulte-

---

[13] No. 8, Vladimir, *op. cit.*, p. 345; to Yamen, 20/5/20, *Tien kao*, 15/49 *l.*

[14] To Yamen, 20/5/6, *Tien kao*, 15/36; 20/5/17, 15/47.

rior motive, and the troops would not proceed beyond Chemulpo.[15]

Simultaneously Count A. P. Cassini, Russian minister to China, called upon the viceroy on his way home through Tientsin, and the viceroy sounded him also as to whether the Russian government would not take the same course as the British, though now the advice to be given to Japan, as circumstances had changed, was not aimed at preventing the sending of Japanese troops, but at their simultaneous withdrawal with those of China.[16]   Since 1885, Russia had been interested in the question of Korea.   Cassini, therefore, not only readily undertook to consult with his government as requested, but he also declared that his government would never tolerate Japanese interference in Korea.   The next day he despatched home a telegram of seven hundred words,[17] and on the 25th he was able to report that the Russian minister at Tokyo had been instructed to confer with the Japanese government.[18]

The mediation of Russia greatly disturbed Japan.[19]   On the one hand she hastened to assure Russia that she had no ulterior motive and would withdraw her troops as soon as the rebellion was quelled,[20] and on the other she suggested to Great Britain that the British government come forward as mediator.[21]   On learning of Japan's tactics Cassini

[15] From Yamen, 20/5/17, *ibid.*, 15/47 *l.*
[16] To Yamen, 20/5/17, *ibid.*, 15/47.
[17] To Yamen, 20/5/18, *ibid.*, 15/48; 20/15/18, 15/49.
[18] To Yamen, 20/5/22, *ibid.*, 15/51 *l.*
[19] From Wang, 20/5/25, *ibid.*, 15/53 *l.*
[20] To Yamen, 20/6/4, *ibid.*, 16/7 *l.*
[21] From Chang Yin-huan, recd. 20/5/27, *ibid.*, 15/58; reply, 20/5/28, 15/58 *l.*; from Chang, 20/5/28, 15/59; reply, 20/5/28, 15/59 *l.*

hastened to communicate with his government again.[22]
Meanwhile he suggested to the viceroy that a conference
be held between China, Russia, and Japan to see what could
be done with Korea. This suggestion the viceroy showed
himself ready to accept on condition that nothing should
be forced upon Korea against her will and that Japan would
first withdraw her troops simultaneously with China in
accordance with the Li-Ito convention.[23] Nothing, however, developed from the proposal, for on July 9th Cassini reported that the Russian government had decided
not to intervene.[24] With Great Britain Japan was equally
successful. O'Conor joined hands with Komura to work
on the Chinese government, both suggesting that no third
power be included in any conference over the question of
Korea.[25] The viceroy comprehended the tactics of the
Japanese from the very beginning, but he was not unwilling to talk the matter over directly on condition that withdrawal of troops should precede discussion.[26] This situation, however, did not last long. When Japan was sure
that Russia would not intervene, a note in the form of an
ultimatum was communicated on July 14th to the Chinese
government through the Japanese legation in Peking ending in the following words:

The only conclusion deducible from these circumstances
is that the Chinese Government is disposed to precipitate
complications; and in this juncture the Imperial Japanese

[22] To Yamen, 20/5/27, *ibid.*, 15/57.
[23] To Yamen, 20/5/29, *ibid.*, 15/60.
[24] To Yamen, 20/6/7, *ibid.*, 16/72.
[25] From Yamen, 20/5/29, *ibid.*, 19/60 *l.*; reply, 20/5/29,
15/61; from Yamen, 20/6/2, 16/3; reply, 20/6/3, 16/3.
[26] From Yamen, 20/6/5, *ibid.*, 16/8; reply, 20/6/6, 16/8 *l.*;
from Yamen, 20/6/6, 16/9; reply, 20/6/6, 16/9.

Government find themselves relieved of all responsibility for any eventuality that may, in future, arise out of the situation.[27]

On the day of this last note, the Court ordered the viceroy to take precautionary measures.[28] But, while the most sanguine saw a conflict inevitable, a ray of hope suddenly pierced through the darkened cloud even as the fire glows before expiring. Cassini in Tientsin and O'Conor in Peking were simultaneously instructed by their respective governments to coöperate with the representatives of Germany, France, and Italy in both Peking and Tokyo to effect a mediation on the basis of simultaneous withdrawal of troops.

At last the *status quo* was receiving equal attention with Korean "reform". But the world had yet to pay for the slowness of statesmen. When Great Britain came forward to mediate the second time it appeared that she had sought the coöperation of all the powers interested in the Far East.[29] After July 9th Cassini suggested to his government that if Russia would not intervene alone she might join with the other powers.[30] No intervention, however, resulted, for evidently the other powers entertained the belief that Japan would abide by her declaration that she would not resort to extreme measures, and possibly the Russians themselves were of the same belief. If such was the case, they were sufficiently convinced to the contrary after July 14th. But they woke up a bit too late. The

[27] No. 9, Vladimir, *op. cit.*, p. 347; from Yamen, recd. 20/6/12, *Tien kao*, 16/19.

[28] To Yamen, 20/6/4, *ibid.*, 16/21 *l*.

[29] Gresham to Bayard, July 20, 1894, *For. Rel.*, 1894, app. *i*, p. 36; Denby to Gresham, July 6, 1894, *ibid.*, p. 30.

[30] To Yamen, 20/6/20, *Tien kao*, 16/28.

Russian instructions came on the 24th, and the British on the 25th. On the 26th the viceroy, on being requested by Cassini, proposed that both Chinese and Japanese withdraw their troops to the Korean frontier, the Chinese to Ping-yang, and the Japanese to Fusan.[31] On the 25th, the day previous, hostilities, however, had begun, and as China joined issue with Japan the plan for mediation was dropped. Meanwhile the British government confined itself to securing a promise from Japan to regard Shanghai, the commercial metropolis of the Yangtze valley, as outside the field of warlike operations.[32]

Before we leave this phase of the subject we may yet review the attitude of the United States, which was no less interested in the problem of Korea than Russia and Great Britain. On June 22nd, the State Department sent John M. B. Sill, American representative at Seoul, the following telegraphic instruction:

In view of the friendly interest of the United States in the welfare of Korea and its people, you are, by direction of the President, instructed to use every possible effort for the preservation of peaceful conditions.[33]

To this Sill replied on the 24th as follows:

Have received telegram. I have already done and will do as much as possible for the interest of peace. Korean rebellion suppressed by themselves. Thousands Chinese and Japanese troops occupying Korea. Neither of them will withdraw first. In their presence there is much danger. Chinese are in favor of simultaneous departure. Japan

---

[31] To Kung and Hsu, 20/6/24, *ibid.*, 16/31 *l.*; from Kung, recd. 20/6/27, 16/35.

[32] From Kung, 20/6/29, *ibid.*, 16/37 *l.*

[33] Uhl to Sill, June 22, 1894, *For. Rel.*, 1894, app. i, p. 22.

stubborn. Ulterior purpose suspected. She seems to desire war. Korea integrity menaced. The king arduously interceding with government of Japan.[34]

On June 24th the Korean foreign office addressed a note to the foreign representatives at Seoul requesting them to use their good offices to effect an amicable solution of the situation. The next day a joint note from the foreign representatives was accordingly addressed to the Chinese and Japanese representatives.[35] As may be expected, both of the latter replied that they would refer the question to their respective governments. In transmitting the replies to the State Department Sill reported, albeit somewhat naïvely:

I may add that Japan seems to be very kindly disposed toward Korea. She seems only to desire, once for all, to throw off the yoke of Chinese suzerainty, and then to assist her weak neighbor in strengthening her position as an independent state, by aiding her in such reforms as shall bring peace, prosperity, and enlightenment of her people. . . .[36]

The instructions of the State Department to Sill given above were sent at the request of the Korean minister at Washington for " disinterested advice and friendly intervention ". On June 28th, a few days later, the Korean minister paid two further visits to the State Department with the same request and he was informed that " while the United States sympathized with his government and desired to see its sovereignty respected, we must maintain towards it and the other powers an attitude of impartial neutrality; that our influence could be exerted with Japan

[34] Sill to Uhl, June 24, 1894, *ibid.*, p. 22.
[35] For the Korean note and joint note see *ibid.*, p. 23.
[36] Sill to Gresham and enclosures, June 29, 1894, *ibid.*, p. 25.

only in a friendly way, and that in no event could we intervene jointly with other powers ".[37]

On the 28th, when Japan suggested that the British government mediate with China in order that such action might neutralize the Russian mediation, the American legation at Tokyo reported that Japan expected an amicable adjustment, but on the following day the legation again telegraphed asking if the American government would use its good offices to protect the Japanese archives and subjects in China in case Japan withdrew her minister from Peking.[38]

On the latter date Edwin Dun, American minister at Tokyo, was instructed to ascertain Japan's reason for sending a military force to Korea and what demands, if any, were expected to be enforced thereby. On July 11th Dun telegraphed, in consequence of this and another inquiry from the State Department, that he was informed " that the Japanese troops were not kept in Korea to make war in that country, but to insure order, Korean independence, and to prevent a recurrence of rebellion; that Japan desired the removal of official corruption, peculation, and misgovernment, the real causes of discontent; that China's equivocal attitude prevented Korea from adopting needed reforms, thus endangering the peace of the East; that the insurrection there had not been entirely quelled; that, while anxious to withdraw her troops, Japan would do so when, and not before, future order was insured; and that war with Korea was not apprehended ".

On the 8th, three days earlier, the State Department was approached simultaneously by Great Britain and China, the former for a " friendly intervention " to avert war

[37] Gresham to Bayard, July 20, 1894, *ibid.*, p. 36.
[38] See same despatch cited above.

between China and Japan, and the latter for American initiative in urging the Powers to unite in a request to Japan to withdraw her troops from Korea. To both W. Q. Gresham, the Secretary of State, replied that he had used his good offices in the interest of peace and could go no further.[39]

France and Germany were the other powers that were requested, simultaneously with the United States, by China to mediate. Of the two France made the greater effort, but she, like the rest, achieved but little.[40]

Sec. 3. War and Peace Attempts

On June 26th, Otori, Japanese minister at Seoul, submitted to the king at audience a memorandum on reforms.[41] On July 18th an imperial edict accepted Yuan Shih-kai's request for leave to return to China, and appointed Mr. Tang Shao-yi, his assistant, to act in his place. On the 23rd at 4 A.M., Japanese forces seized the Korean palace and compelled the aged Ta-yuan-chun to appear as regent, the king in distress vainly appealing to the foreign representatives at his court.[42] Up to about this time China had only the small contingent of troops originally sent to quell the rebellion, and these still remained at Yashan, their landing place, a little south of Chemulpo. Two

[39] See same despatch cited above; also to Yamen, 20/6/13, *Tien kao*, 16/20.

[40] For France see from Kung, recd. 20/6/3 and reply of even date, *ibid.*, 16/4; to Yamen, 20/6/4, 16/7; 20/6/7, 16/10 *l.*; 20/6/10, 16/16 *l.*; 20/6/13, 16/21; 20/6/17, 16/25 *l.* For Germany see to Yamen, 20/6/14, *ibid.*, 16/23; von Rotenhau to Kaiser's party, July 16, 1894, *Lepsius*, ix, 241; from von Kiderlen, July 20, 1894, in note *ibid.*, ix, 242.

[41] For memorandum see *For. Rel.*, 1894, app. i, p. 27.

[42] Sill to Gresham, July 24, 1894, *ibid.*, p. 40.

steamers left the Peiho on July 21st with reënforcements which brought the Chinese force up to 4,500 men. A third, the *Kowshing*, followed with 1,220 men. On the very same day the Korean palace was seized, three Japanese war vessels, the fastest of the Japanese navy, appeared outside Yashan and engaged the two Chinese war vessels stationed there with the Chinese troops,[43] and disabled both of them. Shortly afterwards the Japanese vessels sighted the *Kowshing* and a small transport carrying despatches on her way from Chefoo to Chemulpo, and approached them. The small transport was at once captured. The *Kowshing* was boarded, found to be a *bona fide* British vessel, and ordered to follow. Upon learning of this, the troops requested that they be sent back to the port of departure. This the shipmaster communicated to the Japanese vessel, which in reply ordered the abandonment of the vessel and instantly sank it with all on board. On the 25th the bulk of the Japanese troops at Seoul left for Yashan, and attacked and overpowered the Chinese troops there, the remnant joining the forces that were being gathered in the meantime at Pingyang. When the report of the naval engagement outside Yashan reached China, the Chinese government declared war on Japan. The edict that made the declaration was dated August 1st. On the same day Japan also declared war.[44]

The diligence of the viceroy, Li Hung-chang, to seek a solution of the Korean question with the Japanese by diplomacy rather than by war was undoubtedly due to his desire for peace. But there was also another reason which prompted him to resort to amicable means. In the event

[43] Vladimir, *op. cit.*, pp. 95, 97; to Wang, 20/6/24, *Tien kao*, 16/32.

[44] For texts see Vladimir, *op. cit.*, pp. 370, 372.

of a war with Japan, the forces that could be counted upon would be only the Peiyang Squadron, and the troops of Chihli and Manchuria. As to the troops of other parts of the country, they were not only less dependable, but were also hardly available because of the lack of railway communication, for which the viceroy had fought so hard without avail. As to how a navy neglected since 1885 and an army held jealously in check by the Manchus would fare with a navy created mainly in the previous several years, and an army of the German type, the viceroy had no delusions.

From the very beginning, therefore, the viceroy, on whom as the Defence Commissioner of Peiyang the direction of the campaign fell, was compelled to take a defensive position. The Court, which rightly became incensed at the conduct of Japan, was wrongly anxious to have him take the offensive.[45] In Admiral Ting's opinion, however, the Chinese navy, protected by no destroyers, should only take a chance on the open sea,[46] and in the opinion of the commanders at Pingyang reënforcements of 10,000 troops were necessary for an advance upon Seoul;[47] and the viceroy stood by his subordinates. Even this policy did not help matters. When the commanders at Pingyang reported that their rear was threatened by the landing of Japanese at Wonsan,[48] as well as by projected landing at the mouth of the Yalu, the viceroy hastened to send reënforcements. These were escorted to Tatungkou at the mouth of the Yalu. On September 17th, after the fleet had successfully discharged its duty, it met

[45] Edict, 20/7/16, *Tien kao,* 16/48.
[46] To Yamen, 20/7/3, *ibid.,* 16/38 *l.*
[47] To Yamen, 20/7/16, *ibid.,* 16/48.
[48] *Cf.* statement in Vladimir, *op. cit.,* p. 131.

the Japanese squadron, which had hurried north from the mouth of the Han river to intercept it, and the battle of Tatungkou ensued. As engaged, the two fleets consisted of about the same number of vessels with a tonnage of 35,070 for the Chinese and 40,000 for the Japanese. The Japanese fleet was comparatively more homogeneous and had the advantage in speed and in the number of quick-firing guns. The strength of the Chinese fleet lay only in two ironclads. In the battle several Chinese cruisers were sunk, but in spite of this the Chinese fleet stood its ground and compelled the Japanese to withdraw. The reduction in number, however, was fatal to the Chinese naval power, for it rendered what was left of the fleet unable to engage any reënforced Japanese fleet. As a result, after the battle of Tatungkou, the coast of China was practically at the mercy of Japan. As to Pingyang, reënforcements for that place came too late, for the day previous to the naval engagement it had already fallen into the hands of the Japanese. Having taken Pingyang and crippled the Peiyang Squadron, the Japanese invaded China, both by land and by sea.

After the fall of Pingyang, the government appointed General Sung Ching, senior commander at Port Arthur, to the defence of the Yalu. This proved to be a mistake, for it at once deprived that stronghold of an able leader and sent him to a place where he could achieve little. Before this appointment General Sung had been sent by the viceroy to the front. When the order came, he started without hesitation in spite of his old age, being then over seventy, but in his return message he pointed out the futility of his trip in view of the fact that the troops he was to command were not his own — an essential point in an army organized on old lines — and requested that he be permitted to raise 15,000 men.[49] The old general's fears were confirmed. On the approach of the Japanese on October 24th, there was no unity of action and the Yalu was crossed. Consequently he was compelled virtually to abandon the Yalu and retire to the mountain range that separated it from the Liao. The Japanese followed, but were checked at the pass of Mo-tien-ling on November 11th.

The Japanese who invaded China by sea landed midway between Tatungkow and Port Arthur on October 24th, the same day on which the Yalu was crossed. They captured Kinchow which was weakly defended on November 6th, and marched upon Port Arthur by way of Talien-wan which was evacuated by the Chinese in view of the fact that the navy was not able to protect it. When Port Arthur was invested, the viceroy made an attempt to send a rescue party. But in deference to the opinion of von Hanneken, his German military adviser, and of Admiral Ting Ju-chang, he gave up the attempt.[50] At about the same time General Sung Ching also led an army from Liaoyang southward, but he arrived too late. On November 22nd the stronghold of the navy fell into the hands of the Japanese.

The Japanese who had been stopped at Mo-tien-ling sought to push forward by another route. They left Antung on December 5th, rested at Hsiuyen on the 9th, and pushed their way ahead into Haicheng on the 13th. In the meantime troops from Manchuria were being gathered at Mukden and Liaoyang while those from intra-mural China mustered along the North China Railways.

[49] To Yamen, 20/8/18, *ibid.*, 17/16.
[50] To Yamen, 20/10/13; also other documents, 18/37 *l. et seq.*

About November 25th, the troops from Heilungkiang under General Yi-ko-tang-a began to assume the offensive against the Japanese. After having driven them from the vicinity of Mo-tien-ling, the general made an attempt upon Fenghuan between October 9th and the 14th. The fall of Haicheng, however, compelled him to give up his attempt and to hurry back to Liaoyang, which was now threatened from the south. The same news which hurried Yi-ko-tang-a to Liaoyang also compelled Sung Ching to appear with his new recruits. A battle ensued on the 19th. It resulted in a draw and the Japanese remained at Haicheng. On January 11, 1895, they were joined by their compatriots from the south when the latter pushed their way into Kaiping.

The fall of Pingyang and the crippling of the Peiyang Squadron alarmed the Court, and on September 29th Prince Kung was called from his retirement to head the government. Prince Kung immediately set about to restore peace at any cost. He requested the British minister to have his government initiate a joint intervention of the Powers in the interest of peace. On October 6th Great Britain submitted the proposal to the United States, Germany, Russia, and France on the basis of " Korea's independence being guaranteed by the powers and the payment to Japan of an indemnity for the expenses of the war ". The two first mentioned declined, the United States on the ground that such a move would form a departure " from the wise policy of avoiding foreign alliances and embarrassing positions in guaranteeing the independence of distant states ",[51] and Germany on the ground that in-

[51] Gresham to Denby, Nov. 24, 1894, *For. Rel.*, 1894, app. i, p. 81; Goschen to Gresham, Oct. 6, 1894, Uhl to Goschen, Oct. 10, Gresham to Goschen, Oct. 12, Goschen to Gresham Oct. 14, *ibid.*, 70–71 *passim*.

tervention then, as it was not sure whether it would be followed up, was immature.[52] It appears that the British government then sounded the Japanese government as to whether it would accept the mediation of Great Britain alone. After much delay the Japanese government replied as follows:

The Imperial Government fully appreciates the friendly motives which prompted the inquiry of His Britannic Majesty's Government. Thus far Japan's arms have been attended with complete success; nevertheless the Imperial Government is inclined to think that, in the present stage of the war, affairs have not made sufficient progress to insure a satisfactory result of negotiations. The Imperial Government cannot but refrain from expressing, at this time, their views as to the terms upon which the war could be terminated.[53]

So far the Japanese were victorious, but the young emperor Kuanghsu, many leading Chinese statesmen, and the foreign military advisers were in favor of prolonging the war. On the side of peace, however, were arrayed Prince Kung and his followers, who were restored to power with or by him, and most important of all the Empress Dowager Tsuhsi who, it may be noted, was alone sufficient to turn the scale. In order that a decision might be hastened the viceroy Li Hung-chang sent at the end of October von Hanneken and Detring, his personal military and diplomatic advisers respectively, to Peking to offer their counsel. The Court having decided for peace,[54] the viceroy thereupon obtained permission to send Detring to Japan to ascertain on what terms the Japanese government

[52] Memo. of conversation by von Marchall Oct. 9, 1894, *Lepsius*, ix, 243; von Marchall to von Hatzfeldt, Nov. 12, 1894, *ibid.*, ix, 245.   [53] Dun to Gresham, Nov. 16, 1894, *ibid.*, p. 78.
[54] A. Gérard, *Ma mission en Chine* (1893–1897) (Paris, 1918), p. 10.

would be prepared to open negotiations for peace. Detring carried with him the following credentials from the viceroy:

Our Ta Ching dynasty is in the enjoyment of its traditional policy of peace with every nation save that lately there has arisen an unhappy dispute with your country, whereby the usual friendly intercourse has been exchanged for a state of war. Seeing that no inconsiderable calamities have lately fallen upon the people, it is now proposed that both countries temporarily direct their forces by sea and land to cease hostilities.

Memorializing the throne upon the advisability of this course, the commands of His Imperial Majesty, my august master, have been received as follows:

Whereas Mr. Detring has held office in our Empire for many years and proved himself faithful, true, and worthy of the highest trust, we command Li Hung-chang to inform him fully and completely of whatever has so far been deliberated upon and decided, and ask him to proceed without delay to Japan and effect a settlement as occasion arises. Mr. Detring will inform us confidentially and with due speed by telegram through Li Hung-chang of the progress of negotiations.

In accordance with His Majesty's command, Mr. Detring, an official holding rank of the first grade, has been directed to proceed forthwith to Tokyo to present this despatch and learn the conditions upon which peace may be regained and amicable intercourse be reëstablished as of old.

Therefore, requesting that Your Excellency will discuss with Mr. Detring how friendly relations may be restored, this despatch is written commending the proposal to the favorable consideration of Your Excellency.

November 18, 1894.

Kwang-hsu, 20th year, 10th month, 21st day.[55]

[55] *For. Rel.*, 1894, app. i, p. 92.

The Japanese government apparently did not feel that it had pressed its "victories beyond the limits which will guarantee to them the just and reasonable fruits of the war", and decided to reject Detring's mission on the ground that he was "not properly accredited" by the Chinese government. Detring arrived at Kobe on the 26th; but, before he was informed of the Japanese decesion, he received from Prince Kung a telegram of recall, and he left Kobe on the 29th.[56]

While Detring was on his mission, Prince Kung convoked the representatives of the United States, Great Britain, Russia, France, and Germany at the Tsungli Yamen, evidently at the suggestion of the British minister, and after stating the entire case requested them to transmit to their respective governments a proposal of mediation to secure peace with Japan on the basis of Korean independence and of a war indemnity, the amount of the last to be determined by the Powers conjointly. The ministers had some doubt as to the acceptability to Japan of the basis of peace proposed, as these terms had already been submitted to her once by Great Britain. It was the hope of the Prince, however, that as "Japan had not positively rejected the proposition but had only refused to accede to it at that particular time, . . . its presentation now by the great powers might secure its acceptance". In deference to the wishes of the Prince the foreign representatives forwarded the proposal to their respective governments, but like the former effort this also resulted in nothing.[57]

Meanwhile the United States intimated simultaneously

[56] Dun to Gresham, Dec. 7, 1894, *ibid.*, p. 83; Gérard, *op. cit.*, p. 14.

[57] Denby to Gresham, Nov. 3, 1894; same to same of even date, *For. Rel.*, pp. 73–5; *cf.* Gérard, *op. cit.*, p. 10.

to China and Japan her readiness to tender her good offices
in the interest of peace. It appeared that, either as a part
of his effort to secure a joint mediation through Great
Britain, or independently after its failure, the Prince had
instructed the minister at Washington to approach the
American government with a similar appeal. This the
American government considered favorably and Secretary
Gresham, after satisfying himself that " the motives of
the President were fully comprehended and appreciated
by Japan ", on November 6th instructed Ministers Denby
and Dun to sound the attitudes of both the Chinese and the
Japanese governments officially.[58]   In his instructions to
Dun, Gresham said in part:

If the struggle continues without check to Japan's
military operations on land and sea, it is not improbable that
other powers having interests in that quarter may demand
a settlement not favorable to Japan's future security and
well-being.

On November 17th, the Japanese government replied as
follows:

The Imperial Government does not fail in appreciation
of the amicable sentiments which induced the government
of the United States to tender their good offices in the interest of peace between Japan and China.

The universal success which has thus far during the conflict attended the arms of Japan would seem to relieve the
Imperial Government of the necessity of invoking the co-
operation of friendly powers to bring about a cessation of
hostilities.

The Imperial Government has no wish to press their victories beyond the limits which will guarantee to them the

[58] Gresham to Denby, Nov. 24, 1894, *For. Rel.*, p. 86; Gresham
to Denby and to Dun, Nov. 6, 1894, *ibid.*, p. 76.

just and reasonable fruits of the war. Those limits can not, however, be said to have been reached until China finds herself in a position to approach Japan directly on the subject of peace.[59]

In addition, the American minister at Tokyo was requested to see that " in the event of China's desiring to approach Japan upon the subject of peace it shall be done through the legation of the United States at Peking ".[60] On the receipt of the latter information Gresham instructed Denby and informed the Chinese minister at Washington that " any direct overtures for peace made by China to Japan through the American minister to Peking will be considered ".[61]

Intimation from Gresham that the United States was ready to offer her good offices in the interest of peace reached Peking just after the appeal had been made to the foreign ministers for a joint mediation, and before learning of the result of that attempt the Chinese government hesitated to avail itself of the American offer.[62] But when Gresham's instructions of the 19th to Denby were learnt in Peking, the government was already quite convinced that nothing would come out of its proposal to the Powers and it readily made direct overtures to Japan through Denby.[63] It was in this connection that Detring was recalled.[64]

[59] *Note Verbale*, Tokyo, Nov. 17, *ibid.*, p. 80.

[60] Dun to Gresham, Nov. 17, 1894, *ibid.*, p. 80.

[61] Gresham to Denby, Nov. 19, 1894, to Yang Yu, Nov. 20, *ibid.*, p. 80.

[62] Gresham to Denby, Nov. 6, 1894; same to same, Nov. 8; Denby to Gresham, Nov. 10; same to same Nov. 10, *ibid.*, pp. 76–7.

[63] Denby to Gresham, Nov. 22, 1894, *ibid.*, p. 80; same to same, Nov. 23, *ibid.*, p. 81.

[64] Gérard, *op. cit.*, p. 14.

The Japanese government, as already indicated in the *note verbale* of the 17th, from the very beginning manifested its firm resolution to treat only with China herself directly, not through an intermediary but through regular negotiators sent with full powers to Japan. The terms, which they did not fail to reveal, were, however, more severe than the Court could accept. As a result no mission was sent until December 20th, when Chang Yin-huan, a member of the Tsungli Yamen, and Shao Yu-lien, ex-governor of Formosa, then governor of Hunan, were appointed.[65] The edict of appointment stated:

. . . We now appoint you as plenipotentiaries to confer with the plenipotentiaries appointed by Japan. You will, however, on your part telegraph through the Tsungli Yamen for our direction. The officials of your suite are placed under your control. You shall do your utmost, be attentive to your business, and not disappoint us.[66]

The credentials given to the plenipotentiaries are as follows:

Greetings from the Emperor of China to the Emperor of Japan: Our two countries have the relation of being on the same continent and there has hitherto existed no enmity between us. Recently on account of the affairs of Korea we have both taken up arms, to the suffering of our peoples and the sacrifice of treasures. Can there really be something that we can not avoid! Now that through the mediation of the United States the two countries are to delegate plenipotentiaries to confer upon the conclusion of peace, we have especially appointed Chang Yin-huan, Board President, Senior Vice-President of the Tsungli Yamen, and

[65] *Ibid.*, p. 16.

[66] A translation from Chinese text in Liu Yen, *Diplomatic History of China* (Shanghai, 1921), p. 223.

Shao Yu-lien, Official of the First Grade, Acting Governor of Hunan, as our plenipotentiaries to proceed to Your Majesty's country. It is our hope that Your Majesty will receive them and permit them to fulfil their duties.[67]

As counsellor to the peace mission John W. Foster, ex-Secretary of State and sometime counsellor to the Chinese legation at Washington, was engaged by telegram.

On notifying the Japanese government of the appointment, the Chinese government requested that an armistice be concluded. This request the former refused to entertain. Consequently the two plenipotentiaries did not hasten to depart. Chang left Peking only on January 7th, and having been joined by Shao at Shanghai, proceeded to Japan on the 27th and arrived on the 30th at Kobe, where Foster had been waiting. From Kobe the mission proceeded to Hiroshima, the war capital of Japan, to meet Counts Ito and Mutsu, the Japanese plenipotentiaries.

Upon the arrival of the Chinese mission the ministers of Great Britain, Russia and France expressed to the Japanese government the hope of their governments that there might be a prompt and just conclusion of peace. On February 1st, credentials were exchanged, the Chinese plenipotentiaries submitting the letter from the Emperor of China to the Emperor of Japan, and, on request of the Japanese plenipotentiaries, also the imperial edict. Having examined these the Japanese plenipotentiaries handed to their Chinese colleagues a memorandum asking to be categorically informed in writing whether the papers which had been communicated to them embodied all the authority confided by the Emperor of China. The next day the Chinese plenipotentiaries replied as follows:

[67] Also a translation from Chinese text, *ibid.*, p. 222.

We beg to state in reply that our commissions, handed to you at the same time in exchange, embody full powers given by our Imperial Majesty for the negotiation and conclusion of peace, with authority to conclude articles to that end and to sign them. In order to insure the most prompt execution of the treaty we may agree upon, we shall wire the terms for Imperial sanction and fix the date for signature; after which the same shall be taken to China for examination by His Imperial Chinese Majesty, and, being found proper and in good and due form, will be ratified.[68]

As soon as this note was received an appointment for another meeting was made on the same day by the Japanese. At this meeting Ito read an address of some length citing "the results which history teaches" to support his suspicion of bad faith on the part of the Chinese government in the present mission and then handed the Chinese plenipotentiaries a memorandum stating that their powers were defective and declaring the present negotiations at an end. The Chinese plenipotentiaries protested that their full powers were in the usual form for Chinese envoys and had been recognized by Western nations in treaty negotiations; and the Chinese government, on being advised by telegraph, proposed to the Japanese government the sending of new credentials as desired by Japan. But all this was to no purpose. On the 4th the Chinese plenipotentiaries were escorted to Nagasaki, the Japanese port nearest to China.[69]

[68] *For. Rel.*, 1894, app. i, p. 101.

[69] J. W. Foster, *Diplomatic Memoirs* (Boston, 1909), vol. ii, p. 115; Gérard, *op. cit.*, pp. 16–19. For Ito's address and memorandum see *For. Rel.*, pp. 101–3. For protest of the Chinese mission left with the Japanese plenipotentiaries on departure see Vladimir, *op. cit.*, p. 399.

After the Chinese plenipotentiaries had left Peking, but before their arrival in Japan, the latter had launched an attack upon Weihaiwei, where the remainder of the Chinese fleet had taken refuge. The attack was carried out both by sea and by land. The Japanese having left Talien-wan on January 18th, landed on the coast of Shantung on the 20th. At the last moment the Chinese government ordered Admiral Ting to make a sortie and escape with the remnants of the fleet south.[70] The order, however, came too late to be useful. Before the siege began, the admiral had had the archives of the navy forwarded to Chefoo, thus indicating that he would die at his post. Unlike the commander at Port Arthur who abandoned the stronghold when it fell, all officers in the highest command, military and naval alike, including the admiral, twenty-five years in supreme command, committed suicide.[71] With this the last vestige of the Chinese navy was wiped from the earth, and the long Chinese coast was again exposed to the mercy of the world as it had been two decades before.

Sec. 4.   *The Peace of Shimonoseki*

On February 13th the Court — acting upon hints made by the Japanese government to the Chang-Shao mission, and also through the American legation at Peking — appointed the viceroy Li Hung-chang as peace plenipotentiary, and summoned him to Peking to receive instructions.[72] On learning of the appointment of the new mission the Japanese government by a telegram dated the 17th made known to the Chinese government that the

---

[70] To Yamen, 21/1/13, *Tien kao*, 20/13.

[71] To Yamen, 21/5/17, *ibid.*, 20/15; 21/1/23, 20/16.

[72] Edict, recd. 21/1/19, *Tsao kao*, 79/46.

sending of another mission to Japan would be useless, unless in addition to the full recognition of the independence
of Korea and the payment of a war indemnity, the Chinese plenipotentiary was invested with full power to negotiate on the basis of a cession of territory and an arrangement relating to the future relations between the two
countries, or, in other words, a new commercial treaty.
The viceroy left for Peking on the 19th and stayed there
until March 5th.[73]

The intimation of February 17th from the Japanese
government made the fortnight's stay of the viceroy in
Peking a period of anxiety for him.[74]   Whatever hope of
an honorable peace, if any, had been generated by the
appointment of such a dignitary as himself, was dissi-
pated; and yet peace had to be secured, not so much because the enemy was near as because the Court was not
willing to oppose him any more.   The viceroy, therefore,
on the one hand persuaded the Court to grant him all necessary power to end the war, and on the other appealed to
Great Britain, Russia, France, and Germany[75] to see that
Japan should not take undue advantage of the situation.
Besides conferring with the foreign ministers in Peking,
he instructed the Chinese ministers at London and St.
Petersburg by a telegram dated February 24th to confer
with those governments.   Final report came from London
on March 1st and from St. Petersburg on the following
day.   The reply of both governments was that they could
only determine their policy after they had seen the Japanese terms.[76]   At this juncture the viceroy obtained from

[73] Gérard, *op. cit.*, p. 22.

[74] For a good account see Gérard, *op. cit.*, 23–28.

[75] For Germany see Schweinsberg to Foreign Office, March 3,
1895, *Lepsius*, ix, 252.

[76] To Kung and Hsu, 21/1/30, to Chang Yin-huan 21/2/1,

the Court all necessary powers to end the war, including the authority to cede territory,[77] and a personal telegram from the emperor Kuanghsu to the sovereigns of Great Britain, Russia, and Germany and the presidents of the United States and France " recommending the cause of China and the mission of her ambassador ".[78]

Upon his arrival at Tientsin the viceroy was informed by the Tsungli Yamen that his commission of full powers had been accepted by Japan and that he was expected at Shimonoseki about March 19th.[79] When he first arrived at Peking for his instructions the viceroy requested Minister Denby to intercede with the Japanese government that the latter would grant an armistice to last through his absence on his peace mission, insuring that the province of Chihli of which he had charge as well as the cities of Peking, Tientsin and Shanhaikuan might be free from hostile operations.[80] In the personal letter of the Emperor to the various heads of states the same request had also been made.[81] On February 28th, however, the Japanese army in Shengking, which had for some time remained on the defensive, assumed the offensive and on March 5th and 6th occupied Newchwang and its port, Yingkou. Leaving Tientsin on the 13th, the viceroy arrived at the conference

---

from Hsu, 21/2/2, from Kung, 21/2/2, from Kung, 21/2/5, from Hsu, 21/2/6, *Tien kao*, 21/18 *l.*–20.

[77] Memorial, 21/2/6, *Tsou kao*, 79/47; edict, 21/2/7, 79/49; memorial by the Grand Council, 20/2/7, 79/50.

[78] To Kung, 21/2/6, *Tien kao*, 20/19 *l.*; to Hsu, 21/2/7, 20/20 *l.*; from Yamen, 21/2/14, 20/22 *l.*; from Yamen, 21/2/14, 20/22 *l.*; from Yamen 21/2/17, 20/33.

[79] From Yamen, 21/2/10, *ibid.*, 20/21.

[80] Gérard, *op. cit.*, p. 23.

[81] See to Yamen, 21/2/12, *Tien kao*, 20/21 *l.*

ground on the appointed day, accompanied by his son Li Ching-fang, ex-minister to Japan, John W. Foster, counsellor of the mission, and a number of secretaries, among whom was Wu Ting-fang, later minister to the United States. On the 16th, while he was on his way, a Japanese squadron left Nagasaki to occupy the Pescadores and to attack Formosa. On the 19th Counts Ito and Mutsu, the Japanese plenipotentiaries, also arrived at Shimonoseki.

In the first meeting held at Shimonoseki on the 20th the viceroy, after the exchange of credentials, submitted, as already proposed through the American legation, a plan of armistice providing for a complete suspension of hostilities *in statu quo*.[82] On the 21st, the Japanese submitted a counter proposal giving their terms as follows: (a) occupation by the Japanese troops of Taku, Tientsin and Shanhaikuan, as well as the fortresses and works in the three places; (b) delivery in these three cities, of arms and ammunition of the Chinese army; (c) administration and control by the Japanese authorities of the railway between Shanhaikuan and Tientsin; (d) payment by China of a war contribution calculated on the duration of the armistice. The viceroy at once declared that the terms were too harsh for China to accept, and proposed to enter at once on the peace negotiations. Ito intimated that if this was done hostilities would be pushed on, and the subject of armistice would not again be considered. Thereupon the viceroy asked for an adjournment of three days to refer the question to Peking.[83] The Chinese government after consulting with the foreign ministers in Peking rejected the Japanese proposal. On March 24th the viceroy com-

[82] To Yamen, 21/2/24, *ibid.*, 20/23 *l.*
[83] To Yamen, 21/2/25, *ibid.*, 20/23 *l.*

municated the rejection to the Japanese plenipotentiaries and asked for the conditions of peace. The Japanese plenipotentiaries agreed to submit them in the next meeting, fixed for ten o'clock the following day.[84] On his way to his quarters, the viceroy's life was attempted by a Japanese fanatic, whose shot took effect about an inch below the left eye. An armistice now seemed necessary to make up for the delay in negotiations thus caused, to placate the world and the viceroy. So far as northern China was concerned it was therefore unconditionally granted. A convention was signed on the 30th declaring a complete suspension of hostilities between the two governments in Shengking, Chihli, and Shantung for three weeks to end on April 20th at noon, the Pescadores and Formosa being excluded.[85] The viceroy was not able to leave his quarters until April 10th, when the fourth meeting was held, but in the meantime negotiations were carried on, his son having been invested by the Chinese government with joint powers as a plenipotentiary.

On the very evening he was fired upon, the viceroy communicated with the Japanese plenipotentiaries, requesting that they send him the memorandum containing the promised conditions of peace, now that he could not attend the conference fixed for the next day.[86] On the day the armistice for northern China was signed, he renewed his request.[87] On April 1st the memorandum came.[88] It con-

[84] To Yamen, 21/2/28, *ibid.*, 20/25; to Yamen, even date, 20/25 *l.*

[85] To Yamen, 21/3/3, *ibid.*, 20/27 *l.*; Gérard, *op. cit.*, 33. For convention see Vladimir, *op. cit.*, p. 403.

[86] Foster, *op. cit.*, vol. ii, p. 136.

[87] *Ibid.*, p. 137.

[88] For text see Vladimir, *op. cit.*, 405; to Yamen, 21/3/7, *Tien kao* 20/28.

tained, besides others, the following conditions: (1) recognition by China of the full independence and autonomy of Korea;[89] (2) cession of (a) southern Shengking, (b) Formosa, and (c) the Pescadores;[90] (3) payment to Japan of a war indemnity of 300,000,000 taels;[91] (4) conclusion between the two countries of a new treaty of commerce on the basis of the treaties concluded between China and the Western powers, with, however, additional concessions,[92] these including, besides others, (a) the opening to commerce of Peking, Shashih, Siangtan, Chungking, Wuchow, Soochou, and Hangchou, and the right of inland navigation over waterways leading to those places;[93] (b) commutation on inland taxes on imported goods;[94] and (c) liberty to engage in industry and to import machinery;[95] and, lastly, (5) temporary occupation by Japan of Mukden and Weihaiwei until the completion of the payment of indemnity and the ratification of the new commercial treaty to be concluded.[96]   In the section regarding cession of territory, what affected Shengking was given as follows:

The line of demarcation begins at the south of the River Yalu, and ascends that stream as far as Sanchatsu, thence it runs directly north to Yushutihsia; thence it runs directly west until it strikes the River Liao; it follows from thence the course of that river southward to 41° north latitude; from thence it coincides with that parallel of latitude to the westward as far as 122° longitude east of Greenwich, and from that point of intersection it follows the same meridian of longitude southward to the coast of the Bay of Liaotung, where it terminates.

[89] Art. i.
[90] Art. ii.
[91] Art. iv.
[92] Art. vi.

[93] Clauses 1 and 2.
[94] Clause 3.
[95] Clause 6.
[96] Art. viii.

The cession includes all Islands appertaining or belonging to the province of Shengking situated in the eastern portion of the Bay of Liaotung and in the northern part of the Yellow Sea.

Thus Japan disclosed her hand. She had confined herself to the encroachment on weak neighbors long enough; she would now assume the rôle of dominating the Far East. She was not satisfied with the detachment of Korea together with the destruction of Chinese naval power which might yet prevent the eventual annexation of that poor kingdom; she would also cripple China financially, kill Chinese industries at their infant stage, and advance upon her both from the south and the north by seizing the Pescadores, Formosa, and the Liaotung peninsula in order that she might finally live upon her as a parasite or even devour her like the fabulous birds that feed upon the bodies of their parents.

Prepared as he was for harsh terms, the viceroy could not help being aghast when he received the memorandum. But he had no alternative except to work for mitigation. While communicating the terms to the Chinese government he let Foster draw up a general reply to the Japanese, protesting against the severity of the terms.[97] On the cession of the Liaotung peninsula, which was the most pressing of all questions raised by the Japanese peace terms, Foster had the following to say for the viceroy:

It is the duty of the plenipotentiaries of the two governments, and it is the part of wise statesmanship to negotiate such a peace as will make true friends and allies of these two great nations of the Orient, who are and must remain

[97] To Yamen, 21/3/12, *Tien kao*, 21/31; Vladimir, *op. cit.*, p. 411.

neighbours, and who have in common so many things in their history, literature, art, and commerce. Territory long held by a nation, through many centuries and dynasties, becomes a priceless heritage. Nothing will so arouse the indignation of the people of China and create in them a spirit of undying hostility and hatred, as to wrest from their country important portions of their territory.

This will be especially the case with that portion of territory described in clause (a) of this Article [ii], because it gives Japan a foothold and base for military and naval operations within easy reach of and constantly threatening the capital of the empire, and because it takes from the present dynasty of China a portion of its ancient possessions. In this clause China hears Japan saying: " I am going to be your ever-threatening and undying enemy, with my army and navy ready to pounce down upon your capital when it suits me; and I propose to humiliate your Emperor by taking from him a valuable portion of his ancestors' home ".

The general reply was transmitted to the Japanese plenipotentiaries on the 5th, and in the following day the latter requested the viceroy to formulate definite proposals. On the 8th instructions came from Peking limiting territorial cession to one place and indemnity to 100,000,000 taels, with, however, discretionary power of modification.[98] The viceroy therefore submitted his counter-proposals,[99] comprising: (1) recognition mutually by China and Japan of the independence and autonomy of Korea;[100] (2) cession to Japan of (a) the *hsiens* of Antung and Kungtien, the prefecture of Fenghuang and the subprefecture of Hsiu-

[98] From Yamen, 21/3/14, *Tien kao*, 20/32 *l.*
[99] To Yamen, 21/3/14, *ibid.*, 20/33; to Yamen, even date, 20/34; Vladimir, *op. cit.*, p. 424.
[100] Art. i.

yen, in Shengking, and (b) the Pescadores in the Strait of Formosa;[101] (3) payment of an indemnity of 100,000,000 taels;[102] (4) conclusion between China and Japan of a new treaty of commerce and navigation on the basis of treaties existing between China and Western powers with reciprocal most-favored-nation treatment;[103] (5) temporary occupation of Weihaiwei until total payment of indemnity;[104] and (6) recourse to arbitration in case the two contracting powers could not by usual diplomatic methods agree on the execution or interpretation of the treaties to be concluded between them, the arbitrator to be designated by some friendly power to be selected by mutual accord of the two governments, or by the President of the United States by invitation in case of failure to agree upon the selection of the power.[105]

On the 10th the Japanese plenipotentiaries in their turn replied to the Chinese counter-proposals by submitting a new plan.[106] In this they rejected all counter-proposals made by the viceroy including the mutual recognition of Korean independence, the mutual granting of most-favored-nation treatment, the reference to arbitration of differences that might arise from the treaties to be concluded. But basing their new terms upon the original demands, they made certain concessions — such as the moving of the demarcation line in Shengking a little south to exclude Liaoyang, which they had not captured; the reduction of indemnity from 300,000,000 to 200,000,000 taels; the withdrawal of demands for the opening of new ports as far as they related to Peking, Siangtan, and Wuchou, for the commutation of

---

101 Art. ii.   103 Art. vi.   105 Art. xi.
102 Art. iv.   104 Art. viii.
106 To Yamen, 21/3/16, *Tien kao*, 20/35; Vladimir, *op. cit.*, p. 428.

inland taxes, and for the temporary occupation of Mukden.
The new line of demarcation in Shengking was as follows:

The line of demarcation begins at the River Yalu and
ascends the stream to Anpinghokou; from thence the line
runs to Fenghuang; from thence to Haicheng, and from
thence to Yingkow, where it terminates. The places above
named are included in the ceded territory.

This cession also includes all Islands appertaining or belonging to the province of Shengking situated in the eastern
portion of the Bay of Liaotung and in the northern part of
the Yellow Sea.

In presenting this plan, Ito declared that it was final and
demanded that the viceroy give a categorical reply within
four days. The viceroy spent two hours in vain trying to
persuade Ito to cut another fifty million taels from the indemnity, and to reconsider certain points, such as the inclusion in the territory to be ceded of Yingkou, a treaty port,
and Formosa, which Japan had not occupied. On the next
day Ito made the demand in writing in the form of an
ultimatum.[107] On the 12th the viceroy made his last protest.[108] To this Ito replied the next day by emphasizing the
final character of his demand.[109]

We have seen above that both Great Britain and Russia,
in reply to the approach of the viceroy to see that Japan
should not take undue advantage of the situation, stated
that they could only determine their policy after they had
seen the Japanese terms. When the Japanese demands were
submitted the viceroy accordingly — and with the advice of
his counsellor Foster — requested the Chinese government
to communicate them to the Powers.[110] By the time the

[107] *Ibid.*, p. 432.   [108] *Ibid.*, p. 434.   [109] *Ibid.*, p. 436.
[110] J. W. Foster, *Diplomatic Memoirs* (Boston, 1909), vol. ii,
pp. 152–3; to Yamen, 21/3/7, *Tien kao*, 20/28.

Japanese presented their final ultimatum no definite result, however, came from this move. If anything ever was reported to the viceroy, it was that Great Britain had decided not to intervene.[111] On April 11th, the day after receiving the Japanese ultimatum, the viceroy was advised by Detring as follows:[112]

Mr. de Brandt wires that in discussing cession by China he concurred in disapproval. China ought not to be anxious to sign the treaty.

The viceroy inquired by return wire why the Powers would not intervene. On the 15th he was again advised by Detring as follows:[113] [114]

Telegram received. Have wired to Mr. de Brandt but have received as yet no reply. Would advise signing treaty before expiration of term of ultimatum. Sir Robert Hart concurs in this. It is not likely that the hope of an international conference could be materialized.

In the meantime the viceroy was in constant communication with the Court, advising the acceptance of the Japanese terms. On the 17th he signed the treaty of Shimonoseki as dictated by Japan.[115] On the same day a convention extending the armistice to May 8th was also signed.[116] As it stood, the treaty was ratified by the Emperor on May 2nd, and ratifications were exchanged on the 8th.

[111] To Yamen, 21/3/17, *ibid.*, 20/36 *l.*

[112] From Detring, recd. 21/3/17, *ibid.*, 20/37.

[113] From Detring, recd. 21/3/21, *ibid.*, 20/39 *l.*

[114] *Cf.* statement in note, Tyler Dennet, *Americans in Eastern Asia* (New York, 1922) p. 635.

[115] See correspondence in *Tien kao*, 20/36–40 *passim*; for text of treaty see *Customs*, ii, 1318.

[116] *Ibid.*, ii, 1330.

The heavy indemnity compelled the Chinese government for the first time to resort to foreign loans and to pledge national revenues as security. Between 1895 and 1898 it floated in the markets of Europe three such loans, each amounting approximately to £16,000,000. The first, having come immediately after the war, was raised through the good offices of Russia, and with her guarantee.[117] The second and third were negotiated directly with Anglo-German bankers.[118] All were secured upon the revenues of the Chinese Maritime Customs, but the last was secured with additional *likin* revenues.

The new commercial treaty provided for in Article IV of the peace treaty was taken up later in September by the viceroy, who was transferred from his viceroyalty to the Tsungli Yamen for the purpose, and by Baron Hayashi Tadasu, who had come to Peking as Japanese minister at the end of June. On September 30th Hayashi submitted a plan for the treaty he had then received from Tokyo. On November 19th the viceroy submitted a counter plan. The Japanese government insisted upon taking the Japanese plan as the basis of negotiations. To this the viceroy protested in vain. Shortly thereafter, however, the viceroy was appointed ambassador extraordinary to Russia [119] and the negotiations were entrusted to Chang Yin-huang. The negotiations between Chang and Hayashi lasted until July 21st, when the new commercial treaty was signed and the treaty of reciprocity of 1871 was henceforth replaced by one of unilateral nature.[120]

[117] Memorial by Hsu, 21/7/20, *Tiao yo, K.*, 39/2. For agreement see *ibid.*, 39/5; *MacMurray*, i, 35. For agreement between Russia and the banks, *ibid.*, i, 42; and protocol between China and Russia, *ibid.*, i, 40.   [118] *Ibid.*, i, 85, 107.   [119] See *infra*, sec. 6.

[120] For text see *Customs*, ii, 1332. *Cf.* Gérard, *op. cit.*, pp. 109–112.

During the negotiations the Chinese plenipotentiary repeatedly requested his Japanese colleague to introduce a reciprocal provision regarding the treatment of the citizens of one country in the other, at first on the basis of Article VI of the Burlingame treaty (1868) [121] and later on that of Article I of the treaty of 1869 with Austria.[122] But neither of these bases was accepted by the Japanese plenipotentiary. The former was rejected on the ground that the United States was not within the term " European Powers " of Article VI of the treaty of Shimonoseki, and the latter on the ground that though Austria was within the terms she could not be taken as a prototype since she was far removed from China and would not be frequented by Chinese citizens as Japan would be. So firm was the Japanese on the point that the best concession he would make was a promise to be given in a note after the treaty was signed that Chinese in Japan would be treated with fairness " so long as such is not in conflict with the interest or peace of Japan ".[123]

Another point of much contention was the Japanese attempt to secure in addition to all other privileges an exemption from excise for products of Japanese industries which they had a right to set up in China by virtue of the treaty of Shimonoseki.[124] This the Chinese plenipotentiary strongly resisted on the ground that it would tend either to drive out the Chinese industries since the latter were subject to such taxation, or to deprive the Chinese government

[121] *Customs*, i, 528.

[122] *Ibid.*, ii, 1221.

[123] Chang to Japanese plenipotentiary, 22/6/11, *Tiao yo, K.*, 43/16; Japanese plenipotentiary to Chang, July 21, 1896, *ibid.*, p. 17.

[124] Clause 3, art. vi.

of a legitimate source of income, if, in order to avoid the former evil, exemption was extended also to Chinese industries. Finally, on June 7th, when the Japanese plenipotentiary compelled China to accept a new plan which he had received from Count Okuma of the then new Japanese cabinet, the question was dropped with the reservation that it would be taken up again when specific cases presented themselves.[125]

Thus was China subjected to worse economic exploitation than the kind she had experienced, and started once for all on her way to foreign financial control. But these phases were the less disastrous in comparison with the political. To the latter we may now return.

Sec. 5. The Triple Intervention

In the meeting held on March 24th when the viceroy rejected the Japanese terms for an armistice and asked for the terms of peace, we have a conversation between the viceroy and Ito which Foster preserved for us in his *Diplomatic Memoirs* as follows:[126]

Viceroy Li: If the terms of peace involve the interests of any other country, it would be well to proceed cautiously.

Marquis Ito: Why?

Viceroy Li: Many difficulties may arise. I mention this because of the long intercourse between our countries.

Marquis Ito: This is entirely our affair. Other countries must not meddle with what does not concern them.

---

[125] Memo. of Japanese plenipotentiary, 22/4/26, *Tiao yo, K.*, 43/20; reply to Chang, 22/5/14, *ibid.*, p. 21. For the viceroy's attention on the point see to Sheng, 21/8/21, *Tien kao*, 21/42; from Sheng, 21/8/21, 21/42 *l*.   [126] Vol. ii, p. 130.

Ito had reasons for being so confident in the tone of his reply. As early as March 6th Japan had been informed by Germany that there was a possibility of a European intervention in case Japan demanded territorial cession on the continent.[127] Thus before the opening of the conference at Shimonoseki she had strengthened her position by offering Korean independence to Russia,[128] and most probably also some equally good assurances to Great Britain, the other power that had been active up to that time.

The Liaotung peninsula, with the naval bases of Port Arthur and Talienwan, was such a strategical point that the acquisition by Japan would have ensured her eventual annexation of Korea and at the same time enabled her to dominate entire northern China, leading possibly also to the conquest of China, and with some degree of certainty to the control of Manchuria in one form or another. If this made China literally beg the Powers to intervene in order to prevent it from becoming a fact, it also induced Japan to invite the same Powers to claim shares in the spoils in order to make it a success. On March 31st, the day before the terms of peace were submitted to the Chinese mission, Inouye, at the instance of Mutsu, called on Foster and asked that assurance be given that these would not be made public. Foster replied that he felt sure that the Chinese mission would not make them public in Shimonoseki, but that he could not tell as to the action of the Chinese government.[129] With this Japan believed she had done her part. On April

[127] Von Marschall to von Gutschmid, March 6, 1895, *Lepsius,* ix, 253. Also referred to by M. von Brandt in his *Drei Jahre Ostasiatischer Politik, 1894–1897* (Stuttgart, 1897), p. 125.

[128] Prince Hohenlohe to the Kaiser, March 19, 1895, *Lepsius,* 253.

[129] Foster, *op. cit.,* vol. ii, pp. 152–3; see also to Yamen, 21/3/7, *Tien kao,* 20/28.

2nd, the day after the submission of peace terms, she herself revealed the terms for the cession of the Liaotung peninsula to the Powers and made advances to Russia, Germany, and possibly France, to induce them to forego their opposition to it, if any. What the exact nature of Japan's offer to France was we do not know. Most probably it was a gesture to the effect that French activities lay in the southwestern provinces of China. To Russia she definitely promised a free hand in northern Manchuria,[130] and to Germany "a province in the southeast of China" that "would be much more valuable than all our [German] colonies in Africa".[131]

As we have already stated, Great Britain, after examining the peace terms, decided not to intervene. This took place on April 8th, when the Rosebery cabinet met to consider the question.[132] Great Britain was greatly disappointed in discovering that China was not such a formidable "natural ally" against Russia as she had for years fancied. On the other hand she was undoubtedly pleased to see that, without any effort on her part, she was to enjoy, through the most-favored-nation clause in her treaties with China "many additional commercial privileges".[133] But apart from these considerations, she as yet saw nothing menacing to her interests in the Far East by the change contemplated by the Japanese peace terms, and indeed she appeared to have even seen enormous advantages in them. The ambition and power of Japan, which today form at least quite a problem to some dominions of her empire, were as yet but

---

[130] See Marschall to Hatzfeldt, April 4, 1895, *Lepsius*, ix, 261.

[131] Memo. by *Mühlberg*, April 2, 1895, *ibid.*, ix, 260.

[132] Hatzfeldt to Foreign Office, April 8, 1895, *ibid.*, ix, 266.

[133] Gérard, *op. cit.*, pp. 41–3; also Münster to Foreign Office, April 10, 1895, *Lepsius*, ix, 268.

vaguely comprehended. On the other hand, there was the immediate problem of having someone to take the place of the " natural ally". " Why should we not take what is already provided for us and let the ' natural ally ' die its natural death? " they asked themselves. When Lord Kimberly, the British foreign minister, was approached by Count Hatzfeldt, the German ambassador at London, the former was reported to have even thought that the danger to China in the cession of the Liaotung peninsula might be lessened by moving the Chinese capital to Nanking, or, in other words, by virtually abandoning northern China, including Manchuria.[134]

With Russia the case was different. Korea was situated in such a way that if she passed to Russia she would be a menace to Japan, and if she passed to Japan she would be a menace to Primorskaya. This situation, which must have undoubtedly loomed large in the minds of the Japanese bureaucrats was, evidently, not appreciated by the Russians. Indeed, in view of the latter's ignorance of Japanese ambition and power, it must have been a matter of indifference whether Korea was under China or Japan, and possibly desirable that she might even become independent through China's inability to keep her, and Japan's ability to live up to her words. If this was so, the course of the war must have disturbed their slumber and the Japanese terms for peace finally awakened them.

Just at this juncture the control of Russian diplomacy happily passed over to a man of unusual breadth of view, Prince Lobanov-Rostovski. In the month of March the Prince, who had been Russian ambassador to Turkey, Great Britain, and Austria, was called by virtue of his seniority in the diplomatic service to head the foreign ministry after

[134] Hatzfeldt to Marschall, April 6, 1895, *ibid.*, ix, 264.

the death of the occupant of the post. To him, the idea of permitting Japan to gain a foothold on the continent was like dropping " oil on a sheet of blotting paper ", which would unavoidably spread.[135] Against him neither Japanese assurance of Korean independence, which gulled his predecessor to acquiesce in the war, nor the Japanese proposal of dividing Manchuria between Japan and Russia, which kept his successors between the Russo-Japanese War and the collapse of Tzarist Russia willing slaves to Japanese ambition, made any headway. In taking over the foreign ministry the Prince immediately set up a special commission, consisting of all ministers of state, to discuss the question, and guided it to decide for intervention.

In the meantime the Prince also attempted to secure the coöperation of Germany and France. The latter, of course, constituted no problem, being a new ally of Russia; but from Germany also he found ready response, though for an entirely different reason.

It is very doubtful whether William II of Germany had ever dreamt of seizing Chinese territory before 1894. However, as soon as Port Arthur was invested, and the remnants of the Peiyang Squadron sought refuge in the harbor of Weihaiwei, he immediately constructed for himself a castle-in-the-air colonial empire in the Far East. On November 17th, five days before the fall of Port Arthur, the Kaiser suggested to Prince Hohenlohe, his Chancellor, the seizure of Formosa after coming to a secret understanding with Japan.[136] The suggestion in its brutal form did not find favor with the bureaucrats in the Chancellery, who considered it inopportune, and were afraid that it might

[135] See Baron Rosen, *Forty Years of Diplomacy* (New York, 1922), vol. i, p. 136.

[136] Hohenlohe to Marschall, Nov. 17, 1894, *Lepsius*, ix, 245.

involve complications with the Powers and Japan;[137] but the idea was substantially carried out by them. No sooner than it was suggested steps were taken to prepare the way for some such move as would lead to the acquisition of territory at the expense of China, and to spot a place less pretentious and more substantial to German interests than Formosa. The Germans cast their eyes in turn upon Kiaochou, the Pescadores, and Chusan.[138] They gave up their "undesirable reserve" towards China, while retaining their "royal attitude" towards Japan.[139] They signified to Lord Kimberley their readiness to participate in an intervention when Russia was active in exchanging opinions with Great Britain.[140] They hurried to inform Prince Lobanov when intervention was imminent that they were heart and soul with Russia.[141]

Thus while Great Britain and Russia, who started with one common object, parted company at the end, Russia, France, and Germany, who were actuated by different motives, finally united in common action. Having spent some time in vain to persuade Great Britain to join them,[142] the three continental powers decided to proceed without her. The basis of the "friendly advice" to Japan having been

[137] Marschall to Hohenlohe, Nov. 17, 1894, *ibid.*, ix, 246.

[138] Schweinsberg to Hohenlohe, Nov. 23, 1894, and Marschall to Hatzfeldt, Feb. 1, 1895, *ibid.*, ix, 248.

[139] See, for instance, Schweinsberg to Foreign Office, March 3, 1895, *ibid.*, ix, 252, and Marschall to Gutschmid, March 6, 1895, *ibid.*, ix, 253.

[140] Hatzfeldt to Foreign Office, Feb. 6, 1895, and Feb. 8, 1895, *ibid.*, ix, 250-252. See also footnote on p. 251.

[141] Marschall to Tschirschky, March 23, 1895, *ibid.*, ix, 255; same to same, April 4, 1895, *ibid.*, ix, 261.

[142] Hatzfeldt to Foreign Office, April 13, 1895, *ibid.*, ix, 268; Tschirschky to Foreign Office, April 17, 1895, *ibid.*, ix, 269; same to same, April 20, 1895, *ibid.*, ix, 271.

formulated by Prince Lobanov,[143] the three powers, on April 17th, the very day the viceroy Li Hung-chang signed the treaty of Shimonoseki and left Japan for China, simultaneously instructed their ministers at Tokyo each to communicate a similar note to the Japanese government.[144] This the ministers did on the 23rd.[145] The note [146] in its German version reads as follows:

The examination of the Japanese peace terms forced Germany to the conclusion that the proposed taking possession of Liaotung by Japan will constitute a constant menace to the capital of China and at the same time render the independence of Korea illusory, and that as a consequence it would represent a lasting obstacle to the peace of the Far East. Germany therefore advises refraining from definite occupation of the peninsula.

In view of the mutual jealousy of Great Britain and Russia, of Germany's " loyal attitude towards Japan ", and above all of Russia's indecision before and during the war, the triple intervention must have come to Japan as a surprise. But if Japan was devoid of feeling for the interest of the Far East as a whole, she was quick enough to realize what might come to her if she proved recalcitrant.[147] Accordingly she took up the question with the intervention powers.

On May 1st, Japanese ministers at St. Petersburg, Berlin, and Paris submitted the following terms to the respective

[143] Marschall to Tschirschky, April 8, 1895, *ibid.*, ix, 265.

[144] Marschall to Gutschmid, April 17, 1895, *ibid.*, ix, 270.

[145] Gutschmid to Hohenlohe, April 24, 1895, *ibid.*, ix, 275; Gérard, *op. cit.*, p. 41.

[146] *Lepsius*, ix, 278.

[147] See imperial proclamation of May 10, 1895, *MacMurray*, i, 52.

powers: (1) retention of only Kinchou, including Port Arthur, in return for additional indemnity; and (2) occupation of Mukden until the fulfilment of its obligations by China. They further inquired whether Japan would be allowed to take territories elsewhere as compensation. To the last the powers replied in the negative. As to the two terms, they pointed out the simple fact that occupation of part of the Liaotung peninsula including Port Arthur did not in any sense diminish the menace which formed the basis of the intervention.[148]

On top of the firm attitude of the intervention powers there was already on foot in China a great agitation against the ratification of the peace treaty. On the 5th, by a new reply communicated to the three powers, Japan therefore signified her complete assent, subject to further arrangements as to terms, concerning her claim of an indemnity as compensation, and concerning the manner of evacuation.[149]

In the meantime Prince Lobanov sounded the opinions first of France and Spain — the latter being interested through her possession of the Philippine Islands — and then of Germany.[150] On May 17th, having learnt all their views, the Prince formulated a plan as common basis of negotiation with Japan, and requested the intervention powers to instruct their ministers at Tokyo in similar way.[151] On the question of indemnity, the plan stood for as moderate a figure as possible, for, the Prince pointed out, legally Japan had no right to ask for compensation from China,

[148] Memo. by Marschall, May 1, 1895, *Lepsius*, ix, 282; Marschall to Radolin, May 3, 1895, *ibid.*, ix, 283.
[149] Gérard, *op. cit.*, p. 44.
[150] Radolin to Foreign Office, May 9, 1895, *Lepsius*, ix, 287.
[151] Same to same, May 17, 1895, *ibid.*, ix, 295.

since the retrocession was made without conditions to the three powers and not to China. As to the question of evacuation of the Liaotung peninsula, the plan emphasized the necessity of fixing a term to take effect as soon as possible after the first payments of the indemnity. On May 25th the ministers of the intervention powers at Tokyo commenced their negotiations with the Japanese government.

The negotiations with Japan, however, proved to be lengthy, not because of Japan's obstinacy but because of German obstruction. As might be expected from the sordid motive of Germany's participation, she was forever under the apprehension that she might be left out in dividing the spoils. Just about this time the Russian government was arranging the first of the three sixteen-million-pound loans which China floated in Europe between 1895 and 1898 for indemnity and other services arising from the Japanese War.[152] On June 7th, having learnt of what was going on, the German government instructed von Gutschmid, its minister at Tokyo, not to participate in negotiations, under cover of sickness.[153] On the same day, when the second of the meetings between the Japanese government and the ministers of the intervention powers was held, the former submitted requests that the notes and substance of the negotiations should be kept secret, and that the powers should support Japanese terms of indemnity as well as terms for evacuation, such as dismantlement of the forts of Port Arthur permanently.[154] Gutschmid, of course, could not pretend sickness too long even in hot summer days, and the negotiations with Japan were resumed after some interruption. The question of dismantle-

[152] See *supra*, sec. 5.
[153] Marschall to Gutschmid, June 7, 1895, *Lepsius*, ix, 301.
[154] Gutschmid to Foreign Office, June 7, 1895, *ibid.*, ix, 301.

ment of the forts of Port Arthur did not find favor with the powers. As to indemnity, they let Japan quote her own sum.[155] On July 19th Japan therefore submitted her terms.[156] She asked for 50,000,000 taels as the price of the retrocession. Furthermore, she presented the following:

It [the Japanese government] is ready after the payment of this sum, as well as the first instalment of the war indemnity, to withdrawn its troops on this [the northern] side of the borders of the peninsula Kinchou, and after the payment of the second instalment, as well as after the exchange of ratifications of the contemplated commercial treaty, to evacuate the entire peninsula.

If Germany let Gutschmid recover from sickness, she also decided to resort to other methods of obstruction. When the Japanese terms were communicated to Europe, both Russia and France declared them exorbitant, for they thought, since the retrocession was made rather to the powers than to China, Japan had neither the right to exact a large indemnity nor the right to hold the territory as security for payment of war indemnities.[157] This was not Germany's view. On August 2nd she submitted a note to Russia declaring that the sum of 50,000,000 taels was fair in view of the fact that the territory to be retroceded was an important strategical point, and that what Japan submitted as conditions for evacuation was in line with the terms of Article VIII of the treaty of Shimonoseki concerning Weihaiwei.[158]

[155] Same to same, July 4, 1895, *ibid.*, ix, 305.

[156] Same to same, July 19, 1895, *ibid.*, ix, 306.

[157] Memo. of Rotenham, July 24, 1895, *ibid.*, ix, 307; Memo. of same, August 6, 1895, *ibid.*, ix, 309.

[158] Rotenham to Russian ambassador, April 2, 1895, *ibid.*, ix, 308.

Against the German tactics of obstruction Prince Lobanov was not slow to show resentment. On August 9th he told Prince Radolin, German ambassador to Russia, that he thought China ought not to be further despoiled, that Japan could raise endless difficulties over the contemplated commercial treaty, and that the question of the Liaotung peninsula was independent of the treaty of Shimonoseki. He accused Germany of not coöperating, and the German Chancellery for going counter to the Kaiser's policy, for which he cited a letter William II had written to Nicholas II on July 10th, promising coöperation. He finally ended his two-hour interview by expressing his hope that Germany would give way.[159]

For the next three weeks Germany still kept on haggling over the terms with Russia, giving way first on the question concerning the commercial treaty, and then on the question of indemnity, which she lowered to 30,000,000 taels, but maintaining to the last the necessity of Japan's holding the retroceded territory as security for the indemnity of the retrocession as well as for the first two instalments of war indemnity amounting altogether to 130,000,000 taels, in spite of the fact that, as France pointed out to her, Japan had Weihaiwei for the purpose.[160]

Prince Radolin had raised the loan question in reply to Prince Lobanov's accusation on August 9th. On the 27th, evidently after realizing Germany's object, Russia intimated to Germany the arrangement of a large loan to

---

[159] Radolin to Hohenlohe, August 9, 1895, *ibid.*, ix, 311.

[160] Rotenham to Radolin, August 12, 1895, *ibid.*, ix, 314; Marschall to Radolin, August 19, 1895, *ibid.*, ix, 315; memo. by Marschall, August 22, 1895, *ibid.*, ix, 316; Radolin to Foreign Office, August 24, 1895, *ibid.*, ix, 318; Schoen to Foreign Office, August 30, 1895, *ibid.*, ix, 319.

China in common with her.[161]   Three days later, on Russia's again approaching Germany, the latter yielded on the last point.[162]

The battle having been fought out between Russia and Germany, all followed smoothly.   On September 11th the ministers of the intervention powers presented their terms as agreed upon among the foreign offices in Europe.[163]   On October 7th Japan signified her acceptance of the terms as presented, promising to reduce the indemnity to 30,000,000 taels and to evacuate within three months from the day the said indemnity should have been paid by China.[164]   On the 18th notes embodying the terms were exchanged.[165]

At this point the viceroy Li Hung-chang and the Japanese minister Hayashi, were respectively appointed by the Chinese and Japanese governments to take over the negotiations.[166]   When the Chinese government was first notified by the powers of the terms they had agreed upon with Japan, it sought to obtain a further reduction of the indemnity.   In taking over the negotiations Hayashi, on the other hand, attempted to introduce an additional provision by virtue of which the territory thus retroceded could not be alienated by China to any other power.   After consulting with the Chinese ministers at St. Petersburg, Paris, and Tokyo,[167] the viceroy, on the one hand, advised the Court to give up the attempt, and on the other declined the proposal of Hayashi; and the supplementary treaty was concluded and signed on November 8th with terms practically

[161] Marschall to Hohenlohe, August 27, 1895, *ibid.*, ix, 319.

[162] Same to same, August 31, 1895, *ibid.*, ix, 321.

[163] Gutschmid to Foreign Office, Sept. 11, 1895, *ibid.*, ix, 324.

[164] Same to same, October 7, 1895, *ibid.*, ix, 325.

[165] *MacMurray*, i, 53.

[166] Gérard, *op. cit.*, p. 120.

[167] See correspondence in *Tien kao*, 21/43 *l.*, 44 *l.*

the same as had originally been agreed upon between Japan and the three powers. On November 16th China paid the stipulated thirty million, and on Christmas day the last Japanese invaders left Port Arthur.[168]

Sec. 6. The Russian Alliance

While Russia was lending a helping hand to China by promoting an intervention and guaranteeing a loan, she also approached China for some arrangement to connect southern Primorskaya and Transbakalia by rail across northern Manchuria. The proposal was first made by Serge Witte, Russian minister of finance, to Hsu Ching-cheng, Chinese minister at St. Petersburg, in an informal suggestion that, in view of the menace from Japan which China and Russia were facing in common, China should build railways in Manchuria to connect up the two countries, as well as one part of the Russian Far Eastern possessions lying on one side of Manchuria with another on the other side.

The Russian plan to project the Trans-Siberian Railway across northern Manchuria was widely discussed in the Russian press and naturally reported in the Far East. So, while the matter was being made known to the Chinese government by its representative at St. Petersburg, Chang Chih-tung, viceroy of the Hukuang Provinces, memorialized the Throne, calling for immediate completion of the line already projected into Manchuria,[169] as well as the projection of new lines, to forestall Russian action. In October, while terms for the retrocession of Liaotung were agreed upon between the intervention powers and Japan, the Russian legation at Peking applied for protection for

---

[168] Gérard, *op. cit.*, pp. 50, 160–7; memorial, 29/9/21, *Tiao yo, K.*, 40/2; for text see *ibid.*, 40/5.

[169] *Supra*, chap. iii, sec. 5.

surveyors whom the Russian government was about to despatch into Manchuria. This gave occasion for the Tsungli Yamen to submit the question to the Throne.[170] In a memorial dated October 19, 1895, the Yamen requested the Throne to order the Chinese minister at St. Petersburg to confer with the Russian government on the matter and to report details. In another, bearing the same date, it endorsed Chang's proposal. It pointed out the danger of Russian absorption of Manchuria to meet the argument advanced by the opposition that China could afford neither to develop border provinces before the heart of the empire, nor to expend large sums in addition to the indemnity. It further intimated that measures were being taken to raise foreign loans to carry out Chang's proposal. So far as we know, however, nothing ever came out of the loan plan. Evidently foreign capitalists could not be expected to be as willing to run risks as the Chinese government might be, not to mention the political significance of such loan transactions, which the capitalists had to consider. Then suddenly followed, on February 10, 1896, the appointment of the Grand Secretary [170a] Li Hung-chang as ambassador extraordinary to represent China at the coronation of the ill-fated Nicholas II, a very strange step for the Chinese government of the day to take.

There is a noticeable gap left in the "Works" of the Grand Secretary between 1896 and 1899. It is possible that the documents of this period were not available to the compiler, for, during the greater part of that period the Grand Secretary was a member of the Tsungli Yamen, and as such may not have come to own them. It is also possible

[170] *Tiao yo, K.*, 54/2, 3.

[170a] Li Hung-chang had been Grand Secretary since 1872. Only for convenience have we heretofore referred to him as viceroy.

that those documents were left out by the compiler purposely, for, on the publication of the "Works" the terms of the secret Russian alliance, the conclusion of which we shall presently see, had not expired — although the alliance itself had long become not worth the paper on which it was written, and thus it was considered indiscreet to make public documents that had a bearing upon it. If the latter surmise is correct, there is still some hope that the documents under discussion will soon see daylight; but if the former is correct, they must have found their way, like the rest of the archives of the Yamen, into some foreign ministry of foreign affairs and will remain there until some such event as the Russian Revolution shall unearth them.[171]

In spite of lack of the relevant documents, however, the course of China concerning the alliance is intelligible after we have followed the development of events so far. In view of the Japanese menace and Russian favor, it was neither desirable nor possible for China not to meet Russia in some way. As she was not able to construct railways of her own to connect Russian lines, the alternative was to let Russia construct them under certain conditions.

It appears that at this juncture the matter was taken up by the Grand Secretary. The latter not only sought to safeguard the interests of China as much as possible, but also attempted to convert the move of the Russians into one of mutual benefit. The result was the proposal of an alliance to which the concession for a railway formed only one part, though an important part. The time was also opportune,

[171] The recovery of the archives of the Yamen formed one of the proposals of the Chinese plenipotentiaries in settling the Boxer question with the Powers. The proposal, however, was not entertained by the latter. Is it because archives are considered to be liable to seizure? — or because none was willing to admit the commission of an outrageous act?

for Russian diplomacy was yet in the hands of Prince
Lobanov, and as in the question of intervention Russia re-
sponded readily. As cautious as he was practical, the Grand
Secretary did not yet rest satisfied. He wanted to make sure
that it was not with Cassini, but with the Russian government; no, not even with Prince Lobanov and Witte, but
with the autocrat of all Russias, that he was transacting
business. He therefore journeyed around the world to go
to Russia in spite of his advanced age. In April, after he
had fully discussed the matter with Lobanov and Witte,
and especially after he had been assured by the Tzar in a
private audience in the company of Witte that the arrangement he had made with the ministers of foreign affairs and
of finance had the autocrat's approval, he signed with
Lobanov and Witte a treaty of alliance.[172]

Under the treaty China and Russia were to support each
other in any aggression directed by Japan against either of
them or Korea,[173] and to conclude no peace with the adverse
party without the consent of the other.[174] China, on her
part, further engaged to open her ports to Russia during
military operations,[175] to consent to the construction by her
of a railway across Manchuria,[176] and to grant the free use
of the railway for the transportation and provisioning of
Russian troops in both peace and war.[177] The treaty was
to take effect on the day the contract for the railway across
Manchuria was ratified and to last for fifteen years.[178]

There is no doubt that, had the spirit of the alliance been
observed, Korean independence would have been safe-

---

[172] Abraham Yarmolinsky (ed.), *The Memoirs of Count Witte*
(Garden City, New York, 1921), pp. 89–93. For treaty see *Mac-
Murray*, i, 81. See also Gérard, *op. cit.*, 134–138.

[173] Art. i. [175] Art. iii. [177] Art. v.

[174] Art. ii. [176] Art. iv. [178] Art. vi.

guarded, Japanese aggression would have been nipped in the bud, and the equilibrium of the Far Eastern political system, which the weakness of the Manchu dynasty, the ambition of Japan, and the indifference of the Powers had contributed to upset, could have been restored. Unfortunately, Fate willed differently. On August 30th, only four months after the formation of the alliance, Prince Lobanov died. Adding to this misfortune, his place was taken by Count Michael Nikolaivich Muraviev, whose claim to the office was no better than that he happened to be Russian minister at Copenhagen, which the Tzar often visited. Under Muraviev, as we shall see, Russia not only failed to live up to her words, but was even to act in diametrical opposition to them. Consequently the badly upset equilibrium was further disturbed, not to be restored even until this day. But this was not the fault of the Grand Secretary. It therefore cannot be counted against his patriotism and statesmanship, and, less still, to justify the charge that he traded China's birthright for a bowl of red pottage.

The article in the treaty granting the railway concession reads as follows:

In order to facilitate the access of the Russian land troops to the menaced points, and to ensure their means of subsistence, the Chinese government consents to the construction of a railway line across the Chinese provinces of the Amour, [*i.e.*, Heilungkiang] and of Guirin [Kirin] in the direction of Vladivostok. The junction of this railway with the Russian railway shall not serve as a pretext for any encroachment on Chinese territory, nor for any infringement of the rights of sovereignty of His Majesty the Emperor of China. The construction and exploitation of this railway shall be accorded to the Russo-Chinese Bank, and the clauses of the Contract shall be duly discussed between the Chinese Minister in St. Petersburg and the Russo-Chinese Bank.

The contract was duly discussed and on September 8, 1896, it was signed in Berlin by Hsu Ching-cheng and two representatives of the Russo-Chinese Bank.[179] By means of this contract the Chinese government became a shareholder in the bank to the extent of five million taels,[180] and entrusted to the bank the construction and operation of a railway establishing direct communication between the city of Chita and the Russian South Ussuri Railway.[181] To carry out the trust the bank was to establish a company under the name of the Chinese Eastern Railway Company with the seal given by the Chinese government, with its statutes made in conformity with the Russian usages in regard to railways, and with its president named by the Chinese government but paid by the company. Shares of the company were to be acquired only by Chinese or Russian subjects. The president was to see to the scrupulous fulfilment of the obligations of the bank and of the railway company towards China; to be responsible for the relations of the bank and the railway company with the Chinese government and the central and local authorities; and to examine all accounts of the Chinese government with the bank.[182] The railway company was to have the complete and exclusive right to operate the line for a term of eighty years, at the end of which the line, with all its appurtenances, was to pass free of charge to the Chinese government. The latter, however, was to have the right to buy back the line at the expiration of thirty-six years. It was also to receive as consideration, when the line should

[179] For current English text see *MacMurray*, i, 74. For Chinese text see *Tiao yo, K.*, 45/7 *l*.
[180] For conditions see special contract in *Tiao yo, K.*, 46/2.
[181] Preamble.
[182] Art. i.

be completed, a sum equivalent to the shares it held in the bank.[183]   As to the jurisdiction over the railway, its personnel and the land it traversed, as well as the use of land by the company, there are the following provisions:

Art. V: The said railway and its employees the Chinese government will take measures to protect. As to the personnel, Chinese and foreign, necessary for the operation of the railway, the said company is permitted to employ at will. All criminal cases, lawsuits etc., upon the lands of the railway shall be administered by the local authorities in accordance with treaties.[184]

Art. VI: The land actually needed by the said company for the construction, operation, and protection of the railway as also the land in the vicinity of the line necessary for procuring sand, stone, lime, etc., if this land is state property, will be turned over to the Chinese government free of charge; and if it is private property, will be either paid for at one time or rented from the proprietors annually, both at current price. The said company shall itself provide funds for such purposes. The land belonging to the said company will all be exempt from land tax and will be managed exclusively by the said company which will be permitted to construct thereon buildings and works of various kinds as well as to set up telegraphs, under its own operation, for the exclusive use of the railway. Except in regard to mines for which arrangement will be separately made, the income of the said company, such as the charges for transportation of passengers and merchandise and the receipts from telegrams, will all be exempt from tax or duty.[185]

[183] Art. xii.

[184] A translation from Chinese text. For the stand taken by the Board of Foreign Affairs concerning Chinese as the standard language for the railway contract see to Russian Minister, 34/1/24, *Hsu,* 11/34, *l.*   [185] Also a translation.

As to Russian troops and war materials " despatched in transit over the railway from Russia " it was provided that the company was to carry them through directly " beyond the border " without for any pretext stopping on the way longer than was necessary.[186] As to merchandise it was provided that all despatched in transit over the railway from Russian territory to Russian territory should be free of customs duties and *likin;* that all imported from Russia or exported to Russia over the railway should respectively pay the import and the export duty of the Chinese Maritime Customs, less one-third; that if the import was further transported into the interior it should pay in addition a transit duty equivalent to the half of the import duty collected; and that China was to install customs offices at the two frontier points on the line for the foregoing purpose.[187]

Sec. 7.   The Open Door versus Spheres of Influence

(1) The Powers and China

Russia had thus secured her compensation; but in fact she was not the only nation, nor even the first nation in so doing. M. A. Gérard, the French minister, who, it seems, came to his post in Peking specially for the delimitation of the common frontier between Annam and China, signed with the Tsungli Yamen on June 20, 1895, two conventions,[188] one supplementary to the delimitation convention of June 26, 1887, and the other to the commercial treaty of the same date, which was itself a supplement to a former treaty.

In these conventions M. Gérard did not fail to obtain from China certain provisions besides advantages pertaining to the nature of the two conventions themselves, such as the

[186] Art. viii.   [187] Art. x.   [188] *MacMurray,* i, 26, 27.

delimitation in favor of France or the opening of new markets on the Chinese frontier. The provisions referred to are as follows:

It is understood that China, for the exploitation of its mines in the provinces of Yun-nan, Kwang-si, and Kwang-tung, may call upon, in the first instance, French manufacturers and engineers, the exploitation remaining nevertheless subject to the rules proclaimed by the Imperial Government, as regards national industries.

It is agreed that railways either those already in existence or those projected in Annam may, after mutual agreement, and under conditions to be defined, be continued on Chinese territory.[189]

On the last of the above provisions M. Gérard was able later to persuade the Chinese government to decide upon the construction of a railway between Lungchou in Kuangsi and Dong-dang on the Annam frontier, and to entrust its construction to a French company under the supervision of the Administration of the Lungchou Railway, a government office specially created for the purpose.[190]

After the granting of the Chinese Eastern Railway concession, M. Gérard became active again, and by an identical note exchanged on June 12, 1897, obtained from the Yamen the promise [191] that it would request the same French company to continue the Lungchou Railway after its completion in the direction of Nanning and Pe-se — a privilege the Yamen had formerly declined to grant;[192]

---

[189] Art. v, supplementary commercial treaty.

[190] For text of contract signed on June 5, 1896, see *Tiao yo, K.,* 41/11; and supplementary contract ratified on Sept. 24, 1899, *ibid.,* 41/14; see also memorials by Yamen, 22/2/7, *ibid.,* 41/2; 22/5/21, 41/3.   [191] *MacMurray,* i, 31.

[192] See memorial by Yamen, 22/2/7, *Tiao yo, K.,* 41/2.

that it would improve the upper Red River and the route "from Ho-kou to Man-hao and Meng-tse as far as the provincial capital"; and that it would concede the right to France to construct a railway between the "Annam frontier and the provincial capital, either by way of the Pe-se river region, or by that of the upper Red River" the planning and carrying out of which by China was "to be done gradually".

Soon after the termination of M. Gérard's mission the concession for the Yunnan Railway was definitely granted by China, together with the lease of Kuangchouwan by a convention dated April 10, 1898,[193] but its details were not attended to until after the Boxer Rebellion.[194]

Great Britain suddenly realized that her failure to join in the intervention for the retrocession of the Liaotung peninsula had allowed her traditional rivals to steal a march on her in China. For the time being, however, she had to confine herself to a complaint against the concessions granted to France. Alleging violation of terms in the Sino-British convention of March 1, 1894, by the delimitation treaty with France, she obtained from China a revision of the former by a new convention signed on February 4, 1897,[195] which, besides modifying many points of the old convention in favor of Great Britain and opening ports in Kuangtung and Kuangsi, contained a new provision whereby the Chinese government agreed thereafter to consider whether the conditions of trade justified the construction of railways in Yunnan, and, in the event of their construction, agreed to connect them with the Burmese lines. Great Britain also obtained from France a declara-

[193] *MacMurray*, i, 124.
[194] Signed Oct. 29, 1903, *ibid.*, i, 453.
[195] *Ibid.*, i, 94.

tion, made on January 15, 1896,[196] that there would be
no exclusive commercial and other privileges in Yunnan
and Szechuan, as far as rested with the two Powers.[197]

So far so good, but China had yet another power to compensate.[197a] While Russia and France were active in securing their due portions of compensation, Germany had
for two years lain low. The kind of compensation she had
contemplated — the seizure of territory — was too novel.
It needed not only mitigating circumstances to go with it
before a world not entirely callous; it needed also adjust-
ments with the Powers in view of their interests in China,
since they did not set an example for her to follow as she
all the while thought they would do.

Of the three places upon which Germany had cast an
eye she favored Chusan most, for while the Pescadores
were not as commercially valuable, the Kiaochou Bay
would involve problems of defence comparatively complicated on account of its continental position. To her
disappointment, however, she soon discovered that the desired object was jealously guarded by Great Britain, who
had not only had a non-alienation promise concerning it
from China, but had also undertaken to guard it from
the occupation of other powers.[198] By that time the Pescadores had definitely gone to Japan. So Germany concentrated her attention on the Kiaochou Bay.

Under the terms of the treaty of alliance between China
and Russia, the former was to open her ports to the latter
in a war against Japanese aggression. Among the Chinese

[196] *MacMurray*, i, 54.

[197] Art. iv.

[197a] The writer regrets that when the following pages were
written the volumes of Lepsius' from the 13th on were not available
to him.

[198] For convention see *Tiao yo*, 8/28.

ports that could accommodate a fleet the nearest to Vladivostok was the Kiaochou Bay. Apart from the moral duty of one ally to discountenance any move of a third party inimical to the interest of the other, Russia had therefore the interest of seeing that Kiaochou Bay fell into no other hands. It was evident, therefore, that if Germany was to attain her object, she would have to induce Russia to forego her claim first. There is no doubt that, had Prince Lobanov been living, Germany would have found her way as difficult with Russia as with Great Britain; but with a man like Muraviev at the head of the Russian foreign office, her object was easily attained. In the summer of 1897, during a visit to St. Petersburg, William II of Germany successfully made Nicholas II commit himself on the question.[199]

Having made this adjustment with Russia, the next step for Germany was to seize an opportunity. In this she too was favored. On October 31, 1897, two German missionaries of a Roman Catholic mission were murdered by robbers in the act of plundering in a village in the prefecture of Tsaochou, which was situated in the southwestern corner of the province of Shantung on the coast of which was found the Kiaochou Bay. In spite of stringent and effective measures taken regarding the matter by the Chinese government, Germany seized the Bay on November 13th,[200] and informed the Tsungli Yamen that no evacuation would take place until China not only made full reparation for the murder such as building an imperial tablet to the memory of the murdered, the indemnification of the latter's families, and the degradation per-

[199] Witte's *Memoirs, op. cit.,* p. 101.

[200] MacDonald to Salisbury, Nov. 17, 1897; same to same, Nov. 18; Salisbury to MacDonald, Nov. 19; *China, No. 1* (1898), p. 1.

manently of the governor of Shantung, but also (1) defrayed the cost of the occupation of the Bay, (2) conceded to German engineers the preference in the building of any railway which China might construct in the province of Shantung and also in the working of any mine which might exist along the track of such railway,[201] and (3) granted to Germany a coaling station at Kiaochou.[202]

Taken by surprise the Chinese government naturally turned to Russia, but as might be expected from the commitment Nicholas II had made, it soon found that no assistance could be expected from her, and accordingly early decided to meet the case itself as best it could.

In taking up the case with the German minister, the Chinese government insisted upon treating the Kiaochou question as independent of the Tsaochou incident, and as a full satisfaction of whatever Germany might claim through her part in the joint intervention. To this the German minister could not object, although he never failed to use the missionary incident as a lever whenever it suited his purpose. On January 4, 1898, the missionary case was therefore first disposed of by a protocol of six articles. The missionary case being out of the way, the Chinese government then took up the question of compensation for Germany's part in the intervention. After negotiations which occupied considerable time the question was settled by a railway and mining concession similar to that granted to Russia, and a coaling station at the Kiaochou Bay in the form, not of a territorial cession, but of a non-transferable ninety-nine-year lease.

Germany, however, was not yet satisfied. A little later, on the occasion of the murder by villagers of some Ger-

[201] MacDonald to Salisbury, Nov. 22, 1897, *ibid.*, p. 2.
[202] Same to same, Jan. 31, 1898, *ibid.*, p. 26.

man soldiers of the forces occupying Kiaochou, her minister opened the case, and finally obtained also the concession of a preferential treatment in commercial operations for Germans in Shantung, similar to what had been secured by France concerning the southwestern provinces. The terms as agreed upon were then drawn up in a convention of three sections signed on March 6, 1898,[203] with the following declaration in the preamble:

> The missionary case of the prefecture of Tsaochou has been settled by agreement. As a separate matter China undertakes to compensate Germany for the assistance which the latter had previously rendered her.[204]

The import of the preamble, however, seemed to have undergone much transformation in the current text through the skill of the translator, or the lack of it. Might it not be because the German minister, von Heyking, chose to let his own conscience alone be troubled so that his sixty million compatriots, or as many as had any sensibilities, might sleep in peace?

The seizure of the Kiaochou Bay by Germany had not only had the previous consent of Russia, but was also viewed with friendly interest by Great Britain. In view of this situation, coupled with the fact that by the convention leasing the Kiaochou Bay China had fully liquidated all her obligations towards the intervention powers, one might expect that the trouble would end where it began. Unfortunately this was not the case; for Russia had made up her mind not only to forsake her ally to her fate,

---

[203] Memorials by Yamen, 23/12/23, 24/2/15, *Tiao yo, K.,* 51/2, 5; text of convention, *ibid.,* 51/19; current English version of convention, *MacMurray,* i, 112.

[204] A translation.

but also to join in despoiling her while she was most helpless.

Muraviev, " whose sycophancy was only equalled by his ignorance of public business ", was now to lead his imperial master of an aggravated form of treachery after his failure to prevent him from betraying an ally.[205]   As soon as the Kiaochou affair took place he submitted a memorandum to the Tzar, advising the seizure, after the manner of the Germans, of some Chinese port, preferably Port Arthur or Talienwan, the very ports from which Russia, in company with France and Germany, had two years previously dispossessed Japan.

At this point came the intervention of Serge Witte, the co-signer of the treaty of alliance with Prince Lobanov on the Russian side.   As may be judged by his life, Witte was a mere opportunist; but being a co-signer of the treaty of alliance, coupled with the fact that he was interested in seeing that the project of carrying the Trans-Siberian Railway across Manchuria should not be frustrated by some untoward event, he strongly objected to the scheme as advocated by Muraviev.   His standpoint may be best given in his own words, recording his protest made at a special conference held under the presidency of the Tzar to consider the subject:

I reminded my hearers that we had declared the principle of China's territorial integrity and that on the strength of that principle we forced Japan to withdraw from the Liaotung peninsula, which comprises Port Arthur and Talienwan.   I further pointed out the fact that we had concluded a secret defensive alliance with China, thus obligating ourselves to defend her from Japan's encroachments upon her

[205] Witte's *Memoirs, op. cit.*, pp. 98–104; see also C. L. Seeger (translator), *The Memoirs of Alexander Iswolsky* (London, 1920), pp. 123–4.

territory. Under these circumstances, I declared, the seizure of a Chinese port would be the height of treachery and
faithlessness. Aside from these considerations of an ethical
order, I said, the proposed measure would be extremely
dangerous even from the standpoint of our self-interest.
I called the attention of the conference to the fact that we
were engaged in building a railroad on Chinese territory
and that our step would arouse the country against us, thus
endangering the railroad construction. Besides, the occupied ports, I said, would have to be connected by rail with
the trunk line, which circumstance would drag us into complications likely to have disastrous results.[206]

Through the intervention of Witte the measure was
for a time dropped. In the end, however, the Tzar was
prevailed upon by Muraviev. Accordingly in December,
1897, a squadron of Russian warships occupied Port Arthur
and Talienwan, and in January, 1898, a set of demands
was presented to China for the lease of the Liaotung peninsula to Russia for thirty-six years, without any compensation, and also the construction of a branch railway linking
Port Arthur and Talienwan with the Chinese Eastern
Railway.

The demands of the Russians were naturally resented
by China. Meanwhile Witte attempted to remedy the
situation by calling upon the Kaiser to withdraw from
Kiaochou; but he failed, and, at the bidding of the Tzar,
he turned and helped the Russian plan to success. Through
the agent of the Russian ministry of finance in Peking he
advised the Chinese government to come to terms. Given
thus the alternative of preserving the alliance at the sacrifice of concessions on the one hand, and of resisting the
demands on the other at the certain sacrifice of the alliance, and yet probably without avoiding the concessions,

[206] Page 99.

the Chinese government chose the lesser evil. Accordingly it took up the case in good spirit as it did with the Kiao-chou case, and on March 26, 1898, closed it by a convention.[207]

In this convention China agreed " to place at the disposal of the Russian government, on lease, the Ports Arthur and Talienwan, together with the water areas contiguous to these ports ", for a term of twenty-five years, which may be prolonged subsequently by mutual consent. The purpose of the arrangement was declared to be " to insure that the Russian naval forces shall possess an entirely secure base on the littoral of northern China ", and it was asserted that the act " in no way violates the sovereign rights of His Majesty the Emperor of China " to the territory affected.[208] In line with these declarations, Russia engaged not to invest the authority in charge of the lease with the title of governor or governor-general,[209] and to share with China Port Arthur, an exclusively naval port, as well as the parts set aside in Talienwan for naval use.[210] For the defence of the leased territory the convention further established a " neutral zone " north of the area leased.[211]

The details of the grant were later taken up between Hsu Ching-cheng and Muraviev, and the result of their negotiations was embodied in the additional agreement of May 7, 1898.[212] In this agreement the line of the leased

[207] *MacMurray*, i, 119.

[208] Arts. i and iii.

[209] Art. iv. The Chinese government has always been particular on the provision of this article. See Board of Foreign Affairs to Russian Legation, *K.*, 29/9, *Kuang hsu cheng yao*, 29/34 *l.*, and Board of Foreign Affairs to Bureau of Taxation, *K.*, 33, *Tiao yo*, *K.*, 101/3 *l.*   [210] Art. vi.   [211] Art. v.

[212] *MacMurray*, i, 127.

territory was extended to the north of Pi-tsu-wo, and the neutral zone to the south of Kaiping.[213] The Chinese government was not willing to include in the lease Kinchou, the seat of one of the deputy military governors of Shengking. As a compromise, the administration of police of that city was retained for China,[214] Russia reserving, however, the right to send troops there in case of disturbance.[215] The Chinese government also objected to the provision in the convention of March 27th of a second branch railway " to another more convenient point on the littoral of the Liaotung peninsula between the town of In-tzu [Yingkou] and the estuary of the River Yalu ".[216] By common consent this grant was declared cancelled in exchange for the provision that railway privileges in districts traversed by the line to Port Arthur and Talienwan should not be given to the subjects of other powers, though "as regards the railway which China shall (may) herself build hereafter from Shan-hai-kuan in extension to a point as near as (lit., nearest to) possible to this branch line, Russia agrees that she has nothing to do with it ".[217] On the other hand, Russia obtained from China the engagement not to grant any concession in the " neutral zone " or open any port on its coasts.[218]

Shortly afterwards, a detailed agreement was also drawn up concerning the branch line connecting Port Arthur and Talienwan with the Chinese Eastern Railway. This branch line was given the name, the Southern Manchurian

[213] Arts. i and ii.

[214] Art. iv.

[215] Russian Ministry of Foreign Affairs to Chinese Minister, May 7, 1898, *Tiao yo, K.*, 52/11.

[216] Art. viii.   [217] Art. iii.

[218] Art. v; see also memorial by Hsu and Yang, 24/inter. 3/20, *Tiao yo, K.*, 52/6.

Branch.[219]   In order to facilitate the bringing in of materials and provisions needed in the construction of the line the company was permitted by the agreement to build temporary branch lines from that line to Yingkou and to ports in the " neutral zone ", these lines to be removed " at the notice of the Chinese government " after the completion of the work, *i.e.*, " within eight years from the date of the survey and determination of the line and the appropriation of the land for its construction ".[220]

What then were the other powers doing in the meantime?   Probably, in order to forestall any possibility of Germany's seizing Chinese territory in the neighborhood of Annam France had, on March 15, 1897, secured from the Tsungli Yamen a declaration of non-alienation concerning the island of Hainan.[221]   When Germany had seized the Kiaochou Bay, Great Britain hurried up and, after the example of France, secured a similar declaration concerning the Yangtze region;[222] and as if the opportunity must be fully utilized, she also at the same time sought to neutralize whatever effect the Franco-Russian loan of 1895 might have upon the Chinese Maritime Customs by securing another declaration that China would appoint a British subject to the post of Inspector-General of the Chinese Maritime Customs as long as in " the trade at the various ports British merchants are in the majority ".[223] France was as quick in measuring up with her rivals as in following the footsteps of her ally. She came up again when the lease of Kiaochou was definitely granted, and by two notes, both dated April 9, 1898,[224] secured on the one hand a ninety-nine-year lease at Kuangchouwan,[225] and on

---

[219] *MacMurray*, i, 154.

[220] Art. iii.

[221] *MacMurray*, i, 98.

[222] *Ibid.*, i, 104.

[223] *Ibid.*, i, 105.

[224] *Ibid.*, i, 123, 124.

[225] For details see convention of May 27, 1898, *ibid.*, i, 128.

the other declarations of non-alienation for the provinces bordering on Tongking and of China's readiness to consider French recommendations for the post of the Director of the Postal Service, when it should be organized separately from the Customs. Great Britain, too, did not disdain imitation. When the lease of Port Arthur and Talienwan was definitely granted, she, too, came up again and received by a convention [226] signed on June 9th a lease at Kowloon for ninety-nine years, and, by another [227] signed on July 1st, a lease at Weihaiwei " for so long a period as Port Arthur shall remain in the occupation of Russia ".

Following in the wake of the European powers Japan also secured a declaration [228] of non-alienation for Fukien, half of which, across the channel, she had seized several years before.

(2) *Great Britain and Russia*

In the last chapter we followed the development of railways in China down to the Japanese War. Like practically all other phases of Chinese national life railway development was affected by the hostilities. The result of the war demonstrated the strategical value of railways and removed opposition to them on that score. Thus immediately after the peace of Shimonoseki the construction of the abandoned section from Tientsin to Peking was taken up and soon completed. But the trend of events did not stop at mere removal of obstacles; it was also to give impetus. This latter came in the form of Russia and France seeking railway concessions. Consequently the Chinese government not only took measures to hasten the completion of the lines already projected, such as the Peking-Hankow Railway and the extension of the North China

[226] *Ibid.*, i, 130.   [227] *Ibid.*, i, 152.   [228] *Ibid.*, i, 126.

Railways, but also to project new lines. In doing this it
was necessary that the principle of employing only Chinese capital should be abandoned. This was done, and
loans were therefore negotiated with foreign interests.

For the extension of the North China Railways from
Chunghouso to Hsinmin, with a branch line to Newchwang, as well as for the redemption of existing loans
on that line, a preliminary contract for 16,000,000 taels
was signed between the administration of the North China
Railways and the Hongkong and Shanghai Banking Corporation on June 7, 1898.[229] The security for this loan
was to be the permanent way, rolling-stock, and entire
property, together with the freight and earnings of the
existing sections and the proposed sections when constructed,
as well as the rights of mining retained by the administration on both sides of the proposed sections.[230] Provision
was also made in the preliminary contract for consultation
with the corporation in case a new chief engineer was to
be appointed and for the services of a European railway
accountant.[231] As to the Peking-Hankow line there was
already material for the construction of the Peking-Paoting
section. To secure the capital for the rest, a contract[232]
for a loan of 112,500,000 francs was signed on June 26,
1898, between the Chinese company to which the government had granted the concession and a Belgian company
after a chequered career of two years' negotiations.[232a]
The loan was secured by the entire line as well as its sta-
tionary and rolling-stock and receipts[233] and further guar-

[229] Art. i.   Text in *MacMurray*, i, 179.
[230] Art. ii.
[231] Art. iii.
[232] *MacMurray*, i, 135.
[232a] In these negotiations American interests were also involved.
[233] Art. x.

anteed by the Chinese government; [234] and the Belgian company was to have the privilege of constructing the line from Paoting southward for the account of the Chinese company and of operating the entire line. [235] In accordance with the operating contract signed on the same day, this privilege was to last for thirty years, but was terminable any time the loan should be refunded. [236] Under the latter provision the Chinese government took over the line in 1908. [237]

The making of the two contracts in a political atmosphere such as the one existing was not fortunate, for it tended to intensify the situation, already extremely critical. When the news of the signature of the Belgian contract reached London, Lord Salisbury gave orders for a general advance in his " battle of concessions ". Immediately Sir Claude M. MacDonald, the British minister at Peking, protested to the Tsungli Yamen against the provisions of the said contract. This was naturally ignored by the Yamen which went ahead to ratify the contract. Thereupon MacDonald alleged that some member of the Yamen had promised to inform him before ratification, feigned great injury, and demanded on August 20th that China grant the British syndicates the privilege of contracting for a number of railways on the same terms given the Belgian syndicate. These were the lines from Tientsin to Chinkiang, Honan and Shansi to the Yangtze, Kowloon to Canton, Pukow to Sinyang, and Soochou to Hangchou, with an extension to Ningpo. In reply the Yamen observed that all of those lines were already under discussion and assured him that they would be satisfactorily dis-

[234] Art. vii. [235] Art. xix.
[236] Art. v. Text of contract in *MacMurray*, i, 143.
[237] Note, *ibid.*, i, 152.

cussed. Thus Sir Claude won his "battle" without
bloodshed — indeed without even "any precise threats"
except the intimation that "the fleet is concentrating"
which was, of course, as he pointed out, known to the
Yamen; and soon he was able to write to Lord Charles
Beresford that the British did "not seem to have come
out second best", as, he proved by a table enclosed, they
had secured nine railway concessions with a total of 2,800
miles as against ten with a total of 3,620 secured by the
Russians, Germans, Belgians, French, and Americans together, besides the advantage that their lines as compared
with others were far more paying.[238]

While Great Britain dreaded the southward march of
Russian influence through the Belgian syndicate, Russia
was no less uneasy about the possibility of a British control
of the extra-mural section of the North China Railways;
and, when the terms of the loan for the extension of the
latter became known to her, she likewise protested. After
some discussion, it was agreed between the Tsungli Yamen
and the Russian *chargé d'affaires*, Pavloff, that this particular section would neither be mortgaged nor fall under the
control of foreigners and that it was to be constructed with
Chinese capital, which, it was understood, might be money
borrowed on any other guarantee than the control of or a
mortgage on the section in question.[239]

When the matter was taken up by the British govern-

[238] Salisbury to MacDonald, July 13, 1898, *China, No. 1*
(1899), p. 164; same to same July 16, *ibid.*, p. 164; MacDonald to
Salisbury, Sept. 4, *ibid.*, p. 216; same to same and enclosures, Aug.
19, *ibid.*, p. 260; same to same and enclosures, Sept. 21, *ibid.*,
p. 285; MacDonald to Beresford and enclosures, Nov. 27, *ibid.*,
p. 344.

[239] Scott to Balfour, Aug. 18, 1898; Balfour to Scott, Aug. 19,
1898, *China, No. 2* (1899), pp. 8, 9.

ment with the Russian, the latter denied that its action involved a breach of treaty rights any more than the British action in connection with the question of Sir Robert Hart's succession, and suggested that the difficulties of the situation might be met by an agreement between Russia and Great Britain by which the latter should be bound not to interest herself in railway or mining concessions in Manchuria, Russia on her part binding herself in a similar manner with regard to the Yangtze region — a region, it never failed to point out, much richer and more populous.[240]

When the "battle" for railway and mining concessions was first opened Salisbury instructed MacDonald that it was desirable to acquire the rights to the Peking-Hankow line in exchange for those over the extra-mural extension of the North China Railways.[241] Great Britain being not unprepared to strike a balance with the Russians as proposed, her minister to Russia was instructed on August 19th to take up the matter.[242] Meanwhile, to smooth matters, the Hongkong and Shanghai Banking Corporation, evidently at the instance of the British government, eventually agreed to relinquish its rights to a lien on the extra-mural extension,[243] but in compensation it obtained a half interest in some coal mines in the Chao-yang *hsien* just off the line but within the extra-mural section of Chihli,[244] as well as a government guarantee for the loan over and above the securities given after the model of the Belgian

[240] Balfour to Scott, Aug. 12, 1898, *ibid.*, p. 6.

[241] Salisbury to MacDonald, July 16, 1898, *China, No. 1* (1899), p. 164.

[242] Scott to Balfour, Aug. 18, 1898; Balfour to Scott, Aug. 19, *China, No. 2* (1899), pp. 8, 9.

[243] Art. iii of definitive contract signed Oct. 10, 1898, *MacMurray*, i, 173.

[244] Contract, *ibid.*, i, 181.

contract.[245]   As to the proposed agreement to meet the difficulties of the general situation, a long discussion ensued and it was not until April 28, 1899, that notes embodying its terms were exchanged.[246]

In order to complete this phase of the interesting episode of history under review let us add that a little less than half a year earlier Great Britain, in order to allay possible German opposition to her leasing Weihaiwei, declared to Germany that in so doing she had no intention of injuring or contesting the rights and interests of Germany in Shantung or of creating difficulties for her in that province, and that she would especially not construct any railway from the leased territory to the interior.[247]

(3) *The United States and the Powers*

The idea of acquiring ports in China, as initiated by Germany and Russia, was viewed with favor by Great Britain from the very time it was first advocated.[248]   When it was put into practice, she maintained the same attitude but declared her apprehension lest, through this practice, customs barriers hostile to others and favorable to the special powers concerned, might be put up in accordance with protectionist traditions on the coast of China.[249]   Either

[245] Art. iv; MacDonald to Salisbury, Oct. 11, 1898, and enclosures, *China, No. 2* (1899), p. 37.

[246] *MacMurray*, i, 204.   For details of discussion see *China, No. 2* (1899), *passim*.

[247] For details of negotiation see Lascelles to Salisbury, April 4, 1894; Balfour to Lascelles, April 6; same to same, April 7, *China, No. 1* (1899), p. 5; same to same, April 19, 1898, *ibid.*, p. 27.

[248] Salisbury to O'Conor, March 24, 1898, *China, No. 1* (1898), p. 53; Valentine Chirol, *The Far Eastern Question* (London, 1896), p. 194.

[249] Speech of Balfour, *The Times*, London, Jan. 11, 1898.

because she was anxious to placate Great Britain or because her claim to Shantung was too shadowy to support a protectionist policy, Germany from the very beginning assured Great Britain that the port was to be opened to the commerce of the world,[250] and on September 5, 1898, formally declared Kiaochou a " free port ".[251]   Following the example of Germany, Russia also gave assurance to Great Britain during her negotiations with China for the lease of Port Arthur and Talienwan that any outlet for her commerce she might secure from China would be opened to the ships of all the powers,[252] and this agreement she carried out on August 11, 1899, by establishing Talienwan as a " free port ".[253]

When the Shantung Railway concession was being pressed by Germany, Great Britain warned the Chinese government that " His Majesty's Government will demand equality of treatment for British subjects according to the Treaty rights possessed by Great Britain, and . . . will require compensation on any points in respect to which those rights may be disregarded ".[254]   It occurred to her later, however, that this would not save her trade from being strangled in localities where concessions were in the control of rival hands by the application of preferential rates in such matters.[255]   Accordingly, when she entered into

---

[250] Salisbury to Lacelles, Jan. 19, 1898, *China, No. 1* (1898), p. 23; Lascelles to Salisbury, Jan. 25, *ibid.*, p. 29; same to same, Jan. 28, *ibid.*, p. 31.

[251] Note in *MacMurray*, i, 115.

[252] Salisbury to O'Conor, Feb. 2, 1898, *China, No. 1* (1898), p. 32.   [253] Russian Imperial Order, *MacMurray*, i, 121.

[254] MacDonald to Yamen, Dec. 10, 1897, *China, No. 1* (1898), p. 28.

[255] Salisbury to MacDonald, July 13, 1898, *China, No. 1* (1899), p. 164.

negotiations with Russia for the agreement which finally was signed on April 28, 1899, she sought to provide against this in the following language:

It is further agreed between the two governments that no preferential railway rates or differential treatment are to be established on lines in the aforesaid regions [*i.e.*, Manchuria and the Yangtze district] for which they may obtain concessions.[256]

This, however, did not appear in the final agreement, because, according to Witte, the question of rates was too technical a one to be prematurely inserted in a preliminary agreement, but one which might be left to be settled between the two governments in the spirit of such an agreement when the time came for its necessary consideration.[257] The time never did come, for before long the subject was treated in a more comprehensive way in the Hay note.

While the "battle" was being waged in China the Spanish-American War of 1898 broke out. This for the time being directed the attention of the United States from the affairs of China, but finally, by giving to her the possession of the Philippine Islands made her more interested in them than before. On December 5, 1898, shortly after peace had been concluded at Paris, President McKinley had announced in his annual message that "if no discriminating treatment of American citizens and their trade be found to exist or hereafter develops, the desire of this government would appear to be realized".[258] On September 6, 1899, John Hay, the Secretary of State, instructed

[256] For draft agreement see *China, No. 2* (1899), p. 23.
[257] Scott to Salisbury, Feb. 6, 1899, *ibid.*, p. 59.
[258] *Moore*, vol. v, p. 533.

American ambassadors at London, Berlin and St. Petersburg to ask from the respective governments a declaration that each, within its respective sphere of whatever influence in China —

First, will in no way interfere with any treaty port or any vested interest within any so-called "sphere of interest" or leased territory it may have in China.

Second, that the Chinese treaty tariff of the time being shall apply to all merchandise landed or shipped to all such ports as are within said "sphere of interest" (unless they be "free ports"), no matter to what nationality it may belong, and that duties so leviable shall be collected by the Chinese government.

Third, that it will levy no higher harbor dues on vessels of another nationality frequenting any port in such "spheres" than shall be levied on vessels of its own nationality, and no higher railroad charges over lines built, controlled, or operated within its "sphere" or merchandise belonging to citizens or subjects of other nationalities transported through such "spheres" than shall be levied on similar merchandise belonging to its own nationals transported over equal distances.

Great Britain was the first to give a written reply to the proposal. Lord Salisbury wrote on November 30th announcing his readiness to make the declaration in the sense desired with the usual reservations that a similar one should be made by other powers concerned. Russia followed a month later. Count Muraviev's note of December 30th to the American ambassador in St. Petersburg was as follows:

I have the honor to receive your excellency's note dated the 8th–20th of September last, relating to the principles which the Government of the United States would like to see adopted in commercial matters by the powers which have interests in China.

In so far as the territory leased by China to Russia is concerned, the Imperial Government has already demonstrated its firm intention to follow the policy of " the open door " by creating Talienwan a free port; and if at some future time that port, although remaining free itself, should be separated by a customs limit from other portions of the territory in question, the customs duties would be levied, in the zone subject to tariff, upon all foreign merchandise without distinction as to nationality.

As to the ports now opened or hereafter to be opened to foreign commerce by the Chinese government, and which lie beyond the territory leased to Russia, the settlement of the question of customs duties belongs to China herself, and the Imperial Government has no intention whatever of claiming any privilege for its own subjects to the exclusion of other foreigners. It is to be understood, however, that this assurance of the Imperial Government is given under condition that a similar declaration shall be made by other powers having interests in China.

With the conviction that this reply is such as to satisfy the inquiry made in the aforementioned note, the Imperial Government is happy to have complied with the wishes of the American government, especially as it attaches the highest value to anything that may strengthen and consolidate the traditional relations of friendship existing between the two countries.

In November Hay also instructed the American representatives in Japan, Italy, and France to ask from the respective governments each a similar declaration. All these gave a favorable reply in writing, France on December 16th, Japan on December 26th, and Italy on January 7th. On February 19th Germany also sent in a favorable reply.

And on March 20th Hay instructed the various American representatives to inform the respective governments that the United States considered the assent given by each to the principle as final and definitive.[259] Such in substance was the Open Door declaration. .

[259] *Ibid.*, vol. v, pp. 534–46.

Chapter V

THE BOXER REBELLION

Sec. 1. Li Hung-chang and the Boxer Rebellion[1]

THE Japanese War took place in spite of the conciliatory policy of the Grand Secretary Li Hung-chang, and
the scramble for leases and concessions followed closely
on the heels of his appeal to the Western powers to restore
the balance of the Far East. Upon this superficial appearance of things his political enemies now insisted on
holding him responsible for all the disasters that had come
to China since 1894. Finally the young emperor Kuanghsu
decided to dispense with his services by dismissing him from
the Tsungli Yamen on September 7, 1898, the very moment when all was over, but when, indeed, reconstruction
might have commenced.

The people who replaced the Grand Secretary — the
so-called reformers — however, found themselves unable
to do any better than resorting to a *coup d'état*. History
has yet to pass its final judgment when this interesting episode fades further into the distance. People who remember that China is an ancient country have condemned the
reformers on the ground that they attempted to bring about

[1] The present section, strictly speaking, is beyond the scope of
this work. It has been added mainly because it treats of an important phase of the Rebellion that has hitherto been neglected and
might thus help to complete the picture of this all-important episode
of modern Chinese history.

an abrupt change. Abrupt, indeed, the change undoubtedly was. But it may be recalled that the shock of events of the preceding three years was no ordinary shock, that some of the measures of reform were indeed initiated before the reformers took charge, and that within years that could be counted on the fingers of one hand practically all of the changes were put into practice, though not by the same reformers. There is no doubt that, had they co-operated with the elder statesman, instead of ousting him, and, more important still, had they also abstained from interfering with the natural relation of Tsuhsi and Kuanghsu, of aunt and nephew, they would have saved China, if not from all the ill effects of foreign aggression, at least from plunging into wilder chaos. However this may be, when the reformers resorted to a *coup d'état*, they were no match for the woman already forty years the ruler of the empire; and one hundred days of Utopian dreams ended with the return of the Empress Dowager. Disappointed in her ministers, she instinctively turned towards her kinsmen. Deprived of Prince Kung by death,[1a] she naturally turned towards Prince Tuan. But Prince Tuan had his own way of reform, even as the reformers had theirs. Hence the reorganization of the army became the enlistment of the Boxers; hence the resisting of aggression took the form of exterminating foreigners and things foreign; hence the ship of state sailed in stately fashion into the chaos of 1900.

One of the acts of the Empress Dowager after her return was the appointment of the Grand Secretary to Canton as viceroy of the Kuang Provinces — an unimportant post, indeed, in comparison with what he had held before, but nevertheless one step to full restoration. As soon as she

[1a] May 29, 1898.

began to suspect the wisdom of her kinsmen, she summoned the Grand Secretary to proceed to Peking. This step, though early under ordinary conditions, was taken too late in view of the quick march of events, for shortly afterwards, on June 17, 1900, the foreign admirals, except the American who rightly abstained,[2] seized the Taku forts, gave opportunity to the blind reactionaries to espouse openly the cause of the Boxers, and created a situation in which it was possible for the German minister to be murdered and the legations besieged, and the course of events to pass beyond the control of any Chinese statesman.

When the rebellion first came to a head in the organized attack on government guards on the Peking-Paoting Railway and the destruction of the line, the Grand Secretary had urged the government to take steps to suppress the rebellion.[3] On receiving the edict summoning him to Peking he submitted a memorial on June 20th,[4] repeating his former warning. On the other hand, the very next day he requested the ministers to Great Britain, France, Germany, Russia, and Japan, powers that had taken part in the seizure of Taku, to inform the respective governments of his summons to Peking and to sound them as to two questions: (a) whether they considered a state of war in existence through the hostility at Taku, which he declared was not, so far as China was concerned, by order of the government; and (b) whether they would be ready to suspend hostilities pending his proceeding north to suppress the rebellion first, and then to discuss terms of settlement.[5] Reports came in during the next few days. Japan and

---

[2] See Message of President, *For. Rel.*, 1900, p. xi.

[3] To Liu, 20/5/17, *Tien kao*, 22/20.

[4] To Grand Council, 26/5/24, *ibid.*, 22/26 *l*.

[5] To five ministers, 26/5/25, *ibid.*, 22/28 *l*.

Germany were non-committal on both questions; Great Britain, Russia, and France were favorable to the first but thought the state of affairs in the north such as not to warrant their consideration of the second. As these reports were coming in the Grand Secretary forwarded them to Prince Ching and Yung-lu, members of the Grand Council for submission to the Throne.[6] In forwarding those from London and Tokyo he added:

As matters have come to such a pass, I beseech you at the risk of my life not to let the Tung troops make any silly move. If the legations can be saved, there is still hope of saving the situation: otherwise, I cannot bear to think of the consequences. My coming will not help.

In forwarding the report from Berlin he added:

Until now I have not learned of any edict ordering effective suppression of the Boxers. There is nothing to appease the Powers. Even if I should come, I would not be able to save the situation. Please do something.

In forwarding that from Paris he added:

Report of a foreign source has it that the American consulate [at Tientsin] has been destroyed by shells. It seems that government troops must have taken part. This is what Salisbury referred to when he said " the rebellion is in the ascendency and conditions have been changing ". It seems that the government has no means of suppressing the rebellion. But if the rebellion is not suppressed, the partition of the nation will become a fact. My coming is really useless.

But in forwarding the report from St. Petersburg he added:

[6] To Grand Council via Tsinan, two dated 26/5/26 and two dated 27/5/26, *ibid.*, 32/31 *l.*, 33, 35, and 35, *l.*

Russia has massed troops. If we provoke hostility, ensuing wars will bring about the partition. If we can control the mob and soldiery in time, then, judging by the attitude of Great Britain and Russia, there is still hope of settlement. Please decide and give instructions.

But instructions never came. Instead, on the 27th, the Grand Secretary received the official news of the declaration of war through an imperial edict issued to the viceroys and governors dated the 25th.[7] This meant the victory of the reactionaries over the sane elements, at least for the time being, and he decided to postpone his trip.[8]

The attitude of the coastal and riverine viceroys and governors, as shown in the understanding they established with the Powers, and the excess of the reactionaries — which culminated on June 25th in the invasion of the Palace itself — could not but cause the Empress Dowager to reconsider her decision.[9] On the day the invasion of the Palace took place orders were given that the foreign envoys in Peking be protected. On July 3rd appeals in the name of the Emperor were despatched to various heads of states and an order was issued summoning the Grand Secretary to proceed north " without the slightest delay ".[10] A little later another order was issued, appointing the Grand Secretary to his old post, the viceroyalty of Chihli.[11] On receiving the summons the Grand Secretary embarked for Shanghai on the 18th.[12]

On arriving at Shanghai several days later, the Grand

[7] *Via* Paoting, 26/6/1, *ibid.*, 23/2 *l*.

[8] See also *Ching-shan Diary*, 262, 264, 266.

[9] *Ibid.*, 282.

[10] See from Liu, 26/6/18, *Tien kao*, 23/37; edict *via* Paoting, 26/6/16, *ibid.*, 23/28 *l*.

[11] *Via* Paoting, 26/6/22, *ibid.*, 23/47 *l*.

[12] To five ministers, 26/6/17, *ibid.*, 23/30.

Secretary learnt that Tientsin, the seat of his viceroyalty, and the arsenal there, together with the stock of arms built up since the Japanese War, had fallen into the hands of the allies, leaving him neither the seat to exercise his authority nor the means. Furthermore he found that not only were the reactionaries opposed to him but the entire foreign community, merchants, troops, and missionaries were all hostile. This meant that he would place himself between the devil and the deep sea if he went north, and he decided to proceed no further.

In the meantime the Empress Dowager grew impatient and anxious, and by an edict dated July 23rd, received at Shanghai on the 25th, reprimanded him for delay and ordered him to hurry north by land or sea.[13] Shortly afterwards she repeated her order in reply to one of his memorials.[14] Conditions, however, soon changed for the worse. Throughout the month of July the reactionaries were held more or less in check, but towards the end of the month, perhaps because of the unsettled state of affairs, they gradually got more and more out of control. It was at this time that there occurred the death of Yuan Chang, Hsu Ching-cheng[15] and Chang Yin-huan, the last having been in exile since the *coup d'état* of 1898. The Grand Secretary therefore applied for twenty days' sick leave on August 4th.[16]

The Grand Secretary thus definitely decided to remain at Shanghai, but the situation in the north had to be saved in some way. Prince Ching and Jung-lu had proposed to

---

[13] *Via* Tsinan, 26/6/29, *ibid.*, 23/53; *via* Paoting, 26/6/22, *ibid.*, 23/47 *l.*

[14] *Via* Paoting, 26/7/7, 24/16.

[15] *Ching-shan Diary*, 293.

[16] *Via Tsinan*, 26/7/10, *Tien kao*, 24/19.

the envoys that the latter be safely escorted to Tientsin. This the Grand Secretary considered practical, for it would not only carry out what the Powers were trying to do but would also deprive the reactionaries of the most important lever through which they had control of the situation. He therefore memorialized the Throne on July 27th, urging it to issue specific orders for the safe conduct of the envoys to Tientsin,[17] and on the next day instructed the ministers at London and St. Petersburg to inform the respective governments of the step he had taken and to request them to coöperate by despatching no more troops and by halting the detachments already despatched.[18]

The Court promptly issued the order on August 2nd as requested,[19] and the Grand Secretary instructed the ministers abroad to take up the matter officially with the various governments on the basis of the instructions he had already given to ministers at London and St. Petersburg.[20] The foreign envoys in Peking, however, rejected the overtures of the Chinese government to carry out the imperial order as they did with the proposal of Prince Ching and Yung-lu a little while earlier. Besides, the time was not opportune. The advance from Tientsin had started on August 4th and the Powers were not willing to arrest it.[21] The Grand Secretary, however, did not give up hope. Although the foreign troops had started, he still attempted to halt them on the way at Tungchou.[22] But events now

[17] To Liu, Chang and Yuan, 26/7/4, *ibid.*, 24/6 *l.*

[18] To ministers, London and St. Petersburg, 26/7/5, *ibid.*, 24/7.

[19] *Via* Tsinan, 26/7/10, *ibid.*, 24/19.

[20] To minister, St. Petersburg, 26/7/11, *ibid.*, 24/20/ *l*; to minister, Tokyo, 26/7/11, *ibid.*, 24/20 *l.*

[21] For replies see *Tien kao*, 24, *passim.*

[22] To Lo and Li, 26/7/21, *ibid.*, 24/30 *l.*

moved even faster. On the 14th the foreign troops entered Peking and raised the siege of the legations which they had by their own rash acts precipitated on June 17th.

On the 7th the Court appointed the Grand Secretary plenipotentiary to effect a settlement with the Powers.[23] On receiving the appointment, the Grand Secretary pointed out to the Court that, as it had failed to escort the envoys to Tientsin and to suppress the rebellion itself, the task of appeasing the Powers was beyond his ability, and that when the time came he would have to make request for more colleagues.[24] After the fall of Peking he therefore requested and secured the appointment of Prince Ching, Yung-lu and the viceroys Liu Kun-yi and Chang Chih-tung.[25] On September 1st he received an edict issued by the Court on the way to Taiyuan ordering him to open negotiations speedily with the Powers.[26] He thereupon submitted a long memorial in three parts urging upon the Throne to issue an expiatory edict and to punish the reactionaries.[27] On the 7th he received another edict dated August 24th, granting him " full power ",[28] and five days later he received another dated the 8th granting him all requests either in specific cases or in principle made in his memorial of the 1st.[29] Feeling that he had done everything he could do at the moment the Grand Secretary left Shanghai for Tientsin on the 14th and thence set out on October 3rd for Peking. Owing to objections raised by the Powers Jung-lu was excused. On the other hand, the

[23] *Via Tsinan*, 26/7/15, *ibid.*, 24/23 *l.*
[24] To Grand Council *via* Tsinan, 26/7/17, *ibid.*, 24/26.
[25] To Li, 26/8/2, *ibid.*, 25/4.
[26] To Lo and Li, 26/8/8, *ibid.*, 25/23 *l.*
[27] *Via* Hsian, 26/8/9, *ibid.*, 25/26.
[28] To Li and Yang, 26/8/14, *ibid.*, 25/47 *l.*
[29] To same, 26/8/19, *ibid.*, 26/13.

two Yangtze viceroys, of course, could not leave their respective seats of government. Thus the Grand Secretary and Prince Ching were the only plenipotentiaries in the negotiations with the Powers.

Into the details of the negotiations that settled the Boxer Rebellion with the Powers we will not enter.[30] As might be judged from the attitude of the Grand Secretary revealed above, the Chinese plenipotentaries were prepared to meet all reasonable demands. On the other hand, the Powers had divergent objects in view and were not able to submit their preliminary terms until December 24th. This delay, however, was not all. Within two days the terms were accepted by the Court at Sian, but it yet took more than nine months before the Powers fully recovered their senses and agreed among themselves. It was, therefore, not until September 7, 1901, that the Final Protocol was signed. But neither was this further delay deemed sufficient. By that time all those who were responsible for the disaster had received their full portion of punishment. But for the mad act of these few culprits China was yet made to pay a lump sum of 450,000,000 taels, evidently calculated to absorb for a period of forty years the balance of the revenues of the Chinese Maritime Customs and of the " native customs " under its administration — in other words, what was left over by the Japanese indemnity service — together with the total revenues of the salt gabelle.

Sec. 2. Russian Occupation of Manchuria

At the outbreak of the rebellion Yuan Shih-kai was governor of Shantung. With the energy which had al-

[30] For fuller information see P. H. Clements, *The Boxer Rebellion* (1915, New York); also Morse, *op. cit.*, vol. iii, chap. xii.

ready characterized him in Korea he successfully held the rebellion's southward tendency in check. In the north, however, there was no such able man. Consequently the rebellion spread into Shengking.

At the first sign of trouble in Shengking reported through Russia, the Grand Secretary sent messages to the authorities of the three Manchurian provinces, enjoining upon them the duty of protecting the railways.[31] No reply came from Mukden. As it transpired later, disturbance in that province had then gone beyond control, for not only was the government unable to suppress the rebellion that had spread into that section of the country, but the military lieutenant governor of Shengking also had adopted a policy independent of his superior, the military governor, and sided with the rebels. Replies from Kirin and Heilungkiang came after considerable delay, for telegraphic communication was cut in Shengking as in Chihli. The military governor of Kirin reported that he had already taken measures to protect the railway; that the province was not affected by the rebellion; but that the Russians had massed troops at both ends of the railway with the intention of occupying it. He therefore requested the Grand Secretary to intercede with the Russian foreign ministry to arrest the advance with the assurance that each province would take upon itself the duty of protecting the railway.[32] The military governor of Heilungkiang reported that there were already 20,000 Russian troops along the railway; that in addition there were 80,000 to 90,000 massed on the long frontier ready to march upon him; that he had telegraphed to the Russian government, asking it to arrest the advance

[31] To Sheng, 26/6/4 *ibid.*, 23/7 *l.*; see also Scott to Salisbury, June 29, 1900, *China, No. 3* (1900), p. 93.
[32] To Yang, 26/6/8, *ibid.*, 23/15 *l.*

with the assurance that he would be responsible for the
protection of the railway; and that as he was afraid that
his intercession might not take effect, he had reinforced
the thirty-six battalions under his command with a new
enlistment of fifteen to prepare for the worst.[33]   The
Grand Secretary had both reports communicated to the
Russian government.   The latter, however, refused to stay
the advance of the troops, but said that it had no other
object than the pacification of the disturbance, and that
the troops would be withdrawn as soon as this object was
attained.   It also advised the military governors to co-
operate with, instead of opposing the advance of its troops.
The Grand Secretary had this reply transmitted to the
military governors and advised them " to act in accordance with the dictates of wisdom so that disaster might be
averted ".[34]   In order to show them where the saner fac-
tion of the government stood he also had a copy of the
letter above referred to from the Emperor to the Tzar
forwarded to the military governors.[35]

The advice of the Grand Secretary, if it ever reached
the military governors, arrived too late, for, while the
messages carrying them were despatched from Canton on
July 13th and 14th respectively, hostilities had commenced
in Heilungkiang a few days earlier.   On the 13th, 16th,
and 28th the Grand Secretary successively received three
telegrams from the viceroy Liu at Nanking, transmitting
messages from the military governor of Heilungkiang.
The first telegram [36] merely reported that hostilities had
commenced in Shengking.   The second [37] reported that on

[33] To Yang, 26/6/11, *ibid.*, 23/20 *l.*
[34] From Liu, 26/6/17, *ibid.*, 23/31 *l.*
[35] 26/6/18, *ibid.*, 23/33 *l.*
[36] 26/6/17, *ibid.*, 23/31 *l.*
[37] 26/6/20, *ibid.*, 23/43.

the night of the 11th, the Russian engineer stationed near Tsitsihar had suddenly burnt his own residence and fled to Harbin; that on the very morning the message was despatched several thousand Russian troops came up the Sungari on steamers; and that he had received a telegram alleging attack on his part as cause for the fleeing of the engineer and holding him responsible for the safety of the railway. He added that he would readily face the consequences, but would request the viceroy Liu to give the facts to the press in order that the public might be able to judge for themselves. The third telegram [38] reported that on the 14th hostilities had commenced at Aigun as a result of resisting the landing of Russian soldiers; that he had safely escorted all Russian workers and guards in the cities to Harbin or across the border, but that those in the country refused to leave; that the Russians had seized sixteen cars of silver belonging to the treasury of Kirin and had slaughtered many innocent people in Shengking; that on the 17th they drove five thousand Manchus left by the treaty of Aigun on the northern bank of the Amur into the river and of those only a little over two hundred had escaped death by drowning in the river or suffering slaughter on the bank; and that after the 11th they persecuted Chinese in Harbin, one of the methods employed being burning them alive. He ended with a similar request that the facts be published in newspapers.

In order to appease the Powers the Grand Secretary recommended for punishment all who had resisted them.[39] As a result the part played by the gallant soldier Shou-san, the military governor of Heilungkiang, was not known to

[38] 26/7/3, *ibid.*, 24/5.

[39] To Yang, 26/7/30, *ibid.*, 24/45 *l.*; edict *via* Tsinan, 26/ inter. 8/6, *ibid.*, 27/6.

the world. Whatever we might think of his wisdom in resisting 150,000 Russians with 24,500 men, including 6,500 new recruits, we must say that his gallantry deserved as tall a bronze statue as Muraviev Amursky's. But there is an even more important point which we can not pass unnoticed. The Russian government gave as the occasion for the invasion of Manchuria the unprovoked attack of the Manchu garrison of Aigun upon Blagovchensk. The seriousness of the occasion, of course, pales before the light thrown by the account given in Witte's *Memoirs* and the messages we have just given. In the interest of history it may be permissible to reproduce the account of a Chinese historian of the commencement of hostilities, written, let us add, not at all for foreign consumption. The account is as follows: [40]

On the 15th day of the 7th moon [August 9] Shou-san ordered Feng-hsiang, the deputy military governor at Aigun, to take precautionary measures. On the morning of the 17th when five Russian war vessels and a number of transports were seen coming down the river with troops, Shou-san ordered the troops at Aigun to move out and take up a position at the landing places along the river. Next day the Russian commander brought troops and arms to Aigun, and our commander opened fire to resist them and killed two of their officers. On the 21st the Russians sent mounted troops to the city of Aigun,[41] burning and looting, and Feng-hsiang sent Colonel Wang Chung-liang with three hundred mounted troops across the river to drive them away. This was successful. On the 26th six thousand

[40] *Kuang hsu cheng yao*, 26/17 *l.*

[41] On the trans-Zeya Chinese territory on the left bank of the Amur reserved to Manchu colonists in the treaty of Aigun. It was the original site of Aigun and is given here as "city" for distinction.

Russian troops, mounted and foot, secretly crossed the river at Wu-tao-ho a little above Hei-ho. Next day they entered Aigun.

The disturbance in Shengking could have been easily handled from Port Arthur, and, as events have proved to us, only troops from that point were ever employed for that purpose. The disturbance in one province, however, served as a pretext for the Russians to occupy all three provinces, beginning with the two not affected by rebellion. In spite of assurances given by the authorities of Heilung-kiang and Kirin, which were not materially different from those given by the Yangtze viceroys, they marched 150,000 troops into the two provinces by four routes,[42] from both ends of the railway, from the Sungari, and from Aigun along the post road to Bergen and Tsitsihar. As may be expected from the tone of the reports given above, the military governor of Kirin desisted from offering resistance, but the military governor of Heilungkiang vainly fought the invaders and died with the fall of the capital city, Tsitsihar.

On August 12th, the Russian governor-general of the Amur proclaimed " as having passed under the jurisdiction of Russian authorities the former Manchu territory of the trans-Zeya, the inhabitants of which, according to the stipulations of the treaty of Aigun, have hitherto remained under Chinese authority, as also the Manchu territory occupied by our toops on the right bank of the Amur river ",[43] presumably to as far as the watershed.[44] On

[42] General Kuropatkin, *The Russian Army and the Japanese War* (London, 1909), vol. i, p. 155.

[43] Extract from the *Amur Gazette* of August 4 (17), 1900, *China, No. 5* (1901), p. 14.

[44] See extract from the *Journal de Saint Petersbourg* of Sept. 19 (Oct. 2), 1900, *ibid.*, p. 15.

September 7th, " on the Chinese bank of the Amur, on the burned ashes of Sakalin, a solemn thanksgiving service in memory of the relief [capture?] of this place by the Russian forces together with the ceremony of renaming the post Ilinsky, was held. . . . The High Priest Konoploff said ' now is the cross raised on that bank of the Amur which yesterday was Chinese. Mouravieff foretold that sooner or later this bank would be ours ' ".[45]

In Shengking, the place where trouble actually occurred, the Russians on the contrary did very little at that time. In the early part of July the railway employees and guards gradually retreated to a point called Ta-shih-chiao, where a temporary branch line begins which connects Yingkou with the South Manchurian line. There towards the end of the month they began to provoke trouble with Yingkou and on August 4th took it by force.[46] After the relief of the legations, when military operations were really no longer necessary, the Russians proceeded with their plan of occupation. On September 24th they entered New-chwang,[47] and within a short space of time they had occupied all the towns along the Southern Manchurian branch of the Chinese Eastern Railway and the extra-mural section of the North China Railways. In Shengking as in Kirin the military governor offered no resistance.[48]

[45] Extract from the *Novoe Vremya* of September 2, 1900, *China, No. 1* (1901), p. 184.

[46] For details see Fulford to Salisbury, Aug. 13, 1900, *ibid.*, p. 190.

[47] Correspondence, Newchwang, *Herald,* Oct. 17, 1900.

[48] Letter from military governor of Shengking, enclosed in to Grand Council, 26/9/19, *Tien kao*, 28/33. On the conduct of the Russians in Newchwang see Witte's *Memoirs, op. cit.,* 107–114.

Sec. 3. The Question of Evacuation

Shortly after the outbreak of the Boxer Rebellion and the despatch of large Russian forces from Port Arthur to Tientsin, Muraviev died and the direction of Russia's Far Eastern policy passed mainly into the hands of Witte. Probably because of Muraviev's death, diplomatic Russia showed her correct attitude towards China throughout the crisis in spite of the acts of the military men in Manchuria. Before the relief of the legations, it was Russia alone who replied favorably to the proposal of the Grand Secretary to escort the envoys to Tientsin, and instructed M. N. de Giers, her minister to China, to act accordingly.[49] After that event it was again Russia alone who first acted upon the request of the Grand Secretary to withdraw the relieving forces from Peking,[50] and then took the initiative of inquiring whether the Powers would not follow her example of withdrawing her legation and troops to Tientsin or recognize the full powers of the Grand Secretary and Prince Ching and enter into negotiations with them.[51] Some of these acts, such as the recognition of the full powers of the Grand Secretary and Prince Ching, which, it may be observed, was similar to the step taken by the United States,[52] were salutary. Some of them, such as the withdrawal of legations and troops from Peking, which was belated on account of the rapid shifting of circumstances, caused difficulty instead of bringing help to China.[53] But all was evidently done in the right direction.

[49] To Grand Council, *via Tsinan*, 26/7/19, *Tien kao*, 24/27 *l.*

[50] To Liu and Chang, 26/8/6, *ibid.*, 25/15 *l.*; Salisbury to Scott, Aug. 28, 1900, *China, No. 1* (1909), p. 113.

[51] *For. Rel.*, 1901, app. p. 23; *China, No. 1* (1901), p. 172.

[52] Hill to Wu, Sept. 21, 1900, *For. Rel.*, 1900, p. 293.

[53] To Yang, 26/inter. 8/11, *Tien kao*, 27/14 *l.*

The question of Manchuria though forming fundamentally a part of the bigger problem was, for the simple reason that it involved only Russia, susceptible of separate treatment. Therefore, while the Powers were unwilling or unable to enter into negotiations with him, the Grand Secretary naturally took up the Manchurian question with Giers, the Russian minister at Peking. The Grand Secretary, however, soon found that Giers [54] who, in addition to his training in the last three years in the school of Muraviev, had come through the unpleasant experience of the siege of the legations, was not the kind of man with whom he could discuss the matter.[55] He therefore readily availed himself of the offer of Giers himself to transfer the negotiations to St. Petersburg, and recommended to the Court the appointment of Yang Yu, Chinese minister to Russia, as plenipotentiary with full powers for the purpose, which the Court did in the first days of 1901.[56]

In the negotiations that followed, Russia, for practical purposes, was represented by Witte. If one expected, however, to see a continuation of the policy at first so happily resumed in the early days of the Boxer Rebellion, this hope was doomed to be disappointed.

In his *Memoirs*, Witte has laid all blame for the occupation of Kirin and Heilungkiang — provinces that were not affected by rebellion at all — on General Kuropatkin, his colleague in the ministry of war. In view of the fact that Kuropatkin was a mere militarist, what Witte said of

[54] For Giers see to Yang 26/10/28, *ibid.*, 29/29 *l.*

[55] On several occasions the Grand Secretary attempted to have men not prejudiced by the siege appointed plenipotentiaries by the Powers. The appointment of W. W. Rockhill speaks highly for the calibre of the men of the McKinley administration.

[56] To Grand Council 20/11/10, *ibid.*, 30/16; from Grand Council *via* Shanghai, 26/11/13, *ibid.*, 30/21 *l.*

him is believable. Witte, however, after all an opportunist as we have remarked before, now did not fail to
reap the result of what he had just condemned in his
military colleague.[57]

The Russian terms for the evacuation of Manchuria
were drawn up in twelve articles. As transmitted in sum-
mary by Yang Yu to the Grand Secretary on February 16,
1901 [58] they were as follows: Claims for damages against
China for the destruction of the railway line, for the loss
of property belonging to the railway administration and its
employes, and for delay in carrying on the construction
of the line, — all this was to be kept apart from the settle-

[57] It is interesting to note that, throughout Witte's *Memoirs* we
cannot discover the slightest trace of a reference to the all-important
negotiations he had with the Chinese minister at St. Petersburg.
Could he have failed to realize the significance of the steps he
took in those negotiations, or have forgotten about them altogether
when he came to write his *Memoirs?* Witte was an opportunist
through and through. He had utilized the triple intervention to
project the Trans-Siberian Railway across northern Manchuria; he
had utilized the seizure of Port Arthur to extend the Chinese Eastern
Railway to Talienwan. He now attempted to utilize the occupation
of Manchuria to convert extra-mural China into an exclusive
Russian sphere of influence. If he can defend himself in the first
instance, that the measure was also beneficial to China in view of
the Japanese menace which the two nations were facing in common,
and in the second instance that the measure was a natural sequence to the lease of Port Arthur, what has he to say in the last
instance when the measure was not only neither beneficial to China
nor a natural sequence to the occupation of Manchuria, but was
also both opposed by all the Powers and running counter to the
declared Russian policy of maintaining the *status quo?* Witte is
no better than Muraviev and Kuropatkin, the very men he condemned in his *Memoirs*. He may be more clever, for he knew how
to cover himself up and let others take the blame.

[58] To Grand Council, 27/1/2, 32/11 *l*. For a more or less
accurate translation see *China, No. 6* (1901), p. 110.

ment which Russia would make with China in concert with the Powers, and was to form the subject of a separate arrangement between China and the railway administration.[59] These claims as well as others might by agreement with the administration be commuted either in part or in whole for other privileges including the revision of the railway contract in favor of the administration;[60] but China was first to admit in principle that Russia had the right of constructing a line from either the Chinese Eastern Railway or the Southern Manchurian branch in the direction of Peking up to the Great Wall,[61] or, in other words, she was to sell the extra-mural section of the North China Railways no matter whether she would commute the claims or not. As to privileges besides those mentioned, these remained, of course, indefinite, but an idea may be obtained from a conversation Yang had with Witte a month before[62] in which Witte undertook to tell him confidentially the terms Russia intended to ask from China. There the privileges were given as the exclusive employment of Russians in the customs service in Manchuria; exemption from *likin* of goods imported by land; monthly instead of semi-annual payment of interest on the Franco-Russian loan of 1895; and non-redemption of the Chinese Eastern Railway and its extension before the final payment of claims.

As to evacuation, this was to take place only when order in Manchuria was restored and the terms concerning the claims had all been carried out.[63] China was first to agree not to station an army in those provinces before the completion of the railway line and its opening to traffic; to consult with Russia as to the strength of the troops she

[59] Arts. ix and x.   [60] Art. xi.   [61] Art. xii.
[62] To Grand Council, 26/12/3, *Tien kao*, 31/3 *l.* [63] Art. ii.

might subsequently wish to station there; to prohibit importation of munitions of war into Manchuria; to deprive of office any high official, on representations being made by Russia, " whose conduct of affairs may prove antagonistic to the maintenance of friendly relations "; to consult with Russia as to the strength of the police force and to exclude artillery from its armament and subjects of other powers from its service.[64]

These points were not all. In addition to the right to build a railway in the direction of Peking up to the Great Wall, China was to grant other concessions. These were non-employment of subjects of other powers in the military and naval services in " northern China ";[65] modification of the provision in the convention of May 7, 1898, governing the neutral zone in the Liaotung peninsula, including the abolition of the administration of police in the city of Kinchou hitherto reserved to China;[66] withholding from other powers and their subjects, without the consent of Russia, privileges with regard to mines, railways or other matters in regions co-terminous with Russia such as Mongolia and the sections of Sinkiang known as Tarbagatai, Ili, Kashgar, Yarkand, and Khotan; non-construction of any railway by China herself in the same regions without the consent of Russia; and non-granting to subjects of other powers of leases of land in Manchuria outside of Newchwang.[67]

The Russian terms were highly embarrassing for the Chinese government. Liability to pay indemnity had been admitted by China from the very beginning,[68] and guaran-

---

[64] Arts. iv and v.   [65] Art. vi.   [66] Art. vii.   [67] Art. viii.

[68] Art. ii of draft of a preliminary convention submitted to the Powers by the Chinese delegation on Oct. 15, 1900, *China, No. 5* (1901), p. 39; *For. Rel.*, 1901, app., p. 40.

tees for the future formed an important feature of the French note which led to final settlement,[69] but the principle of compensation for the evacuation had neither been admitted by China nor claimed by the Powers. Other considerations apart, if China were to concede this she would naturally invite the Powers to change their attitude on this point, which might lead to the inclusion of similar demands in the general settlement or, even worse, to some episode like the scramble of 1898.[70]

On the movements of Russia in Manchuria Japan cast an anxious eye. As soon as she learned of the appointment of Yang Yu as plenipotentiary, she came out and inquired of Russia as to the nature of the arrangement, and at the same time asked Great Britain to join her in the matter.[71] In Great Britain Japan found a natural ally in the question of Manchuria, as it appears that through the coöperation of Great Britain pressure from all the leading Powers was also brought to bear upon China. Between February 15th and 22nd the Grand Secretary received separate advices from Japan, Great Britain, Germany, Italy, Austria-Hungary, and the United States, to the effect that no arrangement affecting territorial rights in the Chinese Empire ought to be concluded between the Chinese government and any one of the Powers separately.[72]

[69] *China, No. 5* (1901), p. 5; *For. Rel.*, 1901, app., p. 26.

[70] See to Grand Council, 27/1/7, *Tien kao*, 32/17; to Yang, 27/1/13, *ibid.*, 23/28.

[71] Lansdowne to MacDonald, Jan. 12, 1901, *China, No. 6* (1901), p. 11.

[72] From Li, 26/12/27, *Tien kao*, 31/46; to Grand Council, 26/12/29, *ibid.*, 31/47 *l.*; from Wu and reply, 27/1/4, *ibid.*, 32/9 *l.*; Lansdowne to MacDonald, Feb. 13, 1901, *China, No. 6* (1901), p. 41. See also Lansdowne to MacDonald, Feb. 5, 1901, *China, No. 2* (1904), p. 4; Memo. submitted to Eckardstein by

In reporting the conversation he had with Witte, to which we have already referred, Yang Yu commented upon the ambition of Russia and the possibility of complications with other Powers, and advised that the matter be dropped quietly without further pressure. This advice was endorsed by the Grand Secretary [73] and accepted by the Court, [74] and for one month Yang did not again broach this subject with the Russian government. On receiving the advice from Japan which came the earliest, the Grand Secretary immediately directed Yang to arrange with the Russian government to have the affairs of Manchuria discussed as a part of the questions then being taken up in Peking. [75] The instructions, however, reached St. Petersburg after the Russian terms given above were handed to Yang, who therefore thought it not expedient to do as directed. [76] Consequently, the Grand Secretary on the one hand obtained from the Court new instructions for Yang [77] to negotiate with the Russian government on the basis of the Russian terms, and on the other hand directed the ministers to the United States, Great Britain, Japan, and Germany to ask the Powers to withdraw their opposition. [78] In order to facilitate Yang's negotiations the Grand Secretary also disclosed to Giers the main features of China's objection. [79]

Lansdowne, Feb. 7, 1901, *ibid.*, p. 9; Lansdowne to Lascelles, Feb. 12, 1901, *ibid.*, p. 6; Choate to Lansdowne, Mar. 2, 1901, *ibid.*, p. 9.

[73] To Grand Council, 26/12/3, *Tien kao*, 31/3 *l.*

[74] From Grand Council *via* Shanghai, 26/12/11, *ibid.*, 31/12.

[75] To Yang, 26/12/28, *ibid.*, 31/47.

[76] To Grand Council, 27/1/6, 32/15 *l.*

[77] To Yang, transmitting edict, 27/1/13, *ibid.*, 32/28.

[78] To Wu, Li, and Lu, 27/1/10, *ibid.*, 32/22; also Lansdowne to Satow, Mar. 2, 1901, *China, No. 6* (1901), p. 105.

[79] To Grand Council, 27/1/7, *Tien kao*, 32/17.

Negotiations went on swiftly in St. Petersburg, and on March 15th the Grand Secretary received the substance of the modifications Russia was willing to make.[80] In the question of indemnity it was added that in the arrangement to be made between China and the railway administration the principle agreed upon by the representatives of the Powers and approved by their governments was to be adopted. In the question of guaranties, the terms as modified would read as follows:

For protecting the construction and operation of the Chinese Eastern Railway and for preserving peace on the Russian border, China shall consult with Russia as to the strength of troops and the number of military posts to be maintained in Manchuria. Prohibition of the importation of munitions of war into Manchuria shall be enforced in accordance with the provisions of the treaty to be concluded with the Powers. In the meantime China shall prohibit this herself.

With a view to safeguarding the interests of the territory in question, China shall, on representations being made to Russia, at once transfer any military governor or other high official, whose conduct of affairs may prove antagonistic to the maintenance of friendly relations. A police force, consisting of mounted and unmounted units, may be organized in the interior of Manchuria. Its numbers shall be determined after consultation with Russia, and before order is completely restored artillery shall be excluded from its armament. Only Chinese subjects shall be employed in connection therewith.

In the question of compensation, the articles on the employment of foreigners in military and naval services in

[80] To Grand Council, 27/1/25, *ibid.*, 33/15 *l.* Also *China, No. 6* (1901), p. 134.

" northern China " and on the new rearrangement concerning the neutral zone were dropped; the article on the construction of a railway to the Great Wall was retained but made more specific by substituting " at the point where Chihli and Manchuria meet " for " in the direction of Peking "; and that concerning concessions was modified to apply only to Manchuria instead of the entire Chinese border coterminous with Russia, and was made to read as follows:

China shall not, without previous consultation with Russia, grant to other powers, or the subjects thereof, privileges of railway construction, mining, and all industrial and commercial matters anywhere in Manchuria.

The Grand Secretary considered the terms as modified the best he could obtain under the circumstances, and thought that, with certain reservations as well as certain modifications in language, China ought to accept them.[81] In the meantime, however, Japan and Great Britain had made their intervention a factor in the decision of the Court. Failing to influence it through the plenipotentiaries at Peking they had worked successfully through the Yangtze viceroys whose counsel the Court could not ignore in view of the part they played during the Boxer Rebellion. But the intervention of Japan and Great Britain had not been effective with China alone. It also worked well on Russia, though in a different way. Fearing that she might be placed in an embarrassing situation in case China finally declined to accept the terms, she limited the time for accepting them to a fortnight and, worse still, refused to consider any new overtures from China in the meantime. Between the hesitation of the Court and the determination

[81] To Yang, 27/1/26, *Tien kao,* 33/20.

of Russia, nothing was possible and the terms thus lapsed with the fortnight without the signature of Yang.[82] [83]

In the general negotiations with the Powers Russian claims arising out of Manchuria were settled like any other claims, but the question of evacuation was not touched upon. After the Final Protocol of September 7, 1901, the question was taken up by the Grand Secretary, as president of the newly created Board of Foreign Affairs, with the Russian minister at Peking. The question of indemnity having been settled, what remained to be discussed were those of guaranties and compensation. In view of what the Powers had exacted — such as the maintenance of legation guards and the garrisoning of the road to the sea — Russia could not be persuaded to forego all she had demanded concerning guaranties. As to compensation, she had no precedent to cite, and she was willing to leave what remained of her demands in the revised terms reviewed above to be discussed between the Chinese government and the Russo-Chinese Bank.[84] However, on November 7th, before anything could be definitely settled, the Grand Secretary, who by that time was literally worn out, died, aged seventy-nine.

With the death of the Grand Secretary, China lost the only man who could control the situation, and for the

[82] See correspondence, *ibid.*, bks. 33 and 34; also *China, No. 6* (1901) *passim.*

[83] For the much talked of but comparatively insignificant Tseng-Alexiev convention see from Tseng-chi, 26/12/18, *Tien kao*, 31/25; from Tseng-chi, even date, *ibid.*, 31/26 *l.*; *China, No. 6* (1901), p. 72.

[84] Board of Foreign Affairs to Liu and Chang, 27/12/27, *Tiao yo, K.*, 67/4; Conger to Hay, Dec. 3, 1901, *For. Rel.*, 1902, p. 271; same to same, Dec. 12, 1901, *ibid.*, p. 272; same to same, Jan. 29, 1902, *ibid.*, p. 273.

developments of the next five years we have to go out of China to look for the guiding force.

Sec. 4. " Special Interests " versus Chinese Integrity

On July 2, 1900, while most of the Powers seemed to be only marking time, Delcassé, minister of foreign affairs of France, instructed French representatives in St. Petersburg, London, Berlin, Vienna, Washington, and Rome to submit to the respective governments the proposal that these governments should send identical instructions to the commanders of their forces in Chihli, inquiring as to the number of troops they judged indispensable to accomplish their mission. In submitting this consideration for common action he prefaced his instructions with the following:

From the beginning of the Chinese crisis there has been an understanding among the Powers on three points:

First, the rescue of their representatives and nationals in Peking and in the rest of the Empire;
Second, the maintenance of territorial *status quo;*
Third, the demand for effective guarantees against the recurrence of the disasters which they have rightly deplored and may still dread.[85]

The French proposal brought forth no definite result; [86] but, it seems, it gave occasion for the celebrated circular of John Hay of July 3rd,[87] announcing to all governments diplomatically represented at Peking the attitude, purposes, and policy of the United States. In this circular Hay

[85] *Chine* (1899–1900) (French Yellow Papers), p. 61.
[86] See Delcassé to Harmond, July 5, 1900, Delcassé to de Montebello, July 5, 1900, *ibid.,* p. 71.
[87] Hay to Thiebaut, July 3, 1900, *ibid.,* p. 64; *For. Rel.,* 1900, p. 299; app. p. 12.

stated that the United States regarded the condition at Peking as one of virtual anarchy, in which power and responsibility practically devolved upon the local provincial authorities; that they would act concurrently with the other powers in opening up communication with Peking, in protecting American life, property, and legitimate interests in China, and in coöperating to prevent a spread of disorders and their recurrence; and that she would seek —

a solution which may bring about permanent safety and peace to China, preserve Chinese territorial and administrative entity, protect all rights guaranteed to friendly powers by treaty and international law, and safeguard for the world the principle of equal and impartial trade with all parts of the Chinese Empire.

When in the latter part of the month W. W. Rockhill, a person well versed in Chinese affairs, was sent as special commissioner to China, to examine and report on the situation,[88] he was directed to be guided by the foregoing circular with regard to policy.[89]   Later, on August 8th, when the American *chargé d'affaires* at Berlin inquired, on the solicitation of the German government, whether the United States would put her forces under the chief command of Field Marshal Count von Waldersee, the United States accepted the proposal with the declaration that such was for "attaining the purposes declared by this government in the circular note delivered to the Powers under date of July 3".[90] [91]

The power next in stating its views was Russia.   She made the statement in connection with her belated attempt

[88] *For. Rel.*, 1900, p. 156.
[89] Hay to Rockhill, July 27, 1900, *ibid.*, p. 157.
[90] Adee to Jackson, Aug. 10, 1900, *ibid.*, p. 331.
[91] See *Moore*, v, 481 *et seq.*

to meet the request of the Grand Secretary that the legations be withdrawn to Tientsin. In the circular note she addressed to the Powers on August 8th she declared that she had no designs of territorial acquisition in China; that, equally with the other powers, she had sought the safety of the legations at Peking and to help the Chinese government to repress the trouble; that incidental to necessary defensive measures on the Russian border, she had occupied Newchwang for military purposes, and " as soon as order is re-established will retire troops therefrom if the action of other powers be no obstacle thereto ".[92]

The occupation of Newchwang referred to in the note had taken place four days previously, but it formed only the beginning of the campaign for the occupation of Shengking, which Russia carried out in the following fortnight. This, accomplished after the Boxer Rebellion was practically over, coupled with the occupation of Kirin and Heilungkiang which, like the rest of the empire outside Chihli, Shansi, and Shengking, were not involved in the rebellion, could not but arouse universal suspicion as to Russia's ulterior motives, in spite of her outward declaration.

On October 16, 1900, therefore, there appeared an Anglo-German agreement.[93] By this agreement the two contracting powers were to uphold the principle that " the ports on the rivers and littoral of China should remain free and open " to the nationals of all countries " for all Chinese territory as far as they can exercise influence "; to abstain from making use of the existing complications to obtain for themselves any territorial advantages in Chinese dominions and to direct their policy towards maintaining undiminished the territorial condition of the Chinese Em-

[92] *For. Rel.*, 1901, app., p. 19; *China, No. 1* (1901), p. 113.
[93] *MacMurray*, i, 263.

pire; to come to a preliminary understanding as to the eventual steps to be taken for the protection of their own interests in China in case of another power's not so abstaining; and to invite Austria-Hungary, France, Italy, Japan, Russia, and the United States to accept these principles.

When, however, the question of Manchuria came up, Count von Bülow, the German Chancellor, declared to the Reichstag that the agreement was in no sense concerned with Manchuria.[94]   Great Britain, however, was not to travel alone after Germany parted company with her.   On July 30, 1902, when less than a year had elapsed, there transpired an Anglo-Japanese alliance.[95]   In the treaty of alliance the two contracting powers " having in view . . . their special interests, of which those of Great Britain relate principally to China, while Japan, in addition to the interests which she possesses in China, is interested in a peculiar degree politically as well as commercially and industrially in Korea, . . . recognize that it will be admissible for either of them to take such measures as may be indispensable in order to safeguard those interests if threatened either by the aggressive action of any other powers, or by disturbances arising in China or Korea, and necessitating the intervention of either . . . for the protection of the lives and property of its subjects ".[96]   If either, in doing so, "should become involved in war with another power, the other . . . will maintain a strict neutrality, and use its efforts to prevent other powers from joining in hostilities

[94] Lascelles to Lansdowne, March 16, 1900, *China, No. 6* (1901), p. 131.

[95] *MacMurray*, i, 324. On the negotiations see A. M. Pooley, ed., *The Secret Memoirs of Count Tadasu Hayashi* (New York, 1915), pp. 115–199.   [96] Art. i.

against the ally" and, should another power or powers join in hostilities against that ally, " come to its assistance, . . . conduct the war in common, and make peace in mutual agreement ".[97] They also agreed to enter into no agreement with another power to the prejudice of the interests above described without consulting each other, and to communicate with each other " fully and frankly " when those interests were in jeopardy.[98] The treaty was to remain in force for five years and remain binding automatically for another year unless it was denounced one year before the expiration of the five-year term, or until the conclusion of peace in case either ally was engaged in war.[99]

In reply to the Anglo-Japanese treaty of alliance, Russia in concert with France declared that they " reserve to themselves the right to consult . . . as to the means to be adopted " in case " either the aggressive action of a third Power, or the recurrence of disturbances in China, jeopardizing the integrity and free development of that Power, might become a menace to their own interests ".[100]

What actually took place between the Japanese and the Chinese foreign offices after the formation of the Anglo-Japanese alliance we have no means of knowing at present. But judging by what Japan did when she had only the moral backing of Great Britain we can easily imagine what she would do now that she had the support of an alliance. There is no doubt that as soon as she was sure of her ground she immediately — of course, in concert with Great Britain — started to intervene more actively. Whatever this intervention may have been, we see that Prince Ching, who was reported, when he took over the negotiations after the death of the Grand Secretary, to be in favor of

---

[97] Arts. ii and iii. [99] Art. vi.
[98] Arts. iv and v. [100] *MacMurray*, i, 325.

accepting the Russian terms more or less as they had virtually been agreed to by the Grand Secretary, was now reported by the beginning of March to have declined to entertain the idea of an agreement with the Russo-Chinese Bank and stood for limiting the application of the term of the guarantees to the period before evacuation.[101] Furthermore, we see also a fundamental change in Russia's attitude towards the matter. She no longer insisted upon the severe terms objected to by China and gracefully signed the convention of April 8, 1902, without them.[102]

By the terms of this convention Russia was to evacuate Manchuria in three periods of six months each — first, the southwestern portion of Shengking up to the Liao; then, the remainder of that province and the whole of Kirin; and finally, the province of Heilungkiang.[103] She was also to restore the extra-mural section of the North China Railways as the territory it traversed was evacuated. China engaged, on the other hand, in addition to other things, to discuss with Russia, " should in the course of time extension of the line in Southern Manchuria or construction of branch lines in connection with it, or the erection of a bridge in Newchwang, or the moving of the terminus there, be undertaken ".[104]

Fate, however, decreed that Russia should not be consistent in this wise measure of retreating from her untenable position in Manchuria in the face of a solid front of opposition presented by Japan and Great Britain. The evacuation of the southwestern portion of Shengking and the restoration of the railway therein were carried out on time, but, when the time came for the restoration of the

---

[101] Conger to Hay, March 4, 1902, *For. Rel.*, 1902, p. 277.

[102] *MacMurray*, i, 362.

[103] Art. ii.   [104] Art. iv.

remainder of Shengking and the whole of Kirin, her policy, through the influence, it seems, of those interested in a timber concession on the Yalu river, suddenly underwent a change.[105] The second stage of the evacuation, which was due to end on April 8, 1903, was suddenly stopped by order of Admiral Alexiev. An Imperial Lieutenancy was created by an ukase on April 13th out of the Russian Amur region, the leased territory of Port Arthur and Talienwan and presumably the so-called railway zone of the Chinese Eastern Railway, and Admiral Alexiev was put in control as Imperial Lieutenant of all this region, invested with full administrative powers, the command of naval and military forces and the control of diplomatic relations of the Lieutenancy with neighboring states, in the exercise of all of which he was subject only to the control of a special committee presided over by the Tzar himself.[106] On the 18th de Plançon, Russian *chargé d'affaires* at Peking, presented a note to Prince Ching with seven demands as conditions precedent to further evacuation. These were as follows: (1) the restored territories, in particular Newchwang and localities on the Liao river, were under no circumstances to be transferred to another power; (2) the existing administrative system in Mongolia was not to be altered; (3) new ports in Manchuria were not to be opened, nor consuls admitted without previously informing Russia; (4) foreigners other than Russians were not to be employed in administrative matters in Manchuria and Mongolia; (5) the existing telegraphic line between Port Arthur, Yingkou, and Mukden was to be retained by Russia; (6) the Russo-Chinese

[105] On the Yalu timber concession see Kuropatkin, *op. cit.*, ii, 306–313.

[106] Scott to Lansdowne, Aug. 13, 1903, *China, No. 2* (1904), p. 84; Spring-Rice to Lansdowne, Oct. 14, 1903, *ibid.*, p. 90.

Bank was to be kept as customs bank at Newchwang after the evacuation of the Russians, and finally (7) a sanitary committee at Newchwang was to be appointed to carry on the work of a sanitary board already established there by the Russians.[107]

The foregoing demands of the Far Eastern Lieutenancy were evidently more extreme than the Russian government was prepared to back up. When they became known to the world, Count Lamsdorv, foreign minister of Russia, as well as Russian representatives abroad, except Plançon, categorically denied their existence, and even Plançon tried to cover them up by assuring his British colleague that "the delay in evacuation was due to the military party in Russia".[108]

When the terms were rejected by the Chinese government, Russia, instead of pressing for them, merely presented a note asking to be assured of certain alleged reports that China contemplated a cession of territory in the Liao river region to some power; that China intended to assimilate the administration of Mongolia to the system in force in the provinces; and that China was to give permission for the appointment of foreign consuls to other places in Manchuria than to Newchwang. To this note Prince Ching replied that "there had never been any question of ceding territory in the Liao river district to a foreign power; that the question of altering the administrative system of Mongolia was not under consideration for the present, as, al-

[107] For text see *For. Rel.*, 1903, p. 56.

[108] Hay to Conger, April 29, 1903, *For. Rel.*, 1903, p. 54; Scott to Lansdowne, April 28, 1903, *China, No. 2* (1904), p. 58; Herbert to Lansdowne, April 29, 1903, *ibid.*, p. 59; Scott to Lansdowne, April 29, 1903, *ibid.*, p. 59; Townley to Lansdowne, April 30, 1903, *ibid.*, p. 61.

though the matter had been discussed, the Throne had refused its assent; and that the extent of the development of the trade of Manchuria could alone decide the question of the opening of treaty ports, and the appointment of foreign consuls would probably result therefrom ".[109] Later a similarly worded question respecting the employment of foreign advisers in Manchuria was also put to the Prince, who replied that " in Manchuria no foreign advisers are employed at present ".[110]   In speaking to his British colleague about the reply of the Prince to the first three questions, Plançon said he thought " the explanations given would suffice to allay their [the military party's] anxiety ". He also added that in his opinion Newchwang would shortly be evacuated.

The new Russian retreat appeared to be quite sincere. On May 2nd the British consul at Newchwang reported to his government that, with the exception of Fenghuang and Liaoyang, Russian troops were all withdrawn from the province of Shengking.[111]   On May 20th Sir Claude MacDonald reported from Tokyo that, " from the latest information ", on or about May 8th a party of sixty Russians, eighty Koreans, and forty Chinese settled down at a small village called Yong-am-po on the left bank of the Yalu and near its mouth, with the proclaimed purpose of establishing a station in connection with a timber concession they had secured from the Korean government.[112]   On July 11th he again reported that, according to the latest accounts, there were no Russian troops on the Yalu with the exception of a small guard at the mouth, looking after

[109] Townley to Lansdowne, April 30, 1903, *ibid.*, p. 61.
[110] Townley to Lansdowne, May 8, 1903, *ibid.*, p. 67.
[111] Same to same, May 5, 1903, *ibid.*, p. 65.
[112] MacDonald to Lansdowne, May 20, 1903, *ibid.*, p. 76.

the men employed on the timber concession.[113] Nor do we hear any more of the demands except the one respecting the opening of ports. This last demand was made as a result of the attempt of the United States to induce the Chinese government to open Mukden, Antung, and Harbin. Even this demand soon was dropped when the United States waived its request as to Harbin for future negotiations.[114]

While metamorphosing what were originally garbed as demands into inquiries, Russia also hurried P. M. Lessar, minister to China, back to Peking, and at the same time sent General Kuropatkin out to the Far East to study the situation on the spot. On his mission General Kuropatkin first visited Japan, and there he met with the " most cordial and kind-hearted reception " and " became convinced that the government [of Japan] desired to avoid a rupture with Russia, but that it would be necessary for us [the Russians] to act in a perfectly definite way in Manchuria, and to refrain from interference in the affairs of Korea ".[115] Then he held a council at Port Arthur attended by Admiral Alexiev, Lessar, minister to China, Pavloff, minister to Korea, and several others, including the promoter of the Yalu timber concession. In this council they agreed on July 2nd and 3rd that the occupation of the whole of Korea, or even of the northern part, and the annexation of Manchuria, would be unprofitable and therefore undesirable. As to the Yalu Timber Company, they decided on the 7th on " at once taking measures to give the affair an

---

[113] Same to same, June 11, 1903, *ibid.*, p. 80.

[114] Conger to Hay, June 18, 1903, *For. Rel.*, 1903, p. 65; Lansdowne to Scott, July 11, 1903, *China, No. 2* (1904), p. 79; Hay to Conger, July 14, 1903, *For. Rel.*, 1903, p. 67; Conger to Hay, Aug. 14, 1903, *ibid.*, p. 71.

[115] Kuropatkin, *op. cit.*, vol. i, p. 175.

exclusively commercial character, to exclude from it officers
of the regular army, and to commit the management of the
timber business to persons not employed in the service of the
empire ". As to the Chinese Eastern Railway, one of those
attending the council was entrusted with working out a
policy to reduce the deficit on that line, keeping in view the
effect such policy might have on the economic situation of
Amursk.[116]

Kuropatkin tells us himself that he expressed the opinion
before the Boxer Rebellion that northern Manchuria had
greater value to Russia than southern and its control was
less likely to lead to " misunderstanding " with China and
complications with Japan,[117] and that he submitted memoranda on the Manchurian question once on October 28th
and once on December 6th, advocating the termination of
military occupation of southern Manchuria and the confinement of Russian activity to the northern part of the
country.[118] After the council at Port Arthur what is told
by Kuropatkin seems on the whole to have been the Russian
policy.

The demands of April 18th, though having an application wider than Manchuria, related essentially to southern
Manchuria. We have seen that they were not afterwards
pressed. In their place Russia submitted sometime in the
autumn a new series of six demands. First of all, China
was to declare that she would neither alienate any part of
Manchuria to another power, nor grant land for the purpose of foreign settlements. Next, she was to give permission to Russia (a) to establish landing stages on the
Sungari, to connect them by telegraph and to station Russian troops for their protection; (b) to establish post stations
along the road from Tsitsihar to Blagovestchensk. In ad-

[116] *Ibid.*, 181-3. [117] *Ibid.*, 160-164. [118] *Ibid.*, 188-193.

dition she was to grant the same special treatment in the matter of import duties to goods brought into Manchuria by rail as had been accorded to goods transported by road or river. Finally China was (a) to undertake after the evacuation the protection of the branches of the Russo-Chinese Bank with Chinese troops at the expense of the bank, and (b) to appoint a Russian doctor to the sanitary board at Newchwang. On these conditions, the note added, Russia would withdraw from Newchwang and other places in Shengking on October 8th, from Kirin " at the expiration of four months, and from Heilungkiang at the end of one year ".[119]

According to the report of the British minister from whom we quote, the Chinese government was not at all unprepared to discuss the demands in order to end the trouble. Of these demands, the two most important were those relating to the establishment of landing stages on the Sungari with troops to protect them, and to post stations along the road from Tsitsihar to the Amur. China objected to the establishment of post stations on the ground that such would duplicate what were already in existence. But she was willing to entertain the idea of establishing stages along the Sungari provided Russia would not insist upon protecting these with troops. Negotiations, however, were before long interrupted by Japanese armed intervention.

Sec. 5. Special Interests in Conflict

After the war of 1894–5 there was no longer any suzerain power in the way of Japan in Korea, and she therefore proceeded to " reform " the latter until the queen was murdered, the king, or rather emperor, fled to the Rus-

[119] Satow to Lansdowne, Sept. 10, 1903, *China, No. 2* (1904), p. 93.

sian legation and Japan herself had to accept whatever terms Russia chose to dictate. By one agreement, dated May 14, 1896, between the representatives of the two powers at Seoul, Japan undertook to restrain her political bravoes in exchange for the earlier return of the king, and to limit with Russia the number of guards to be maintained in Korea.[120] By another, dated June 9th of the same year, between Marquis Yamagata and Prince Lobanov, she agreed to come to a common accord on the question of rendering financial assistance to Korea and to abstain with her from meddling with the Korean army and police force.[121]

If Japan had previously lost through her own folly, she was soon to profit by the folly of others. When Russia changed her diplomatic front and seized Port Arthur and Talienwan she could not expect also to maintain her position in Korea; and Baron Nishi, Japanese minister of foreign affairs, conveniently obtained a new arrangement from Baron Rosen, Russian minister at Tokyo. The new arrangement was embodied in the convention of April 25, 1898.[122] It provided for mutual abstention from interference in the internal affairs of Korea and from nominating military instructors and financial advisers without having previously arrived at a mutual accord on the subject. It also contained the following:

In view of the great development of the commercial and industrial enterprises of Japan in Korea, as also of the considerable number of Japanese subjects residing in that country, the Russian Imperial Government shall not obstruct the development of the commercial and industrial relations between Japan and Korea.[123]

[120] *Japan Treaties*, p. 391.
[121] *Ibid.*, 393.   [122] *Ibid.*, 394.   [123] Art. iii.

Japan's success, however, was not limited to advantages secured by a single Russian blunder. We have had occasion above to speak of Japan's intervening when the Russian terms for evacuation of Manchuria were made known, and of her bringing force to bear upon that power by entering into an alliance with Great Britain. In doing all this she could not have been moved by altruistic purposes, nor even by motives of self-defence, for judging by the real situation in the summer and autumn of 1903, as well as by the conventions in force, Japan had little to fear from Russia. But here was a power who had not only alienated one of her two allies and driven her traditional rival to join hands with her sworn enemy, and thus to neutralize the value of the other ally, but who had also on top of this announced to the world that she was not to live up to the terms of the evacuation convention she had solemnly entered into with China. If this was not an opportunity for Japan, there can never be one worthy of the name.

On July 28, 1903, Japan invited Russia to enter upon an " examination of the condition of affairs in the Extreme East where their interests meet, with a view to a definition of their respective interests in those regions ".[124] On August 12th she submitted her prosposals whereby the two powers should agree [125] (a) to respect the independence and territorial integrity of the " Chinese and Korean Empires " and to maintain the principle of equal opportunity for the " commerce and industry " of all nations therein; (b) to recognize " Japan's preponderating interests in Corea " and " Russia's special interests in railway enterprise in Manchuria " and of the right of each to take necessary measures to protect those interests; (c) to abstain

[124] Komura to Kurino, July 28, 1903, *R-J Corres.*, 3.
[125] Same to same, Aug. 3, *ibid.*, 7.

from impeding the " industrial and commercial activities "
of each in these respective regions; (d) to despatch no more
than sufficient troops in case they are necessary for the protection of their interests or for the suppression of "insurrection or disorder calculated to create international complications " in the respective regions and to immediately
recall them when their missions should have been accomplished; (e) to recognize the exclusive right of Japan " to
give advice and assistance in the interest of reform and
good government in Corea, including necessary military
assistance "; and (f) to abstain from impeding the
" eventual extension of the Corean railway into southern
Manchuria so as to connect with the East China and
Shanhaikuan-Newchwang lines ".

At the request of Russia the negotiations were transferred to Tokyo.[126] On October 5th Baron Rosen, after
repairing to Port Arthur for consultation with Admiral
Alexiev, submitted Russia's counter proposals.[127] According to these, Russia accepted all Japanese proposals concerning Korea, passed over that concerning the " eventual extension of the Corean railway into southern Manchuria ",
and substituted all references to China and Manchuria by
an engagement to be made by Japan, recognizing " Manchuria and its littoral as in all respects outside her sphere
of interest ". In addition Russia made the following new
proposals: that the two powers agree (a) to abstain from
using any part of the territory of Korea for strategical
purposes and from undertaking on the coasts of Korea any
military works capable of menacing the freedom of navi-

[126] Kurino to Komura, Aug. 12, *ibid.*, 11; same to same, Aug.
24, *ibid.*, 11; Komura to Kurino, Sept. 9, *ibid.*, 21.
[127] Komura to Kurino, Sept. 24, *ibid.*, 22; same to same, Oct. 5,
ibid., 22.

gation in the Strait of Korea; and (b) to consider that part
of the territory of Korea lying to the north of the 39th
parallel as a neutral zone into which neither of the contracting parties should introduce troops.

On October 30th, after some discussion, Japan submitted
a new list of proposals.[128] She raised no objection to Russia's accepting her proposals concerning Korea, but did not
fail to reintroduce the more important references to China
and Manchuria, as embodied in her original proposals (a)
and (b). She reintroduced, too, her proposal (f) which
Russia had passed over, but this time in a less offensive
form, modifying it to read to the effect that neither party
would impede the connection of the Korean and " East
China " railways " when those railways shall have been
eventually extended to the Yalu ". She met Russia's proposal that Japan recognize Manchuria as outside her sphere
of special interest, by introducing a similar clause concerning Russia and her claim to Korea. She further added the
provision that they were to abstain from interfering with
" commercial and residential rights and immunities " belonging to each in virtue of treaty engagement with Korea
by Russia and with China by Japan. As to the additional
Russian proposals she accepted the half of (a) referring to
the freedom of navigation in the Strait of Korea and
rejected the other half referring to the employment of
Korean territory for strategical purposes, and substituted
for (b) one of hers, constituting a neutral zone extending
fifty kilometres on each side of the Korean-Manchurian
frontier.

The Japanese proposals were referred to the Russian
government.[129] On December 12th Rosen submitted Rus-

[128] Komura to Kurino, Oct. 30, *ibid.*, 28.
[129] Same to same, Nov. 1, *ibid.*, 30.

sia's list of new counter-proposals.[130] In this, though maintaining most of her old counter-proposals, Russia made the
concession of suppressing the proposal referring to Japanese
recognition of Manchuria as outside her sphere of interest
and embodying Japan's modified proposal referring to the
connection of railways.

On December 21st, Japan instructed her minister at
St. Petersburg to submit a *note verbale* [131] regretting that
" the Imperial Russian Government did not see their way
in those proposals to give the compass of the suggested
understanding the same territorial extension as was deemed
essential by Japan ", asking it to reconsider its position on
the subject, and suggesting the suppression of the additional
Russian proposal (b) concerning a neutral zone and the
elimination in (a) of the clause " not to use any part of
the territory of Corea for strategical purposes " as she had
insisted before.

Russia replied on January 6th,[132] keeping her proposal
(b), accepting the Japanese suggestion as to (a) and offering to revive the suppressed proposal in the following modified form, in case the last two conditions were agreed to:

Recognition by Japan of Manchuria and its littoral as
being outside her sphere of interest, while Russia, within
the limits of that province, will not impede Japan, nor other
powers in the enjoyment of rights and privileges acquired
by them under existing treaties with China, exclusive of the
establishment of settlements.

The Russian part in this, it may be observed, was substantially what she had declared to the Powers in the previous

[130] *Ibid.*, Dec. 12, 41.
[131] *Ibid.*, Dec. 21, 42.
[132] *Ibid.*, Jan. 7, 1904, 46.

summer when the question arose of opening ports in Manchuria.[133]

On the 13th Japan submitted another *note verbale*.[134] She accepted all Russian concessions of January 6th except the reference to the " establishment of settlements " and maintained her position with regard to the Russian additional proposal (b), taken in her last *note verbale*, and with regard to her original proposals (a) and (b), taken in her list of new proposals, except that she substituted for the reference to " China " a reference to " Manchuria " in (a).

On January 26th Lamsdorv showed the Tzar the Japanese note. On the 28th a conference of the Russian ministers of foreign affairs, war, marine, and other authorities concerned met for the consideration of the question. On February 1st and 2nd Grand Duke Alexis, with the minister of marine, and Lamsdorv with the minister of war in turn reported to the Tzar. From the very beginning of the negotiations, Japan had been " anxiously awaiting a definite reply ". After the presentation of the last note the balance between her anxiety and her patience seemed to tip greatly to the advantage of the former. Between the 23rd and the 30th of January Japan instructed her minister at St. Petersburg four times to find the day on which the reply was to be given. The report was that the earliest date was on February 2nd, when the Tzar would have heard all reports of his ministers and have made his decision; and further that Lamsdorv intimated that the delay was due to the fact that the opinions of the ministers concerned and Admiral Alexiev had to be brought into harmony, but that he would not fail to use his efforts to hurry the matter. On Febru-

[133] See Hay to Conger, July 14, 1903, *For. Rel.*, 1903, p. 67.
[134] Komura to Kurino, Jan. 13, *R–J Corres.*, 47.

ary 5th at 2:15 P.M., Japan instructed her minister to inform Russia officially of her decision to terminate the negotiations and " to take such independent action as she may deem necessary to defend her menaced position and to protect her rights and interests ". The next day at the same hour she went through the same procedure with regard to her decision to sever her diplomatic relations with Russia.[135] [136]

On February 10, 1904, the Chinese government was informed by both Russia and Japan of the declaration of war one against the other. Two days later China sent the following note [137] to the two belligerents, and transmitted copies of it to the neutrals:

At present Russia and Japan have severed their peaceful relations. The Court, being on friendly terms with both and wishing to respect this good relationship, has already issued an edict declaring neutrality.[138] All provinces have been given strict instructions and enjoined to observe them uniformly. Stringent orders have also been given throughout the empire to maintain the peace and to give thorough protection to foreign commerce and missionary work.

Mukden and Hsingching being the sites of imperial mausoleums and palaces, the military governor has been ordered to guard them with care and reverence. The cities, public buildings, and the life and property of the people of the Eastern Three Provinces, it is incumbent upon the two belligerents not to destroy. Likewise, they and the Chinese troops originally stationed there shall mutually abstain from

[135] See correspondence, *ibid.*, 50–59.

[136] In connection with this it is interesting to read Rosen, *op. cit.*, pp. 237–242.

[137] Translation from Chinese text in Liu Yen, *op. cit.*, p. 377; *cf.* translation in *For. Rel.*, 1904, p. 121.

[138] For edict, *ibid.*, p. 121.

interfering with each other. As to the west of the river Liao, all territory that has been evacuated by the Russian troops the Imperial Commissioner of Peiyang will detail forces to station.

Throughout the Provinces, along the frontier and in Inner and Outer Mongolia the law of neutrality will be enforced, and neither belligerent shall be permitted to enter. Should there be any violation, it would be incumbent upon China to prevent this and such should not be considered as contrary to peaceful relations. But at such places in Manchuria as are not yet evacuated by the Powers [because of conditions growing out of the Boxer Rebellion] it would be difficult, as China's power cannot at present reach these places, to enforce the law of neutrality. Nevertheless, the sovereign rights and territory of the Eastern Three Provinces should still be restored to China, no matter which belligerent shall be victorious, and are not subject to the right of conquest.

On the same day when the declaration of war was officially communicated to China by each of the belligerents, John Hay, the Secretary of State, sent the following note to the two belligerents as well as to China,[139] and transmitted copies to all the powers signatory of the Final Protocol of September 7, 1901, requesting each of them to make similar representations to Russia and Japan:

You will express to the minister of foreign affairs the earnest desire of the government of the United States that, in the course of the military operations which have begun between Russia and Japan, the neutrality of China and in all practical ways her administrative entity shall be respected by both parties, and that the area of hostilities shall be localized and limited as much as possible, so that undue excitement and disturbance of the Chinese people

[139] *For. Rel.*, 1904, p. 2.

may be prevented and the least possible loss to the commerce and peaceful intercourse of the world may be occasioned.

On the 13th Japan replied that she was prepared " to respect the neutrality and administrative entity of China outside the regions occupied by Russia, as long as Russia, making a similar engagement, fulfills in good faith the terms and conditions of such engagement ". On the 19th Russia also replied accepting the American proposal on condition that China observed her neutrality and Japan her engagement and that " neutralization in no case can be extended to Manchuria, the territory of which, by the force of events, will serve as the field of military operations ".

Sec. 6. *The Treaties of Portsmouth and Peking*

In the ensuing war Russia fared no better with the Japanese than had China in 1894, either on land or at sea, and perhaps much worse in the latter arena, and she was equally anxious to come to terms, though, it seems, with much less necessity. When, in June, 1905, President Roosevelt made a proposal for peace negotiations at the instance, it is said, of Japan, Russia accepted his proposal.

At the beginning of July the emperor Kuanghsu sent a confidential message to President Roosevelt,[140] expressing China's gratitude for the part he had played in her behalf and the hope that he would still exert his influence for her in the peace conference. About the same time the Board of Foreign Affairs also made a declaration to Russia and Japan, and transmitted copies to the neutrals to the effect that " no provision affecting China without the approval of China previously obtained, which the treaty of peace may

[140] *Ibid.*, 1905, p. 816.

contain, will be recognized as valid ".[141]   In communicating a copy of the declaration to the State Department Minister Rockhill added that " the motif of this declaration is the apprehension felt that Japan may seek to secure at the peace negotiations the reversion of the various concessions made to Russia or to Russian companies of rights in Manchuria ".[142]

On September 5, 1905, a treaty of peace was signed between Serge Witte and Baron Roman Rosen for Russia, and Baron Komura and Takahira Kogoro for Japan, at Portsmouth, New Hampshire.   By this treaty Russia agreed to let Japan have a free hand in Korea;[143] ceded to Japan the southern part of the island of Sakhalin;[144] obligated herself to grant to Japanese subjects certain fishing rights along the coast of the Russian Far East;[145] and transferred and assigned to Japan, with the consent of China, the lease of Port Arthur and Talienwan and the railway south of Changchun.[146]   In addition the treaty contained the following provisions:

Art. III. — Japan and Russia mutually engage:

1. To evacuate completely and simultaneously Manchuria except the territory affected by the lease of the Liaotung Peninsula, in conformity with the provisions of additional Article I annexed to this Treaty; and

2. To restore entirely and completely to the exclusive administration of China all portions of Manchuria now in the occupation or under the control of the Japanese or Russian troops, with the exception of the territory above mentioned.

[141] *Ibid.*, p. 818.
[142] Rockhill to Secretary of State, July 8, 1905, *ibid.*, p. 818.
[143] Art. ii, *MacMurray*, i, 522.
[144] Art. ix.   [145] Art. xi.   [146] Arts. v and vi.

The Imperial Government of Russia declares that they have not in Manchuria any territorial advantages or preferential or exclusive concessions in impairment of Chinese sovereignty or inconsistent with the principle of equal opportunity.

Art. IV. — Japan and Russia reciprocally engage not to obstruct any general measures common to all countries, which China may take for the development of the commerce and industry of Manchuria.

The additional Article I annexed [147] to the treaty referred to in Article III, related to the evacuation of Manchuria which the two powers agreed to complete within eighteen months. It, however, contained the following provision:

The High Contracting Parties reserve to themselves the right to maintain guards to protect their respective railway lines in Manchuria. The number of such guards shall not exceed fifteen per kilometre and within that maximum number, the Commanders of the Japanese and Russian Armies shall, by common accord, fix the number of such guards to be employed, as small as possible having in view the actual requirements.

The consent of China for the transfer of the lease of Port Arthur and Talienwan and the section of the railway south of Changchun was later effected by the treaty of Peking signed on December 22, 1905, between Baron Komura Jutaro and Uchida Yasuya for Japan, and Prince Ching, Chu Hung-chi, and Yuan Shih-kai for China.[148] For this consent Japan made the following engagement: [149]

The Government of Japan engages to earnestly observe the original agreements entered into between China and

[147] *MacMurray*, i, 526.   [148] *Tiao yo, K.*, 95/4.   [149] Art. ii.

Russia respecting the lease and the construction of the railway, and to promptly consult and determine with the Government of China as matters come up in the future.[150]

On the same day and between the same parties there was also signed an additional agreement.[151]   In this Japan promised that she would take similar steps with Russia " in the event of Russia's agreeing to the withdrawal of her railway guards, or in case other proper measures are agreed to between China and Russia ", and that at any rate she would withdraw her railway guards " simultaneously with Russia " " when tranquillity is restored in Manchuria and China is [thus] able to give full protection to the life and property of foreigners ".[152]

In this agreement also China made two important concessions.   The one concerned the conversion of the military line Japan built during the war between Antung and Mukden into a commercial line.[153]   The term for the concession was fifteen years, which, by counting from the end of three years — two being allowed for the work of improvement and one for delay due to service in transporting evacuated troops — was to end on " the forty-ninth year of Kuanghsu ", *i.e.*, 1923–4.   At the expiration of the term the railway was to be sold to China at a price to be determined through the appraisement of all its property by an expert of a third nationality to be mutually chosen.   Prior to such sale the transportation of Chinese troops and munitions of war was to be governed by rules laid down with the Chinese

[150] There is no such phrase as " as far as circumstances permit," nor such term as " exploration " in the original text.   For current text see *MacMurray*, i, 549.

[151] *Tiao yo, K.*, 95/6.

[152] Art. ii; *cf.* current text in *MacMurray*, i, p. 551.

[153] Art. vi.

Eastern Railway. Regarding the manner in which the improvements of the railway were to be effected, the person undertaking the work for Japan was to consult with the officer especially appointed by China for the purpose. As to the affairs of the railway, " the government of China will appoint an officer to inspect and manage as is provided in the Chinese Eastern Railway contract ". The other concession was for the establishment of a Sino-Japanese timbering company to exploit the forests on the right bank of the Yalu, with details to be determined later.[154]

By the additional agreement China also engaged herself to open the following ports: [155] Fenghuancheng, Liaoyang, Hsinmin, Tiehling, Tungkiangtze, and Fakumen, in Shengking; Kirin City, Harbin, Ninguta, Hungchun, and Sansin in Kirin; and Tsitsihar, Hailar, Aigun, and Manchuli in Heilungkiang.

On February 10, 1904, the emperor of Japan, in his declaration of war against Russia, declared that the integrity of Korea was a matter of constant concern to his empire, not only because of Japan's traditional relations with that country, but because the separate existence of Korea was essential to the safety of his realm, and that the absorption of Manchuria by Russia would render it impossible to maintain the integrity of Korea and preserve the peace in the Far East.[156] On the 23rd of the same month Japan drew up a protocol [157] with Korea, by which Korea agreed to place full confidence in Japan and adopt its advice with regard to improvements in administration, while Japan agreed to insure the safety and repose of the " imperial " house of Korea and to " definitely guarantee the independence and territorial integrity of the Korean Em-

[154] Art. x.
[155] Art. i.
[156] *For. Rel.*, 1904, p. 414.
[157] *Ibid.*, p. 437.

pire ". On August 19th she obtained another agreement[158] by which Korea undertook to employ a Japanese subject as financial adviser and a Westerner as diplomatic adviser, both to be recommended by Japan. On May 30, 1905, she obtained still another agreement[159] by which Korea undertook to transfer and assign the control and administration of the post, telegraph, and telephone services in Korea to Japan. On August 27th, at an audience accorded to the Japanese minister and the Japanese financial adviser, arrangement was made to place the Korean maritime customs under the ministry of finance, controlled by the Japanese financial adviser.[160]

Reference has been made to Korea in reviewing the treaty of Portsmouth. By that treaty Russia " recognizing that Japan has predominant political, military, and economic interests in Korea, agrees not to interfere or place obstacles in the way of any measure of direction, protection, and supervision which the Imperial Government of Japan may deem necessary to adopt in Korea ".[161] On August 12th, Great Britain, in the treaty of alliance with Japan, had also made a similar acknowledgment, which reads:

Japan, possessing paramount political, military, and economic interests in Korea, Great Britain recognizes the right of Japan to take such measures of guidance, control, and protection in Korea as she may deem proper and necessary to safeguard and advance those interests, provided always that such measures are not contrary to the principle of equal opportunities for the commerce and industry of all nations.[162]

[158] *Ibid.*, p. 439.
[159] *Ibid.*, 1905, p. 625.
[160] Morgan to Secretary of State, Aug. 28, 1905, *ibid.*, p. 625.
[161] Art. ii.   [162] *MacMurray*, i, 516.

No more express recognition other than those from the enemy and the ally seemed necessary. On November 22nd Japan declared [163] that the measures hitherto taken "have been purely advisory, but the experience of recent years has demonstrated the insufficiency of measures of guidance alone" and to remove the "unsatisfactory condition of things" she by arrangement [164] with Korea under date of November 23rd assumed control and direction of the external relations of that nation.

With the last days of Korea's shadowy existence we do not need to busy ourselves. Ito, now a Prince, was appointed first resident-general. He was first succeeded by Viscount Sone and then by Count Terauchi. By a series of agreements, Korea's internal administration was part by part transferred to Japan. And, finally, on August 22, 1910, annexation followed. In taking this last step Japan declared to the world that "the existing system of government in that country has not proved entirely equal to the duty of preserving public order and tranquillity", "notwithstanding the earnest and laborious work of reform [undertaken by her] in the administration of Korea . . . engaged in for more than four years"![165] Less than a year previously, on October 26, 1909, in Harbin, where Ito repaired to discuss, it is said, the fate of Korea and Manchuria with the Russian delegated for that purpose, he had fallen a martyr to his cause by the hand of a Korean patriot.

What, then, was China doing in the meantime? "Man," says Mencius, "lives in difficulties and dies in

---

[163] *For. Rel.*, 1905, p. 613.   [164] *Ibid.*, p. 612.

[165] *State Papers*, 1912, p. 688; for other documents relating to events of those four years, *ibid.*, 1909, p. 937; 1910, p. 992; *Rockhill*, sup., nos. 66 and 67, pp. 280–1.

comfort." If the Empress Dowager Tsuhsi had grown jealous of Prince Kung and ousted him at a time when China had just got on her feet after the Taiping Rebellion, she was to share the control of the destiny of the nation with liberal statesmen now that she had experienced a decade of disasters. In the nation the reforms, which the liberal statesmen had inaugurated, and the radicals and reactionaries had brought to naught, she reintroduced and vigorously carried out. In Manchuria the century-old policy of Kienlung she, with one stroke of her pen, reversed. In October, 1906, shortly after the Russo-Japanese War, she appointed Prince Tsai-chen and Mr. Hsu Shih-chang to make a study of conditions of Manchuria and to recommend measures for its reconstruction. On January 7, 1907, the two commissioners reported.[165a] On April 20th there appeared the following memorable edict:[166]

In the Eastern Three Provinces (Tungsansheng) the government is perfunctory and our people are suffering. Let these provinces be thoroughly reconstructed to the end that abuses may be eliminated and responsibility become determinable. Let the military governorship of Shengking be replaced by a viceroyalty to be known as the Viceroyalty of the Eastern Three Provinces, the incumbent of which is to assume also the duties of the military governors of the three provinces and to visit his office in each from time to time. Let governorships also be instituted in Fengtien, Kirin, and Heilungkiang to assist in government. We hereby appoint Hsu Shih-chang Viceroy of the Eastern Three Provinces, with duties of the former military gov-

[165a] Edict, 32/12/–, *Hsu*, 32/55 *l.*; *Herald*, 1906, iv, 325, 435, 661; 1907, i, 59; ii, 30, 197–8, 199.

[166] A translation. For the Chinese text see *Hsu*, 33/24. *Cf.* the current text in *Herald*, 1907, ii, 197.

ernors of the three provinces, as well as of the Imperial Commissioner of Mukden; Tang Shao-yi, Governor of Fengtien; Chu Chia-pao, Acting Governor of Kirin; Tuan Chih-kuei, with the brevet rank of Pu-cheng Ssu, Acting Governor of Heilungkiang. You, Viceroy and Governors, being entrusted with such a great task, be whole-hearted and cautious, disregard susceptibilities, try to bear both complaints and hardships, consider as a whole the affairs that you need to attend to, and carry them out in an orderly manner that you may measure up to the trust reposed in you. As to details of reorganization, you are to discuss among yourselves and report to us.

The reconstruction of Manchuria in consequence of this edict forms an important part of our investigation in the next chapter. As part of the policy of reconstruction Chinese immigration was promoted, not only for the country already colonized, but also for the outlying districts along the Amur and Ussuri rivers where, on account of the Manchu policy of exclusion, Chinese colonists had not yet arrived in their northward march. Consequently, the process of colonizing Manchuria, or what was left of Manchuria after the mid-century descent of the Russians, was also completed.[167]

[167] As it existed in the early days of the Republic there were thirty-three *hsiens* in Fengtien, thirty-seven in Kirin and twenty-three in Heilungkiang, grouped into three, four, and three *taos*, respectively — prefectures and other intermediate administrative units between the province and the *hsien* having been abolished under the Republic — with the following towns as the seats of government for the *taoyins*, *i.e.*, deputy governors: Mukden, Antung, Taonan, Kirin, Harbin, Yenchi, Sansin, Tsitsihar, Suihua, and Aigun. For the establishment of new administrative units after the Boxer Rebellion, see memorial by Committee on Reconstruction, *K.*, 30/12, *Kuang hsu cheng yao*, 30/54 *l.* For that after the edict of April 20, 1907, see *Hsu*, vols. 2–3 and 5–8.

CHAPTER VI

THE RECONSTRUCTION OF MANCHURIA

Sec. 1. Regional Problems

THE policy of the Hsu administration followed two broad lines. On the one hand it attempted to confine the activities of the Russians and the Japanese to what was provided in the treaties; on the other, it promoted the development of the provinces to forestall any further foreign encroachment. In the carrying out of the latter line of policy the administration immediately came into conflict with the advancing Japanese in two regions, the Cherim prairie, and the left bank of the Tumen river.

(1) The Left Bank of the Tumen

We have seen how the Manchus attempted to keep the Chinese from Manchuria. They had put up bars against all other peoples also, though in the latter case it was a matter of principle — the principle of non-expatriation — and not a matter of policy. The Koreans on a certain section of the upper Yalu were among the first to declare their allegiance to the Manchus and it is said that the first "banner" forces enrolled about 10,000 of them. On account of this relation Koreans there were allowed to cross the river at will,[1] but elsewhere along the long frontier the rule of mutual exclusion was strictly enforced throughout the Tsing dynasty down to the Taiping Rebel-

[1] *Lin chiang pao kao*, p. 11.

lion. In 1875 local authorities first reported that Koreans were found on the isolated spots on the left bank of the Tumen neglected by frontier inspection.[2] Kirin had then been thrown open to Chinese colonization; besides, the Tumen region was then exposed to the Russians. Consequently, the government was not only indisposed to reenforce the law, but also regularized the situation even as was done in the case of Chinese immigration. In 1881 these Korean settlers were first put under local jurisdiction by Wu Ta-cheng, then Defence Commissioner of Kirin Frontiers. In 1885 special bureaus were even established for Korean immigrants and parts of the bank of the Tumen were reserved for their accommodation. In 1894 they were also admitted to regions further inland. In 1890 by a memorial[3] submitted by the Tsungli Yamen the Korean settlers were finally given title deeds to the land they cultivated and made liable to land tax as full Chinese citizens.

In 1882 when the first Korean settlers were put under local jurisdiction, the king of Korea, evidently unaware of the change of policy on the part of the Chinese government, hastened to memorialize[4] the Throne, apologizing for failure to prevent his subjects from violating the imperial law, and asking grace for the offenders whom he promised to remove across the boundary. A year for this purpose was granted him. The Korean commissioners sent to carry out the task, however, found it beyond their ability, because in place of a few frontier stragglers, as the case used to be, they would have to move whole villages. In order to escape the dilemma, they recommended to the

[2] For a history of Korean colonization of the left bank of the Tumen, see *Yen chi pao kao*, bk. 4.

[3] For text see *ibid.*, p. 4.   [4] *Ibid.*, p. 2 *l.*

Korean government that it request a delimitation of the boundary.[5] Thus two joint inspections were made in 1885 and 1887 and the question of removing the Koreans back to Korea was dropped.

The Yalu and the Tumen had been officially taken as the boundary between China and Korea ever since the Ming dynasty; as to the section between the head waters of the two rivers, this was not determined until the fifty-first year of Kanghsi (1712) when, at the order of the emperor, an inspection was made by Mu-ko-ting, a frontier stone with inscription set up, and the Korean government notified. In the joint inspections of 1885 and 1887 the stone, however, was found in a place which both parties agreed was not the original place, and a new survey was made. According to the report of the Chinese commissioners there were three rivulets, any one of which could be taken as the source of the Tumen, but in their opinion the middle agreed more with the inscription on the stone, and they recommended that it be so taken. This was accepted by the Chinese government. Although the Korean commissioners dissented from the opinion, they made no complaint against China's ruling or against the measures adopted by her in consequence.

After Korea had become independent, China and her former vassal agreed, in the commercial treaty of 1899, that from that time forward migration across the frontiers was to be prohibited on both sides " in order to avoid complications ", but that " all persons who have already crossed the frontier and reclaimed ground shall be allowed to pursue their avocations in peace and enjoy protection for their lives and property ".[6]

[5] For a history of the boundary question see *ibid.*, bk. 5 and appended documents.   [6] *MacMurray*, i, 213.

So long as Korea remained independent all seemed to go well, but as soon as Japan established a protectorate over it the trouble began. The Tumen is full of sand beaches, of which the biggest one is ten *li* in length and one *li* in width, situated opposite to Kuang-chi-ku and known as Chia-chiang. In 1881 the Korean settlers opened up a channel near the left bank of the river in order to divert water for cultivation purposes.[7] In course of time the channel was deepened by water until it divided the current with the original course and turned the Chia-chiang into a regular island. In 1903, after the severance of political connection between China and Korea, local Korean authorities for the first time claimed jurisdiction over the island, calling it by the name known to them, "Chientao". China, however, was able to show the history of the island and the Korean claim was dropped.

Taking the incident as a lesson the Chinese minister at Seoul was instructed to propose to the Korean government the appointment of a joint frontier commission to delimit the entire course of the Tumen once for all. The proposal met with a cordial reception, but before it was carried out the Russo-Japanese War broke out, and at the request of Japan the steps were postponed.[8]

After the Russo-Japanese War a certain Japanese wrote a geography of Manchuria and extended the name Chien-tao to cover the whole territory between the Tumen and the Hai-lan-ho, pointed out the strategical value of that region which he had thus christened, and advanced the idea that the sovereignty over it was not yet determined. The

[7] For history of the name Chientao see *Yen chi pao kao*, bk. 6.

[8] Japanese Minister to Board of Foreign Affairs, 30/6/16, *ibid.*, 8/1.

Japanese press was not slow in echoing him. In a short time Japanese public interest was roused and the name was further extended to cover the region where the Tumen, the Yalu, and the Sungari had their common origin, making what was Chientao an area equal to the Japanese island of Kiushiu. The Japanese government then acted. On August 19, 1907, the Japanese *chargé d'affaires* in Peking suddenly forwarded to the Chinese government the following instructions [9] from his government:

The question whether Chientao is Chinese territory or Korean has been left unsettled for a long time. The Koreans who have settled in that district number more than one hundred thousand. They have been constantly subjected to ill-treatment from the bandits and ruffians and have applied to the Korean government for protection. The latter government on account of the fact that the matter relates to the frontier and comes within the sphere of their foreign relations has requested the Japanese government to despatch officers there for the purpose. Before the Russo-Japanese War, the Korean government from time to time sent officials to Chientao for the protection of the Koreans. Now that Korea's foreign relations and the duty of protecting the Korean citizens have passed over to Japan, the Japanese government, having been requested by the Korean government, cannot refrain from giving consideration to the matter, and has decided to have the Residency-General despatch officers to Chientao specially for the protection of settlers. Please notify the Chinese government and request them to instruct the Chinese officials at Chientao in order that there may not be misunderstandings.

On the next day Japanese troops accordingly landed on Chinese territory on the left bank of the Yalu.

[9] Same to same, 33/7/11, *ibid.*, 8/2 *l.*

On the 26th the Board of Foreign Affairs replied to the Japanese note,[10] saying in part:

Between China and Korea the Tumen has been taken as the boundary. There has never been such a place as "Chientao". The territory designated in your note as such consists really of Ho-lung-ko of the sub-prefecture of Yen-chi. It is on the north of the Tumen. The migration of Koreans across the border for settlement has been at various times regulated by the Imperial Commissioner of Peiyang and the Military Governor of Kirin. The posts of the sub-prefect of Yen-chi and of the commissary of Ho-lung-ko had been established since long ago. There is no question as to that section's being Chinese territory. With regard to the statement that the Koreans have been attacked by bandits and ruffians, according to the telegraphic report of the Viceroy of the Eastern Three Provinces there have been no such cases. It is proper that local authorities should continue to have charge of their protection to the end that order and peace may not be disturbed. This government cannot acquiesce in the despatch of troops to that place by the Residency-General as intimated in your note.

With this exchange of correspondence began one of the several regional problems of Manchuria which will probably continue as long as the bigger problem of Manchuria itself remains. We shall take up the case again when it forces itself upon our attention.[11] For the time we may add that, as a result of the Japanese move, the Defence Commissionerships of Kirin Frontiers, which had been swept away a short time before with the rest of the old Manchurian administration, were reinstituted with Colonel

[10] Board of Foreign Affairs to Japanese Minister, 33/7/16, *ibid.*, 8/3.

[11] *Infra*, sec. 5, and chap. vii, sec. 5.

Wu Lu-chen as assistant defence commissioner stationed at Yenchi, Wu having been sent there by the Hsu administration to study conditions several months before the Japanese landing of troops.[12] Wu strictly enforced China's sovereign rights short of expelling the Japanese which he did not have power to do, and made a painstaking study of the boundary question; and thus the Chinese government was not only given time for diplomatic negotiations, but was well supplied with material to carry on the negotiations, which, had it not been for Manchu incompetency, as we shall have occasion to see later, might have resulted in the successful ending of the problem.

(2) *The Cherim Prairie*

Another section of the country that seriously engaged the attention of the Hsu administration was the Cherim prairie.[13] The sections of the prairie that bordered on the Liao, Sungari, and Nonni rivers had been settled, as we have seen above, but the rest, by far the greater part, was less fertile and was still undeveloped as before. After the Russo-Japanese War the Russians and the Japanese vied with each other in extending their influence at this place. While the Russians tried to do it by befriending the Mongol princes, the Japanese concentrated on the people, and bureaus were established by the respective parties in Harbin and Kuangchengtze to forward their objects.

The problem of this region will be treated below in connection with the railway development.[14] For the time being we will merely recount the history of the projects adopted by the Hsu administration to anticipate trouble.

[12] *Hsu*, 2/9.
[13] *Hsu*, bks. 9 and 10. See especially the memorials.
[14] *Infra*, sec. 2.

In 1908, the Court sent Prince Shu to Inner Mongolia on a mission similar to that of Prince Tsai-chen and Mr. Hsu Shih-chang. On his return Prince Shu recommended the policy of extensive colonization of the land with the object of absorbing the Mongols there into the Chinese nation even as had happened with the Manchus themselves. Geographically the Cherim prairie formed a part of Manchuria, and so the matter was referred by the Court to the Hsu administration. Accordingly, Mr. Chu Chi-chien was first appointed to study and report, and later as special commissioner to carry out his own recommendations.[15]

One of the recommendations of Mr. Chu was the establishment of a system of colonization stations on strategical points with headquarters at Taonan. Before the introduction of railway communication into Manchuria there were two postal roads from Tsitsihar to Peking, one of which, after traveling the settled section of the Cherim prairie, crossed the Palisade and entered Shanhaikuan, while the other, after traveling the unsettled section of the same prairie, struck across the Jehol hills and headed for Hsifengkou. In order to avoid offending the susceptibility of the Mongol princes as much as possible, Mr. Chu proposed[16] to establish stations more or less along these old roads, though with such modifications as to avoid the settled sections on the north and the east and the hilly section in the south. As projected, there were to be a main road from Tsitsihar to Mukden by way of Faku, Liaoyuan, and Taonan, with twenty-six stations, and two branch roads, one from Taonan to Tao-lai-chao on the Chinese Eastern Railway by way of Hsin-cheng with twelve stations, and the other from Faku to Hsinmin on the Peking-Mukden Rail-

---

[15] Memorandum submitted by Chu, *Hsu*, 10/16.

[16] *Ibid.*, 10/45.

way with two stations. In each of these stations there was to be a set of officials with jurisdiction extending ten *li* on each side of the road, whose duty it would be not only to transmit government mails as before, but also to convert the nomads into settlers and to provide all facilities for immigrants with power to allot land and to extend protection to them.

Sec. 2. Development Projects

We have seen that, in the conference that led to the conclusion of the treaty and additional agreement of December 22, 1905, Japan obtained from China the concession of the Antung-Mukden Railway. In that conference Japan also demanded concessions for two smaller lines, the Mukden-Hsinmin and the Kirin-Changchun. On the Mukden-Hsinmin line, as on the Antung-Mukden, Japan had laid a light railway during the war with Russia; but as the line formed a part of the projected extension of the North China Railways which had then been built as far as Hsinmin, the Chinese plenipotentiaries declined to entertain the Japanese proposal. As to the Kirin-Changchun line — a concession which was granted to the Chinese Eastern Railway in 1902,[17] but cancelled with its consent after the Russo-Japanese War — it was then in the process of construction by the Kirin provincial authorities [18] and the Chinese plenipotentiaries likewise refused to consider the Japanese proposal. However, after some discussion a compromise was reached. By this Japan was to sell to China the light line she had laid between Mukden and Hsinmin, while China was to borrow from Japan one-half of the necessary capital for the section of the railway

[17] For preliminary agreement see *MacMurray*, i, 296.
[18] Hsu Hsi, *op. cit.*, 453.

east of the Liao on terms similar to those of the loan agreement for the North China Railways. In addition, China was to borrow from Japan for the Kirin-Changchun line on the same terms, in case foreign capital was necessary. This still seemed unsatisfactory to the Japanese. Some time afterwards, when China approached Japan to carry out the understanding regarding the Hsinmin-Mukden line, she further exacted from China the concession of borrowing one-half of the capital for the Kirin-Changchun line, as well as a promise to borrow from her in case foreign capital was necessary for the construction of an extension or a branch from the same railway.[19] Upon this latter basis, a convention was signed on April 15, 1907,[20] providing for a loan for eighteen years for the Hsinmin-Mukden line east of the Liao, and another for twenty-five years for the Kirin-Changchun line.[21] After the completion of the work of reconstruction on the Hsinmin-Mukden line, the section of the North China Railways from Peking to Mukden was renamed the Peking-Mukden Railway.[22]

For the development of Manchuria it was the opinion of the Hsu administration that a system of railways should be projected in addition to the Chinese Eastern and the South Manchurian Railways which were originally built with a view to the interest of Russia rather than of China. According to the original plan the North China Railways were to be extended to the Tumen by way of Kirin. The need of such means of communication with eastern Kirin had not been met since the nineties. On the other hand,

---

[19] Memorials by Board of Foreign Affairs, 33/3/11, *Tiao yo, K.*, 99/2.   [20] *MacMurray*, i, 627.   [21] Art. iii.
[22] Memorials by Board of Communications, 33/10/4, *Tiao yo, K.*, 99/4.

now that Japan was in control of Korea, frontier problems had become even more tense. Consequently the administration decided to carry out the plan as originally projected,[23] though in order to meet existing conditions the line was to run from Mukden direct to the Tumen by way of Hailung, following closely an abandoned post road, instead of the Kirin route, and the terminus was to be at Yenchi instead of Hungchun.

Another section of the country which stood in need of development no less urgently was Heilungkiang, the province which had just been officially thrown open to the Chinese. Before the creation of the viceroyalty, plans had been on foot to extend the North China Railways from Hsinmin to Aigun by way of Petuna and Tsitsihar, with branch lines from the left bank of the Sungari, then known as the granary of Manchuria. When the plans were taken over by the Hsu administration, the development of the Cherim prairie also had just been projected, and consequently the trunk line was modified to run by way of Taonan instead of Petuna.[24] Of the two projected lines, the administration decided to begin with the latter and in the autumn of 1907 a contract for the section between Mukden and Fakumen was signed with a British contracting firm.[25]

When this line was being surveyed, the Japanese minister at Peking protested,[26] on the ground that the Chinese plenipotentiaries to the Peking Conference of 1905 had declared that for the protection of the interests of the South Manchurian Railway the Chinese government would not construct any trunk or branch lines parallel to it before the purchase of that railway from Japan. At the request

[23] Hsu Hsi, *op. cit.*, 457–59.   [25] Hsu Hsi, *op. cit.*, 459.
[24] *Hsu*, 10/77–81.   [26] *Hsu*, 11/46.

of the Board of Foreign Affairs the Board of Communications submitted a memorandum stating that, as the extension of the railway from Hsinmin was for the purpose of increasing the value of the existing railway, the Board never intended to invite competition by paralleling the South Manchurian Railway, and that in the case of the extension being constructed the Board would undoubtedly follow precedents of similar cases in Europe and America in order that neither party should suffer through it. The Japanese minister, not being satisfied with the memorandum, the Board of Foreign Affairs finally replied in a formal note.[27] In speaking of the understanding reached in the Conference, the note had the following to say:

Your Excellency refers to the minutes of the Sino-Japanese Conference, and declares that the Chinese government has disregarded her engagement and taken action prejudicial to the interest of the South Manchurian Railway. Probably your Excellency is not aware of the fact that at the time the plenipotentiaries of China and Japan discussed the matter, the plenipotentiaries of China maintained that the word "parallel" was too comprehensive and that it was necessary to give distance in miles, stating definitely that within so many miles no parallel line could be constructed. The Japanese plenipotentiaries, however, thought that if the number of miles were fixed, it might create the impression in other countries that there was an intention to restrict Chinese railway enterprise. The Chinese plenipotentiaries then asked that the number of miles between the parallel lines be fixed in accordance with the practice of Europe and America. The Japanese plenipotentiaries said the practice was not uniform and that no statement was necessary. And they added a declaration that Japan would do nothing to prevent China from any

[27] *Ibid.*, 11/46 *l.*

steps she might take in the future for the development of Manchuria. The declaration was made in all sincerity and with consideration for the interests of a friendly nation. This is what we both ought to observe.

The Board then went on to point out that, quite contrary to Japanese apprehension, the line, when opened, would tend to increase the traffic of the South Manchurian Railway, since commerce served by such a line would naturally take the route to Talienwan, as Tientsin and Yingkou were ice-bound ports. Yet the Japanese minister was not satisfied with even this reply.

At this juncture Mr. Chu had just returned from his study of the condition of the Cherim prairie. On being consulted, he submitted a memorandum [28] advising the change of the southern terminal of the line to Chinchou, where the ice-free port of Hulutao had just been discovered, his main argument being that thus the line would serve also the Jehol hills, the development of which, like the Cherim prairie, had been decided upon. According to his plan the line would run from Chinchou to Chaoyang, thence to Taonan and Tsitsihar by way of Suitung, with a possibility of extending the line westward to connect with the Peking-Kalgan Railway by way of Chihfeng. The new project was well received by the administration and immediately forwarded to Peking for consideration.

Under the Hsu administration a number of new governmental activities were introduced in addition to the reorganization of the government of the three provinces; measures were taken to safeguard China's rights, such as the maintenance of a frontier bureau at Yenchi, or the assumption from the Russian and Japanese of debts privately contracted by the Mongol princes; and a broad policy was adopted to develop the country by opening up the sec-

[28] *Ibid.,* 10/82.

tions not yet settled and promoting immigration from intra-
mural China. And all these steps meant increase in expenditure. Under efficient administration, local revenues
of the three provinces increased by one-half, and this increase was sufficient to meet the additional activities.[29]
For the reorganization of the government a special grant
was made by the imperial government. The extraordinary
expenses incurred in remedial measures were met by special grants also as they came up.

As to the expenditure required for carrying out the
broad policy of Manchurian development, the imperial
government was unable to make any more grants, having
at its disposal only a flat conventional tariff of five per
cent *ad valorem*, further burdened by an indemnity calculated to sap all that it might yield for yet another thirty-
three years. It was imperative, however, that Manchuria
should be developed, and the imperial government, therefore, gave the administration permission to make a foreign
loan. In the summer of 1907 the new administration had
requested E. H. Harriman, the American financier, through
W. F. Straight, then American consul-general at Mukden,
and previously secretary to the last American minister to
Korea, to undertake a loan of $20,000,000. Owing to
the panic which occurred in the United States in the
autumn, no active steps were taken until the summer of
1908, when on August 12th, a memorandum of agreement was signed between Mr. Tang Shao-yi and Straight
which, with the approval of Mr. Elihu Root, the Secretary of State, was referred to a New York banking firm.[30]

On October 8, 1907, ex-President Taft, then Secretary

[29] *Ibid.*, 24/1–4.
[30] Willard Straight, *The Politics of Chinese Finance*, an address
(New York, 1913), p. 5. Also Herbert Croly, *Willard Straight*,
(New York, 1924), p. 269, *et seq.*

of War, passed through Shanghai on his way to the Philippine Islands to open the first legislative assembly of that American possession. In a speech,[31] made " as an American citizen," Mr. Taft reiterated the policy of the United States towards China as set forth in John Hay's celebrated circular of July 3, 1900; declared that "the American-China trade is sufficiently great to require the government of the United States to take every legitimate measure to protect it against diminution or injury by the political preference of any of its competitors " ; and that " the United States . . . will encourage this great Chinese Empire to take long steps in administrative and governmental reforms, and in the development of her natural resources and the improvement of the welfare of her people " so that " she will add great strength to the position as a self-respecting government, may resist all possible foreign aggression seeking undue, exclusive and proprietary privileges in her territory, and without foreign aid can enforce an open door policy of equal opportunity to all ".

On May 25, 1908, the Congress by a joint resolution authorized the President to return to China a portion of the Boxer indemnity as an act of friendship. On July 20th Mr. Tang Shao-yi was by an imperial edict given the brevet rank of Board President and appointed special envoy to the United States, " to carry the grateful thanks of their Imperial Majesties for this further token of United States' friendship towards China ".[32] Mr. Tang, after signing the memorandum referred to above, left on his mission, arriving at Washington on October 30th.[33]

After his arrival Mr. Tang entered into negotiation with

---

[31] Text in *Herald*, 1907, iv, 100.

[32] *Ibid.*, 1908, iii, 230.

[33] *Ibid.*, 1908, iii, 353, 354, 777; iv, 20–22.

the Secretary of State for securing a portion of the re-
mitted Boxer indemnity for the service of the Manchurian
loan. At the same time he also proposed that China issue
a loan of $300,000,000 to be utilized for a program of
industrial development of China, for currency reform, and
to finance the Chinese administration during the period
following the intended abolition of *likin,* and until the
consent of all the treaty powers should be obtained to an
increase in the customs tariff, and that the United States
take the lead in the matter. The proposal for the second
loan was also met with favor, and Mr. Root, with the
approval of President Roosevelt, introduced Mr. Tang to
American bankers.[34] Before proceeding further with this
phase of Manchurian reconstruction, however, we must
first return to a review of the attempts at readjustment the
Hsu administration had in the meantime made with Russia
and Japan.

Sec. 3. Readjustment with Russia

Of the more important readjustments made with Russia,
the first in point of time was embodied in a note[35] dated
July 6, 1907, addressed by the Board of Foreign Affairs
to the Russian minister in Peking informing him that
China had decided to install custom houses at Manchuli and
Suifenho in accordance with the provision of Article X of
the Chinese Eastern Railway contract; and that as to the
manner in which merchandise transported by the railway
was to be exempted from duty or to be subject thereto, the
Chinese and Russian governments had agreed upon four
" experimental regulations ".[36]

[34] Willard Straight, *China's Loan Negotiation,* an address (New
York, 1912), p. 9. Also Croly, *op. cit.,* p. 277 *et seq.* See also
ibid., p. 249. [35] *Tiao yo, K.,* 103/2. [36] *MacMurray,* i, 648.

According to these regulations, which were put into operation two days afterwards, certain areas around the stations of the Chinese Eastern Railway were reserved, within which merchandise shipped by the railway was required to pay the two-thirds import duty. Of these areas, the one around Harbin had a radius of ten *li* from the railway station; those around fourteen other stations each a radius of five *li*, and those around the rest each a radius of three *li*. In accordance with the regulations for trade by land annexed to the treaty of St. Petersburg, February 24, 1881, the hundred-*li* free zone was maintained on both ends of the railway. This covered Manchuli and Suifenho, which would otherwise have fallen into the class of the fourteen stations.[37]

Second in point of time to the above were four agreements[38] on questions of expropriation of land, on timbering and on coal mining, signed on August 30, 1907, and on April 5, 1908, between the railway company on the one part and the authorities of Kirin and Heilungkiang, either jointly or separately, on the other. All these were rendered necessary by the liberal interpretation the Russians had made of the provision of Article VI of the railway contract during the military occupation, and in some cases by the irregularity of the situation arising from agreements made between minor officials and the railway administration never ratified by the Board of Foreign Affairs. In all of these cases the company agreed to give up some of their claims in exchange for the recognition by the provincial authorities of other claims. In the case of timbering, it is estimated that only one-fifth of the land originally claimed by the company was retained by it.[39]

[37] Regs. i and ii.   [38] *MacMurray*, i, 658, 663, 667, 671, 721.
[39] *Hsu*, 11/3; 12/27.

In the case of coal mining, the sixty-*li* zone provided in
an unratified agreement [40] was accepted. On the other
hand, it was agreed that the company was to have only the
right to be consulted as against foreign or semi-foreign
companies prospecting coal in the zone,[41] instead of the
exclusive right of prospecting coal within the zone, and of
the right to be consulted concerning the same outside the
zone as provided in the unratified agreement.[42] In addition, the presence of Chinese officials was also provided
for in the exploration and operation of coal mines by the
company as well as their intervention in transactions between the company and the people.[43]

The third readjustment with Russia concerned municipal administration along the Chinese Eastern Railway.
Ever since the military occupation, the company had maintained police on its lands. In order to put an end to this
irregularity the Hsu administration as it installed bureaus of
foreign affairs on the principal stations along the railway
also sent police to those points. This called forth protests
from the company and became a subject of correspondence
between the Russian minister and the Board of Foreign
Affairs.[44]

The question of police, however, was soon lost in a
larger question — that of municipal administration.[45] In
the fall of 1907 a copy of municipal regulations drawn
up by the Russians in Hailar first came to the hands of
the Hsu administration. Shortly afterwards a municipal
council was reported established in Harbin. These being

[40] *MacMurray*, i, 661.

[41] Art. ii; for Chinese text see *Hsu*, 11, ii/21.

[42] Art. ii.

[43] Arts. i, iv, v, viii and xii.

[44] *Hsu*, 11/10.

[45] For a full account and relevant documents see *ibid.*, 11/12-44.

duly brought to the notice of the central government, the Board of Foreign Affairs launched a protest on January 27, 1908 [46] to the Russian minister. On February 10th the latter replied,[47] justifying the act by the provision of Article VI of the Chinese Eastern Railway contract, quoting the phrase " The land belonging to the said company . . . will be managed exclusively by the said company ", without the continuing clause " which will be permitted to construct thereon buildings and works of various kinds as well as to set up telegraph, under its own operation, for the exclusive use of the railway ", nor considering that the subject of the article was entirely commercial in nature and not political. Such claims of political jurisdiction over lands granted for a commercial purpose the Board found no difficulty in repudiating, in a note,[48] dated February 18th, to the Russian minister and a circular,[49] dated February 25th, to the foreign representatives in Peking.

While the matter was still under discussion the Russians at Manchuli and Hailar proceeded to impose municipal taxes upon Chinese residents and on September 4th the Board of Foreign Affairs drew the attention of the Russian legation to the matter.[50] In replying on September 26th [51] the Russian minister, while still claiming the right on the basis of Article VI of the railway contract, advanced the contention that, since China acquiesced in the establishment of municipal councils in foreign settlements in treaty ports, she could not deny the privilege to the Russians on the land of the company. To this the Board replied on October 29th [52] pointing out that the contract

[46] *Ibid.*, 11/31.
[47] *Ibid.*, 11/31 *l.*
[48] *Ibid.*, 11/32 *l.*
[49] *Ibid.*, 11/33.

[50] *Ibid.*, 11/35 *l.*
[51] *Ibid.*, 11/36.
[52] *Ibid.*, 11/37 *l.*

was made especially for the construction and operation of the railway and that it contained no provision that its land was for trade or residence of foreigners and that no other meaning could be read into it.

China had granted to the company a wide stretch of land and had consented to make every station along the railway a special area in matters of customs duties. The creation of special municipal administration in towns of considerable size along the same line would mean but one step further, and it took a strong government to avoid submission. At this point the Board of Foreign Affairs showed itself ready to entertain proposals that might lead to settlement. Accordingly conferences were held between Major General Horvath, general manager of the railway, and Messrs. S. K. Alfred Sze and Yu Szu-hsiang, delegates of the Board of Foreign Affairs, and on May 10, 1909, a preliminary agreement was drawn up.[53] In this agreement China consented to the establishment of municipal bodies in commercial cities of a certain importance situated on the land of the railway,[54] with power to deal with all local questions of public utility [55] on certain conditions. These conditions may be seen in the following provisions: All residents without difference between the Chinese population and that of other nationalities were to enjoy the same rights and be subjected to the same obligations,[56] including the right to vote with certain qualifications,[57] and the right to be president of the assembly of delegates,[58] the president of the assembly being *ex officio* president of executive committee.[59] The municipal bodies

[53] *MacMurray*, ii, 1185.
[54] Art. vi.
[55] Art. x.
[56] Art. vii.
[57] Art. viii.
[58] Art. ix.
[59] Art. xii.

were to submit all decisions arrived at by the assemblies
to the president of the Bureau of Foreign Affairs and the
general manager of the railway for their joint approval,[60]
these to have a suspensive veto power,[61] and to refer important questions having reference to the public interest
or the finances of the municipalities for the consideration
and approval of the Chinese President of the company conjointly with the head office of the railway administration.[62]
In case the president of the Bureau of Foreign Affairs and
the general manager of the railway disagreed on decisions
submitted for their joint approval, the Chinese and foreign
residents were each to choose one representative and the
two officials jointly another, with no distinction of nationality, to form a committee of five with the two officials to
settle the difficulty on the basis of common agreement.[63]
In addition, the Chinese chamber of commerce at Harbin
was to have the right to nominate three members, and
each of those at Hailar and Manchuli to nominate two to
the executive committee of the respective towns to participate in its affairs upon the same footing with the other
members of the committee. As to detailed regulations in
regard to the municipalities and police, as well as the scale
of taxation, they were to be determined on the basis of the
general arrangement.[64]

Simultaneously with the conclusion of this preliminary
agreement, an exchange of notes concerning treaty rights
of other powers was effected between the Board of Foreign
Affairs and the Russian minister, of which the Russian
note is as follows: [65]

[60] Art. xiii.   [63] Art. xiii.
[61] Art. xiv.   [64] Art. xvii.
[62] Art. xv.
[65] Translation. For text see *Tiao yo, H.*, 1/4.

The land of the railway in the Eastern Three Provinces is Chinese territory. Now that the agreement declaring China's sovereign rights, establishing municipal bodies, and determining general rules, is about to be signed, I specially declare that in the said land my Government will fully respect the rights and privileges the subjects of other powers enjoy under the treaties between China and other powers.

The declaration of China's sovereign rights referred to in the note, it may be added, was made in the first few articles of the preliminary agreement.

Another point of readjustment with Russia, though not made by the Hsu administration but by its successor, may for convenience be also reviewed. It is embodied in the memorandum concerning the provisional regulations relating to navigation and trade on the Sungari, signed on August 8, 1910.[66]

Ever since the Russians had absorbed the half of Manchuria beyond the Amur and the Ussuri they had repeatedly attempted to navigate the upper Sungari. In doing this, as in absorbing the trans-Ussuri country,[67] they did not fail to take as the point of departure a provision of the treaty of Aigun. In this case it was the provision that " the navigation of the rivers Hei-lung [Amur], Sung-hua [Sungari] and Ussuri shall hereafter be reserved to the vessels of the Ta Tsing and Russian Empires ", by which rivers the negotiators had only in mind the sections that formed the common boundary for the drawing of which the treaty was made. Having failed in their attempt on account of the diligence of local Chinese authorities, the Russians sought to attain their object in another way. When, in 1880, the question of the evacuation of Ili came up, they asked as a condition the right to navigate the upper Sun-

[66] *MacMurray*, i, 807. [67] *Supra*, chap. ii, sec. 3.

gari up to Petuna, and succeeded in inserting a provision to the effect into the treaty of Livadia. This concession formed one of those to which the Chinese government raised the strongest objection. Consequently, the Russians were constrained to drop it from the treaty of St. Petersburg, which replaced the last-mentioned treaty in the following year.[68] However, they obtained a declaration that the provision of the treaty of Aigun concerning the navigation of the Sungari held good.[69]

Russia, of course, meant only to drop the question for the time being. Her time came again during the Boxer Rebellion. Under the cover of military occupation of Manchuria she began to navigate the upper Sungari to Harbin, and when she presented her note on April 18, 1903, concerning northern Manchuria, one of the demands, as we have seen above, was permission to establish landing stages along the river. War intervened and the demand, like the rest of its kind, was dropped, though navigation continued as before.

Having succeeded in navigating the upper Sungari, as if it were within the provision of the treaty of Aigun, Russia logically also claimed exclusive navigation with China in accordance with that provision. In 1909 China was about to establish customs offices at Aigun, the river front of Harbin, Sansing, and Lahasusu, as well as to regulate the navigation of the upper Sungari, as a result of her engagement [70] with Japan to open those ports. On this occasion Russia immediately asked to be consulted with regard to the last of the two measures.[71] The successor of

---

[68] See memorial by Tseng ki-tze, *K.*, 7, *Tiao yo*, 5/2.

[69] Art. xviii, *ibid.*, 5/20.   [70] *Supra*, chap. v, sec. 6.

[71] Board of Foreign Affairs to Russian Minister, 1/6/19, *ibid.*, *H.*, 9/1.

the Hsu administration, for reasons we shall presently see, was not in a position to resist Russia. After the details of the regulations had been discussed and agreed upon at Harbin between Mr. S. K. Alfred Sze, *taotai* of the Harbin customs, and the Russian delegates, the memorandum mentioned above was signed between the Board of Foreign Affairs and the Russian legation on August 8, 1910. In the preamble it was declared that the memorandum was agreed upon "in accordance with Article XVIII of the treaty of St. Petersburg concluded between Chinese and Russians in the seventh year of Kuanghsu (1881)".

Sec. 4. Readjustment with Japan

We have seen above that the question of the Hsinmin-Mukden and Kirin-Changchun lines was settled with Japan by a convention signed on April 15, 1907. Second in point of time to this settlement was that concerning the Yalu timber exploitation granted by Article X of the additional agreement to the treaty of Peking.

When the question came up in the fall of 1906 the Japanese minister interpreted the term "the right bank of the Yalu" to cover also the basin of the Hun river, a tributary of the Yalu. To this the Chinese government could not agree and the case dragged on for more than a year, until both parties made concessions.[72]

Under the terms of the agreement[73] signed on May 14, 1908, the area for exploitation was limited to a zone of 60 *li* on the right bank of the Yalu from the *hsien* of Linchiang to the 24th rivulet near the source of the river.[74] In places beyond this marked area in the Yalu basin, as

[72] Memorial by the Board of Foreign Affairs, *Hsu*, 12/5.
[73] *MacMurray*, i, 731.
[74] Art. i.

well as in the forests of the Hun river the woodcutters
were to apply to the company for loans to carry on their
industry and all timber cut by them — with the exception
of cross-ties for the railway companies in the Kiangsu and
Chekiang provinces, and timber for the use of the inhabitants along the river — was to be sold exclusively to the
company.[75]   In carrying out the exploitation, a Sino-Japanese company was to be formed [76] with a capital of
$3,000,000 (Mex.), of which Chinese and Japanese were
to contribute a half each,[77] and with the *Taotai* of Tung-
pien as superintendent and one Chinese and one Japanese
appointed by the respective countries as co-managers.[78]   As
to the term of the concession, it was fixed at twenty-five
years, with a possible extension at its expiration, if the
Chinese government should be satisfied with the working
of the company.[79]

Apart from the two foregoing cases, attempts at readjustment with Japan were, on the whole, less fortunate.
One of the attempts related to the Fushun coal mines.[80]
In 1902 two Chinese merchants each secured a concession
from the government to work the coal deposits at Fushun.
Later, one of them admitted $60,000 (Mex.) from the
Russo-Chinese Bank as shares in his enterprise.   Still later,
the same concessionaire bought out the right of the other
and applied to the central government through the military
governor of Fengtien for incorporation.   In view of the
fact that there was a foreign interest in the proposed company the Board of Foreign Affairs thought a special permission from the Throne was necessary, and advised the
military governor to apply for it.   Meanwhile the Russo-

[75] Art. v.   [78] Art. viii.
[76] Art. ii.   [79] Art. vi.
[77] Art. iii.   [80] For details see *Hsu*, 11, ii/3–5.

Japanese War broke out and the matter was left as it stood.

During the war the Russians took possession of the mines and connected them with the Southern Manchurian branch of the Chinese Eastern Railway by a short line to facilitate transportation. Later, when the Russians were driven off from the vicinity, the Japanese in turn occupied them. After the war, on the petition of the concessionaire, the Board of Foreign Affairs communicated with the Japanese minister requesting their restoration. After referring to Tokyo, the latter replied in April, 1907, that his government regarded the property in question as Russian and thus as having passed over to it by the provision of Article VI of the Portsmouth treaty.[81] About the same time news also came that the Japanese had occupied three more small coal mines ten *li* from Fushun worked by other Chinese than the concessionaire referred to.[82]

Another attempt related to the Yentai coal mines.[83] In the Yentai district there were ten coal beds, the operation of which dated back to the eighteenth century. In 1900 five of these beds were leased by their owners to some Russian merchants. In the next year four were worked by some Chinese merchants and one by the provincial government of Fengtien. Of the four worked by the Chinese merchants three were located close to one another and were generally known as one, reducing the number to five for the Russians and three for the Chinese.

When the Japanese reached the Yentai district after the Russians had fled from its vicinity, they closed the five

[81] *Ibid.*, p. 3.
[82] *Ibid.*, 11, ii/15.
[83] For details see *ibid.*, 11/6–8.

Russian beds, but issued orders to leave the three Chinese beds in operation as before, after verifying them by a map in the possession of their commander in charge. In July, 1906, however, the Japanese suddenly took possession of the two beds worked by private individuals. When the military governor took up the matter with the Japanese consul-general at Mukden, the latter replied [84] that they were taken under Article VI of the agreement relating to the Southern Manchurian branch, in which China granted the railway company the right to mine such coal as might be needed for the construction and operation of the railway. He further refused to consider the military governor's contention that such grant did not give an exclusive right as shown in the same article, which went on to say that " the price of which coal . . . shall not exceed the royalties paid by other parties in the same locality ".

A third attempt related to the Penhsihu [85] coal mines. These mines were situated about two *li* south of the An-tung-Mukden Railway. During the war the Japanese first worked them for the operation of the railway. After the war they turned them over to a private Japanese company, but when the military governor protested they gave assurance that the working was still for military purposes. In March, 1907, when the Japanese evacuation was about to finish, the Japanese company approached the provincial government for a joint enterprise. The military governor was reported to be well disposed. But before anything had yet been done, a note came from the Japanese consul-general at Mukden stating that, according to instructions from his government, the mines in question, being in the vicinity of the Antung-Mukden line, must naturally be worked by the Japanese, citing as precedents the cases of the Chinese Eastern and Shantung Railways, and invoking the aid of Article XII of the additional agreement to the treaty of Peking, which provided that most favorable treatment should be reciprocally extended in the matters dealt with in the treaty and the additional agreement. In reply the military governor went over Article VI of the additional agreement and the minutes of the Peking Conference to show that the two cases cited by the Japanese were not applicable, and pointed out that reciprocity as provided in Article XII of the additional agreement was entirely lacking in the Japanese proposal. Nothing, however, resulted from the effort of the military governor.

In addition to the preceding cases, there was the case of the mines of the metallic ores along the Antung-Mukden Railway worked or occupied by Japanese private individuals with the acquiescence of the Japanese military authorities. This last, probably because no Chinese concessionaire's interest was involved, had not yet been discussed with the Japanese when the Hsu administration took over the government.

The Hsu administration having entered upon its duties, all pending cases were taken up. The Japanese evidently had made up their minds by this time to treat the mines along the Antung-Mukden Railway as being on a different footing from those along the South Manchurian Railway and attempted to secure a monopoly for the latter and a half interest for the former, irrespective of whether private or government interests were affected. On the other hand, the Hsu administration held, as did the military governor before it, that a line should be strictly drawn between what was private and what was government prop-

erty; and, while willing to concede as much as possible
in case of the latter, was insistent that satisfaction should
be fully made for the former, irrespective of whether it
was on one or the other railway.

No difficulty arose, therefore, over the Penhsihu coal
mines, because they happened to be both on the Antung-
Mukden Railway and government property. Here the
Japanese consul-general retreated from the ground he had
previously held, and agreed to the proposal to turn these
mines into a Sino-Japanese enterprise.[86] For the same
reason no difficulty arose in regard to the mines of the
metallic ores. After some negotiations a memorandum of
agreement on them was therefore drawn up on August
24, 1907.[87] According to this, Japanese were allowed to
work coal, iron, tin, and lead mines along the Antung-
Mukden Railway conjointly with Chinese, subject to the
approval, first, of the commissioners of the two countries,
then, of the Viceroy of the Eastern Three Provinces and
the Governor of Fengtien, and finally of the Throne.
As to conditions under which the mines were to be worked,
they were to be similar to those provided in the contract
concerning the Lincheng mines on the Peking-Hankow
Railway,[88] with a right on the part of the concessionaires
to ask for equal treatment in case better terms were granted
to operators of other nationalities, for metals in Fengtien
and for coal in other localities.[89] The privileges thus
granted concerned mining along the Antung-Mukden Railway. In order that the line might not be changed in course
of reconstruction to take in mines elsewhere, the Hsu ad-

---

[86] For agreement signed May 22, 1910, see *MacMurray*, i, 793.
[87] Text in *Hsu*, 14/23; also *MacMurray*, i, 791.
[88] Art. iii.
[89] Arts. iv and v.

ministration insisted upon a declaration from the Japanese consul-general that no other route should be taken than the one in existence. This was accordingly made and embodied in the memorandum.[90]

The willingness of the consul-general to discuss pending cases, however, ended with the above. When the principles governing mines along the Antung-Mukden Railway were first agreed upon, the administration requested that the coal mines along the South Manchurian Railway be in turn discussed. On that occasion the consul-general said he would have to secure instructions on the subject.[91] Now that the principles had been embodied in a memorandum the administration fully expected that those cases would be discussed. They were, however, soon to be disappointed. What actually took place in the meeting next to the one in which the memorandum referred to was drawn up, probably cannot be better told than by reproducing in part the minutes: [92]

Viceroy and Governor: What do you wish to discuss today, please?

Consul-General: We do not need to discuss any other question today. Have you received instructions from your government on the memorandum concerning mines along the Antung-Mukden Railway?

V. & G.: Questions concerning mines along the South Manchurian and the Antung-Mukden Railways shall be reported to the government together. Now that the memorandum relating to mines along the latter has been agreed upon, let us proceed to discuss mines along the former. Have you received instructions from your government?

90 Art. i. See also *Hsu*, 11/48.
91 Minutes of third meeting, 33/7/7, *ibid.*, 14/6.
92 Minutes of sixth meeting, 33/7/20, *ibid.*, 14/24.

C.-G.: Yes. But since you have not secured yours I deem it unnecessary to discuss mine. [Here the consul-general went on to accuse the Hsu administration of delay in settling cases, which was followed by a reply from the viceroy that the consul-general had made settlement difficult.] I do not understand you. I do not think that I have demanded more than during the administration of Military Governor Chao. Take the case of the mines along the Antung-Mukden Railway. It is an entirely different case from that of those along the South Manchurian Railway, and yet you have to report them to your government together. You have been rather confused in this matter. That is not my fault.

V. & G.: These meetings are held to take up cases left over by the administration of Military Governor Chao. Some of these cases arise out of treaty provisions and some do not, as is admitted in your correspondence with us. Take the mines along the Antung-Mukden Railway and the Penhsihu coal mines. They do not arise from treaty provisions. In your notes you have requested us to take them up like those along the South Manchurian Railway. In consideration of the good relationship of the two nations, we have consented to take up even these for an open-minded discussion. Now that these have been settled, it is but right that the mines along the South Manchurian Railway — cases arising from treaty provisions — should be discussed next. On the contrary, although you have instructions from your government, you have refused to discuss these with us. You have indeed failed to meet our cordiality. We hope you realize that to take the cases connected with the South Manchurian and Antung-Mukden Railways together is to accommodate you. Our correspondence is still here to be our witness. You have not yet repudiated it. How can you put the blame on us? [Here the administration continued with illustrations of the consul-general's unreasonableness from another case

under discussion, in which the consul-general failed to restore private residences evacuated by military forces. Then
the consul-general retorted with an intimation that he
might take back those already restored pending the settlement of all cases.] . . . This is most unreasonable. If
you mean to resort to forcible measures, please declare it
expressly and we shall telegraph to the government to have
our negotiations terminated.

C.-G.: Since you do not fulfil your duties, I cannot
fulfil mine. [Here follows a long and heated exchange
of accusations into which other cases were brought.] . . .
May I ask whether it is not your intention to intimate that
the mines along the South Manchurian Railway must be
discussed first before you would sign the memorandum
concerning those along the Antung-Mukden Railway?

V. & G.: Yes. They all concern mines and must be
settled and signed together.

And so the memorandum was not signed. Later all
unsettled cases were transferred to Peking. In order to
have his advice, Mr. Tang Shao-yi was summoned by the
Board of Foreign Affairs. Mr. Tang was, however, soon
appointed special envoy to the United States, and these
cases were therefore left as they stood.

Another case which also baffled the efforts of the parties
to settle, though of much less importance, concerned the
Tashichiao-Yingkou line.[93] In the agreement concerning
the South Manchurian branch of the Chinese Eastern Railway, the railway company was permitted to build temporary branch lines from the main line to Yingkou and to
the seaports in the " neutral zone " to facilitate the construction of the line, with the understanding that, within
eight years from the date of the survey and determination
of the line and the appropriation of the land for its con-

[93] For details see *ibid.*, 11/50.

struction, they were to be removed.[94]　In accordance with
this provision a branch line was constructed by the Chinese
Eastern Railway company from the main line at Tashichiao to Yingkou.

In the autumn of 1907, when the time for the removal
of that branch line had almost arrived, the Japanese prepared to move its Yingkou terminal five *li* nearer town.
The Board of Foreign Affairs therefore drew the attention of the Japanese minister to the provision referred to
above.　When this branch line was taken up in the Peking
Conference, the Japanese plenipotentiaries insinuated that
neither China nor Russia ever intended to remove it in
spite of the treaty provision.　To this the Chinese plenipotentiaries frankly replied that it was China's intention to
reconstruct it herself when the term for its removal was
up.　Finally, both parties agreed that the matter be left
for future discussion when the time came.　Now that the
question was taken up by the Board of Foreign Affairs,
the Japanese minister asserted that it was already settled
in the Peking Conference.　In consequence, this case, like
the mine cases, was left unsettled.

Sec. 5.　*Japan and the Regency*

On April 8, 1904, Great Britain signed three agreements with France, removing causes of possible conflicts
concerning Egypt and Morocco, Newfoundland and West
Africa, and Siam.　On August 31, 1907, she further
signed three agreements with Russia removing conflicts
concerning Persia, Afghanistan, and Tibet.

Of the rapprochement of Great Britain and her traditional rivals, of which the above six agreements formed
only a landmark, Japan, being an ally of hers, was not

[94] Art. iii, *MacMurray*, i, 155.

slow to take advantage. On June 10, 1907, she entered into an agreement [95] with France, ally of her enemy in the late war, by which the two contracting parties —

. . . being agreed to respect the independence and integrity of China, as well as the principle of equal treatment in that country for the commerce of subjects or citizens of all nations, and having a special interest in having order and a specific state of things guaranteed, especially in the regions of the Chinese Empire adjacent to the territories where they have the rights of sovereignty, protection or occupation, engage to support each other for assuring the peace and security in those regions, with a view to maintaining the respective situation and the territorial rights of the two Contracting Parties in the Continent of Asia.

On July 30th she entered into two agreements,[96] one open and one secret, with Russia her late enemy. By the open agreement the two contracting parties agreed to respect each " the actual territorial integrity " of the other, and " all the rights accruing to one and the other party from the treaties, conventions and contracts in force between them and China " from the Portsmouth treaty " as well as from the special conventions concluded between Japan and Russia " ; and to " recognize the independence and the territorial integrity of the Empire of China and the principle of equal opportunity in whatever concerns the commerce and industry of all nations in that empire " as well as to " sustain and defend the maintenance of the *status quo* and respect for this principle by all pacific means within their reach ". By the secret agreement the two powers recognized each the interests of the other, Japan in Korea and Russia in Mongolia, and furthermore a line

[95] *MacMurray*, i, 640.　　　　[96] *Ibid.*, i, 658.

of demarcation was drawn across Manchuria dividing it into two mutually exclusive spheres of influence.[97]

Of the Powers that were interested in the Far East, only Germany and the United States were thus left without a special understanding with Japan. Germany, of course, was out of the question. As to the United States one, however, was soon concluded. It appeared that, while Mr. Tang was on his way to America, an understanding with regard to their respective positions in the region of the "Pacific Ocean" was being negotiated by the Japanese ambassador with the State Department. On the very day of Mr. Tang's arrival at Washington (October 30) when the State Department had had time to inform him of the contents of the agreement, identical notes embodying it were exchanged.[98]

"The exchange of views between us", Baron Takahira's note says, "has shown that Japan and the United States holding important outlying insular possessions in the region of the Pacific Ocean, the Governments of the two countries are animated by a common aim, policy and intention in that region". The note gave an outline of their understanding of that "common aim, policy, and intention" as follows: (1) Encouragement of free and peaceful development of their commerce "on the Pacific Ocean"; (2) Maintenance of the existing *status quo* in the region of the Pacific Ocean and defence of the principle of equal opportunity for commerce and industry in China; (3) Respect for the territorial possessions belonging to each other in the region of the Pacific Ocean; and (4) Preservation of "the common interest of all powers

[97] A. L. P. Dennis, *The Foreign Policies of Soviet Russia* (New York, 1924), p. 271.

[98] *MacMurray*, i, 769; Croly, *op. cit.*, p. 274.

in China by supporting by all pacific means at their disposal the independence and integrity of China and the principle of equal opportunity for commerce and industry of all nations in that Empire ". The note then provided that " should any event occur threatening the *status quo* as above described or the principle of equal opportunity as above defined, it remains for the two Governments to communicate with each other in order to arrive at an understanding as to what measure they may consider it useful to take ".

But a change of greater significance also took place at about the same time. On November 15, 1908, while Mr. Tang Shao-yi was still on the Pacific Ocean, the Empress Dowager Tsuhsi, who had needed two losses of Peking and two flights from her capital to convince her of the solidarity of interest between the Manchu dynasty and the Chinese nation, died, and her place, to control the destiny of the nation, was taken by Prince Chun, a young man who was without natural talent for government and at the same time lacked the experience of misfortune which is so often a good teacher.

On January 2, 1909, Yuan Shih-kai was summarily dismissed from all his offices in the government. On the 8th Mr. Tang, who was to proceed to Europe to study " the systems of financial administration and to report to the Throne thereon " after fulfilling his mission in the United States, was hastily recalled. On February 9th, Mr. Hsu Shih-chang was removed from the viceroyalty of the Eastern Three Provinces and given a post in Peking as president of the Board of Communications, and General Hsi-liang, a Manchu, then the viceroy of the Yun-Kuei Provinces, was appointed in his place. On July 8th, Mr. Tang, having returned to Peking, was com-

manded to vacate his post as Governor of Fengtien, and
was virtually retired from government service.[99]

On the arrival of the new viceroy the Chancery and the
Advisory Council, two important bodies of the viceregal
government of Manchuria, as well as the Commission for
Mongolian Affairs, were abolished.[100] After this the governorship of Fengtien was also done away with,[101] and the
reality of a viceroyalty as conceived by the edict of April
20, 1907, accordingly disappeared; for henceforth the
viceroy was but a colleague, with a superior rank, to the
governors of Kirin and Heilungkiang and not their superior, and there was no person or organ to plan and work
for the three provinces as a whole.

What, then, was the fate of the reconstruction measures? In the beginning of 1909 Japan first approached
China on the matter of the Antung-Mukden Railway, for
the reconstruction of which by Japan China had given
her consent in the additional agreement to the treaty of
Peking. The Board of Communications accordingly sent
officers to make a joint survey; and, when it had been
completed as far as Chen-hsiang-tun, a little distance from
Mukden, the matter was referred to the viceroy. Suddenly, on August 7th, Reuter's Agency reported that Baron
Ijuin, Japanese minister, had informed the Chinese government that Japan was going to proceed independently
with the work of reconstructing the railway without waiting for Chinese coöperation,[102] and a few days later Eitaké,
Japanese consul-general at Shanghai, made a statement to

99 *Herald*, 1909, i, 382; ii, 713; iii, 147.

100 Memorial by Hsi-liang, *Hsu sin fa ling*, 5/16.

101 Memorial by Hsi-liang, *ibid.*, 6/19.

102 *Herald*, 1909, iii, 361.

the foreign community of that port, which said in part: [103]

. . . China, having recourse to her well-known policy of obstruction and procrastination, evaded the just and reasonable demands of Japan and raised questions regarding the police authority in the railway zones and the withdrawal of railway guards. Finally, on July 24th last, they sent a reply which, if concurred in, would wholly nullify the provisions of the arrangement of 1905 and disregard the survey agreed to by the Commissioners of the two Governments.

That reply, besides reviving the questions of railway guards and police authority, and raising other immaterial subjects which would appropriately lend themselves to separate negotiations, declared that the work of improvement must be confined to the existing track and that no broadening of the gauge could be permitted.

. . . China still maintains an unyielding and unaccommodating attitude, which gives no promise of anything but vain and unprofitable negotiations.

In this situation the Imperial Government is compelled to take independent action and, without waiting for the coöperation of the Chinese authorities to proceed to carry out the necessary works of reconstruction and improvement and in harmony with the survey of the Commissioners of the two Governments.

On the evening of the very day (August 6) when Ijuin informed the Chinese government of Japan's intention, orders were given to the South Manchurian Railway company to commence work. The next day the railway company reported that the order was instantly transmitted; that the construction of the difficult Fuchinling tunnel was

[103] *Ibid.*, 389.

already begun; that the whole line of about one hundred and eighty miles was divided into fourteen sections to be completed in two years and a half, at a cost of 23,000,000 *yen*, and that proper military precautions were being taken for the protection of the work.[104]

To the Japanese note the Board of Foreign Affairs replied the next day.[105] It stated that China never objected to the broadening of the gauge nor to any other improvement of an engineering character — a point which the Japanese had capitalized — but had insisted, and still insisted, that the gauge, when broadened, should conform with the standard adopted by the Peking-Mukden Railway and that no other change must be made than those entailed by the necessity of engineering. It also stated that no extension of military control or patrolling of railways in Manchuria would be permitted and that China would furnish police to guard the line, and then concluded by repudiating any responsibility for past delay.

About the same time the Board also issued a statement [106] of the case to Chinese representatives abroad. To the accusation made by Japan it had the following to say:

We have been compelled to lay particular emphasis on the question of military protection of the railway and the constitution of the police force. If Japan had conceded these points, the matter could have been settled long ago, and she would have been under no necessity to attempt to lay blame for any delay at the door of China.

The matter was finally referred back to Mukden, where, between the viceroy and the Japanese consul-general, a

104 *Ibid.*, iii, 450.

105 Substance given in the statement given to Chinese representatives abroad cited below.

106 *Herald*, 1909, iii, 451.

memorandum was drawn up on August 19, 1909.[107] The gauge insisted upon by the Chinese government was adopted, but as to the question of military guards and police nothing was said.

The effect of this Japanese coup was not entirely lost upon the Prince Regent. He awoke; he found himself helpless; and he surrendered. Sensing the danger he also commanded that all pending cases be settled; and so they were all settled. On September 4th two agreements were signed between China and Japan, one concerning mines and railways, and the other concerning the so-called Chientao dispute. The first [108] of the two agreements was simple. China engaged that, in the event of her undertaking to construct a railway between Hsinmin and Fakumen she would arrange with Japan. China agreed that the railway between Tashichiao and Yingkou should be delivered up to herself simultaneously with the South Manchurian Railway. China recognized the right of Japan to work the Fushun and Yentai mines. China consented that all mines, not only along the Antung-Mukden Railway, but also along the main line of the South Manchurian Railway, except those at Fushun and Yentai, should be exploited as joint enterprises of Japanese and Chinese subjects, under the general principles provisionally agreed upon between the Hsu administration and the Japanese consul-general.

As to the so-called Chientao dispute, after the way the Bureau of Frontier Affairs at Yenchi went about the whole matter, Japan had for some time shifted her basis of action from the question of boundary to the question of protection of Koreans. In November, 1908, when Mr. Tang

[107] *MacMurray*, 787.
[108] *Ibid.*, 790.

Shao-yi passed through Japan on his way to America, the Japanese government had suggested to him that the case be settled on the basis of China's conceding to Japan the right to protect her Korean subjects there as in the treaty ports, promising at the same time that Japan would not interfere with the Koreans that had been or might be willing to become naturalized.[109]   In communicating the Japanese suggestion to the government, Mr. Tang gave as his opinion that China might open several ports on the left bank of the Tumen to meet the Japanese.

In the agreement [110] now signed, it was declared that the Tumen was recognized as forming the boundary between China and Korea and that, in the region of the source of that river, the boundary line would start from " the boundary monument and thence follow the course of the stream Shihyishwei ".[111]   Following this, China engaged to open Lungchingtsun, Chutzuchia, Toutaokau, and Paitsaokau to the residence and trade of foreigners, where Japan might establish consulates or branch offices of consulates;[112] and recognized the residence of Korean subjects, as heretofore, on agricultural lands lying north of the Tumen within certain limits.[113]   Concerning these Korean subjects, China was to exercise jurisdiction over them, but Japan was to have the right to be represented at all court proceedings, to receive previous notice before the hearing of important cases, and to apply for new trial in decisions not properly rendered.[114]   An examination of the terms of the agreement will show to what a shadow Mr. Tang's suggestion to the Chinese government had been reduced, and how the agreement was drawn to Japan's

[109] *Hsu*, 3/2.
[110] *MacMurray*, i, 796.
[111] Art. i.

[112] Art. ii.
[113] Art. iii.
[114] Art. iv.

entire satisfaction upon the proposal she had made. But this was not all. In the agreement China was made to undertake, apart from the boundary question or the question of protection of Koreans, to extend the Kirin-Changchun Railway to the southern boundary of Yenchi opposite to Hueining, on the Korean side, upon the same terms as the Kirin-Changchun Railway, and upon consultation with Japan as to the date to commence work.[115] This line, be it noted, covers precisely the last section of the extension of the North China Railways as it was originally projected, and is parallel to the Mukden-Yenchi line designed by the Hsu administration to replace that section. And it was after this and the foregoing concessions that Japan, on her part, as if to show her magnanimity, consented to withdraw within two months "the Chientao branch office of the Residency-General, as well as all civil and military offices attached thereto." [116]

By the foregoing two agreements were nullified practically all the efforts of the Hsu administration in restricting Japanese activities to strict treaty basis. What, then, about the development of Manchuria? The execution of this latter policy involved just as much statesmanship as the former. Since the Prince Regent and his henchmen had failed in one, it would not be reasonable to expect them to succeed in the other. Indeed, in carrying out the development projects, all the initiative that characterized the Hsu administration was entirely lacking with the Regency. As we shall see, the original project of a Manchurian bank through which a program of industrial and railway development was to be carried out, soon degenerated into the mere grant of a Chinchou-Aigun Railway concession, and a mere loan for Manchurian industrial development; and

[115] Art. vi.   [116] Art. vii.

what should have been carried out by China herself, with the assistance of the United States, by a combination of circumstances — the incompetency of the Regency and the activities of the Taft administration it seems — came to be handled by the United States with weak, though whole-hearted, support from China; so much so that the development of the second line of policy handed down by the Hsu administration could be better reviewed from another angle in the following pages.

Sec. 6. *Japan and the United States*

(1) *The Knox "Neutralization" Scheme*

In the message of President Taft to the Prince Regent [117] sent on July 15, 1909, in connection with American participation in the Hukuang Railways loan, the President said:

I have an intense personal interest in making the use of American capital in the development of China an instrument for the promotion of the welfare of China, and an increase in her material prosperity without entanglements or creating embarrassments affecting the growth of her independent political power and the preservation of her territorial integrity.

American good will towards China, which had hitherto been confined mainly to diplomatic actions, had assumed the additional form of financial assistance by the Taft administration. In the summer of 1909, when the Hukuang Railways loan was being negotiated by China with the bankers of Great Britain, France, and Germany, the State Department, relying upon certain claims, secured

[117] *For. Rel.*, 1909, p. 178.

American participation and caused the formation of the American group of bankers for the purpose.[118] The message, part of which we have quoted, was sent at the time the State Department had experienced difficulties with the other powers over the question of equality of right of participation.

In August, W. F. Straight, who had become the representative of the American group, arrived at Peking. On the arrival of Straight, the Regency approached him to revive the Manchurian bank discussion and to undertake the Chinchou-Aigun Railway project.[119] On October 2, 1909, a preliminary agreement [120] providing for the financing, construction, and operation of the Chinchou-Aigun Railway was signed between the provincial authorities at Mukden and Straight, together with the representative of the British interests that had contracted for the construction of the extension of the North China Railways from Hsinmin to Fakumen, the line that had been abandoned in favor of the Chinchou-Aigun Railway. Then the matter was referred by the American bankers to the State Department as part of a bigger Manchurian railway project.

American interest in Manchurian railways had, indeed, had its origin in a much earlier date. In September, 1905, E. H. Harriman, working closely with Lloyd Griscom, American minister to Japan, drew up with Prince Ito and Count Katsura, the premier of Japan, a memorandum stipulating that the South Manchurian Railway be financed by an American loan, and operated under joint Japanese and American direction. The scheme, however, was blocked by Marquis Komura. During 1906–1907 the Rus-

[118] Croly, *op. cit.*, pp. 292, 295, 299.
[119] *Ibid.*, p. 300.
[120] *MacMurray*, i, 800.

sian government proposed to certain American bankers that they purchase from Russia the Chinese Eastern Railway, stating that Russia was willing to sell in case Japan could be persuaded to take similar action. When Mr. Tang Shao-yi was in Washington, the scheme was discussed with him, and he expressed his readiness to coöperate. An important Japanese financier, who had been informally advised of it, however, stated that Japan would be unwilling to acquiesce therein. In the summer of 1909 Harriman, through a leading Paris banker, approached Kokovtsev, Russian minister of finance, and was assured that on the latter's return from a trip to Vladivostok upon which he was about to start, he would recommend the sale of the Russian railway. This he did in a public address on his return to Moscow.[121]

At this juncture Harriman died. In order that his plan might not miscarry, Straight, who had throughout been coöperating with Harriman, undertook to acquaint the American bankers with it. The following letter of Straight's is worth quoting:[122]

The proposition (Mr. Harriman's plan) was as follows: The Russian government and the French interest in the Russo-Chinese Bank, are not satisfied with the present policy of that institution into which a large German element has been introduced. It is proposed therefore either (a) to inject new life and thus oust German control, or (b) to extend the activities of the semi-government Siberian Bank to Manchuria and China in order to check the growth of Japanese influence. In either case English and American,

[121] Willard Straight, *China's Loan Negotiations*, pp. 5 *et seq.* Memorandum of Department of State to Russian Embassy, Feb. 8, 1910, *For. Rel.*, 1910, p. 258. Croly, *op. cit.*, pp. 238, 295.

[122] Croly, *op. cit.*, p. 306.

together with French capital, would be used to bolster waning Russian prestige in the Orient, besides ensuring for themselves the political support of the Russian government in their enterprises in Manchuria and Mongolia.

Leaving Siberia out of the discussion, the most promising field for the Group's Eastern activities would be Manchuria and Mongolia. It should in these regions be possible to act as partners, not as lenders alone, for the political situation, particularly in the former, forces China to grant terms more favorable than could be secured elsewhere, while in neither region is popular sentiment, a growing obstacle to foreign investment in the South, an important factor.

These being the premises, the following program is suggested:

I. Coöperating Anglo-American interests should, as already proposed, secure the contract for financing, constructing, and operating the Chinchou-Amur Railway, Russian political acquiescence, at least, if not support, being assured either by permitting the Russo-Chinese Bank to handle Pauling's construction accounts or by giving that institution a share in the flotation.

II. The Manchurian Bank should be taken up as part of the general scheme, but would not necessarily be the next step, which should be —

III. The purchase of the Chinese Eastern Railway by the China-American-British Company, which shall operate the Chinchou-Amur line. Prior to such purchase the American government should interchange with Russia notes similar to those exchanged with Japan on November 30, 1908. Russia, in order to secure such a political *entente*, would be willing before selling the railway to withdraw the railway guards and recognize fully China's sovereignty and administrative right within the so-called " Railway Settlements ", over

which the Chinese Eastern Railway now claims jurisdiction.

IV. The withdrawal of the railway guards and the abandonment of the claim to administrative rights would
force Japan, in view of her obligations under the
Treaty of Portsmouth and the Komura agreement,
either to follow suit or to stand convicted of international bad faith.

Considering her alliance with England and Russo-Japanese and Anglo-Russian *ententes,* and the notes exchanged
with us in November last, Japan's opposition to a Russo-
American *entente* would hardly be a diplomatic probability.
The possible extension of a participation which would satisfy Japanese *amour propre* and not produce Chinese dis-
trust, timely reference to the contract which Mr. Harriman
signed for the joint operation of the South Manchurian
Railway and which was ignored but never canceled by
Japan, and the judicious manipulation of the American and
European attitude toward the war loan conversion and
treaty revision which Japan now contemplates, should render impossible any overt act of hostility or any very serious
intrigue which could in any way be attributed to Japan.

It is difficult to tell whether it was the fault of the
bankers or of the State Department, or of both, that the
tactics of Harriman were not followed when the matter
was transferred from the bankers to the State Department.
On November 6th, P. C. Knox, the Secretary of State,
submitted to Great Britain [123] the entire project as conceived by Harriman without, however, the essential condition of Russian support or acquiescence. Knox said in
part in his proposal to the British government:

[123] *For. Rel.,* 1910, p. 234.

First, perhaps, the most effective way to preserve the undisturbed enjoyment by China of all political rights in Manchuria and to promote the development of those Provinces under a practical application of the policy of the open door and equal commercial opportunity would be to bring the Manchurian highways, the railroads, under an economic, scientific, and impartial administration by some plan vesting in China the ownership of the railroads through funds furnished for that purpose by the interested powers willing to participate. . . .

Second, should this suggestion not be found feasible in its entirety then the desired end would be approximated, if not attained, by Great Britain and the United States diplomatically supporting the Chinchou-Aigun arrangement and inviting the interested powers friendly to complete commercial neutralization of Manchuria to participate in the financing and construction of that line and of such additional lines as future commercial development may demand, and at the same time to supply funds for the purchase by China of such of the existing lines as might be offered for inclusion in this system.

On the 25th Sir Edward Grey replied to the proposal.[124] He stated that the general principle involved " entirely commends itself to His Majesty's Government, so far as the preservation of the open-door policy and equal commercial opportunities are concerned and would in their opinion be well adapted to securing to China full control in Manchuria ". But he continued:

I am, however, of the opinion, that until pending negotiations for the Hukuang loan have been completed, it would seem undesirable to consider the question of another international loan for China's railway undertakings, and I would suggest, therefore, that, for the present at any rate,

[124] Grey to Reid, *ibid.*, p. 235.

it would be wiser to postpone consideration of the first scheme. As regards the alternative proposal contained in your Excellency's note, I observe with satisfaction that the coöperation of interested powers forms part of the scheme, and I have the honor to suggest, for your Excellency's consideration, that as a preliminary step towards attaining this desirable end the two Governments should unite in endeavoring to persuade the Chinese Government to admit the Japanese to participation in the Chinchou-Aigun line, as being the parties most interested. The question of supplying funds for the purchase by China of existing lines to be connected with the Chinchou-Aigun line could be considered subsequently.

No sooner was the proposal made to the British government than it was publicly discussed in Europe and the Far East, especially Japan. In order to prevent its prospects from being prejudiced, Knox hastened on the one hand to notify Great Britain, on December 14th,[125] of his reason for not being able to postpone the consideration of the first scheme and his acceptance of her suggestion as to the second; and on the other, submitted the proposal, on the next day, to China, Japan, Russia, Germany, and France.[126]

Germany and France were the least interested. As was expected, the former expressed a general concurrence, while the latter inclined to support her ally, Russia. China, Russia, and Japan were the most interested, either legitimately or illegitimately. When the proposal first reached China, the government showed no small amount of hesitation; but, in order to give moral support to a proposal which, good or bad, was conceived in its interest, an edict was issued on January 20, 1910, publicly ratifying the

[125] Knox to Reid, *ibid.*, p. 236.
[126] Knox to O'Brien, *ibid.*, p. 236.

preliminary agreement concerning the Chinchou-Aigun Railway.[127]

What then was the attitude of Japan and Russia? On December 21st replies came from both Tokyo and St. Petersburg. Both maintained that nothing appeared to have threatened either China's sovereign rights or the " open door " policy in Manchuria and that therefore there was no reason for them to entertain the proposal. Both maintained, also, that " the substitution of an international in place of a national régime " would not be satisfactory from a financial standpoint, and that therefore the proposal was not worth entertaining. With these general observations the two governments then went on each to give its specific objections. With regard to the chief scheme Russia said:

The development of Manchuria and the exploitation of its natural resources are not the only purposes pursued by the Chinese Eastern Railway. The latter is of a public interest of the first order to Russia. It constitutes the principal line of communication between the Russian possessions in the Far East and the rest of the Empire; it is also the great artery by which these possessions are supplied with Russian merchandise. In this way the line is but an integral part of the great Trans-Siberian Railway, which is used by almost all of western Europe in its relations with the Far East. It is this consideration that decided the Russian Government to guarantee, at very considerable expense, the capital invested in the construction of the Chinese Eastern Railway and to cover the deficit resulting from its operation. It can not, therefore, be a matter of indifference to the Imperial Government whether it is an international organ that administers a line of such importance, or, on the contrary, a Russian stock company which is obliged not to

[127] See documents *ibid.*, pp. 245–255 *passim.*

fix the rates and conditions of transportation of merchandise by the Chinese Eastern Railway without the consent of the Russian Government, and which, by the nature of the concession obtained, is closely connected with the interests of the nation.

As to the alternate scheme, Russia said:

The Imperial Government considers itself obliged to declare that it regards the project of construction of the Chinchou-Tsitsihar-Aigun Railway as being of capital importance to Russia. Its accomplishment will open up a new route giving access from the south not only to the Chinese Eastern Railway, but directly to Russian possessions at Aigun. This shows adequately the strategic and political importance of the enterprise. Moreover, the construction of this line will essentially modify the conditions under which Eastern Mongolia and the north of Manchuria are served by the Chinese Eastern Railway. Now, the Imperial Government cannot realize the consequences of this proposition and decide on the attitude which it ought to assume in regard thereto unless it is informed of the basis on which it reposes. For these reasons the Imperial Government, while being willing in principle to take this question under consideration, hopes that it will be enabled to know the basis of the proposition in due time in order that it may, after a thorough examination, reach a final attitude with regard to the proposition itself as well as to participation therein.

Russia then went further and declared that " it is the same in any future project concerning a financial participation in the construction of railways in Manchuria ".

Japan, on the other hand, did not seem to be so favored by the condition of things as to be able to put forth arguments of the same force, false as they might be. Against the chief scheme she said:

The most serious objection to the proposal in question lies in the fact that it contemplates a very important departure from the terms of the treaty of Portsmouth. That treaty was designed to establish in Manchuria a permanent order of things, and the Imperial Government firmly believed that in a strict and loyal adhesion to its provisions are to be found the highest guarantees of enduring peace and repose in this part of the world and of the orderly advancement of Manchuria. Not the least difficult of the many difficult and important problems that were definitely solved at the Portsmouth conference was the question of railways. That adjustment subsequently received the deliberate confirmation of the Chinese government in the treaty of Peking, and the railway operations now carried on in southern Manchuria are consistent with the original concessions which were with equal deliberation granted by the same power.

When Japan came to the alternate plan she did not seem to have even an argument to advance, and she contented herself with the following words:

The observation which I [the foreign minister] have now the honor to present to your Excellency and which I venture to hope may prove as convincing to your Excellency's Government as they are convincing to my own, have reference to the plan in its widest sense, but they are, I should add, no less applicable to the scheme in its more restricted form, since the two plans are in principle the same and differ only in degree.

And these were then qualified by the following:

In conclusion, I wish to express to your Excellency the sincere appreciation of my Government for the courteous intimation of the United States concerning the projected Chinchou-Aigun line, and to say that in principle the Imperial Government will be prepared to participate in the enterprise with the other powers interested in the question. But as that question is clearly distinguishable from the main subject of your Excellency's note, I will, with your permission, reserve this minor point for separate and independent attention when the necessary details regarding the matter are known.

With these replies, not only the neutralization scheme proper, but also the Chinchou-Aigun Railway project, were destined to be buried. In Peking notes identical in tone and spirit were presented by the ministers of Japan and Russia to the effect that, in view of their interests, China should consult with them before concluding the details of the agreement concerning the Chinchou-Aigun Railway.[128] In Washington, the Russian ambassador claimed that Russia was " entitled to expect " that the conclusion of that agreement would not take place before his government had had an opportunity to express its views in regard to it, since, he declared, the United States had invited Russia to take part in the enterprise.[129] Knox declined to entertain the Russian claim but declared that he still adhered to the principle of participation and friendly coöperation of the " interested powers ".[130]

On February 8th, previous to the foregoing exchange of views, Mr. Knox had submitted a memorandum to Russia [131] explaining the position of the United States. This

[128] Fletcher to Knox, Feb. 7, 1910, *ibid.*, p. 257.

[129] Memorandum from Russian Embassy, Feb. 2, 1910, *ibid.*, p. 255.

[130] Memorandum to Russian Embassy, Feb. 14, 1910, *ibid.*, p. 260.

[131] Memorandum to Russian Embassy, February 8, 1910, *ibid.*, p. 257.

did not help. On the 24th Russia informed the State Department [132] that she was convinced by a study of the Chinchou-Aigun Railway project that such a railway would be "exceedingly injurious both to the strategic and to the economic interests of Russia", and that as China in 1899 had "engaged not to build railroads to the north of Peking with foreign capital other than Russian", Russia "could be willing not to insist on the execution by China of this obligation only under the conditions that railways built with capital provided by international syndicates should not be an evident menace to the security of the Russian frontier, and should not injure the interest of Russia's railway enterprise in Manchuria". She further suggested that China and the Anglo-American interests build, in place of the Chinchou-Aigun Railway, a railway between Kalgan and Urga with a right on the part of Russia to connect it with the Trans-Siberian Railway at Kiakhta.

On April 18th Knox replied.[133] He declined the counter-proposal. He contended that the Russian position, in invoking such an alleged agreement as that referred to above in derogation of general treaty rights, amounted to a nullification of stipulations of treaties between China and foreign powers and a curtailment of the rights of the nationals of other countries. He intimated that he was still prepared to use his influence with the American interests and the Chinese government to secure the full and friendly consideration of such modifications of the Chinchou-Aigun Railway project as Russia might wish to propose. Finally, he requested Russia to withdraw her re-

[132] Memorandum from Russian Embassy, Feb. 24, 1910, *ibid.*, p. 261.

[133] Memorandum to Russian Embassy, April 18, 1910, *ibid.*, p. 264.

monstrance at Peking " a deference for which due to Russia's universally recognized interests ", he said, " has alone delayed the efforts of those concerned ". On the 24th the American ambassador at St. Petersburg reported [134] that the Russian finance minister intimated that a surveying party was being sent out from Harbin to go over the proposed line to study different aspects of the question, expecting a full report by July on which to hold a full discussion.

July finally came, and on the 4th, the American Independence Day, the world witnessed instead the signing of the Russo-Japanese agreement of 1910.[135] By this the two powers, in order " to develop the results of the convention of July 17, 1907 " agreed —

(1) " to lend each other their friendly coöperation with a view to the improvement of their respective lines of railway in Manchuria, and to the perfecting of the connecting service of the said railways, and to refrain from all competition unfavorable to the attainment of this result;

(2) " to maintain and to respect the *status quo* in Manchuria as it results from all the treaties, conventions, or other arrangements hitherto concluded, either between Russia and Japan, or between these two powers and China ", which arrangements they had exchanged; and

(3) " in case any event of such a nature as to menace the above-mentioned *status quo* should be brought about ", " to enter into communication with each other, for the purpose of agreeing upon the measures that they may judge it necessary to take for the maintenance of the said *status quo* ".

Since then the world has discovered a secret counter-

---

[134] *Ibid.*, 367.
[135] *MacMurray*, i, 803.

part [136] affirming mainly the secret arrangement of 1907.

On receiving copies of the open agreement from the Russian and Japanese ministers at Peking the Board of Foreign Affairs made its acknowledgment,[137] in which, after observing that the convention " accords with and confirms the principles of the engagements " made between Japan and Russia by the Portsmouth treaty and between China and Japan by the treaty and additional agreement of Peking, it declared:

The Imperial Government will, therefore, in the future act in accordance with the principles declared in the Russo-Japanese Treaty of Peace, and execute the provisions of the Treaty and Agreement [of Peking] with Japan, maintaining with increased efforts such matters as arise from the exercise of China's rights of sovereignty, the principle of equal opportunity, and the development of the commercial and industrial prosperity of the three Manchurian provinces, with a view to the promotion of the best interests of all parties.

(2) *The Manchurian Industrial Development Loan*

After the failure of the Chinchou-Aigun Railway project, the Manchurian bank project had yet its course to run. This, however, had, since passing over to the hands of the Regency, shrunk into a mere loan for Manchurian development. The loan was proposed to the American government on October 2, 1909, as part of a larger loan for the reform of the Chinese currency already proposed on September 23rd,[138] which itself was but a humble shadow of the loan

---

[136] Dennis, *op. cit.*, p. 272.

[137] *MacMurray*, i, 804.

[138] Croly, *op. cit.*, p. 345.

project which Mr. Tang Shao-yi proposed simultaneously with the Manchurian bank loan in 1908. The combined loan, amounting to 50,000,000 taels, met with the approval of the State Department, and on October 27th a preliminary agreement was signed in Peking between the Board of Finance and an agent of the American group acting in place of Straight during the latter's absence in America.[139] While the American government still held firm to its policy, the bankers had begun to hesitate about their support. Disheartened by the failure already met with, and terrified by possible responsibility for international complications that might yet result, some of these bankers wanted to withdraw from the group, and all were in doubt as to the wisdom of continuing on the same course. On September 3rd they interviewed Secretary Knox, and advised him to the effect that, while continuing to serve as the financial agents of the State Department, they would remain under no obligation to seek or accept contracts which aroused the irreconcilable opposition of other powers.[140]

The unwillingness of the bankers to support an aggressive policy tended to magnify the advantage of coöperation with bankers of Great Britain, France, and Germany already in the field. This in turn caused the American bankers to offer voluntarily to share the new loan concession with their European colleagues in the Hukuang Railways loan, and to bring about the formation of a four-power consortium for " all loans and advances for railway purposes to be floated out of the Chinese Empire ".[141] An agreement to the latter effect was signed in London on November 10, 1910.[142] On April 15, 1911, the Chinese government having previously given its consent to the par-

[139] *MacMurray*, i, 851.

[140] Croly, *op. cit.*, pp. 339, 342.

[141] *Cf. ibid.*, p. 351.

[142] *MacMurray*, i, 828.

ticipation of the other three powers, a final agreement was signed between the Board of Finance and the representatives of the four national groups.[143]

According to its provisions, the loan was to be a first charge partly on the duties on tobacco and spirits and production and consumption taxes of Manchuria, and partly on the surtax on salt newly added, all of which, it was declared, were free from other charges. In case these revenues were insufficient, the balance was to be made up first from Manchuria, and then, if necessary, from other sources.[144] The loan was to run for forty-five years [145] with an option on the part of the Chinese government to redeem the outstanding amount from the eleventh year on.[146] If additional funds from foreign sources were needed " to continue or complete the operations contemplated under this agreement " or if foreign capitalists were to be invited to " participate with Chinese interests " in these operations, the signatory banks were to be given the option.[147]

In the agreement there was also a provision requiring the Chinese government to hand to the banks a statement showing the expenditure of the loan.[148] The statements so handed showed the expenditure, so far as the Manchurian industrial development was concerned, to be for (a) the promotion of immigration, reclamation, and pastoral enterprise; (b) forestry and other agricultural enterprise in Heilungkiang; (c) gold mining at Mo-ho, Kuang-yin-shan, and Sansin, and other mining enterprises; and (d) branch mints.[149]

[143] *Ibid.*, i, 841; for details see documents in *For. Rel.*, 1912, 88–94.

[144] Art. v.   [147] Art. xvi.
[145] Art. xii.   [148] Art. viii.
[146] Art. xiii.   [149] *MacMurray*, i, 849.

The loan, which was thus far promising, proved, however, to be as ill-fated as the Chinchou-Aigun Railway project. Encouraged by the success in the opposition to the "neutralization" scheme, Japan and Russia were not slow to come forward and see what they could do with this. Judging by the published correspondence on the subject, Japan must have begun to plan out her work very early, for we see that the State Department instructed the American ambassador at Tokyo on April 29th [150] that the question of Japanese participation finally rested with the financing group; and, on May 11th,[151] that in case Japan should apply for participation on an equal footing with others not now parties to the quadruple agreement, the Department would be prepared to support such an application.

However this may have been, we see that on May 13th Japan came out squarely on the subject. On that day the Japanese government inquired [152] whether participation, if granted, would place Japan in a position superior to an ordinary bondholder, for, they declared, Japan was greatly concerned in the loan, especially as to the purpose of the Manchurian allotment. On that day also, the American ambassador at St. Petersburg reported [153] that exchange of views on the loan was taking place between Japan and Russia, and that this might result in the presentation of observations relating to the use of the loan. On the 18th the American minister at Peking reported [154] that the French were holding back advances for Manchuria because of Russian pressure. On July 11th, after some correspond-

[150] See Knox to O'Brien, May 11, 1911, *For. Rel.*, 1912, p. 96.
[151] See *ibid*.
[152] O'Brien to Knox, May 13, 1911, *ibid.*, p. 96.
[153] Rockhill to Knox, May 13, 1911, *ibid.*, p. 96.
[154] Calhoun to Knox, May 18, 1911, *ibid.*, p. 97.

ence, into which we do not need to enter, the Japanese ambassador handed to the Secretary of State a copy of a *note verbale* presented by the Japanese government to the French on June 26th.[155] In this *note verbale* Japan declared:

Japan possesses in the region of southern Manchuria special rights and interests, and while she is fully prepared in the future as in the past to respect the rights of others, she is unable to view with indifference measures which tend not only to menace these special rights and interests but to place her subjects and institutions at a disadvantage as compared with the subjects and institutions of any other country.

On the same day Russia submitted a note to the State Department taking a similar stand.[156] Shortly after this the Revolution of 1911 broke out, and the loan project, like the Manchu dynasty, passed into history.

What happened then to the other phases of American policy? If the Americans could seek the company of the British, the French, and the Germans to further their objects, their opponents could also join the same company to hinder this. The Revolution brought Yuan Shih-kai and Tang Shao-yi back to power. Seeking to finance the administration over the period of financial chaos resulting from the upheaval, as well as to revive the far-reaching national reorganization which formed part of Mr. Tang's mission of 1908, the government of the Republic proposed to the four-power consortium the flotation of a large loan. At this juncture the Japanese and the Russians followed up their success and effected their admission into the financial consortium by a six-power agreement, dated June 18,

[155] *Ibid.*, p. 99.
[156] Koudacheff to Knox, July 11, 1911, *ibid.*, p. 100.

1912.[157]   In doing so, they did not fail to state as their understanding [158] that, before concluding any business exact information as to the nature of the objects for which the loan was intended would be communicated to each group for consultation with its government; that each group was not bound to entertain business to which its government might object; and that —

. . . in the event of the Russian or Japanese groups disapproving of any object for which any advance or loan under the agreement shall be intended to be made, then, if such advance or loan shall be concluded by the other groups or any of them and the Russian Government or the Japanese Government shall notify the other governments concerned that the business proposed is contrary to the interests of Russia or Japan as the case may be, the Russian Group or the Japanese Group, as the case may be, shall be entitled to withdraw from the agreement.

Following the entrance of Japan and Russia into the consortium came the insistence by the latter of strict supervision over the expenditure of the Reorganization loan and, later, withdrawal of American participation therein. A reorganization loan, as its name indicates, is different from a railway loan or an industrial development loan. By its nature it admits no strict supervision by the lender. First, strict supervision would leave no room for the exercise of discretion by the borrower when policies were involved.   Next, strict supervision in administrative expenditure would lead directly to political control without even the intervening step of economic control.   And yet the consortium not only demanded it, but also demanded it insistently.   Could the same set of Chinese officials have

[157] *MacMurray*, ii, 1021.   [158] *Ibid.*, ii, 1024.

become untrustworthy over night? Or rather could it not be because that body had undergone a fundamental change in its nature and purpose since the entrance of Japan and Russia? In any event, it is evident that the American loan policy could hardly serve its end after reaching the then existing stage. Its termination by the incoming Wilson administration [159] was, therefore, salutary, apart from the unfortunate considerations that shall occupy our attention below.[160]

For an intimate knowledge of the situation at the last stage of the American policy, as well as to have the criticism of one of those who had part in carrying out the policy we may, by way of conclusion, quote the report of W. G. Calhoun, American minister to China, dated February 12, 1912: [161]

Sir: I have the honor to report that the international situation here is critical, and at times very much strained. Despite the concerted action agreed upon, there is much jealousy and suspicion of each other manifested by the representatives of the six leading powers. The tendency seems to be for the English and Japanese to work together, and the intimacy between the French and Russians is marked. These combinations are, for many reasons, to be expected, but they leave the Germans and the Americans very much to themselves. . . .

All of the powers are more or less suspicious of the Americans. They seem to think we have some exclusive or personal policy in mind; that our professions of altruism are a mere blind; and that we hope or intend, somehow or somewhere, to secure an advantage, either in prestige or

[159] For statement of President Wilson, March 18, 1913, see *ibid.*, ii, 1025.

[160] Chap. vii.

[161] *For. Rel.*, 1912, p. 64.

substance, in which the rest will have no share. . . . It was all right so long as we released indemnities, educated Chinese youth at home, and sent missionaries to China. But when we rather forcibly injected ourselves into the Hukuang loan, tried to neutralize the Manchurian railways, proposed to build the Chinchou-Aigun railway, and finally negotiated a preliminary contract for the currency loan, we were then and are now believed to entertain an active and aggressive policy, which is competitive, if not hostile, to all other foreign interests in China. . . .

It is, therefore, probable that for some time to come American influence in China will be obstructed in every way possible. It is not enough that the Chinese people may be friendly to us. They have been, and doubtless will continue to be, the subject of foreign coercion of one kind and another that deprives them of freedom of action. They will not dare to oppose either Russia or Japan. They know that all the support we can give them is sentimental and philanthropical in its character. . . .

If the necessities of market conditions once came home to the American people in such a way as to make them support a national policy in the Far East that insured the " open door " and equal opportunities, the attitude of other nations towards us might be very different. As it is, we are comparatively helpless. Diplomacy, however astute, however beneficent and altruistic it may be, if it is not supported by the force which not only commands but demands respect and consideration, will avail but little.

CHAPTER VII

DEVELOPMENTS SINCE THE REVOLUTION

Sec. 1. Japan and the Revolution

THE reconstruction of Manchuria was but a phase of a broader policy which the Empress Dowager Tsuhsi and the liberal Chinese statesmen of the time attempted to carry out for the nation in the post-Boxer Rebellion days. In this broader policy, no less than in its Manchurian phase, the Regency proved itself to be an absolute failure. Close at the heels of foreign aggression followed, therefore, domestic troubles. Almost simultaneously, Outer Mongolia, Tibet, and the Provinces were all in revolt. In its difficulty it turned to Yuan Shih-kai, the man whom it had ousted.

Ever since Kienlung had initiated the decline of the dynasty, the Chinese, in consideration of the interests of the nation, had once and again saved the dynasty from destruction. Had the Manchus not demonstrated their utter incompetency in the quarter of a century immediately preceding, the Chinese might yet, for the same reason, have saved it again. But Prince Chun, the Regent's father, Prince Tuan, and the Regent himself — the three Manchus who in turn took charge of the destiny of the nation since 1884 — had already pulled the nation into the mud, and the result of ridding China of the dynasty could not place her in more dire straits. Thus, Yuan Shih-kai and his supporters let the dynasty go, and it went out of existence.

China was thus rid of one of her curses, which was the worst and the most fundamental; but even as the tide that does not ebb when the moon reaches the zenith, so the effect of the curse was yet to reach its full flow before receding. The abdication of the Manchu emperor was not the end of all. The evolution of a moral headship to take the place of the defunct dynasty still needed time. In these circumstances foreign aggression was to assume an even worse form, and the following pages will yet record a more serious impairment of China's political entity.

Japan had just brought the Regency to its knees and the policy of the Taft administration to a standstill. When the Revolution came, it was reported that Japan fully expected a call from the browbeaten Manchu court for armed assistance.[1] The Manchus acted, however, more sagaciously, and entrusted their destiny to Yuan Shih-kai. Accordingly, Japan submitted to the United States and Great Britain[2] a proposal of joint intervention for the establishment of " a Chinese rule under nominal reign of the Manchu Dynasty ", to be guaranteed by " the concert of powers having important interests in China ".[3] The Taft administration, and apparently also the British government, acted more correctly, and flatly rejected the proposal.[4] Japan, therefore, for the time being had to confine her activities to particular regions instead of extending them to China as a whole.

The Republic having been successfully established, Japan suggested to the Powers that, prior to the recognition of any

[1] Schuyler to Knox, Oct. 15, 1911, *For Rel.*, 1912, p. 50.

[2] Memo. by Japanese legation Dec. 18, 1911, *ibid.*, p. 56; memo. by same, Dec. 21, 1911, *ibid.*, p. 58.

[3] For Japan's corresponding move in Peking, see Croly, *op. cit.*, p. 431.

[4] *Aide memoire* to Japanese legation, Dec. 21, 1911, *ibid.*, p. 57.

new government, a confirmation of all foreign rights, privileges, and immunities in China should be secured.[5] To this Secretary Knox replied that the American government would be glad to reply more definitely when more explicitly informed.[6] No such explanation, however, was forthcoming, but on March 8, 1912, in communicating with the American government on the subject of the Japanese proposal, Russia declared that she " holds in Northern Manchuria, Mongolia, and Western China special interests and rights founded on her treaties and conventions with China ";[7] and on May 16th the Japanese ambassador informed the State Department that in view of the Russian reservation Japan must also make one as to eastern Inner Mongolia " in which quarter Japan is naturally interested," lest " silence might be misconstrued ".[8] Then, on August 31st, the American minister in Peking reported that the British minister presented a memorandum in which Great Britain " recognizes China's suzerainty and not sovereignty over Tibet ".[9] In the summer, while Russia was energetically engaged in intervention in the Urga secession, which we shall presently review, Japan sent Count Montono to Russia on a special mission, and wrested from the latter power, as embodied in a third secret agreement dated July 8th, the recognition of her " special interests " in Inner Mongolia east of a line drawn north and south on the meridian of Peking.[10]

In the Revolution Japan had seen her opportunity for a

[5] Memo. by Japanese legation, undated, *ibid.*, p. 68.

[6] Memo. to Japanese legation, Feb. 27, 1912, *ibid.*, p. 69.

[7] Bakhmetieff to Knox, March 8, 1912, *ibid.*, p. 74.

[8] Memo. of conversation with Japanese ambassador, May 18, 1912, *ibid.*, p. 79.

[9] Calhoun to Knox, Aug. 31, 1912, *ibid.*, p. 86.

[10] Dennis, *op. cit.*, p. 272.

second advance upon China — this time also upon eastern Inner Mongolia. She had cleared her way of all obstacles except the United States. But she did not have long to wait, for soon the latter power voluntarily stepped out. On March 18, 1913, when the Wilson administration was asked by the American group of bankers if it would renew the request of the government to participate in Chinese loans, especially the Reorganization loan which was then under discussion, the administration expressly declined, on the ground that " it did not approve the conditions of the loan or the implications of responsibility on its own part ".[11]

No sooner was the policy of the Wilson administration made known than Japan approached China for a number of railway concessions in southern Manchuria and eastern Inner Mongolia. On September 26th Japan obtained a release from the six-power agreement of June 18, 1912, with regard to industrial and railway loans, reducing the scope of the agreement to cover only administrative loans.[12] By October 5th the Ministry of Foreign Affairs had to inform the Japanese legation [13] that " the question of Chinese railway loans has often been raised by you and discussed many times "; that China agreed to contract for a loan from Japanese capitalists in the terms of the Pukow-Sinyang Railway loan agreement [14] for the construction of railways (a) from Ssupingkai *via* Chengchiatun to Taonan, (b) from Kaiyuan to Hailung, and (c) from the Changchun station of the Kirin-Changchun Railway across the South Manchurian Railway to Taonan; that she agreed also to apply to Japanese capitalists first in case foreign capital was

[11] *MacMurray*, ii, 1025.

[12] See British Foreign Office to American Embassy, Aug. 14, 1918, *Scott*, p. 6.

[13] *MacMurray*, ii, 1054.

[14] See *ibid.*, ii, 1068.

necessary for the construction of railways (a) from Taonan to Jehol (Chengte), and (b) from Hailung to Kirin. Shortly after this Japan started to construct the Ssupingkai-Taonan line.[15]

As might be expected, the Russians followed suit. On March 27, 1916, the Chinese government had to enter into an agreement [16] with the Russo-Asiatic Bank for a loan of 50,000,000 rubles for the construction of a railway from Harbin to Heiho opposite to Blagovchensk by way of Mergen with a branch line connecting Mergen with Tsitsihar, with a view to connect it with the Chinese Eastern Railway *via* the short line in existence between Tsitsihar and the latter railway.

The Ssupingkai-Taonan and Changchun-Taonan lines, all converging upon the centre of the Cherim prairie, were undoubtedly designed as a double-edged weapon to extend Japanese influence into the heart of eastern Inner Mongolia, and to tap the region the Chinchou-Aigun Railway intended to serve. The Taonan-Jehol line, as the Japanese later frankly admitted,[17] was designed to further nullify whatever effort might be made to revive the Chinchou-Aigun Railway project. The Kaiyuan-Hailung line, and its extension to Kirin, was evidently intended to forestall any further railway construction by China west of the South Manchurian Railway, besides further exploiting the region safely within Japanese grasp. It is unnecessary to add that the Russian lines, particularly the so-called branch line from Mergen to Tsitsihar, was precisely the northern section of the proposed Chinchou-Aigun Railway, and that it also ran over the same route on which Russia had failed to secure the

---

[15] Hsu Hsi, *op. cit.*, 473.
[16] *MacMurray*, ii, 1267.
[17] *Infra*, Sec. 5.

right of maintaining post stages. So, taking advantage of the Revolution and the withdrawal of the United States from the financial consortium, Japan, with Russia dragged behind her victorious chariot, finally rode triumphantly not only over the last vestige of Manchurian reconstruction, but also to the control of eastern Inner Mongolia in addition to southern Manchuria.

Sec. 2.   *Russia and the Urga Secession*

In the summer of 1911, still several months before the Revolution, the political storm in Mongolia had gathered to a head. We have seen how Russia attempted to convert extra-mural China into an exclusive Russian sphere of influence in exchange for the evacuation of Manchuria after the Boxer Rebellion, and how, in the first two secret agreements with Japan she was promised by her partner a free hand in Mongolia. Now that there was opportunity to exercise that free hand she readily availed herself of it. In the latter part of August her minister at Peking was instructed to declare to the Regency [18] that the Russian government had received an appeal from Mongol princes and lamas for intervention, on the ground that Chinese authorities refused to suspend measures newly introduced, such as the training of troops, opening of schools, and reclamation of lands; and that, as Mongolia was coterminous with Russian territory, unless China suspended all the measures Russia would take steps to protect her own interests. Early in October large numbers of Russian troops also arrived at Urga under the pretext of protecting the Russian consulate there.[19]

---

[18] Chen Chung-tsu, *Contemporary Outer Mongolia* (in Chinese) (Shanghai, 1922), bk. 1, p. 6.   [19] *Ibid.*, p. 7.

At this juncture the Chinese Revolution broke out, and on October 30th the Kutuktu of Urga sent the Imperial Commissioner stationed there a note [20] declaring the independence of Mongolia and announcing himself as khan. Following this the Imperial Commissioner left Urga. In the following January the secessionists pushed both eastward and westward, taking Hailar on the Chinese Eastern Railway in the Hulun region of Heilungkiang, and Uliassutai, the seat of the Military Governor of that name. Concurrently the Russian minister at Peking was instructed to demand from China [21] that the latter grant to Russia the right to construct a railway from Russian territory to Urga; concede autonomy to Mongolia; undertake as towards Mongolia not to station troops in or colonize that country; and enter into an engagement with Russia not to adopt measures affecting the *status quo* of Mongolia without consulting her.

In February, 1912, immediately after the Republic was established, President Yuan Shih-kai began to correspond with the Kutuktu with a view of persuading him to cancel his declaration of independence. In both of his telegrams he pointed out the folly of secession and promised to accord special treatment to the Mongols; and in the second, he added that he would appoint a commissioner to proceed to Urga to arrange the matter. The Kutuktu, however, declined to enter into direct negotiations, and asked that the matter be discussed with the Russian minister.[22] Conditions being such, the government of the Republic decided upon an appeal to arms. But at this juncture Russia again appeared. On the one hand she notified the Chinese govern-

[20] *Ibid.*, p. 11.
[21] *Ibid.*, p. 19.
[22] For correspondence see *ibid.*, bk. i, pp. 14–17.

ment [23] that Russia could not view with indifference the despatch of troops to Mongolia; on the other hand, she proceeded to create a state out of the nomadic Mongols.

Measures to the latter effect followed in quick succession. On April 26, 1912, Sazanov, her minister of foreign affairs, announced in the Russian diet [24] that Russia would see to it that China should henceforth cease to colonize Outer Mongolia, or to station troops there, or to interfere in its government. About the same time the Russian government sent an army officer with a dozen assistants to Urga to organize a Mongolian army, consigned to Outer Mongolia a large quantity of war materials, including 40,000 rifles and eight guns, and granted it a loan of 2,000,000 rubles. A little later it also sent two financiers to organize a Mongolian banking system.[25] In July, after the Mongols had failed to take Kobdo, which was still held by the Assistant Military Governor of that name with the assistance of the inhabitants who were Oelot, and not Khalka Mongols, the Russians, in conjunction with the secessionists, intercepted Chinese troops sent from Sinkiang to the rescue of Kobdo, and enabled their protégés to force the evacuation of that city in August.[26][27] Finally, on November 3rd, Korostovetz, authorized agent of Russia, concluded with the Mongols an agreement,[28] engaging Russia to assist Mongolia " to maintain the autonomous régime which she had established, as also the right to have her national army and to admit neither the presence of Chinese troops on her

[23] *Ibid.*, p. 25.

[24] *Ibid.*, p. 23.

[25] *Ibid.*, pp. 25–28.

[26] *Ibid.*, p. 29.

[27] On August 15th the secessionists also captured Taonan in western Fengtien, but there they did not have the benefit of Russian protection and were easily defeated and driven away.

[28] *MacMurray*, ii, 992.

territory nor the colonization of her land by the Chinese ";
and securing from the Mongols direct, in a protocol annexed, substantially the rights which Russia had enjoyed
under treaties with China. Following this, Russia also entered into another agreement [29] in December for the establishment of a mining company with practically unlimited
right of exploitation, apparently as part compensation for
her intervention.

On learning of the conclusion of the Russo-Mongolian
agreement of November 3rd, the Chinese government
lodged a protest with the Russian legation on the 7th. But
the question was not one that could be solved by protest, for
it was the question whether China was ready to fight the
Russians or do the best she could on the basis the latter
might choose to dictate. The result was the commencement
of negotiations between Mr. Lou Tseng-tsiang, Minister
of Foreign Affairs, and B. Kroupensky, Russian minister,
as to some mode by which an agreement could be reached.
After thirty meetings, which lasted from November 30,
1912, to May 20, 1913, they agreed upon the following: [30]

Art. I. Russia, recognizing that Mongolia forms an integral part of the territory of China, hereby engages not to
be in the way of the continuation of that relation, and to
respect all rights China has had in virtue of that relation.

Art. II. China engages not to alter the system of local
self-government which Outer Mongolia has had, and, as
the Mongols of Outer Mongolia have the responsibility of
defence and maintenance of order, to grant exclusive right
of organizing military and police forces. She engages also
to grant the right of excluding non-Mongolian people from
colonization within the boundary.

Art. III. Russia, on her part, engages not to despatch

[29] Chen, *op. cit.*, bk. i, p. 35.
[30] Translation from Chinese text *ibid.*, bk. ii, p. 11.

troops to Outer Mongolia except the guards of consulates; not to colonize the territory of Outer Mongolia; and, except the consulates provided for in treaties, not to station there other officials representing Russia.

Art. IV. China, desiring to employ peaceful methods to exercise her rights in Outer Mongolia, hereby declares that in response to the mediation of Russia she will act in the spirit of the preceding articles in deciding upon her methods of handling Outer Mongolia and in causing the central authorities there to admit the status of local officials under China as before.

Art. V. The Chinese Government, in appreciation of the mediation of the Russian Government, grants to Russian subjects the following commercial privileges in Outer Mongolia. [Here follows the privileges as enumerated in the protocol annexed to the Russo-Mongolian agreement.]

Art. VI. Henceforth, if Russia enters into agreement of an international character with Outer Mongolia concerning its status, such agreement will become effective only after direct negotiation between China and Russia and after the consent of China.

The foregoing agreement was submitted by the Cabinet to the House of Representatives of the National Assembly on May 28th. On June 13th the House returned it to the Cabinet with the suggestions that "non-Mongolian" in Article II be substituted by "non-Chinese"; that the Russian consular guards in Article III be limited to sixty as had been the practice; that "central" in Article IV be eliminated; that the term of ten years as provided in commercial treaties with Russia be added to Article V. Concerning the provisions of Article II the House also declared that it was understood that (a) "Outer Mongolia" was to denote the four Khalka divisions; that (b) the local self-government was to be regulated in accordance with Article II of the terms granted by the Republic to the Manchu dynasty at the latter's abdication; that (c) military and police forces were to be subject to the control of the Chinese government as in the Tsing dynasty; and that (d) the non-colonization provision was not to affect privileges pertaining to commerce. The Russian minister, however, declined to entertain the suggestions of the House, and on July 8th on the advice of Mr. Lou the agreement was passed by the House as submitted.

Democratic control of diplomacy evidently has its limitations. The agreement had finally come out of the House safely. But it had yet to go through the Senate. Besides, by this time, after so much discussion in the House and so much echoing outside of it, its foundation in the confidence of the Russian minister in himself as a diplomat was also shaking. The fate of the agreement therefore was far from being decided. The end, however, came soon. On the 11th came the rejection by the Senate. On the 13th came a note from the Russian minister stating that the Russian government in opening negotiations with China declared as a basis the Russo-Mongolian agreement and its annexed protocol; that this purpose was defeated by the phraseology employed by the Chinese government; that the public also misunderstood the meaning of the draft agreement as shown by discussion in the national legislature and in the press; that there would be misunderstanding if the agreement should be put in force; and that his government was therefore compelled to repudiate it. Following this Mr. Lou resigned from his post as Minister of Foreign Affairs.[31]

For two months the case was therefore left as it stood. China, however, had no alternative but to negotiate again.

[31] For the foregoing see *ibid.*, bk. ii, pp. 12–14.

This was taken up by Mr. Sun Pao-chi, who succeeded Mr. Lou, and on November 5th, after ten meetings which lasted from September 18th to 31st, a protocol was signed and additional notes exchanged.[32] The protocol was not submitted to the national legislature on the ground that it did not come within the constitutional provision requiring this.[33] According to the protocol Russia recognized Outer Mongolia as under the suzerainty of China, and China the autonomy of Outer Mongolia.[34] China bound herself not to intervene in the internal administration of autonomous Mongolia on questions of a commercial and industrial nature relating to that country, not to send troops or to keep any civil or military official there; and not to colonize that country. Russia on her part bound herself in a similar way. Russia, however, might station guards at consulates, while China might appoint a " dignitary " to Urga accompanied by the necessary subordinates and an escort, and maintain agents for the interests of her nationals in certain localities to be determined.[35] China declared herself ready to accept the good offices of Russia for the establishment of her relations with Outer Mongolia in conformity with the principles thus set forth and the provisions of the Russo-Mongolian agreement. As to " questions pertaining to the interests of Russia and China in Outer Mongolia and resulting from the new state of affairs in this country " they would be subjects of subsequent conferences.[36]

In the notes exchanged it was stated that Russia recognized that the territory of Outer Mongolia formed a part of the territory of China; that the Chinese government would come to an agreement with the Russian government

[32] *MacMurray*, ii, 1066.
[33] Chen, *op. cit.*, bk. ii, pp. 14–17.
[34] Arts. i and ii.

[35] Art. iii.
[36] Art. v.

as regards questions of a political and territorial nature, through negotiations in which the authorities of Outer Mongolia would take part; that the conferences referred to in the protocol would take place between the three interested parties, who would designate for that purpose a place where their delegates would meet; that autonomous Outer Mongolia would comprise the regions which had been under the jurisdiction of the Imperial Commissioner of Urga, the Military Governor of Uliassutai, and the Assistant Military Governor of Kobdo.

The place designated for a tripartite conference was Kiakta, where the delegates of the three parties finally met on September 8, 1914. The conference lasted until the latter part of May, 1915, in which forty-eight formal and about forty informal meetings were held. The length of time and the number of meetings clearly indicates that the conference was by no means a smooth one. On several occasions the Chinese delegates requested their government to recall them, but each time they were asked to be patient. Indeed, the government could not have advised differently, for it was then confronted with the notorious Twenty-one Demands.[37] On June 7, 1914, a tripartite agreement was signed.[38]

Among questions that occasioned difficulty in the conference were those of post and telegraph, of customs tariff, and of colonization by Chinese along the border of Outer Mongolia; the first of these was settled in Articles XVII and XVIII; the second in Article XII; the last by an exchange of notes between the Ministry of Foreign Affairs and the Russian legation.[39] On May 25, 1913, Russia ob-

[37] See Chen, *op. cit.*, bk. ii, pp. 25, 52, 54.
[38] *MacMurray*, ii, 1239.
[39] Chen, *op. cit.*, bk. ii, pp. 54–55.

tained a concession from Outer Mongolia for a telegraphic line connecting Kobdo with Russian territory.[40] When the question of post and telegraph came up for discussion in the conference, she again obtained another concession for another telegraphic line connecting Uliassutai with Russian territory on the one hand, and Urga on the other.[41] Thus while China granted to Outer Mongolia the section of Kalgan-Urga-Kiakta telegraphic line in Outer Mongolia Russia obtained from Outer Mongolia two concessions. At the same time that she obtained the last of the two telegraphic concessions, Russia also obtained an agreement [42] in which the Mongols engaged to " deliberate and decide with Russia upon the most advantageous direction in which the railways were to extend which are to serve Mongolia and Russia, as well as upon the manner in which the construction of such railways is to be provided for ", in exchange, it seems, for the recognition on the part of Russia that Mongolia had the perpetual right to build railways within the confines of its own territory!

The day the tripartite agreement was signed the President invested the Kutuktu of Urga as Khan of Outer Mongolia.[43] On the 16th he appointed Chen Lu, one of the two delegates plenipotentiaries, Resident-General at Urga. On the 22nd he also appointed three assistants to be stationed at Uliassutai, Kobdo, and Kiakta.[44] On January 10, 1916, the Khan despatched a tribute mission to Peking.[45] On July 8, 1916, the investiture was formally carried out at Urga.[46] At the close of the same year the government established, with the concurrence of Outer Mongolia, one

[40] *MacMurray*, ii, 1038.
[41] *Ibid.*, ii, 1179.
[42] *Ibid.*, ii, 1176.
[43] Chen, *op. cit.*, bk. ii, p. 63.
[44] *Ibid.*, p. 64.
[45] *Ibid.*, p. 89.
[46] *Ibid.*, p. 70.

more assistant-resident at Ulianghai, which, in spite of the protest of autonomous Outer Mongolia which Russia had helped to create, was then occupied by the Russians.[47]

In Chapters I and II we have seen that China first established a military governor at Uliassutai to govern Outer Mongolia, then moved his assistant to station at Kobdo; then later established an imperial commissioner at Urga to take charge of frontier, and hence Russian, affairs. At the end of the Tsing dynasty the government, in order to tighten its control over Outer Mongolia, not only practically turned these three dignitaries into three military governors for Outer Mongolia, but also added a fourth by moving a colleague of the Assistant Military Governor of Kobdo to reside at Cheng-hua-ssu under the title of the Imperial Commissioner of Altai. Now that Altai was the only portion unprovided for, it was first constituted into a special territory and later, on June 1, 1919, converted into a *tao* and incorporated into the province of Sinkiang.[48]

We have seen in the last chapter that the Cherim prairie was made part of Fengtien at the end of the Tsing dynasty, while the Jehol hills, which in the time of Kienlung had become part of Chihli, were constituted into a special territory in the Republic. The last of the two events took place in January, 1914, as part of the reorganization of Inner Mongolia that followed the signing of the protocol with Russia concerning Outer Mongolia. In that reorganization two more special territories were created. One was known as Chahar, consisting of the section of Chihli and Shansi originally the Chahar country and the territory of the Silinghol League north of the Great Khingan range. The other was known as Suiyuan, consisting of the section of Shansi — originally the Tumet country — the Ordos

[47] *Ibid.*, bk. iv, p. 152.   [48] *Ibid.*, bk. iv, p. 130.

country, and the territory of the Ulan Chap League north
of the Yinshan range.   As to Alashan, it was incorporated
into the province of Kansu.

The Hulun region, the trans-Khingan section of Heilungkiang which lay east of Outer Mongolia, was originally part of the land of the Solons and Daurians.   During
the campaigns against the Russians in the 17th century
the Buriates, who deserted the Russian camp and joined the
Chinese, were accommodated there.   Later, during the
Oelot War, it was also made an asylum for the captives.
Consequently it had become more the land of desert nomads
than of Manchurian nomads.

We have seen that the Urga secessionists captured Hailar,
the principal city of the Hulun region.   After the question
of Outer Mongolia had been settled, Russia also came forward to treat with China about this region.   On November
6, 1915, she finally obtained from China the creation of a
special district [49] to be ruled by a governor appointed by the
President of China from among the natives; [50] and the
engagement to give Russia advance notice in case detachments of troops were to be sent there to suppress disorder;
to withdraw them as soon as order was reëstablished; [51] to
abstain from colonizing the region; [52] to apply first to
Russia in case foreign capital was necessary for the construction of a railway there; [53] and to confirm " contracts
that have already been concluded between Russian investors
and the authorities of Hailar " during the Mongol occupation. [54]

[49] *MacMurray.*, ii, 1247.   [52] Art. vi.
[50] Arts. i–iii.   [53] Art. vii.
[51] Art. iv.   [54] Art. viii.

Sec. 3. The High-Water Mark

The crisis created by getting rid of the Manchu dynasty was thus fraught with great difficulties and at great price tided over. But, as if it had been predestined, greater disasters were yet to befall China before she could get on her feet.

Late in the summer of 1914, when she was about to settle down for a period of reconstruction, there came the war in Europe. On August 6, 1914, shortly after its outbreak, China declared her neutrality. On the 23rd Japan entered the war on the side of the *Entente* powers. On September 3rd she landed troops at Lungkou on the north of the Shantung peninsula, one hundred and fifty miles from the nearest point of the leased territory of Kiaochou, to begin an attack upon Tsingtao. China protested in vain and was compelled to follow the precedent set in the Russo-Japanese War to regard the territory affected as a hostile area.[55] Thereafter Japan, with the assistance of Great Britain, which landed troops within the leased territory, took Tsingtao, and then proceeded alone to occupy the Shantung Railway.

China was yet disorganized. The European powers were fully absorbed in a life and death struggle, and the Wilson administration had made clear that its interest in the Open Door was to enter it rather than to maintain it. This was the opportunity for Japan to consummate her old ambition of dominating China, which the success of the war of 1895 had roused, but which the international situation since the triple intervention for the retrocession of Liaotung had prevented. If this were not the opportunity, there never would be one, and the Japanese pounced upon it. On

[55] *MacMurray*, ii, 1367.

January 9, 1915, on the occasion of China's requesting
Japan and Great Britain to withdraw their troops as the
war, so far as the Far East was concerned, was long over,
Japan presented to China a set of twenty-one demands.

The demands were drawn up in five groups. The first
was designed to make sure of Japan's succession to all
German claims relating to Shantung. With the exception
of this group, none of them had even the slightest connection with the region affected by the war, not to say with the
specific question of evacuation. Group II was designed to
snatch southern Manchuria and eastern Inner Mongolia
from China, short of outright cession; Group III for the
control of the Hanychping Company, the only domestic
source of China's iron supply; and Group IV with a view
to a supposedly prior claim to the entire coast of China by
a non-alienation declaration. The last group dealt with
questions of advisers, police, military supply, missionary
propaganda, Yangtze valley railways, and the province of
Fukien. While the last items of the last group would
open a third line of advance upon the heart of China, and
at the same time cut right across the so-called British sphere
of influence, the first items were undoubtedly meant to
bring China half way to the fate of Korea. The twenty-
one demands together revealed that Japan not only wished
to succeed Germany, as she did Russia, and deprive China
of important regions of her country, but that she also intended to oust Great Britain after having checkmated the
United States, and add China to the list of Liuchiu and
Korea.

If China could not fight the vanquished Russia, even less
could she resist the victorious Japan. So, in this case, as in
the Russian intervention at Urga, her only alternative was
to negotiate. During the course she, nevertheless, con-

stantly consulted the American minister " in an unofficial way ". The United States was the only power that yet could do something. It was the opinion of the Chinese government that if the United States could only say, to use Minister Reinsch's expression, " Such matters concerning foreign rights in China, in which we have an interest by treaties, policy, and tradition, cannot be discussed without our participation ", the danger would largely dissolve.[56] It never occurred to President Wilson, however, that the United States could be of such service. As early as February 8th he wrote the following characteristic letter to Minister Reinsch:[57]

I have had the feeling that any direct advice to China, or direct intervention on her behalf in the present negotiations, would really do her more harm than good, inasmuch as it would very likely provoke the jealousy and excite the hostility of Japan, which would first be manifested against China herself. . . . For the present I am watching the situation very carefully indeed, ready to step in at any point where it is wise to do so.

Such an opportune point never presented itself to President Wilson. In the meantime Japan sent large bodies of troops to southern Manchuria and Shantung " with a view ", she declared, " to preserving the peace of the Far East ".[58] On April 26th, after twenty-four meetings over details, Japan presented a new set of twenty-four so-called revised demands, with the request that China accord her acceptance without delay;[59] and on the memorable May 7th, which has

[56] Paul S. Reinsch, *An American Diplomat in China* (Garden City, 1922), p. 139.

[57] Reinsch, *op. cit.*, p. 137.

[58] *S–J Negotiations*, p. 4.

[59] *Ibid.*, pp. 14, 21–26.

since been observed in China as a national "humiliation day", Japan delivered an ultimatum compelling acceptance of all with the exception of Group V, outside the item relating to Fukien, which group she reserved for "future discussion".[60]   On the 25th treaties and notes embodying the terms were signed or exchanged.

In the recent Washington Conference the group relating to Shantung was disposed of through the good offices of Secretary Hughes and Lord Balfour, by an agreement between China and Japan in which Japanese claims were reduced to what would arise from a fifteen-year loan secured upon the Kiaochou-Tsinan Railway.   As to the rest of the demands that affect intra-mural China, now that the European War is over and the normal international situation in the Far East has been restored, they would probably become less injurious than they might have been, even as most of the forms of the post-bellum foreign aggressions of 1897–98 in that region have become.   But the group relating to southern Manchuria and eastern Inner Mongolia have become fastened upon China even as Russian designs upon Manchuria of the same memorable period at the close of the last century had been.   Indeed, as we shall see, it became from now on the centre of the problem that forms the theme of the present work so far as its Japanese phase is concerned.

This group, as presented by the Japanese, was as follows: [61]

The Japanese Government and the Chinese Government, since the Chinese Government has always acknowledged the special position enjoyed by Japan in South Manchuria and Eastern Inner Mongolia, agree to the following articles:

[60] *Ibid.*, p. 36.   [61] *Ibid.*, p. 19.

Article 1. The two Contracting Parties mutually agree that the term of lease of Port Arthur and Dalny and the term of lease of the South Manchurian Railway and the Antung-Mukden Railway shall be extended to the period of 99 years.

Article 2. Japanese subjects in South Manchuria and Eastern Inner Mongolia shall have the right to lease or own land required either for erecting suitable buildings for trade and manufacture or for farming.

Article 3. Japanese subjects shall be free to reside and travel in South Manchuria and Eastern Inner Mongolia and to engage in business and in manufacture of any kind whatsoever.

Article 4. The Chinese Government agrees to grant to Japanese subjects the right of opening the mines in South Manchuria and Eastern Mongolia. As regards what mines are to be opened, they shall be decided upon jointly.

Article 5. The Chinese Government agrees that in respect of the (two) cases mentioned herein below the Japanese Government's consent shall be first obtained before action is taken:

(a) Whenever permission is granted to the subject of a third Power to build a railway or to make a loan with a third Power for the purpose of building a railway in South Manchuria and Eastern Inner Mongolia.

(b) Whenever a loan is to be made with a third Power pledging the local taxes of South Manchuria and Eastern Inner Mongolia as security.

Article 6. The Chinese Government agrees that if the Chinese Government employs political, financial, or military advisers or instructors in South Manchuria or Eastern Mongolia, the Japanese Government shall first be consulted.

Article 7. The Chinese Government agrees that the control and management of the Kirin-Changchun Railway shall be handed over to the Japanese Government for a term of 99 years dating from the signing of this agreement.

The Chinese government had no alternative but to work for mitigation over this group as over the rest. It only contended as to Articles I and III that eastern Inner Mongolia could not be considered in the same light as southern Manchuria, as the former, it asserted, was not " an enlightened region as yet " and the conditions existing there were " entirely different " from those prevailing in the latter; and that inland residence for Japanese, even in southern Manchuria, was " incompatible with the treaties China has entered into with Japan and other Powers ". But for all that, the Chinese government was constrained to make certain concessions. It proposed to open commercial marts in eastern Inner Mongolia in lieu of what was demanded with respect to that section of country. It accepted in principle the demand for the right of residence in southern Manchuria, but suggested that settlers should be under Chinese jurisdiction. The Japanese minister declined to accept these counter-proposals. Thereupon the Chinese government reconsidered and revised them " five or six times, each time making some definite concession ", and finally went so far as to concede that all civil and criminal cases between Chinese and Japanese be arranged according to existing treaties, with only cases relating to land or lease contracts reserved to Chinese courts " as a mark of China's sovereignty over the region ".[62]

In the revised set of twenty-four demands which the Japanese presented on April 26th, the Japanese changed the term " special position " in the preamble of the group into " economic relations ", and took out the questions relating

[62] *Ibid.*, p. 28.

to eastern Inner Mongolia and made them into four separate demands, of which the last was as follows: [63]

In the event of Japan and China desiring jointly to undertake agricultural enterprises and industries incidental thereto, the Chinese Government shall give its permission.

As to their position regarding the question of jurisdiction arising out of inland residence no change was made.

In replying to the revised demands the Chinese government made further concessions on the question of jurisdiction arising out of inland residence, in the following counter-proposal: [64]

The Japanese subjects referred to in the preceding two articles, besides being required to register with the local authorities passports, which they must procure under the existing regulations, shall also observe police rules and regulations, and pay taxes in the same manner as Chinese. Civil and criminal cases shall be tried and adjudicated by the authorities of the defendant's nationality and an officer can be deputed to attend the proceedings. But all cases purely between Japanese subjects, and mixed cases between Japanese and Chinese, relating to land or disputes arising from lease contracts, shall be tried and adjudicated by Chinese Authorities and the Japanese Consul may also depute an officer to attend the proceedings. When the judicial system in the said Province is completely reformed, all the civil and criminal cases concerning Japanese subjects shall be tried entirely by Chinese law courts.

Of the four new articles relating to eastern Inner Mongolia two had been agreed to by the Chinese government as part of Article V of the original demands, while a third embodied its proposal to open trade marts in place of grant-

[63] *Ibid.*, p. 25.   [64] *Ibid.*, p. 32.

ing the right of inland residence, and to these three it
readily acceded. As to the last, it felt that it contained
exactly what it at the first instance rejected, and it declined
as before to give it consideration.

The Japanese government, however, refused to entertain
these and other counter-proposals and delivered an ultimatum to compel acceptance of all, as already referred to.
In an explanatory note accompanying the ultimatum, there
was the following concerning the group relating to southern
Manchuria and eastern Inner Mongolia: [65]

Article 2 of Group II relating to the lease or purchase
of land, the terms " lease " and " purchase " may be replaced by these terms, " temporary lease " and " perpetual
lease " or " lease on consultations ", which means a long-
term lease with its conditional renewal.

Article 4 of Group II relating to the approval of laws
and ordinances and local taxes by the Chinese [Japanese ?]
Consul may form the subject of a secret agreement.

The phrase " to consult with the Japanese Government "
in connection with questions of pledging the local taxes for
raising loans and the loans for construction of railways in
Eastern Inner Mongolia, which is similar to the agreement on Manchuria relating to the matters of the same
kind, may be replaced by the phrase " to consult with the
Japanese capitalists ".

The article relating to the opening of trade marts in
Eastern Inner Mongolia in respect to location and regulations, may, following the precedents set in Shantung, be
the subject of an exchange of notes.

As signed on the 25th, the treaty relating to southern
Manchuria and eastern Inner Mongolia is as follows: [66]

[65] Arts. iv and v, *ibid.*, p. 38.
[66] *Ibid.*, p. 49.

With a view to developing their economic relations in South Manchuria and Eastern Inner Mongolia:

Article 1. The two High Contracting Parties agree that the term of lease of Port Arthur and Dalny and the terms of the South Manchuria Railway and the Antung-Mukden Railway, shall be extended to 99 years.

Article 2. Japanese subjects in South Manchuria may, by negotiation, lease land necessary for erecting suitable buildings for trade and manufacture or for prosecuting agricultural enterprises.

Article 3. Japanese subjects shall be free to reside and travel in South Manchuria and to engage in business and manufacture of any kind whatsoever.

Article 4. In the event of Japanese and Chinese desiring jointly to undertake agricultural enterprises and industries incidental thereto, the Chinese Government may give its permission.

Article 5. The Japanese subjects referred to in the preceding three articles, besides being required to register with the local Authorities passports, which they must procure under existing regulations, shall also submit to the police laws and ordinances and taxation of China.

Civil and criminal cases in which the defendants are Japanese shall be tried and adjudicated by the Japanese Consul; those in which the defendants are Chinese shall be tried and adjudicated by Chinese Authorities. In either case an officer may be deputed to the court to attend the proceedings. But mixed civil cases between Chinese and Japanese relating to land shall be tried and adjudicated by delegates of both nations conjointly in accordance with Chinese law and local usage.

When, in future, the judicial system in the said region is completely reformed, all civil and criminal cases concerning Japanese subjects shall be tried and adjudicated entirely by the Chinese law courts.

Article 6. The Chinese Government agrees, in the interest of trade and for the residence of foreigners, to open by China herself, as soon as possible, certain suitable places in Eastern Inner Mongolia as Commercial Ports.

Article 7. The Chinese Government agrees speedily to make a fundamental revision of the Kirin-Changchun Railway Loan-Agreement, taking as a standard the provisions in railway agreements made heretofore between China and foreign financiers.

When in future more advantageous terms than those in existing railway loan agreements are granted to foreign financiers in connection with railway loans, the above agreement shall again be revised in accordance with Japan's wishes.

Article 8. All existing treaties between China and Japan relating to Manchuria shall, except where otherwise provided for by this Treaty, remain in force.

The notes exchanged as the treaty was signed were seven in number. Of these, four appeared to relate to the provisions of the treaty itself, and three with independent subjects concerning the same localities which formed the subject of the treaty. One of the first four notes stated, with reference to Article I of the treaty, that the term of the lease of Port Arthur and Talienwan was to expire in 1997; that the dates for restoring the South Manchurian and Antung-Mukden Railways were to be set at 2002 and 2007 respectively; and that the provision in Article XXI of the original agreement relating to the South Manchurian Railway that that railway might be redeemed by China after thirty-six years from the day traffic was opened, was cancelled.[67] A second stated that the term " lease by negotiation " contained in Article II of the treaty was to be

[67] *Ibid.*, p. 51.

understood to imply a long term lease of not more than thirty years and with the possibility of its unconditional renewal.[68] A third stated that the Chinese authorities would notify the Japanese consul of police laws and ordinances and the taxation to which Japanese subjects were to submit according to Article V " so as to come to an understanding with them before their enforcement ".[69] The last stated that, on the selection of places to be opened as provided in Article VI and the drawing up of regulations therefor, decision would be made by the Chinese Government " after consulting the Minister of Japan ".[70]

In one of the last three notes the Chinese government granted the privilege of mining in nine localities in southern Manchuria, six being in Fengtien and three in Kirin.[71] In another it declared that " hereafter, if foreign advisers or instructors on political, financial, military, or police matters are to be employed in southern Manchuria, Japanese may be employed first ".[72] In the last note there was the following declaration:[73]

China will hereafter provide funds for building necessary railways in South Manchuria and Eastern Inner Mongolia; if foreign capital is required China may negotiate for a loan with Japanese capitalists first; and further, the Chinese Government, when making a loan in future on the security of the taxes in the above-mentioned places (excluding the salt and customs revenue which have already been pledged by the Chinese Central Government) may negotiate for it with Japanese capitalists first.

It may be observed that if the exchange of notes of October 5, 1913, ended whatever there was left of the Chinchou-

[68] *Ibid.*, p. 59.
[69] *Ibid.*, p. 60.
[70] *Ibid.*, p. 53.
[71] *Ibid.*, p. 54.
[72] *Ibid.*, p. 58.
[73] *Ibid.*, p. 56.

Aigun Railway project, the note last quoted ended whatever there was left of the Manchurian Industrial Development Loan plan.

In 1910, when the Russo-Japanese joint enterprise in Manchuria was a success, the agreements of July 30, 1907, were strengthened by a new set. Now that the joint enterprise in the Republic of China was a success, it seemed natural that the understanding of July 8, 1912, should thus be converted into an alliance. Accordingly on July 3, 1916, there was signed by the same Montono with the Russian government a new secret agreement under the cover of an open one.[74] In this open agreement the two nations merely engaged, " for the maintenance of permanent peace in the Far East ", to abstain mutually from becoming party to any " arrangement or political combination " directed against each other and to confer in regard to the measures to be taken " with a view to the support or coöperation " to be given each other in order to " safeguard and defend " " the territorial rights or the special interests " of either party in the Far East in case these " should be menaced ". In the secret agreement their object was not so much for the maintenance of " permanent peace in the Far East " as for strengthening " the firm friendship between them established through the secret agreements of July 17–30, 1907, June 21–July 4, 1910, and June 25–July 8, 1912 ". And for this " firm friendship " they mutually obligated themselves " in the future at all times ", when circumstances demanded, to enter " with open-hearted dealings, based on complete trust ", in order to take necessary measures with the object of " preventing the possibility of occurrence " of " the political domination " over China " of any third power whatsoever, having hostile designs against

[74] *MacMurray,* ii, 1327.

Russia and Japan ",[75] and to come to each other's aid in the event of war declared by any third power on either in consequence of measures taken by mutual consent, and not to conclude peace with the common enemy without the consent of its ally.[76] This secret agreement was to continue in force until July 1/14, 1921, one day beyond the Anglo-Japanese alliance, and, in case neither party denounced it one year before the end of the term, still to continue in force in the same manner as the last mentioned alliance, *i.e.*, indefinitely for a period of one year after one of the parties should have denounced it.[77]

Sec. 4. Recession of the Tide

(1) *Southern Manchuria and Eastern Inner Mongolia*

With one group of the Twenty-one Demands postponed for future discussion, and an alliance with Russia to fight off any chance or intentional intruder, it is plain that Japan did not mean to stop with the treaties and notes of May 25, 1915.

The leaders of the Republic had for some time been casting about for a way to get out of the intolerable situation of foreign aggression. They saw in monarchy the shortest way to that end, and they set their minds upon it. Monarchism was destined to give place to republicanism after the Revolution, even as universalism had given way to nationalism since Japan had asserted her independence of the Far Eastern political system. In trying to lead the nation out of difficulties by running counter to the current of the time the leaders courted more disasters for her. Hardly before the monarchical movement of 1915–16 in favor of President Yuan Shih-kai was started, opposition

[75] Art. i.   [76] Art. ii.   [77] Art. v.

was developed in the country and the nation was again in a turmoil. In consequence, the unification which the formal establishment of the Republic had brought about in 1912 was undone, and even not now has the prospect of its reappearance come anywhere within sight.

Fortunately the President in general acted correctly. As soon as he saw unmistakable signs of disapproval from the people, he repudiated the movement. Furthermore, on his death, which soon followed, he turned over his office in accordance with constitutional provisions, in spite of the fact that the man thus to succeed him was of an entirely different political feather. Through this patriotism of the President, which seems to have lain deeper in his person than his ambition, the ill consequences of the mistaken policy did not take effect until 1917. But then the international situation, which had favored Japanese aggression in China had changed. With the entrance of the United States into the European War, not only was the early termination of that conflict presaged, but the United States would be so armed as to enable her to demand that kind of respect for her diplomacy for which Minister Calhoun in vain craved in 1912. Consequently, Japanese aggression in China, after the Twenty-one Demands, never again approached that high-water mark. On the contrary, it receded with time even as the tide in spite of favorable Chinese conditions.

In the monarchical movement of 1915–16 Japan was no less alert than in the Revolution of 1911. As soon as the movement was started,[78] she invited the Powers to offer

[78] For the following pages see an account given by Baron (now Viscount) Goto Shimpei, given textually in Liu Yen, *Sino-Japanese Relations during the European War* (in Chinese), (Shanghai, 3rd ed. 1921), pp. 67–74.

" friendly counsel " to the Chinese government against the movement, and at the same time gave assistance to the opposition in the country to prolong disorder. The movement having been suddenly terminated, the Japanese not only saw their plans frustrated, but were to find themselves caught in an awkward position. Nevertheless the Japanese were not willing to leave empty-handed.

The best known instance of Japan's giving assistance to the opposition in the country was the financing of and giving facilities to the retired Manchu officials at Dairen to assemble 2,000 Manchurian bandits in that port and to equip 5,000 Mongolian bandits in the desert — the bandits who were in the pay of Japan during the Russo-Japanese War — for a joint descent upon Fengtien. After the cessation of the monarchical movement, the Manchus at Dairen also gave up their attempts; but the Mongolian bandits, who were guided by lust for loot rather than loyalty to the republican or the Manchu cause, were not as ready to refrain from action, and as originally planned they marched upon Taonan in July. In spite of their number and foreign equipment the Mongolian bandits as soon as they entered Manchuria were held at bay by the Twenty-eighth Division of the Chinese army which had been sent to meet them. At this juncture the Japanese came forward and informed the commander that no hostility would be permitted near the South Manchurian Railway, and soon there took place a fracas in the headquarters of one of the regiments of the division then in Chengchiatun, between the soldiers of that regiment and some Japanese soldiers whose presence in that inland town in the heart of eastern Inner Mongolia dated back to the time of the Twenty-one Demands, when China refused to treat that part of the country in the same light as Manchuria.

As a result of the fracas four Chinese and twelve Japanese soldiers were killed and some others wounded. When
this took place, the Japanese reinforced their troops at
Chengchiatun and despatched other detachments to station at points on the highway between Chengchiatun and
Ssupingkai. Before the Japanese the Twenty-eighth Division could not but retire and the Mongolian bandits headed
for Kuochiatien on the South Manchurian Railway.

While the bandits were safely on the land of the railway, the Japanese at Mukden requested General Chang
Tso-ling, military governor of Fengtien, to let them leave
unmolested. At the same time they also permitted them to
be reinforced by eight hundred Manchurian bandits from
Dairen with full equipment of arms and ammunition. The
Fengtien authorities therefore issued orders for immediate
attack, the Japanese being duly notified. In the ensuing
battle some of the Japanese mounted troops who were
" guarding the railway zone " were injured and a Japanese
flag shot through. The Japanese therefore concentrated
their troops at Chao-yang-po " to prevent a recurrence ".
Meanwhile Kirin troops attacked the bandits from the rear
and threatened to envelop them. At this juncture the
Japanese again came forward and requested cessation of
hostilities, undertaking at this time to disarm the Manchurian bandits and to see the Mongolian bandits out of
Fengtien.

The Japanese were evidently not satisfied with merely
fulfilling their moral obligations to the bandits.[79] On
September 2nd their minister in Peking submitted a memorandum to the Chinese government containing three de-

[79] For the following pages see " The Chengchiatun Affairs "
appendix G in M. T. Z. Tyau, *Treaty Obligations between China
and Other States* (Shanghai, 1917), pp. 268–280.

mands and four desiderata.[80]   The first two of the demands concerned punishment of those who had taken direct part in the fracas and of their superior officers as well as the issuance of a proclamation against " provoking the Japanese forces, or soldiers, or other Japanese subjects, by either word or act ".   The last two of the desiderata concerned apology to be given by the military governor of Fengtien and compensation for the Japanese sufferers.   The remaining demand was as follows:

To agree that the Japanese Government may, with a view to the protection and government of the Japanese subjects in South Manchuria and Eastern Inner Mongolia, send Japanese police officers to function at those places where considered to be necessary; also to let the Chinese officials in South Manchuria employ more Japanese to serve as police advisers.

The remaining desiderata were as follows:

(a) Every Chinese army headquarters stationed in South Manchuria and Eastern Inner Mongolia to employ a certain number of Japanese military officers as advisers.

(b) Chinese military cadet schools to employ a certain number of Japanese military officers as instructors.

The Chinese government deemed it inexpedient to examine into the cause of the case, and proceeded to discuss the memorandum.   While ready to agree in principle to other questions, the government found itself unable to make concessions on the three points we have given textually above.

The stand taken by the Chinese government did not satisfy the Japanese minister, especially as regarded the question of police.   On January 5, 1917, the minister

[80] *Ibid.*, p. 272.

handed to the Chinese government three *notes verbales*. In the one [81] relating to the question of police he attempted to justify the Japanese position on the ground that the right claimed therewith was but " a corollary of the right of extra-territoriality ", and declared that, in order to give adequate protection to and establish effective control over the increasing number of Japanese subjects in southern Manchuria and eastern Inner Mongolia in consequence of the operation of the treaty of 1915, the Japanese government would be " constrained to carry it into effect in case of necessity " notwithstanding the lack of concurrence on the part of the Chinese government.

In its reply [82] to the *notes verbales* the Chinese government pointed out that protection and control of the increasing number of Japanese subjects in southern Manchuria and eastern Inner Mongolia had been provided for in Article V of the said treaty, in which it was stipulated that Japanese subjects in those localities were to submit to Chinese police law and ordinance. As to the right of stationing police officers in that region as a corollary to extra-territoriality it said that " ever since the conclusion of extra-territoriality treaties between China and the foreign powers for several decades no such claim has ever been heard ", not to say that in view of the provision of the above-mentioned article there was no such necessity. It finally requested the Japanese government to abandon the matter. Meanwhile the cause of the case became well known to the public and the Japanese government did not deem it expedient to press the police matter any further.

Shortly after the foregoing exchange of correspondence, the impending disorganization of the nation took place in the form of a civil war (1917–18) between the national

[81] *Ibid.*, p. 276.   [82] *Ibid.*, p. 277.

legislature and the Anfu Club. On this occasion, as in the monarchical movement, the Japanese took sides with one of the hostile camps, but, whereas they had sided with the opposition on the former occasion, now they sided with the government, and instead of financing and equipping bandits they financed and equipped the Anfu government.[83] The following is a table of loans and advances [84] that are known to have been made to that government during that period:

Date	Alleged Purposes	Amount in Million Yen
1917		
Aug. 28	Advance upon proposed reorganization loan	10
Sept. 28	Loan to Bank of Communications	20
Oct. 12	Loan for the Kirin-Changchun Railway	6½
1918		
Jan. 6	Second advance upon proposed reorganization loan	10
April 30	Loan for improvement of the telegraphs	20
June 18	Advance upon loan for the Kirin-Hueining Railway	10
Aug. 2	Loan for gold mining and forestry in Heilungkiang and Kirin	30
Sept. 28	Loan for European War participation	20
Sept. 28	Advance upon loan for railways in Manchuria and Mongolia	20
Sept. 28	Advance upon loan for the Shantung Railway extensions	20
Total		166½

[83] For contract and alleged contract for supply of arms see *MacMurray*, ii, 1414; Liu Yen, *op. cit.*, 139, 145.

[84] For these loans see *MacMurray*, ii, 1382, 1387, 1390, 1400, 1424, 1430, 1434, 1446, 1448, 1450.

A glance at the foregoing list is sufficient to reveal that the loans and advances, apart from prolonging civil war in China, were designed to secure control over the Chinese nation in general and Shantung and Manchuria in particular, very much like the Twenty-one Demands, though in a disguised friendly way instead of an open hostile one. In view of the fact that the Shantung question has been settled, and that in a normal international situation designs to catch the nation as a whole cannot work well, the shackles, even as in the case of the Twenty-one Demands, have been fastened upon no other part of the country as firmly as upon Manchuria.

Of the four loans and advances that were charges upon Manchuria and eastern Inner Mongolia, the so-called loan for the Kirin-Changchun Railway [85] was alleged to be made in accordance with Article VII of the treaty of 1915 relative to southern Manchuria and eastern Inner Mongolia. Its amount was $6,500,000; its terms thirty years; and its security, the property and receipts of the Kirin-Changchun Railway. [86] The rights of administration of the line were vested in the Chinese government which would have a chief of the administration (Chu-chang), who would exercise supervisory powers over all the affairs of the railway, [87] but the actual administration was to be entrusted to the South Manchurian Railway Company during the term of the loan. [88] If in the future the government should require foreign capital to construct branch lines or extensions, priority was to be given to that company. [89] As to the rights of policy, administration, jurisdiction, and taxation on the railway and on the land used by the railway, they were " naturally vested in the government ". [90]

[85] *Ibid.*, 1390. [87] Art. ii. [89] Art. xvii.
[86] Art. i. [88] Art. iii. [90] Art. xii.

The so-called advance upon loan for the Kirin-Hueining Railway,[91] $10,000,000 in amount, was made, " without any deduction for commission " upon the conclusion of a preliminary agreement for a loan alleged to be " for the purpose of constructing the railway from Kirin to Hueining ",[92] the formal agreement to be concluded within six months.[93]   The term of the loan was to be forty years, redemption to begin from the eleventh year from the date of issue;[94] and its security was the property owned by and the revenue due to the railway " either at present or in the future ".[95]   When the construction of the railway should take place the Chinese government was to build the railway bridge over the Tumen river " conjointly with the Railway Department of the Office of the Japanese Governor-General of Korea ", and was to share half of the expense.[96] As regards particulars not provided for in the preliminary agreement, they were to be decided in accordance with the Tientsin-Pukow Railway loan agreement of January 13, 1908.[97]

The so-called loan for gold mining and forestry in Heilungkiang and Kirin [98] was alleged to be made " for the development of gold mining and forestry in Heilungkiang and Kirin ".   Its amount [99] was $30,000,000 " to be delivered without discount ";[100] its term ten years, with a provision for extension by mutual consent at its expiration,[101] and an option on the part of the Chinese government to repay a portion of it after the lapse of five years;[102]

[91] *MacMurray*, ii, 1430.

[92] Art. ix.

[93] Art. viii.

[94] Art. i.

[95] Art. v.

[96] Art. iv.

[97] Art. vii, *MacMurray*, i, 684.

[98] *Ibid.*, ii, 1434.

[99] Art. i.

[100] Art. vi.

[101] Art. ii.

[102] Art. iii.

and its security the gold mines, national forests, and the government's revenue therefrom.[103] During the period of operation of the agreement the lenders were to have the right of being first consulted in case further loans were to be made in respect to objects of the securities or disposal contemplated thereof,[104] but the agreement was subject to cancellation as a result of the repayment of principal and interest.[105]

The so-called advance upon loan for construction of railways in Manchuria and Mongolia,[106] $20,000,000 in amount, was made [107] "without deduction for commission",[108] upon the conclusion of a preliminary agreement for a loan alleged to be " for the purpose of building " a railway between Jehol and Taonan, a railway between Changchun and Taonan, a railway between Kirin and Kaiyuan by way of Hailung, and " a railway from a point on the Jehol-Taonan Railway to a certain seaport " to be decided upon by consultation between the government and the banks,[109] formal agreement to be concluded within four months.[110] The term of the loan was to be forty years, redemption to begin " after eleven years " from the date of issue,[111] and its security " all the property and revenue of the Four Railways of Manchuria and Mongolia, at present and in the future ".[112]

Of the four loans and advances we have reviewed, the first was declared to be based upon Article VII of the treaty of 1915 relating to southern Manchuria and eastern

[103] Art. viii.
[104] Art. ix.
[105] Art. x.
[106] *MacMurray*, ii, 1448.
[107] Art. xi.

[108] Art. xii.
[109] Art. i.
[110] Art. viii.
[111] Art. iii.
[112] Art. v.

Inner Mongolia. As to the other three, one evidently took as the point of departure Article VI of the agreement of 1910 relating to the Tumen river, while two related to notes accompanying the treaty of 1915 above referred to. It must be observed, however, that Article VII of the treaty of 1915 did not contemplate the administration of the Kirin-Changchun Railway by the South Manchuria Railway Company, and that the engagements of Article VI of the agreement of 1910 and of the notes of 1915 were such that China had discretion as to the time to carry them out. Aside from other misdeeds, for these few loans and advances alone the Anfu government would have fully deserved its fate in 1920.

Japan was not to profit by only these ill-advised measures of the Anfu Club. When some of the loans were not yet made to the Anfu government the question of intervention in Siberia had been mooted. Japan having had a financial string tied around that government, it did not take much ingenuity to secure an agreement, dated May 16, 1918, for Sino-Japanese military coöperation in the mooted enterprise.[113] As Japan was thus enabled to carry out her campaigns against Siberia from northern Manchuria, in the last analysis the agreement meant nothing but permission to Japan to establish a military occupation of the latter region. This they actually did when intervention was decided upon by the *Entente* powers. Fortunately there then came to China's rescue a succession of events — the failure of the Kolchak régime in Siberia, the withdrawal of the *Entente* powers from intervention, the establishment of the Far Eastern Republic, and the restoration of peace in Europe.

[113] For this agreement and relevant documents see *MacMurray*, ii, 1407–15.

On January 28, 1921, the agreement with Japan was terminated.[114]

From the *Entente* intervention in Siberia as from the monarchical movement of 1915–16 Japan therefore reaped no great harvest, but on this, as on that occasion, she was not willing to leave empty-handed. On October 2, 1920, according to the Japanese report, some Korean revolutionaries, in the company of Siberian and Manchurian bandits to the number of three hundred, suddenly crossed the frontier from Russian territory into Hungchun and set fire to the Japanese consulate, as well as the Japanese settlement there, which resulted in the death of one dozen Japanese and the injury of another dozen, besides considerable material losses.[115] On the 6th and 7th Japanese troops, 10,000 strong, marched upon southeastern Kirin from Korea, from Vladivostok, from the Ussuri Railway, from the Chinese Eastern Railway, which Japan then still occupied after her evacuation of Siberia, and from the South Manchurian Railway, and occupied the entire section of country from the Tumen river to Ninguta and the Chinese Eastern Railway.[116] On the 9th the Japanese minister at Peking called upon the Minister of Foreign Affairs to give China's consent to a joint military operation against the bandits. On the same day the Japanese foreign office in an announcement [117] accused the Chinese government of failure to end Korean revolutionary activities in the Korean settlement north of the river Tumen as well as for alleged participation of Chinese troops in the attack on the Japanese at

[114] For notes exchanged on that occasion see Liu Yen, *op. cit.*, p. 305.

[115] *Ibid.*, 293.

[116] *Ibid.*, 294.

[117] For text see *ibid.*, 295.

Hungchun. Upon their arrival in the Tumen region the Japanese troops started a campaign to clear the Korean settlements of Korean revolutionaries. According to the appeal of the Catholics to the Pope, as far as they knew, the Japanese burnt in that campaign more than one thousand dwellings, twenty-one chapels, seven schools, and killed about twenty-one hundred Korean Catholics besides several hundred Chinese.[117a]

China protested. But in the meantime Japan had done everything to her heart's content and, as she was not able to prove that Chinese troops were involved in the attack at Hungchun, she slackened her grasp and withdrew some of her troops after establishing in all the principal occupied cities Japanese police agencies. Even up to the Washington Conference some of her troops were found still lingering there as on the Chinese Eastern Railway.

(2) *Northern Manchuria and Outer Mongolia*

In proportion to the change of circumstances experienced by Russia as compared with Japan, Russian aggression was hit even harder. Indeed, at a certain period of time after the Russian Revolution, it seemed as if Russian encroachments upon northern Manchuria and Outer Mongolia were to end forever.

On the eve of the European War[118] the number of Russian troops stationed along the Chinese Eastern Railway amounted, it was estimated, to 90,000, of which one-third were concentrated at Harbin. During the war some of these were withdrawn, but a considerable portion was still left behind. After the Russian Revolution of 1917 dis-

[117a] *Ibid.*, 297.

[118] For the following pages see Liu Yen, *Diplomatic History of China* (in Chinese) (3rd edition, Shanghai, 1921), p. 608. *et seq.*

sension appeared among these troops, and General Horvath, general manager of the Chinese Eastern Railway and Russian consul-general at Harbin, soon practically lost his control over them. Conditions being thus, the Chinese government was moved to take action. On January 10, 1918, it gave orders to the authorities of Kirin to disarm the Russian troops, hand them over to General Horvath to be deported to Russia, and take over the protection of the railway in accordance with Article V of the railway contract of 1896. At the same time it also appointed the Military Governor of Kirin President of the Chinese Eastern Railway in accordance with Article I of the said contract. Both rights, it may be observed, China had been prevented from exercising since the Boxer Rebellion.

Two years elapsed. Then, on March 11, 1920, the third anniversary of the Russian Revolution, the railway employees, in revolt against the Russian general manager, requested that he transfer his authority over the railway to the provisional government at Vladivostok, which had then been set up by the Soviets there, and went on strike when the request was ignored. Conditions being such, the Chinese government was again moved to action. The Chinese President of the railway, while maintaining order among the employees, advised the Russian general manager to resign. This the latter did, and the railway was provisionally placed under a joint Sino-Russian, instead of an all-Russian, management. According to an arrangement made a little later (October 2, 1920) between the Chinese government and the Russo-Asiatic Bank,[119] the control of the railway was vested in a board of directors consisting of four Chinese and five Russians, with the President of the railway as its chairman with one vote, as well as a deciding vote in case

[119] *Ibid.*, 611.

of a tie, and the operation of the railway was entrusted to a body of officers equally representative of China and Russia from the general manager down to bureau chiefs.

So much for northern Manchuria. As to Outer Mongolia, the secession of that region was, as might be expected, not at all a spontaneous movement among the Khalkas, and less so with the Oelots of Kobdo and the Urianghais of Kobdo and Tannu Urianghai. Before the protocol of November 5, 1913, was signed between the Russian minister in Peking and the Minister of Foreign Affairs, some of the chieftains under the jurisdiction of the Kobdo authorities had deserted the Khalkas for China, and this movement continued until by the Russian Revolution only about one-half of the Kobdo district was left to autonomous Outer Mongolia.[120] Then, as soon as the first Assistant-Resident arrived at Uliassutai the Urianghais of Tannu came to him for assistance to free themselves from the Russians. China accordingly took the matter up with Russia. Nothing, however, resulted, and finally in the fall of 1919 that territory had to be recovered by a joint Sino-Mongolian expedition.[121] After the Oelots and the Urianghais, came the Khalka themselves.

Under the tactful rule of Chen Lu, the first Resident-General, a change of attitude came over the Khalkas. Both the lamas and the princes reflected regretfully upon the price they had paid for Russian assistance, and the princes, in addition, upon the personal sacrifice of pensions which they used to receive from the Chinese government, and of political power which they had now to share with

[120] Report of Kobdo Residency, Feb. 16, 1920, Chen, *op. cit.*, bk. ii, p. 164.

[121] Report of Urga Residency-General, Feb. 1, 1920, *ibid.*, bk. ii, p. 152.

the lamas. Then came the Russian Revolution, which let loose the Russian lawless elements to plague Outer Mongolia, culminating in the attempt of Semenov, backed by Japan, to utilize the Buriates to seize Outer Mongolia, and create for himself an empire east of Lake Baikal.[122] Finally a movement was started by the princes to cancel the autonomy.[123]

Under the circumstances the princes easily carried the lamas with them, but their easy success also made them less considerate towards the latter. They proceeded to draw up an agreement with the Resident-General as basis of reunion without previous consultation with their colleagues of the church, and when the latter protested against certain provisions, they ignored them and submitted the draft to the Chinese government. In order to safeguard their interests the lamas appealed to Peking.

Into this delicate internal situation of Outer Mongolia unfortunately entered a new factor. General Hsu Shu-cheng, of the Anfu Club, arrived at Urga just at this time as Defence Commissioner of Northwestern Frontiers. Apparently with the object of gaining prestige the general usurped the function of the Resident-General and took the question of the reunion into his own hands. There is no doubt that if the matter had been left to the Resident-General the latter would have sought first to meet the wishes of the lamas. Such a policy was evidently too delicate for the general. In the typical manner of a militarist he bluntly proposed to the lamas the cancellation of autonomy without condition, promising merely to take up the question of their rights afterwards. Thus a natural

[122] *Ibid.*, July 26, 1919; *ibid.*, bk. ii, p. 146.
[123] *Ibid.*, bk. iii, pp. 1–7.

movement, instead of being allowed to run its course, was forced.

On November 17, 1919, the Urga Kutuktu submitted a petition to the President of the Chinese Republic for the cancellation of the autonomy of Outer Mongolia. When the petition was granted, the Russian minister in Peking protested on the ground that a unilateral termination of the Russo-Mongolian agreement of 1912 and the tripartite agreement of 1915 was inadmissible. In reply the Minister of Foreign Affairs stated that the cancellation of the autonomy, like the declaration of independence, originated with Outer Mongolia; that the agreements of 1912, 1913, and 1915 concerning Mongolia, having flowed out of " mediation voluntarily offered " by the former Russian government, were of a different category from ordinary international engagements and their termination, therefore, could not be governed by rules governing the latter kind; and that China had no intention of doing away with privileges enjoyed by Russian traders so long as they were not in conflict with China's sovereign rights or the interests of Outer Mongolia.[124]

Following the cancellation of autonomy of Outer Mongolia, the Hulun region, the trans-Khingan section of Heilungkiang, also applied for the cancellation of the special arrangement made between China and Russia concerning it, which was accordingly granted.[125]

---

[124] For text see *ibid.*, bk. iii, p. 8.

[125] Report of Inspector-General of Manchuria, Jan. —, 1920, *ibid.*, bk. iii, p. 8.

Sec. 5.   The United States and Japanese "Vested Interests"

Throughout the greater part of the Wilson administration the attitude towards the developments in the Far East was one of waiting. The policy of the Taft administration, although it had been shattered, formed nevertheless a line of defence for the political entity of China. For a long time after its termination, none seemed to have been evolved to take its place.

In 1913, China was made to agree to give priority to Japanese capitalists in case a railway was to be built between Taonan and Jehol. This line covered practically the southern section of the Chinchou-Aigun Railway and in fact has been admitted by Japan as such in her correspondence with the State Department relating to the formation of the four-power financial consortium of 1919. So far as we know, the Wilson administration made no protest.

During the Twenty-one Demands, when not only Shantung and Manchuria were at stake, but the sovereignty of China was also threatened, the Wilson administration was silent. It was not until all was over that it made the following notification to both China and Japan:[126]

In view of the circumstances of the negotiations which have taken place and which are now pending between the Government of China and the Government of Japan and of the agreements which have been reached as a result thereof, the Government of the United States has the honor to notify the Government of the Chinese Republic (or Japan) that it can not recognize any agreement or undertaking which has been entered into or which may be entered into between the Governments of China and Japan impairing the treaty rights of the United States and its

[126] *MacMurray*, ii, 1236.

citizens in China, the political or territorial integrity of the Republic of China, or the international policy relative to China commonly known as the Open Door Policy.

In the fall of 1917, after Japan had arrived at understandings with Great Britain, France, Italy, and Russia regarding ultimate disposal of German rights in Shantung and the Pacific Ocean,[127] she sent Viscount Ishii Kikujiro to the United States to have conversations with the Secretary of State touching the " questions of mutual interest " relating to China. On this occasion the Wilson administration actually entered into an agreement with Japan. In the Lansing-Ishii notes [128] published on November 2nd " in order to silence mischievous report ", it was stated that " the Governments of the United States and Japan recognize that territorial propinquity creates special relations between countries, and consequently, the Government of the United States recognizes that Japan has special interests in China, particularly in the part to which her possessions are contiguous ", although, it may be added, a number of denials and affirmations were also made such as are commonly seen in agreements entered into between Japan and various powers since her first treaty of alliance with Great Britain.

With the experience thus acquired the Wilson administration, however, soon began to feel the necessity of doing something, and when in 1918 Japan resorted to the loan policy which we had occasion to review above, it suggested to the American bankers that they, to put it in plain language, get into the game. The bankers, as in 1910, were

[127] For text of correspondence between Japan and the four powers containing the understanding, see *New York Times*, April 22, 1919, p. 192.   [128] *MacMurray*, ii, 1394.

not ready to undertake the adventure alone, and on July 8, 1918, suggested to the State Department the formation of a new financial consortium consisting of American, French, British, and Japanese bankers. This was accepted by the State Department, which shortly afterwards had the plan officially proposed to the three powers concerned.[129]

The Japanese were not slow to play their part. No sooner was the plan officially proposed than they made haste to complete their loan policy as well as to strengthen their position in the regions affected by that policy. Of the ten loans and advances listed above the four made in August and September were by far the most harmful to Chinese interests. They amounted to more than one-half of the sum total of the loans and advances, and were charges upon Shantung, Manchuria, and Mongolia.

But the Japanese were not to stop at these activities. They were even to make use of the opportunity to secure the recognition of the Powers, particularly the United States, to the positions they had adversely acquired in China since the Chinese Revolution, and, if failing in this, at least to make sure that the consortium would do no harm to those positions.

The American proposal having been accepted by the three powers, on May 12, 1919, the bankers met at Paris and drew up an agreement.[130] Article II of this agreement read in part as follows:

This agreement relates to existing and future loan agreements which involve the issue for subscription by the public

[129] Bankers to State Department, July 8, 1918. State Department to Bankers, July 9, 1918. British Foreign Office to American Embassy, August 14, 1918. State Department to French, British and Japanese Embassies, October 8, 1918. *Scott*, pp. 1, 3, 6, 10.

[130] *Cmd.*, 1214 (1921), p. 20.

of loans to the Chinese Government . . . but does not relate to agreements for loans to be floated in China. Existing agreements relating to industrial undertakings upon which it can be shown that substantial progress has been made may be omitted from the scope of this agreement.

In addition to the agreement the bankers also passed a number of resolutions of which No. 2 is as follows: [131]

(a) That in addition to future business all existing loan agreements and options which involve the issue for subscription by the public of loans be pooled, with the exception of agreements and options relating to industrial undertakings (including railways) upon which substantial progress has been made;

(b) That the groups will surrender to the consortium any such agreements and options which they themselves possess or control;

(c) That the groups will use their best endeavors to induce other parties who may possess or control any such agreements or options to surrender the same to the consortium.

Upon the agreement being concluded, the Japanese made their move. On June 18, 1919, Mr. Odagari, representing the Japanese group, wrote to Mr. T. S. Lamont of the American group [132] that he had instructions from his principals in Japan that all the rights and options held by Japan " in the regions of Manchuria and Mongolia, where Japan had special interests ", should be excluded from the arrangements for pooling provided for in the proposed agreement. The ground he went on to give, was that the very special relations " which Japan enjoys geographically and historically " with the regions referred to, had been recognized

---

[131] *Ibid.*, p. 19.   [132] *Scott*, p. 19.

by Great Britain, the United States, France, and Russia on many occasions — pointing specially to the Lansing-Ishii agreement — and had formed the subject of a special reservation made by the Japanese bankers on June 18, 1912, when discussing the agreement for the Reorganization loan with the bankers of the other five groups. On June 23rd, after consulting with his British and French colleagues, Mr. Lamont replied.[133] He denied that the " special interests " referred to ever had anything to do with economic matters. He drew the attention of the Japanese bankers to the fact that the reservation they made on June 18, 1912, was not accepted by the British, French, and American groups on the ground that they were not competent to deal with political questions. He stated that he and his British and French colleagues would refer the matter to their respective governments.

The matter having been taken up by the United States and Great Britain with the Japanese government, the latter submitted at the end of August a memorandum [134] accepting the terms as agreed upon among the bankers at Paris, with the reservation that such acceptance " shall not be held or construed to operate to the prejudice of the special rights and interests possessed by Japan in South Manchuria and Eastern Inner Mongolia ".

On October 28th, Mr. Lansing replied [135] that the American government reluctantly found itself unable to assent to the Japanese proviso on the ground that it was " an intermixture of exclusive political pretensions in a project which all the other interested governments and groups have treated in a liberal and self-denying spirit and with the purpose of eliminating, so far as possible, such disturbing and complicating political motives "; and that

[133] *Ibid.*, p. 20.   [134] *Ibid.*, p. 30.   [135] *Ibid.*, p. 31.

from the viewpoint either of the legitimate national feeling of China or of the interest of the Powers in China "it would be a calamity if the adoption of the consortium were to carry with it the recognition of a doctrine of spheres of interest more advanced and far-reaching than was ever applied to Chinese territory even in the period when the break-up of the Empire appeared imminent". Mr. Lansing then went on to point out that the wording of the agreement plainly excluded those enterprises which were already developed "such as the South Manchuria and Ssupingkai-Chengchiatun Railways, the Fushun collieries, et cetera", and "might fairly be interpreted" to exclude likewise the existing options for the extension of railways already in operation "for instance the proposed continuation of the Ssupingkai-Chengchiatun Railway to Taonan and to Hueining of the Kirin-Changchun Railway". In conclusion he observed that the Japanese government should be amply content with the understanding that certain specific enterprises were exempt.

On March 2nd the Japanese government submitted another memorandum to the United States.[136] It defended its claims on the ground that the regions in question, "being contiguous to Korea" stood in "very close and special relation to Japan's national defense and her economic existence". It justified its insistence upon the reservation by pointing to the "direful influences" of the Russian Revolution which, it declared, might effect their penetration through those regions "into Japan and the Far East to the instant menace of their security". It finally proposed a new reservation for acceptance of the terms as agreed upon among the bankers at Paris. The new reservation runs as follows:

[136] *Ibid.*, p. 34.

In matters . . . relating to loans affecting South Manchuria and Eastern Inner Mongolia which in their opinion are calculated to create a serious impediment to the security of the economic life and national defence of Japan, the Japanese government reserves the right to take the necessary steps to guarantee such security.

In line with Mr. Lansing's specifications of exempt enterprises the Japanese government also supplied a list of enterprises which it claimed to fall into that category. These were: (1) the "South Manchurian Railway and its branches, together with the mines which are subsidiary to the Railway"; (2) The Kirin-Changchun, Hsinmin-Mukden, and Ssupingkai-Chengchiatun Railways; and (3) the Kirin-Hueining, Chengchiatun-Taonan, Changchun-Taonan, Kaiyuan-Kirin, and Taonan-Jehol Railways, and "the railway connecting a point in the Taonanfu-Jehol Railway with a seaport". It intimated, however, that in case of any loan being floated in future in connection with the railways of the third category the European and American market would be invited to subscribe to it.

On March 16th the State Department replied.[137] It regretted that the Japanese reservation was "in terms so exceedingly ambiguous and in character so irrevocable" that it might be held to indicate a continued desire on the part of Japan to exclude the Powers from participating in the development of important parts of China. It maintained that the right of national self-preservation was one of universal acceptance in the relations between states, and therefore would not require specific formulation as to its application in any particular instance; that "the recognition of that principle is implicit in the terms of the notes exchanged between Secretary Lansing and Viscount Ishii

[137] *Ibid.*, p. 38.

on November 2, 1917 "; and that by reason of " the particular relationships of understanding thus existing between the United States and Japan, and those which, it is understood, similarly exist between Japan and the other powers proposed to be associated with it in the consortium, there would appear to be no occasion to apprehend on the part of the consortium any activities directed against the economic life or national defence of Japan ". It observed that it was difficult to believe that " in order to meet the necessities of Japanese economic or political security " it was essential for Japan alone to construct and control a railway line of such a character as the one projected from Taonan to Jehol and thence to the seacoast.

In the meantime Mr. Lamont had proceeded to Tokyo to effect an agreement with the Japanese bankers on the specific enterprises to be exempt from the operation of the consortium. On April 3rd, while he was there, the Japanese government submitted another memorandum to the United States.[138] It expressed its satisfaction that it was " not so much to the principle of their [Japanese] proposal as to its form " that the United States took exception. It noted the assurance of the United States that the right of national self-preservation, " which forms the basis of the guarantee required by Japan " was not only one of universal acceptance, but one of which " the recognition is implied in the terms of the notes exchanged between Secretary Lansing and Viscount Ishii, so that the new consortium would in no case embark upon any activities directed against the national defence and the economic existence of Japan, and so that the powers associated in the consortium would refuse their countenance to any enterprise inimical to the vital interests of Japan ". Then " relying upon that assurance of the

[138] *Ibid.*, p. 46.

United States", it accepted "most willingly" the suggestion of the United States to forego the general reservation and to include the Taonan-Jehol Railway and "the line connecting a point thereon with a seaport" in the operation of the consortium. The latter, however, was made on the following condition:

In the event of the new Consortium projecting in future a scheme of extending the Taonanfu-Jehol Railway to the north with a view to connection with the Eastern Chinese Railway, the assent of the Japanese government thereto must be obtained beforehand through the Japanese group, inasmuch as such an extension being tantamount to a renewal of the so-called Chinchou-Aigun Railway scheme against which a protest was lodged by Japan when the question was motioned some years ago, is calculated to have a serious effect upon the South Manchuria Railway.

In the meantime Mr. Lamont had reached an agreement with the Japanese bankers [139] embodying substantially what might be gathered from the correspondence thus far reviewed. On April 3rd, the State Department replied [140] to the Japanese memorandum of March 2nd. It signified its readiness to agree to the terms of the compromise proposed by Mr. Lamont, and objected to the veto power the Japanese sought to retain with respect to the Chinchou-Aigun Railway project, on the ground that the granting of such power would be "contrary to the principles upon which the idea of the consortium is based". On May 8th the Japanese government submitted another memorandum [141] "explaining" that the point concerning the Taonan-Jehol Railway was just raised as "one of the

[139] President of the Yokohama Specie Bank to Lamont, May 11, 1920, *ibid.*, p. 60.   [140] *Ibid.*, p. 54.   [141] *Ibid.*, p. 56.

actual examples of enterprises prejudicial to Japan's vital interests which formed the subject matter of the general assurances given by the American Government ". Japan had by this time obtained practically all she wanted. She had had all projected railways in Manchuria and eastern Inner Mongolia, with the exception of the Taonan-Jehol line, exempted from the operation of the consortium irrespective of whether " substantial progress " had been made or not. She had had also an assurance that the consortium was not directed against the " economic life or national defence of Japan ". She had succeeded in maintaining her position in southern Manchuria and eastern Inner Mongolia which she had consolidated since the Chinese Revolution at the expense of China and in defiance of the United States: what else could she want? Her government, therefore, waived an explicit assurance from the United States concerning the Taonan-Jehol Railway project.

Over the correspondence between Japan and Great Britain we do not need to go. Suffice it to say that the stand taken by the latter power was substantially the same as that taken by the United States.[142]

Sec. 6.   Respective Positions

(1) *China and Japan*

The Harding administration did not depart from the policy formulated under President Wilson. Shortly after taking office it approved the consortium as already approved by its predecessor.[143] About the same time, when a conference for discussing the question of the limitation of armament was being proposed, President Harding also sug-

[142] See nos. 14, 17, 21, 24 *ibid.*, pp. 28, 33, 44, 52.
[143] *New York Times*, March 30, 1921, p. 17, cols. 1 and 2.

gested that as such questions had a close relation to Pacific and Far Eastern problems, the powers especially interested in these problems should undertake in connection with the conference " the consideration of all matters bearing upon their solution with a view to reaching a common understanding with respect to principles and policies in the Far East.[144]

Towards the proposal the Japanese government was as cautious as towards the formation of the consortium. It appears that it first asked for a fuller statement of the nature and scope of the Pacific and Far Eastern problems, which were to be discussed, and when the American government expressed the hope that it would not press for the statement, Japan accepted the proposal with the understanding that the main object of discussing those problems was " to reach a common understanding in regard to principles and policies in the Pacific and the Far East ", and that " introduction therein of problems such as are of sole concern to certain particular powers or such matters that may be regarded as accomplished facts should be scrupulously avoided ".[145]

A full review of the conference which was finally held in Washington forms no part of our task. We are only interested in its bearings upon the problem that forms the subject of our study. As might be expected, in course of time the questions relating to southern Manchuria and eastern Inner Mongolia one after another came up for discussion. In point of time that which came first was the question of Japanese troops and police. It was raised in the fifth meeting of the committee on Pacific and Far Eastern

[144] W. W. Willoughby, *China at the Conference* (Baltimore, 1922), p. 4.
[145] *Ibid.*, pp. 5–7.

questions held on November 28, 1921, in connection with the proposal of Mr. S. K. Alfred Sze on behalf of the Chinese delegation that each power should severally declare against and cease from stationing police boxes, or erecting or operating electrical communication installations upon the soil of China without her express consent.[146] According to a memorandum [147] submitted by the Chinese delegation, Japanese troops and police in the regions in question consisted of the following: (a) one full division of Japanese troops with its headquarters in various important localities such as Liaoyang, Tiehling, Harbin, Kungchuling, and Haicheng, besides the leased territory of Port Arthur and Talienwan; (b) sixteen independent battalions of guards along the Chinese Eastern Railway, each composed of 21 officers and 617 men besides (c) the troops then withdrawn from Siberia; and (d) those still maintained in the districts around Hungchun. In addition there were (e) 27 police agencies as reported by local authorities of Fengtien and Kirin in 1917, not counting (f) a number since then established as results of the Chengchiatun fracas and the Hungchun affair in these respective localities.

In reply to the Chinese statement, Mr. Hanihara Masanas of the Japanese delegation stated [148] that the maintenance of troops along the South Manchurian Railway was " conceded and recognized by China under the treaty of Peking, 1905, additional agreement Article II " — a right which Japan could not forego in view of the existing state of affairs in Manchuria, " a region which has been made notorious by the activity of mounted bandits "; that the Japanese troops scattered along the Chinese Eastern Rail-

[146] *Sen. Doc.*, 1921–22, p. 501.
[147] *Ibid.*, 504.
[148] *Ibid.*, 512.

way were stationed "in connection with an inter-allied agreement concluded at Vladivostok in 1919" and for establishing communication between the Japanese contingents in Siberia and southern Manchuria, but would be withdrawn as soon as the evacuation of Siberia by the Japanese troops was effected; that the stationing of Japanese police in the interior, especially in Manchuria, had proved to be of much practical usefulness in the prevention of crimes among Japanese residents, "without interfering with the daily life of Chinese or of other foreign nationals".

In the eleventh meeting, held on December 2nd, Mr. Sze made his statement in reply.[149]   Referring to Japanese troops along the South Manchurian Railway Mr. Sze reviewed Article I of the treaty of Peking, 1905, Articles III and IV of the Portsmouth treaty which the former article confirmed, and Article II of the additional agreement to the treaty of Peking, and said that, while Russia had withdrawn her troops from Manchuria as provided in these treaties, Japan had retained hers; that if Japan, in spite of China's request, continued to maintain the troops on the ground of the alleged existing state of banditry, China might never have an opportunity to show her capacity of affording protection to lives and property of foreigners; and that the mere presence of Japanese troops made for friction with the natives and roused rather than allayed disorders throughout the adjacent territory.

Referring to Japanese troops along the Chinese Eastern Railway, Mr. Sze only observed that the objects and purposes of the inter-allied agreement had long since disappeared and all allied troops other than the Japanese had

[149] *Ibid.*, 529.

long since withdrawn; and that the necessity for maintaining troops along the Chinese Eastern Railway to establish communication between the Japanese contingents in Siberia and southern Manchuria was no argument.

As to Japanese police in Manchuria, Mr. Sze said the reasons advanced by the Japanese delegation had never been regarded in international law and practice as sufficient to justify the institution of police administration, in a foreign friendly country, that the statement that the Japanese police did not interfere with the daily life of Chinese was not correct.

After Mr. Sze had made his statement, the Chairman observed [150] that, as all Japanese statements amounted to the offer to withdraw her troops when China accorded adequate protection of life and property, while those of China amounted to the offer of protection with a request for the immediate withdrawal of the troops, the question was whether China was able to so provide the protection. As to this question which involved facts, he suggested the formation of a subcommittee to study and make recommendations. Mr. Sze agreed, and suggested that the matter of police might as well be left for discussion in the subcommittee.

The French delegation suggested that, since a commission of jurists had been charged with investigating on the spot the question of extra-territoriality, the examination of facts with regard to foreign troops in China might also be referred to it. Mr. Sze objected on the ground that, while extra-territoriality was conceded by treaty, the presence of foreign troops had no legal justification whatever, and that the French proposal would imply a confirmation of the right of one country to maintain armed forces in another against

[150] *Ibid.*, 532.

the will of the latter. The British delegation supported the French proposal, but suggested that the question of foreign troops stationed in China with treaty sanction be also included in the investigation. The Chinese delegation was also assured that the French suggestion was intended to carefully avoid any derogation of the principle laid down, and the suggestions were allowed to go into the sub-committee.

In the thirteenth meeting, held on December 7th, Mr. Hanihara made another statement.[151] Referring to the Japanese troops along the South Manchurian Railway, he said that the withdrawal of Russian troops from Manchuria referred to by the Chinese delegation was the condition of things created by the existing anomalous situation in Russia, and did not prove that Russia had definitely agreed to the withdrawal of her troops contemplated by Article II of the additional agreement to the treaty of Peking. In addition he observed that the same article contained the proviso, " when tranquility shall have been reëstablished in Manchuria and when China shall have become herself capable of affording full protection to the lives and property of foreigners ", as conditions precedent to Japan's withdrawal of troops, and submitted a list giving statistics of lawless conditions along the South Manchurian Railway to prove that tranquility had not yet been reëstablished. Then finally he declared, as a reply to the Chinese contention that China should be given an opportunity to prove her ability to maintain peace and order, that Japanese interests and Japanese security were matters of such importance that she could not afford to take obvious risks.

As to troops along the Chinese Eastern Railway, Mr. Hanihara merely repeated what he had said on the last

[151] *Ibid.*, 553.

occasion without, however, mentioning anything about the maintenance of communication between Japanese contingents in Siberia and southern Manchuria as a justification. As to police, he was altogether silent.

According to the list given,[152] the statistics of lawless conditions along the South Manchurian Railway, cases of attacks by bandits " within the South Manchurian Railway zone ", beyond the leased territory, increased from 9 in 1906 to 57 in 1911, 99 in 1917, and 183 in 1920; cases of Japanese injured by bandits while travelling in southern Manchuria " within the railway zone " increased from 7 in 1913 to 19 in 1917, and 32 in 1920, and " outside the railway zone " increased from 13 in 1913 to 49 in 1917, but decreased from 49 in 1917 to 24 in 1920; and the number of criminals arrested by Japanese authorities and handed over to Chinese authorities totalled 23,595.

Although the Chinese delegation reserved their right to reply, no record of reply is found in the minutes. Evidently there was no necessity for such a reply, for the subject was presently disposed of in the subcommittee proposed by the French delegation. Had there been a necessity, the Chinese delegation would have found no difficulty in refuting the Japanese argument. The treaty provision to the point is found in the latter part of Article II of the additional agreement to the treaty of Peking, embodying a declaration of Japan, made as a result of China's protest, that she would withdraw her railway guards simultaneously with Russia when tranquility should have been established; or, in other words, that she would perform a duty of hers under a certain condition. It is true that the withdrawal of Russian railway guards already effected was caused by the existing anomalous situation in Russia; but it is equally

[152] *Ibid.*, 555.

true that, on account of that very anomalous situation, Russia was not competent to perform her part. Whatever might be said of the relation of that condition to the plain duty of Japan, it is evident that that condition was not operative. Therefore, the question came to this: whether tranquility had been established. It must be borne in mind that the treaty provision was made in consequence of the Russo-Japanese War and in reference to it. What was meant by tranquility there was the condition of things re-established after the termination of belligerency, and not the condition of things which might be brought about by enlightened administration. This being the case one is prompted to ask whether fifteen years constitute a reason-able length of time after a war to permit the return to normal ante-bellum conditions. It is difficult to see why the Japanese delegation attempted to show the lawless con-ditions along the railway. If their exposure of this condi-tion helped in any way at all, it helped to prove that China ought to be given the opportunity to remedy those conditions now that the war which gave rise to them had been over some fifteen years, and, moreover, ought to be given such an opportunity without further delay because those condi-tions had become worse and worse every year as a result, it would seem, of the presence of Japanese railway guards. The question of whether tranquility is reëstablished being a question of opinion rather than of fact, one cannot help also feeling that the proposal to refer it to a subcommittee made in the conference was ill-advised though perhaps well-meant.

The question of Port Arthur and Talienwan came up second in point of time. It was raised in the twelfth meeting, held on December 3rd, in connection with the proposal of Dr. V. K. Wellington Koo on behalf of the

Chinese delegation [153] that all leases in China be annulled
and that, pending such action, fortifications in leased areas
be dismantled, on the ground that "the sole purpose of
maintaining the balance of power in the Far East" among
the Powers concerning China had ceased to exist; that the
existence of the leases prejudiced China's territorial and
administrative integrity and hampered her national defence; that they had more than once involved China in
the complication of the Powers themselves, and that they
were utilized as *points d'appui* for developing spheres of
influence to the detriment of the principle of equal
opportunity.

The question of the lease of Kiaochou was then being
discussed outside the conference. In reply to the Chinese
statement regarding the lease of Port Arthur and Talienwan Mr. Hanihara, on behalf of the Japanese delegation,
made the following declaration: [154]

As to that territory [Port Arthur and Talienwan], the
Japanese delegates desire to make it clear that Japan has
no intention at present of relinquishing the important rights
she has lawfully acquired and at no small sacrifice. The
territory in question forms a part of Manchuria — a region
where, by reason of its close propinquity to Japan's territory more than anything else, she has vital interests in that
which relates to her economic life and national safety.
This fact was recognized and assurance was given by the
American, British, and French governments at the time of
the formation of the international consortium, that these
vital interests of Japan in the region in question shall be
safeguarded.

In the leased territory of Kwantung Province there reside no less than 65,000 Japanese, and the commercial and

[153] *Ibid.*, 538.   [154] *Ibid.*, 541.

industrial interests they have established there are of such
importance and magnitude to Japan that they are regarded
as an essential part of her economic life.

It is believed that this attitude of the Japanese delegation towards the leased territory of Kwantung is not against
the principle of the resolution adopted on November 2d
[the Root Resolution].

In reply to this, Dr. Koo made the following statement
in the thirteenth meeting, held on December 7th: [155]

As to the leased territory of Kwantung Province, namely,
Port Arthur and Dalny, its original term will expire in
1923, and while an extension to ninety-nine years was obtained by Japan in 1915, it was obtained in such circumstances that the dispute about its validity remains one of the
most grave outstanding questions between China and Japan.

Both Port Arthur and Dalny are situated in Manchuria,
which is an important part of Chinese territory. Not only
does the national safety of China depend upon the safeguarding of Manchuria as an integral portion of the Chinese Republic, because these three eastern Provinces, as
Chinese people call Manchuria, have been the historic road
of invasion into China throughout the past centuries, but
also the security of the economic life of the Chinese people
depends in a very vital measure upon the conservation and
development with the surplus capital of the world of the
natural and agricultural resources in Manchuria — a region
where today an abundance of raw material and food sup-
plies are already accessible to all nations, on fair terms and
through the normal operation of the economic law of supply and demand. Moreover, Manchuria is an important
outlet for the surplus population from the congested provinces in other parts of China.

In view of the foregoing facts, it is clear that China
has such truly vital interests in Manchuria that the inter-

[155] *Ibid.*, 551.

ests of any foreign power therein, however important they may be to themselves, can not compare with them. The fact of close propinquity of Manchuria to Korea, if it justifies any claim to consideration, can be equitably appealed to only on the condition of reciprocity.

As to the statement that assurance was given by the American, British, and French Governments at the time of the formation of the international consortium, that the vital interests of Japan in Manchuria shall be safeguarded, the Chinese delegation do not feel in a position, since China was not consulted at the time, to express an opinion as to the question of its accuracy. Should such assurance have been given, they would not, however, conceal their feeling that it can not be reconciled with the principle which was adopted by the conference on November 21st with respect to the sovereignty, the independence and territorial and administrative integrity of China.

The question of the treaties and notes of May 25, 1915, growing out of the Twenty-one Demands was the last to come up. It was raised in connection with the proposal of Dr. C. H. Wang, on behalf of the Chinese delegation,[156] that the Powers make a joint disavowal of all claims to any spheres of influence in China. In the fifteenth meeting, held on December 12th, Dr. Wang made his proposal on the ground that those spheres (a) hampered the economic development of China, (b) were contrary to the policy of equal opportunity, and (c) furthered political ends, under cover of economic claims, of particular powers, threatening the political integrity of China and giving rise to international jealousy and friction. In the next meeting, held on December 14th, he submitted a list of agreements [157] which formed the basis of the spheres and asked to be relieved from their restrictive stipulations.

[156] *Ibid.*, 580.   [157] *Ibid.*, 583.

This list consisted of (a) the Sino-Japanese treaties and notes of May 25, 1915, (b) fourteen inter-power agreements, (c) commitments and agreements which appeared to have been alleged to create or recognize the existence of spheres of interests and (d) non-alienation agreements.

Taking up first the treaties and notes of 1915, as these figured in the list, Dr. Wang reviewed the history and the treaties and notes themselves, pointed out their vital effects upon the " very existence, independence and integrity of China " and urged that in the common interest of the Powers as well as of China, and in conformity with the principles relating to China then already adopted by the committee, these treaties and notes be considered and cancelled. At this point the Japanese delegation signified its unwillingness to have the question discussed in the conference. Mr. Hanihara, while reserving his reply until he could examine Dr. Wang's statement carefully, announced that the Japanese delegation could not agree to any course making the validity of the treaties and notes of 1915 or the change or abrogation thereof the subject of discussion at the conference. He asserted that the question was one to be taken up between China and Japan, and not at the conference, if it were to be taken up at all.

In the thirteenth meeting, held on February 2nd, Baron Shidehara Kijuro made a statement on behalf of the Japanese delegation,[158] declining to have the treaties and notes of 1915 reconsidered on the ground that they were entered into by China " as a free sovereign nation ", and making the following declaration:

1. Japan is ready to throw open to the joint activity of the international financial consortium recently organized

[158] *Ibid.*, 583.

the right of option granted exclusively in favor of Japanese capital, — with regard, first, to loans for the construction of railways in South Manchuria and Eastern Inner Mongolia; and second, to loans to be secured on taxes in that region; it being understood that nothing in the present declaration shall be held to imply any modification or annulment of the understanding recorded in the officially announced notes and memoranda which were exchanged among the governments of the countries represented in the consortium, and also among the national financial groups composing the consortium, in relation to the scope of the joint activity of the organization.

2. Japan has no intention of insisting on her preferential right under the Sino-Japanese arrangements in questions concerning the engagement by Chinese of Japanese advisors or instructors on political, financial, military, or police matters in South Manchuria.

3. Japan is further ready to withdraw the reservation which she made, in proceeding to the signature of the Sino-Japanese treaties and notes of 1915, to the effect that Group V of the original proposal of the Japanese Government would be postponed for future negotiations.

In other words, Japan was willing to forego what she had already relinquished to the financial consortium as in (1), or what she would most probably never enjoy, either because it involved China's discretion as in (2), or because circumstances had changed as in (3).

In giving more fully the ground on which Japan declined to reconsider the treaties and notes of 1915, the statement continued:

It is presumed that the Chinese delegation has no intention of calling in question the legal validity of the compacts of 1915, which were formally signed and sealed by the duly authorized representatives of the two governments, and for which the exchange of ratifications was effected in conformity with established international usages. The insistence by China on the cancellation of those instruments would in itself indicate that she shares the view that the compacts actually remain in force and will continue to be effective, unless and until they are cancelled.

After Baron Shidehara had read his statement, Dr. Wang refuted the implication that China recognized the validity of those treaties and notes. He said that the Chinese government and people had always regarded them as peculiar in themselves owing to the circumstances under which they had been negotiated, and considered the state of things arising under them as a *de facto* situation, without any legal recognition on the part of China. He also reserved his right to reply fully.

In the next meeting, held on the following day, Dr. Wang made his reply.[159] He took note of Japan's concessions. He told how the treaties and notes were extorted from China at a time when the most friendly relation was in existence between the two countries, and how their provisions were in conflict with China's obligations towards other countries, and said:

Because of the essential injustice . . . , the Chinese delegation, acting on behalf of the Chinese government and of the Chinese people, has felt itself in duty bound to present to this conference, representing the powers with substantial interests in the Far East, the question as to the equity and justice of these agreements and therefore as to their fundamental validity.

Then he continued further:

If Japan is disposed to rely solely upon a claim as to the technical or juristic validity of the agreements of 1915 as

[159] *Ibid.*, 776.

having been actually signed in due form by the two governments, it may be said that, so far as this conference is
concerned, the contention is largely irrelevant, for this
gathering of the representatives of the nine powers'has not
had for its purpose the maintenance of the legal *status
quo*. On the contrary, the purpose has been, if possible,
to bring about such changes in existing conditions upon the
Pacific and in the Far East as might be expected to promote that enduring friendship among the nations of which
the President of the United States spoke in his letter of
invitation to the powers to participate in this conference.

The unwillingness of the Japanese delegates, however,
to have the question discussed in the conference remained
the same, and Dr. Wang had to be content with giving the
reasons why the treaties and notes of 1915 should form
the subject of impartial examination with a view of their
abrogation. These reasons were (a) the unilateral character of the agreements in point of benefit, (b) their violation
in important respects of treaties between China and the
other powers, (c) their inconsistency with the principles
relating to China adopted at the conference, and (d) their
being a source of constant misunderstandings between China
and Japan. He then concluded his statement with the
following:

The foregoing declaration has been made in order that
the Chinese government may have upon record the views
which it takes, and will continue to take, regarding the
Sino-Japanese treaties and exchange of notes of May 25,
1915.

(2) *The Powers*

Apart from the differences over specific cases, we see,
however, now as in the past a reign of harmony in the
matter of general principles. So, while the questions of

Japanese armed forces in Manchuria, of Port Arthur and Talienwan, and of the Twenty-one Demands left the conference practically as they entered it, the principles of the Open Door, and the policy for the preservation of China's territorial and administrative entity, as well as its counterpart, the pledge to respect China's sovereignty and independence as found in a number of agreements to which Japan was a party, found their way one after another in a more or less elaborate manner into a nine-power treaty.[160] Discordant notes, of course, were not entirely absent, but these were sounded only when proposals that had retroactive effects were made.[161] But these discordant notes were rare.

In the past the Powers had not only declared certain principles and policies, but also entered into agreements with the declared purpose of upholding those principles and policies. The nine-power treaty evidently did not take care of all these matters. Accordingly among the United States, the British Empire, France, and Japan, the powers which had entered into such agreements, another treaty was concluded.[162] By this treaty the parties agreed "as between themselves to respect one another's rights in relation to their insular possessions and insular dominions in the region of the Pacific Ocean". They also agreed on certain methods for settling controversies relating to those rights arising among themselves and between themselves and other parties. The term "insular possession and insular dominions" as applied to Japan, according to a supplementary treaty, was to include "only Karafuto (or the southern portion of the island of Sakhalin), Formosa and the Pescadores, and the

---

[160] *Ibid.*, 895.
[161] For instances see *ibid.*, 619, 693.
[162] *Ibid.*, 889.

islands under the mandate of Japan ". The treaty was to remain in force for ten years and to continue in force after that period subject to the right of any party to terminate it upon twelve months' notice. On the deposit of ratifications of this treaty the Anglo-Japanese agreement of July 13, 1911, was to terminate.

The Washington Conference rendered a piece of good service in providing an opportunity for the settlement of the Shantung question, for the definition of the future relations of the Powers in the Far East, and for the interment of the outworn Anglo-Japanese alliance. As to the question of southern Manchuria and eastern Inner Mongolia, it did nothing more than give us a bird's eye view of the situation as it then existed. Probably it had never been expected to do better.

With this conference we may take leave of the Japanese phase of our problem. Since then China has served notice upon Japan that her lease of Port Arthur and Talienwan was already up according to the original grant, but nothing resulted. Japan has entrenched herself in southern Manchuria and eastern Inner Mongolia, in addition to annexing Liuchiu, Formosa, the Pescadores, and Korea. She has no intention of quitting the former as she has no thought of giving up the latter.

Sec. 7. *Russia "Comes Back"*

In the summer of 1919, when the Reds first followed the Whites into Siberia, the Soviet government, evidently with the object of weakening the hold of the Whites in the Far East, declared null and void " the agreement of 1896 " [163] between China and Russia, the Peking Final

[163] For text see Chen, *op. cit.*, bk. iii, p. 22.

Protocol of 1901, and the agreements entered into between Russia and Japan between 1907 and 1916, and offered to China the restoration of all Chinese territories seized by the Tzarist government " such as Manchuria, etc."; the unconditional surrender of the Chinese Eastern Railway and all the mines and forests along it; the cancellation of the Boxer indemnity; the repudiation of the right of extraterritoriality; and the removal of all other injustices that China might bring up when conference was held to discuss details. As might be expected, this altruistic attitude of the Soviet government did not survive the necessity which had caused its adoption. In 1920, hardly a year had passed when the Reds had succeeded in ending all White power in Siberia, the Soviet government in a new proposal to China for resumption of normal relations, had already dropped the Chinese Eastern Railway as one of the terms offered.[164] But the Soviets were yet to reveal more clearly their real intent.

After the civil war of 1920 between the Chihli party and the Anfu Club, which ended in the elimination of the latter, Baron Ungern, leader of a band of the Whites who were hard pressed by the Reds, conveniently descended with his men upon Outer Mongolia and, as relief columns sent by the Chinese government did not reach there in time, took Urga on February 2, 1921. At this juncture the Reds intervened, and occupied Urga in turn, against Chinese protests.

In the meantime Russia did not cease to approach China for the restoration of normal relations. Towards the end of 1920 the first Soviet mission, headed by M. Yourin, came to Peking from Chita with the avowed purpose of

[164] *China Weekly*, xxiv (4), 124.

negotiating a trade agreement. This foundered on the rock of the Mongolian question, as the Soviet occupation of Urga took place shortly after the arrival of the mission. In the fall of 1921 a second Soviet mission, headed by M. A. K. Paikaiss, followed from Moscow, with the avowed object of entering into an arrangement with China over the Chinese Eastern Railway. This, too, struck the rock of the Mongolian question, as the Russians refused to discuss the matter when raised by the Chinese government. In the fall of 1922, a third mission, headed by M. Joffe, therefore came with the avowed object of settling all outstanding questions with China. The Soviet being ready to discuss the Mongolian question as well as that of the Chinese Eastern Railway, and not the latter alone, the Chinese government appointed Dr. C. T. Wang to represent China.

After several months of *pourparler*, Joffe suddenly alleged sickness and left for Japan " to recuperate ", and his place was taken by M. L. Karakhan, the author of the declaration of 1919. Since Russia first made overtures to China, it had always been admitted that recognition of the Soviet government would follow as a matter of course after settlement was made. M. Karakhan, however, attempted to reverse the process by proposing recognition before discussion. In order to meet him half-way Dr. Wang accepted his proposal on condition that they should first agree upon certain principles as the basis of discussion.[165] On March 13, 1924, after several months of discussion by no means smooth in its nature, the two representatives finally drew up a draft preliminary agreement embodying the points they had agreed upon, of which the articles concern-

[165] See statement made by Dr. Wang at a reception given by the Ministry of Foreign Affairs, *Chen pao*, March 26, 1924.

ing the two major subjects, the Chinese Eastern Railway and Outer Mongolia, are as follows: [166]

Article III.   The Governments of the two Contracting Parties agree to annul at the Conference as provided in the preceding Article [II] [167] all Conventions, Treaties, Agreements, Protocols, Contracts, etcetera, concluded between the Government of China and the Tzarist Government, and to replace them with new treaties, agreements, etcetera, on the basis of equality, reciprocity and justice, as well as the spirit of the Declarations of the Soviet Government of the years of 1919 and 1920.

Article IV.   The Government of the Union of Soviet Socialist Republics, in accordance with its policy and Declarations of 1919 and 1920, declares that all Treaties, Agreements, etcetera, concluded between the former Tzarist Government and any third party or parties affecting the sovereign rights or interests of China, are null and void.

The Government of China simultaneously declares that all Treaties, Agreements, etcetera, concluded between China and any third party or parties affecting the sovereign rights or interests of Russia, are null and void.

The Governments of both Contracting Parties declare that in future neither Government will conclude any treaties or agreements which prejudice the sovereign rights or interests of either Contracting Party.

Article V.   The Government of the Union of Soviet Socialist Republics recognizes that Outer Mongolia is an integral part of the Republic of China and respects China's sovereignty therein.

The Government of the Union of Soviet Socialist Republics declares that as soon as the conditions for the with-

[166] To the end of the present section, unless otherwise specified, quotations are made from, and statements upon the basis of, documents in Chinese issued for official use by the Chinese government.

[167] Providing for a conference to be held within one month after the signing of the agreement.

drawal of troops from Mongolia — namely, as to the time-limit and the measures to be adopted in the interests of the safety of the frontiers — are agreed upon at the Conference as provided in Article II of the present Agreement, it will effect the complete withdrawal of all the troops of the Union of Soviet Socialist Republics from Mongolia.

Article IX. The Governments of the two Contracting Parties agree to settle at the aforementioned conference the question of the Chinese Eastern Railway in conformity with the principles as hereinafter provided:

(1) The Governments of the two Contracting Parties declare that the Chinese Eastern Railway is a purely commercial enterprise.

The Governments of the two Contracting Parties mutually declare that, with the exception of matters pertaining to the business operations which are under the direct control of the Chinese Eastern Railway, all other matters affecting the rights of the National and the Local Governments of the Republic of China — such as judicial matters, matters relating to civil administration, military administration, police, municipal government, taxation and landed property (with the exception of lands required by the said Railway) shall be administered by the Chinese Authorities.

(2) The Government of the Union of Soviet Socialist Republics agrees to the redemption by the Government of the Republic of China, with Chinese capital, of the Chinese Eastern Railway, as well as all appurtenant properties and to the transfer to China of all shares and bonds of the said Railway.

(3) The Governments of the two Contracting Parties shall settle at the Conference as provided in Article II of the present Agreement, the amount and conditions governing the redemption as well as the procedure for the transfer of the Chinese Eastern Railway.

(4) The Government of the Union of Soviet Socialist Republics agrees to be responsible for the entire claims of the shareholders, bondholders, and creditors of the Chinese Eastern Railway incurred prior to the Revolution of March 9, 1917.

(5) The Governments of the two Contracting Parties mutually agree that the future of the Chinese Eastern Railway shall be determined by the Republic of China and the Union of Soviet Socialist Republics to the exclusion of any third party or parties.

(6) The Governments of the two Contracting Parties agree to draw up an arrangement for the provisional management of the Chinese Eastern Railway pending the settlement of the question as provided under Section (3) of the present Article.

(7) Until the various questions relating to the Chinese Eastern Railway are settled at the Conference as provided in Article II of the present Agreement, the rights of the two Governments arising out of the contracts of August 27–September 8, 1896, for the construction and operation of the Chinese Eastern Railway, which do not conflict with the present Agreement and the Agreement for the Provisional Management of the said Railway and which do not prejudice China's rights of sovereignty, shall be maintained.

In accordance with Section 3 of Article IX of the draft preliminary agreement Dr. Wang and M. Karakhan also drew up a draft agreement for the provisional management of the Chinese Eastern Railway, pending the final disposal of the question concerning it.[168]

The draft agreement contemplated the establishment of a board of directors to be composed of ten persons, of whom

[168] For text see *S. & P. S. Review*, viii (3), 225.

five were to be appointed by the Chinese government and five by the Soviet government. The president and vice-president of the board were to be appointed by the Chinese and Soviet governments respectively from among the members of the board. They were to be also the director-general and assistant director-general of the board and to manage the affairs of the board jointly.[169] The draft agreement also contemplated the establishment of a board of auditors, to be composed of five persons, two to be appointed by the Chinese government, and three by the Soviet government, with the chairman of the board to be elected from among the Chinese members.[170] For the management of the business of the railway there was to be a manager who was to be a Russian, and two assistant managers, one a Chinese and the other also a Russian. These officers were to be appointed by the board of directors subject to the approval of the Chinese and Soviet governments, and their rights and duties were to be defined by the board of directors.[171] The chiefs and assistant chiefs of the various departments of the railway were also to be appointed by the board of directors. The employment of persons in these departments from the chiefs and assistant chiefs downward was to be in accordance with the principle of equal representation.[172] The " estimates and budget " of the railway were to be submitted by the board of directors to a joint meeting of the board of directors and the board of auditors.[173] With the exception of the " estimates and budget " all other matters on which the board of directors could not reach an agreement were to be referred to the Chinese and Soviet governments.[174] All net profits of the railway were to be held by the board of directors pending the final dis-

[169] Art. i. [171] Art. iii. [173] Art. vii.
[170] Art. ii. [172] Arts. iv and v. [174] Art. vi.

posal of the question of the railway.[175]   Finally, it was
stipulated that the board of directors was to revise, within
six months from the signing of the agreement, the statutes
of the Chinese Eastern Railway company, approved on
December 4, 1896, by the Tzarist government, in accordance with the present agreement and the agreement on general principles for the settlement of questions between China
and Soviet Russia.[176]

When the draft agreement on general principles was
submitted to the Cabinet on March 14th, several provisions,
chiefly those relating to Outer Mongolia, were criticized.
It was pointed out that in Article IV while China declared
null and void all her international engagements affecting
Russian interests, Russia's part was confined to those of the
Tzarist régime alone; and that in Article V the provisions
relating to withdrawal of troops from Outer Mongolia
were fraught with possibility of difficulties.   In consequence Dr. Wang was instructed to approach M. Karakhan
for revision on those points.   The latter, however, not only
declined to discuss the matter, but also notified Dr. Wang
on the 16th that if the Chinese government failed to accept the draft as it stood within three days, he would consider himself no longer bound by its provisions and,
furthermore, his government would hold the Chinese responsible for any consequences, should the negotiations be
broken off as a result.   The Cabinet in a communication
to Dr. Wang expressed its surprise at the attitude assumed
by the Russian envoy, justified its stand upon the significance of the issues involved, and shifted back to the Russian
government responsibility for whatever might happen consequent to a breaking off of negotiations.   On the 19th
M. Karakhan forwarded to Dr. V. K. Wellington Koo,

[175] Art. viii.   [176] Art. ix.

the Minister of Foreign Affairs, an instruction from his government. In this document the Russian government asserted that the negotiations with the " official representative " of the Chinese government had been concluded. On this ground it declared that it would absolutely decline to discuss again what had been " agreed upon and signed "; that at the expiration of the three-day period it would consider itself no longer bound by the provisions of the draft agreement; and that not until the Chinese government should have first unconditionally resumed normal relations with Russia, would it again enter into negotiations with China. It also warned the Chinese government not to commit an " irretrievable mistake " that would " affect the future relation of Soviet Russia and the Chinese government ". On the same day M. Karakhan addressed also another note to the Chinese government through Dr. Wang, in which, pointing to a note addressed by the French legation to the Chinese government on March 12th to reserve French interests in the Chinese Eastern Railway, he insinuated that the Chinese government was subservient to the wishes of the Powers who, he declared, were hostile to Soviet Russia. On receiving M. Karakhan's communication to Dr. Koo the Chinese government ordered the Ministry of Foreign Affairs to take full charge of Sino-Russian negotiations.

To M. Karakhan's notes Dr. Koo replied on the 22nd. He expressed surprise at the contents of the note addressed to him. He stated that the Chinese government saw no reason to be bound by the time-limit given by him, since Dr. Wang's signing the draft agreement was not authorized by it, and hence lacked the character of finality. In support of his contention he referred M. Karakhan to Dr. Wang's commission which, while authorizing Dr. Wang to

" negotiate and agree ", plainly stated that the conclusions so reached would be valid only after they were duly signed with the permission of the Chinese government. He assured M. Karakhan that the Powers never did intervene and would under no circumstances be suffered to do so. In conclusion he expressed the wish that M. Karakhan would speedily resume negotiation.

M. Karakhan, however, maintained his position. On the 25th he submitted a memorandum elaborating his views upon the points at issue. On April 1st Dr. Koo therefore replied again. This time he not only rebutted the arguments advanced, but also submitted as conditions precedent to acceptance of the draft agreement by the Chinese government certain specific points of revision. Of these the two that concern us are (a) that a declaration be made by Russia on the international engagements of Soviet Russia similar and additional to what was already made by her in Article IV on those of the Tzarist régime; and (b) that the settlement upon measures concerning the withdrawal of Russian troops from Outer Mongolia be not described as condition therefor.

Against the positive attitude of the Chinese government M. Karakhan could make no headway. In the meantime something that must have appeared to the Russian envoy at least equally disastrous also took place. M. Karakhan, like his predecessor M. Joffe, had taken pains to cultivate favorable Chinese public opinion, and did so, it may be added, with considerable success. In his anxiety to bring the Chinese government to terms he now sought to utilize that force. In the several memoranda spoken of above, which were given wide publicity in local newspapers, he spared no effort in holding up Russia as the best friend of China, and at the same time accusing the Chinese government of unfriendliness and insinuating that it was under the thumb of the Powers. In doing this, however, he made a wrong calculation. The Chinese people, long living under " imperialistic " oppression, were naturally credulous of altruistic professions. But even as the thirsty that would not take poison, they could not suffer their government to be cudgelled to submission. Instantaneously a reaction set in, and M. Karakhan, instead of finding the Chinese government in difficulty, saw the people rallying to its support.

Having failed in his flanking attack, M. Karakhan also gave way on his front. After some more *pourparler* he consented to have the passage relating to the question of withdrawal of troops from Outer Mongolia in Article V modified to read as follows: [177]

The Government of the Union of Soviet Socialist Republics declares that as soon as the questions for the withdrawal of all troops of the Union of Soviet Socialist Republics from Outer Mongolia — namely, as to the time-limit of the withdrawal of such troops and the measures to be adopted in the interests of the safety of the frontiers — are agreed upon at the Conference as provided in Article II of the present Agreement, it will effect the complete withdrawal of all the troops of the Union of Soviet Socialist Republics from Outer Mongolia.

As to the question of the international engagements of Soviet Russia affecting China's interests, M. Karakhan was unwilling to go the full length with the Chinese government. There a compromise was reached, by which he joined with the Chinese government in making the following declaration: [178]

[177] *S. & P. S. Review*, viii (3), 220.
[178] Declaration iii, *ibid.*, 230.

The Government of the Republic of China and the Government of the Union of Soviet Socialist Republics jointly declare that it is understood that, with reference to Article IV of the Agreement on General Principles, the Government of the Republic of China will not and does not recognize as valid any treaty, agreements, etcetera, concluded between Russia since the Tzarist régime and any third party or parties, affecting the sovereign rights and interests of the Republic of China. It is further understood that this expression of understanding has the same force and validity as a general declaration, etcetera, etcetera. M. Karakhan having not made the declaration desired by the Chinese government, on the principles of reciprocity he let the similar declaration made by China in Article IV drop.

Upon the foregoing concessions the attempt of Soviet Russia to resume normal relations with China became a success. On May 31, 1924, the preliminary agreement on general principles, the agreement for the provisional management of the Chinese Eastern Railway and a number of declarations were signed between M. Karakhan and Dr. V. K. Wellington Koo, the Minister of Foreign Affairs. Since then Soviet Russia had been recognized and M. Karakhan appointed as first Soviet ambassador to China. But the conference provided for in Article II of the preliminary agreement, on account of the civil war which took place in the fall of 1924, had not yet been held at the time this study was concluded.

Sec. 8. The Outlook

Of the two major problems of Sino-Russian relations, at least that of the Chinese Eastern Railway is for all practical purposes solved. There the Soviets are content with the economic ownership of the railway divested of all political significance, subject to redemption at any time with Chinese capital. As to the problem of Outer Mongolia, the other major problem, the prospect of a satisfactory solution of it is not as bright; but even there the possibility of trouble is confined to the allusion made to " the measures to be adopted in the interests of the safety of the frontiers". The political upheaval in Russia is a great blow to Russian ambitions in the Far East. So, in spite of the inclination of the Soviets to revive the Tzarist policy with respect to that region, Russian menace to China will, it seems, not become as tense for some time as it was in the last quarter of a century.

With the Japanese menace the case is different. Since Great Britain and Russia have parted company with Japan and the United States no longer recognizes, at least in principle, that " Japan has special interests in China, particularly in the part to which her possessions are contiguous ", it is probable that Japan will not be able to repeat coups such as the Twenty-one Demands and the like in the next few years. But she can afford to wait for a change of circumstances in her favor as long as she is entrenched in southern Manchuria and eastern Inner Mongolia; for in the meantime she can continue to frustrate all such measures for the development of Manchuria as the Chinchou-Aigun Railway project and the Manchurian Industrial Development Loan plan, and when the time comes she can easily overrun China, even as did the Mujungs, the Tobas, the Chitans, the Nuchens, and the Manchus in the past.

According to the original agreements, Japan would have had to give up Port Arthur and Talienwan in 1923, and also let China redeem the Antung-Mukden Railway in the same year, and the South Manchurian Railway about a decade hence. As part and parcel of her attempt to control China by the Twenty-one Demands, she had had the terms of both the railways and the lease extended to ninety-nine years. Ever since then the Chinese government has repeatedly declared that it questioned " the equity and justice of the agreements arising from the Twenty-one Demands ", and therefore " their fundamental validity ", and the Chinese people have made May 7th, the day on which Japan delivered an ultimatum to compel the acceptance of her terms, a national Humiliation Day. There is no doubt that, in proportion to the degree the Chinese nation recovers from the political disorder it now experiences, it will grow more insistent upon shaking off the Japanese shackles. Here lies the hope and the danger.

INDEX

431